ALSO BY BING WEST

No True Glory: A Frontline Account of the Battle for Fallujah

The Village

Naval Forces and Western Security: Sea Plan 2000 (editor)

Small Unit Action in Vietnam

The Pepperdogs

WITH MAJOR GENERAL RAY L. SMITH

The March Up: Taking Baghdad with the United States Marines

THE
STRONGEST
TRIBE

THE
STRONGEST
TRIBE

WAR, POLITICS, AND THE ENDGAME IN IRAQ

BING WEST

RANDOM HOUSE / NEW YORK

Published in the United States by Random House, an imprint of The Random House
Publishing Group, a division of Random House, Inc., New York.

RANDOM HOUSE and colophon are registered trademarks of Random House, Inc.

Library of Congress Cataloging-in-Publication Data
West, Francis J.
The strongest tribe : war, politics, and the endgame in Iraq / Bing West.
p. cm.
ISBN 978-1-4000-6701-5
1. Iraq War, 2003– 2. United States—Politics and government—2001–
3. Iraq—Politics and government—2003– I. Title.
DS79.76.W46 2008
956.7044'3—dc22   2008016565

Printed in the United States of America on acid-free paper

www.atrandom.com

246897531

FIRST EDITION

Book design by Casey Hampton

IN MEMORY OF THEIR VALOR

Maj. Megan McClung
2006, Ramadi

Capt. Travis Patriquin
2006, Ramadi

Spc4 Vincent Pomante
2006, Ramadi

Sheik Sattar Abu Risha
2007, Ramadi

Cpl. Abraham Simpson
2004, Fallujah

Sgt. Jonathan Simpson
2006, Habbaniyah

Lt. Col. Suleiman
2004, Fallujah

Sgt. David Weir
2006, Baghdad

Maj. Douglas Zembiec
2007, Baghdad

CONTENTS

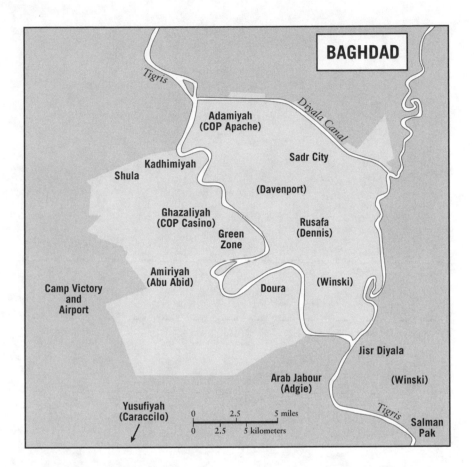

BAGHDAD

Tigris

Diyala Canal

Adamiyah
(COP Apache)

Sadr City

Kadhimiyah

Shula

(Davenport)

Ghazaliyah
(COP Casino)

Green
Zone

Rusafa
(Dennis)

Amiriyah
(Abu Abid)

Doura

(Winski)

Camp Victory
and
Airport

Jisr Diyala

Arab Jabour
(Adgie)

(Winski)

Tigris

Yusufiyah
(Caraccilo)

Salman
Pak

0   2.5   5 miles

0   2.5   5 kilometers

PREFACE

When I first met Capt. Doug Zembiec in 2004, he was sitting on the roof of a shot-up house, nibbling on a cracker and shouting into a headset over the cracks of rifle fire. The fierce battle for Fallujah had been raging for weeks. Black stubble covered his cheeks and his eyes were bloodshot. He flashed a wicked grin and said, "Welcome to chaos."

Crouched behind the sandbags lining the rooftop wall, two snipers sat hunched over rifles with telescopic sights. Zembiec pointed to a few insurgents darting across a street several hundred yards away. One sniper fired a .50-caliber shell, big as a cigar, and the recoil rocked him back. The other took a shot with a smaller M14 rifle. "The corporal with the M14," he said, "has more kills. If we keep knocking them down out there, they'll get the message."

An All-American wrestler while at the Naval Academy, Zembiec took care of his men, adored his wife and baby daughter, bragged about his dad, shared food with the civilians hiding downstairs, stored the china away from the bullet-shattered windows, and shot at every insurgent. He was a fighter, an infantryman. His men had dubbed him "the Lion."

I stayed with Doug and his company inside Fallujah, and several months later caught up with him again on patrols outside the city. We stayed in touch and just missed linking up in May of 2007 in Baghdad, where his unit was hunting down al Qaeda terrorists. Later that month, while leading his team on a raid, the Lion of Fallujah was killed.

From the summer of 2003 until the fall of 2006, we were losing militarily. Sunni and Shiite extremists were threatening to break Iraq apart. Then the tide of war swung. This narrative describes how warriors like Doug Zembiec turned the war around.

There are two broad views of history. By far the more popular is the "Great Man" view: that nations are led from the top. Leaders like Caesar and Lincoln shape history. Most accounts of Iraq subscribe to the Great Man view. The books about Iraq by senior officials like Bremer, Tenet, Franks, and Sanchez have at their core a wonderful sense of self-worth: History is all about them.

The other view of history holds that the will of the people provides the momentum for change. Leaders are important, but only when they channel, or simply have the common sense to ride, the popular movement. "Battle is decided not by the orders of a commander in chief," Tolstoy wrote in *War and Peace,* "but by the spirit of the army."

Iraq reflected Tolstoy's model. Events were driven by the spirit, or dispirit, of the people and tribes. Iraq wasn't a "Great Man" or a generals' war. There wasn't a blueprint and scheme of maneuver akin to what guides units in conventional war. The generals were learning at the same time as the corporals. At the top, it was easiest to talk with those officials who had spent time on the lines and didn't substitute theories to cover up what they didn't know. Generals Casey, Petraeus, Mattis, and Odierno were remarkably candid, willing to share with a fellow grunt their feelings about leadership and operations. I was struck that all four used the word "complex" time and again. Iraq was a kaleidoscope. Turn it one way and you think you see the pattern. Then along comes some unexpected event and the pattern dissolves.

This book has two parts. The early chapters bring us through mid-2006, amidst strategic mistakes and a growing frustration among the troops. At that time, many in the States believed the only course was to leave Iraq, despite the consequences. Then came a remarkable U-turn, described in the later chapters. By 2008, the steadfastness of our soldiers and excellent leadership had reversed the course of the war.

A cottage industry has sprung up in academia to study counterinsurgency as if it were a branch of sociology. In this book—a narrative of war—you meet the troops. War is the act of killing. As a nation, we have become so refined and so removed from danger that we don't utter the word "kill." The troops in this book aren't victims; they are hunters.

———

Iraq was my second insurgency. As a grunt in Vietnam, I patrolled with a Marine squad and Vietnamese farmers in a Combined Action Platoon, or CAP, in a remote village. Later, as a counterinsurgency analyst at the RAND Corporation, I visited Malaysia and Northern Ireland to look at British techniques and wrote a book, *The Village,* about fighting in combined units in Vietnam.

In Iraq, over a span of six years I accompanied, or embedded with, over sixty American and Iraqi battalions. In the course of hundreds of patrols and operations, I interviewed more than 2,000 soldiers, as well as generals and senior officials. In this book I also cite campaign plans, because they illustrate how senior staffs assessed the war, and how difficult it was for senior officials in Iraq, let alone the White House, to understand what was going on.

In conventional war, the locations of the battlefields change as the armies move on. In counterinsurgency war, the goal is to control a population that does not move. The adversaries fight on fixed battlefields—the same cities and villages. What changes is time rather than location. To describe the war, I bring the reader back again and again to the same cities in Anbar Province—the stronghold of the insurgency—and the same neighborhoods in Baghdad, the heart of Iraq. These two locales accounted for most of the fighting and most of our casualties.

This narrative describes how the war was fought by our soldiers, managed by our generals, and debated at home. The tone is not gentle toward those at the top, military and civilian, supporters and detractors of the war alike. After Vietnam, I never envisioned that I would again know so many who died so young. What angered me after six years of reporting from the lines was how so many at the top talked mainly to one another and did not take the time to study the war. The same was true of the war's critics. The turnaround in the war went largely unacknowledged.

The generals, ambassadors, and senators will write their own books. The intent of this book is to deepen the reader's understanding of the performance of our soldiers and the war's complexity. It lays out the mistakes and the learning, drawing conclusions and lessons. Our society imposed restraints and expectations that can lead to failure on a future battlefield. At the same time, no reasonable observer could watch how our military adapted without being impressed by the resilience and learning up and down the chain of command. It was a remarkable turnaround.

———

The confused fighting in Iraq has been distant from our lives at home. Only the families of our soldiers sacrificed. The rest of us stood on the sidelines, applauding the soldiers—whom few of us knew—while criticizing their leadership and their mission. Our domestic politics became ever more divisive and impervious to progress on the battlefield.

Our soldiers deserved better. No nation ever fought a more restrained and honorable war. Having changed its strategy, our military has merited a fresh hearing. Al Qaeda in Iraq has been shattered. The Sunni tribes have aligned with the Americans. Iraqi forces have taken the lead against rogue militias. In 2008, the battlefield is under control and violence has subsided.

Iraq remains a long-term project about which reasonable people disagree. Whether critics of the war can acknowledge the gains as well as the defeats is problematical. Political attitudes have hardened into articles of faith. In an election year, Iraq will be an incendiary topic, with politicians making assertions that aren't true. I hope this book will inform the reader. Understanding the war is the best antidote to demagoguery.

Shortly before he was killed, Doug Zembiec wrote to his family, "I honestly believe we can win this one now."

Our soldiers fought to give us a reasonable choice. We can persist in Iraq at reduced cost or we can leave altogether. Regardless of what we decide, we owe it to the Doug Zembiecs to give a fair hearing to what they accomplished.

THE
STRONGEST
TRIBE

ONE

HOW TO CREATE A MESS

SUMMER 2003

In late March of 2003, Col. Joseph F. Dunford led 5,000 Marines in a wild dash up Highway One to seize Hantush Airfield, a major base south of Baghdad. Hidden behind dirt berms, Iraqi soldiers fired rocket-propelled grenades and machine guns at the tanks and Humvees roaring by. One machine gun concentrated its fire on a lead Humvee, killing Gunnery Sgt. Joseph Menusa.

When the fighting subsided, Dunford sent out a radio message that he was pushing north to Baghdad. As expected, the Iraqis took the bait and scrambled to block the highway, while Dunford shifted his regiment to fall on Baghdad from the east. At the last minute, higher headquarters ordered him to halt.

That night, I asked Dunford what had happened. He slowly took off his boots, choosing his words. He had brought enough foot powder to go for weeks with two pairs of socks, so you could listen to him without gasping. "Higher headquarters changed the mission," he said. "The main effort now isn't Baghdad; it's the supply lines to the rear. We're to wait."

The division commander, Maj. Gen. James N. Mattis, sent higher headquarters an angry message that the enemy would sniff out the planned feint, resulting in American casualties. "We should attack soonest," Mattis wrote. But three days passed before the Marines were allowed to attack, reclaiming the ground where Gunny Menusa had died. The lower levels had opened an opportunity that higher head-quarters suppressed. Obstinately, high-ranking officials later denied that there was an alternative not taken. "There was never a pause," Defense Secretary Donald Rumsfeld told the press. Yet inside the Pentagon, Rumsfeld himself had demanded to know why the attack had stopped. Gen. Tommy Franks, in command of the invasion, was equally disingenuous in his memoir, claiming there never was a pause—because air attacks had continued.

Mattis disagreed. "I didn't want the pause. Nothing was holding us up," he told *Inside the Pentagon*. "The toughest order I had to give the whole campaign was to call back the assault force."

Because the campaign ended triumphantly, the incident seemed trivial. Senior levels had ignored the ground commanders, however, a tendency that would persist for several years because the war seemed impossible to lose. As a colonel in the 82nd Airborne Division said to me, "There's no threat that a well-trained platoon can't handle." To a hammer, every problem looks like a nail. The challenge, though, wasn't how to employ a platoon; it was how to change the conditions so that there would be no need for that platoon.

On the political and military level, roads not taken mark the history of this war. America was so powerful it seemed any road would lead to a quick exit. Until December of 2006, there was never a choice of "do this or lose." In 1862, President Abraham Lincoln knew he had to fire Gen. George B. McClellan or lose the war. In 1943, Gen. Dwight D. Eisenhower knew he had to refuse British entreaties to invade France prematurely, or lose the war. No such historic choices loomed in Iraq.

Indeed, during the first year of the occupation, the going seemed so easy that we split the team and drove down two roads, getting stuck in the sand in both.

ORGANIZING TO FAIL

After al Qaeda destroyed the Twin Towers in 2001, the American public was in no mood for quibbling. In Afghanistan, the Taliban was smashed quickly, while al Qaeda and Osama bin Laden retreated into Pakistan. Based on incorrect intelligence, the administration concluded that Saddam Hussein possessed weapons of mass destruction that he could give to terrorists. Secretary of State Colin Powell argued the case convincingly before the United Nations, and Congress voted to use force.

In the fastest blitzkrieg in history, the American and British forces sped 400 miles from Kuwait to Baghdad, rolling over and around a demoralized Iraqi Army that—having learned from the air bombardment in 1991—abandoned its armor. On April 9, 2003, the massive statue of Saddam was ripped from its pedestal in Firdos Square in Baghdad. Television images of joyous Iraqis dancing beside laughing American soldiers flashed across the globe. President George W. Bush and Secretary of State Powell stood side by side in the Oval Office, savoring the moment. Saddam's reign of terror had ended, but chaos was about to reign.

Throughout the city, American commanders stood off to one side as mobs rushed like locusts into hundreds of government buildings and stripped them clean. As looters danced by in carnival glee, I asked an American colonel what he was going to do to restore order.

"Nothing," he said. "I have no such orders. They deserve whatever they can haul away, after what Saddam did to them."

General Franks, in charge of Central Command, was soon to retire. He had achieved victory the good old-fashioned way—with tanks, air, and artillery, just as Kuwait City had been liberated in 1991 and Paris had been liberated in 1944. Once the war was over, he and Secretary of Defense Rumsfeld had agreed that retired Army Lt. Gen. Jay Garner would serve as the Central Command deputy for Phase IV—the occupation of Iraq.

Yet when fighting petered out in late April, the Phase III commander for combat operations, Lt. Gen. David McKiernan, kept control over all units. Central Command never passed control from Phase III to Phase IV. Garner was supposedly in charge, but the 173,000 soldiers in the invincible coalition did not work for him. He was stranded in Baghdad, his tiny staff out of touch and having to hitch rides to meetings. Garner was a deputy commander with no one to command.

On the Iraqi side, governance had collapsed. Most workers stayed home, electric power was sporadic, and the blast furnace heat of summer was approaching. General Franks flew into Baghdad for a photo op with his conquering generals, while on street corners tanks loitered as looters swarmed past. No one was in charge. Television crews captured the irony of the scene—an American military machine implacable in battle, flummoxed in peace.

For several weeks after Baghdad fell, Central Command was in charge and chose to do nothing. During the invasion, Rumsfeld took pride in showing off a list of fifty things that could go wrong, such as torching of the oilfields or massive oil spills. The error not mentioned was a collapse of the Iraqi government coupled with no American plan to restore it.

The lack of a postwar plan was caused in large part by longstanding Pentagon strategy. For decades, the military had designed force-planning guidance that emphasized fighting and swiftly winning a major war, then withdrawing quickly to be ready to fight somewhere else. This planning method ensured that the budget went to the fighting forces, while ignoring the forces needed for an occupation.

In early May, Ambassador Zalmay Khalilzad and Assistant Secretary of State Ryan C. Crocker visited Baghdad and left shocked by the chaos and the American paralysis. Washington responded not by addressing the systemic failures of a detached military and a rudderless administration, but by replacing Garner.

The administration offered Garner's job to five persons, including former senator Howard Baker (R-TN), a deft politician. Eventually Ambassador L. Paul Bremer III, who was acceptable to both Powell and Rumsfeld, took the job. A graduate of Yale and Harvard Business School, Bremer had followed up a successful career in the foreign service by working in private business for former secretary of state Henry Kissinger. "Jerry [Bremer] is a good man," Kissinger quipped, "but he's a control freak." This elicited raised eyebrows among those who had experienced Kissinger's controlling ways and suggested that the administration didn't know whether a savvy politician or a strong manager was best suited for ruling Iraq.

Bush designated Bremer his proconsul to Iraq, with the mission and resources to establish the new Iraqi government and its security forces. At the same time, he tasked the U.S. military with providing security until the Iraqis took over. The military reported to the secretary of defense, while Bremer bypassed Rumsfeld, using Condoleezza Rice, the national security adviser, as a back door into the White House. With the approval of the U.S. military, Bush had instituted disunity of command. The divisiveness between Bremer and the military was to grow steadily over the next year, severely hampering the war effort.

Franks applauded, warmly endorsing the sacking of his own deputy. Bremer would have more clout, Franks later explained, because he would be close to the president. The White House provided Bremer with a staff called the Coalition Provisional Authority, or CPA, an amalgam of young people living in tight quarters behind huge walls, shut off from Iraq. The staff had no identifiable criterion for selection, save a willingness to serve and approval by the White House.

CentCom was still responsible for Iraq's security. With Rumsfeld's

approval, CentCom appointed Lt. Gen. Ricardo Sanchez, the most junior three-star in the Army, as the senior commander in Iraq. To support Sanchez in his Baghdad headquarters, a pickup staff called Joint
Task Force 7, or JTF-7, was cobbled together from different commands.

THE BAATHIST PURGE

Bremer arrived in Baghdad in early May. Stunned to see looters on the
streets, he suggested shooting a few to make an example. He apologized for the remark, though it did illustrate that he was not hesitant or
weak-minded. He showed that by swiftly issuing an edict banning from
government all Baathists with the rank of colonel or its civilian equivalent.

The Baathist Party was the core administrative strength of Saddam's regime. Few could gain midlevel jobs such as teachers or town
administrators without belonging to the party. In Iraq, the Baath Party
union card was reserved mainly for Sunnis. Although Bremer equated
them to the Nazis under Hitler, Baathists were less virulent or latently
threatening. As a transnational ideology that both predated and survived Saddam's reign, Baathism was a loose amalgam of socialism and
pan-Arabism. In Iraq, millions were Baathists.

Bremer thought he was banning only the top one percent. Saddam,
though, had so inflated military grades that colonels commanded battalions of 400 soldiers. Barring the deflated rank of colonel and its
civilian equivalent threw out the middle-level managers.

Compounding the problem, de-Baathification was placed in the
hands of Ahmed Chalabi, a wily Shiite expatriate with chameleon political adroitness and overarching ambition whose core support lay inside
the upper reaches of the Pentagon. De-Baathification became Chalabi's
calling card to ingratiate himself with the Shiite community. He set about
his task with energy and self-promotion, and the real and perceived effects of what he accomplished went far beyond what Bremer had intended. In his memoir, former director of central intelligence George
Tenet cited 100,000 Iraqis "driven to the brink" by de-Baathification, a
number hotly disputed by Bremer.

THE IRAQI ARMY DISSOLVED

In late April, the U.S. Marines were sent from Baghdad into the south
to occupy a dozen cities containing eight million Shiites spread across
an area the size of Wyoming. Receiving little direction from the Coali-

tion Provisional Authority, the division commander, Major General Mattis, devised his own plan. Called "Mad Dog" for his ferocity in battle, Mattis was a bachelor who lived to lead troops. A devotee of military history, he had built a private library with hundreds of obscure titles. To Mattis, the Shiite south was a return to the days of the Banana Wars in the early twentieth century, when small contingents of marines were sent off to obscure Latin American countries to fight guerrillas and train local constabularies. Drawing on those experiences, the Marines had written their own treatise on government. Called the *Small Wars Manual,* it was full of practical advice—such as how to harness mules—for advancing the principles of John Locke, including how to hold elections. Mattis looked forward to updating the manual. Combat operations were put aside; governance and the restoration of services were now his mission.

His boss, Lt. Gen. James T. Conway, fully agreed. Conway commanded the Marine Expeditionary Force, or MEF, which included the division, an air wing, and a logistics brigade. Conway sent home his artillery and tank units, signaling that the "kinetic" war was over. No more shooting. Infantry battalions would restore basic services and bring back normalcy. Marines would walk the streets without armor or helmets.

If someone shoots at you, Mattis told his troops, kill him and go back to work. The people are not your enemy. Your job is to establish a functioning government. Reorganize the Iraqi Army to provide local security. The MEF has the list of Iraqi units to be recalled to duty. In our sector, the 3rd Iraqi Division will help us.

On May 20, a tired, dirty Mattis walked into his modest division headquarters after visiting his units. He hated PowerPoint briefings. It was his habit to gather his staff, from PFC to colonel, in a circle to discuss the day's events. He liked to force sharp questions, insisting everyone stay until someone challenged him. On this evening, a lieutenant asked if the Marines would provide security after the Iraqi Army was disbanded.

"That's not gonna happen," Mattis said. "We're not homesteading here. The Iraqis have their own army."

The next day, Ambassador Bremer dissolved the Iraqi Army. The American divisions on the ground were not consulted. Instead, Bremer had the concurrence of the White House, the Pentagon, and the top level of the U.S. military. President Bush sent Bremer a congratulatory memo—"I agree fully; you're doing a great job!" The rationale was that the army was the hated enforcer of the Saddam rule, bloated in size, exploitive of the Shiites who formed its enlisted ranks, and commanded by Sunnis who had to be removed. Besides, the army no longer existed; it had dissolved itself, as unit after unit had deserted. At a press conference in Baghdad, the news was greeted as ho-hum.

That night, the lieutenant asked Mattis when all those out-of-work, pissed-off Iraqi soldiers—estimates ranged up to 400,000—would start an insurgency. "He nailed me," Mattis said. "That's what I get for being a wise-ass, challenging smart lieutenants. We generals get too full of ourselves."

IGNORING A "CLASSICAL GUERRILLA-TYPE CAMPAIGN"

During the summer of 2003, the Sunni insurgency predicted by the lieutenant did emerge. Its fuel was the Sunni belief that they had been disenfranchised. Nine million Sunnis had lost their position of dominance over eighteen million Shiites. The decrees about high-level Baathists and about the army, coupled with Bremer rather than an Iraqi appearing on television as the ruler of the country, convinced many Sunnis that a pogrom loomed. The Americans had the power and the Shiites had the motivation. Persecution was the way top-level Baathists had acted. Now payback was coming.

After the invasion, there was no functioning central government and no representatives to the people. The eighteen provinces were left on their own. The mosques were the centers of social discourse and the imams were widely believed. In the Sunni areas, imams were free to preach hate, gloom, and sedition—and many did.

The insurgency blossomed spontaneously as small cells with no centralized leadership sprang up among tribes throughout the Sunni Triangle, which stretched 350 miles west from Baghdad and 400 miles to the north. Some of Saddam's coterie had fled to Syria with carloads of cash. They settled into comfortable villas and sent money and instructions back into Anbar Province, a vast expanse of desert and farmland stretching from the outskirts of Baghdad 280 miles west to Syria.

Separate from the Baathists, a small group of al Qaeda–type extremists led by Abu Musab al-Zarqawi began a bombing campaign against Shiites and soft targets. In the 1990s, with the bombings of the USS *Cole*, the Khobar Towers in Saudi Arabia, and the U.S. embassies in Nairobi and Dar es Salaam, al Qaeda had initiated a campaign of mass killing that reached its apex on 9/11. In Iraq, Zarqawi dispatched suicide bombers to murder mass numbers of innocent Shiites in order to provoke civil war between the Sunnis and Shiites. By blowing up the

United Nations building in Baghdad in August, he drove out of the country both the U.N. staff and those of other nations. Eventually he hoped to set up caliphates in the Sunni provinces and strangle the government in Baghdad. Charismatic and energetic, Zarqawi received support and recruits from the more radical imams.

Tribal fighters comprised most of the insurgents. Determined to drive out the infidel invaders and their Shiite collaborators, they saw themselves as the honorable resistance. They had no overarching political goal. These were eighteen-year-olds with AK-47s and no money, no prospect of marriage or sex, no music, no recreation, no job, and no direction given by elders whose status had been demeaned by invaders who didn't speak the language.

Our military prided itself on "maneuver warfare," probing, finding an enemy's weak spots, and then striking at his central nervous system. Don't, for instance, fight every Iraqi division on the march to Baghdad; instead, flow around them, rush to Saddam's lair, and cut the head off the snake. That was the smart way to fight.

Only now our military was facing an enemy that had no head, no central nervous system, no hierarchical command and control that could be destroyed. There was no structure to the Sunni insurgency. It was like swatting bees.

From a palm grove or behind an overpass, rocket-propelled grenades, RPGs, would zip past a Humvee, followed by wild bursts from AKs. The Humvee crew would swivel its .50-caliber machine gun and pound the suspected firing position. When the guerrillas did not rehearse an escape route, they were cut down. With a Darwinian world demanding a quick learning curve, by midsummer the more foolish attacks had petered out, replaced by bombs or improvised explosive devices—IEDs—along the highways and sniping at longer distances, usually from the far side of a canal or deep ditch.

Rumsfeld refused to admit an insurgency had begun, insisting that the resistance was comprised of "dead-enders." Each morning the president was shown an easel containing fifty-two cards with the faces of wanted leaders of Saddam's regime. A succession of raids was netting an impressive rate of arrests. But the number of attacks was increasing even as the number of fugitives in the deck of cards was decreasing.

In mid-July, Gen. John Abizaid acknowledged that he was facing "a classical guerrilla-type campaign." An Arabic-speaking Lebanese-American with an advanced degree from Harvard, Abizaid was respected by his peers and liked by his staff. He had a knack for getting along with people, including Rumsfeld, who had selected him to re-

place Franks, ignoring the decades-old Army-Marine agreement to rotate that command on an even basis between Army and Marine generals. To his staff, Abizaid's unease with Sanchez as the commander in
Iraq was evident. Too decent a leader to take charge away from the man
on the ground, in referring to "a classical guerrilla-type campaign"
Abizaid was sending a strong signal to Sanchez. Basic doctrine stressed
that raids weren't the solution to an insurgency.

No observable operational change by the JTF followed. The two-
headed coalition command in Baghdad—the CPA and the JTF—had no
coherent outreach program and no credible Iraqi leaders to deal with
the insurgents. The JTF oversaw the 170,000 soldiers in six divisions—
five American and one British—that were spread out among 28 million
Iraqis in a country the size of California. In Baghdad, a few key billets
were reserved for the Brits, and the 5,000 troops from the United Kingdom in the Basra region at the southern end of Iraq were referred to as
British. In the rest of Iraq, the term "coalition forces" was commonly
used, although the Americans comprised 95 percent of the force.

Attacks inside Baghdad during the summer were rare. Over twenty
civilians were killed each month, though, as American soldiers, not
knowing which driver might be a suicide bomber, repeatedly opened
fire on approaching vehicles. It was morally wrenching to pulverize a
car, the bullets shattering the windshield and the tires, the car rolling to
a stop with the engine smoking, waiting for the bomb blast that never
came and walking cautiously forward to prod the blood-drenched
driver, head back and mouth open in death. The first human reaction
was to blame the driver—why didn't he have the sense to stop? The
second reaction was to distance yourself from the Iraqis. It wasn't the
same as killing an American for running a red light in heavy traffic.
Somehow Iraqis were different; they had to be.

In the Sunni Triangle, the security approach was mixed. In Anbar
Province to the west, elements of the 3rd Infantry Division, worn out
after living in the deserts of Kuwait and Iraq for nine months, adopted
a patient, avuncular style with the tempestuous Sunni tribes, balancing
a show of armored force with a willingness to stay out of local affairs.
Crippling the effort was a lack of local Sunni leaders and the refusal
of the CPA to give the military tens of millions of dollars to spend on
projects.

North of Baghdad, the 4th Infantry Division tended to focus on
raids and sweeps after the "dead-enders." These sweeps consistently
netted prisoners—some insurgents and some innocents—with mixed
results that prompted Thomas Ricks in his classic book, *Fiasco,* to

claim that rough tactics were inflaming the insurgency. The numbers supported Ricks. Each month, coalition forces sent about 1,000 insurgents to long-term prison, while killing hundreds more. Thousands more Iraqis were detained for several days and then released. The 82nd Airborne alone detained 3,500 Iraqis in six months. Yet the JTF estimate of the total insurgency remained fixed at 5,000. Even granting the huge unknowns, the JTF was acknowledging that at the least the insurgency was replenishing its losses.

In the far north, the 101st Air Assault Division, commanded by General David H. Petraeus, shifted gears altogether, replacing military operations with civic action. When Max Boot, a fellow at the Council on Foreign Relations, and I visited with Petraeus in August 2003, we were surprised by the scale and the enthusiasm of the effort. Each of the three brigade commanders was acting like a governor in a huge swath of desert and farmland, settling land disputes, adjudicating tribal feuds, and doling out scarce monies for start-up projects. "We're in a race with ourselves," Petraeus told us. "Now we're seen as liberators. Eventually we'll be seen as occupiers."

A large number of officers from the disbanded army had returned to Mosul, and Petraeus knew it was only a matter of time until many were recruited into the insurgency. Before that happened, he wanted to change underlying conditions to take away their incentives to support an insurgency. To him, that meant creating a class of local leaders, each with a personal stake in the new Iraq. That required money to pay the salaries of municipal workers, police, teachers—anyone in government. It meant opening roads and border crossings with Syria to stimulate trade. It meant handing out start-up funds to aspiring entrepreneurs. Inside his division headquarters, Iraqis owned and operated a restaurant that served excellent roasted chicken.

The slogan on the wall of the division's operations center read: "Money is ammunition." The CPA had on hand billions in Iraqi funds, seized after Baghdad fell. Bremer, though, was parsimonious, doling out small sums and insisting on project proposals that placed senior commanders like Petraeus in a paper-chase loop.

"When we arrived, the Iraqis believed in our embodiment of capitalism and democracy," retired Rear Adm. David Oliver, the CPA comptroller, said later. "We [the CPA] had the money to give them. Sending our battalions out into the provinces without big bucks was stupid. We blew it."

Petraeus created his own work-around to defang the de-Baathification order. After hundreds of former Baathists signed a pledge of good faith, he rehired them into middle-level management. In Baghdad, there were grumblings that Petraeus had cut "a separate peace" by his independent wheeling and dealing. In turn, Petraeus warned the CPA that disbanding the Iraqi Army had been a grave mistake.

LOCAL ELECTIONS: THE ROAD NOT TAKEN

In the Shiite south, Mattis had dispatched a battalion to each of seven key cities spread across hundreds of miles. Lacking the helicopter mobility of the 101st, the battalion commanders, to their delight, were on their own. The guidance from Mattis was remarkably similar to that of Petraeus 300 miles to the north. Petraeus had written his Ph.D. thesis at Princeton on counterinsurgency; Mattis studied in his own library. The two men were physically similar, fit and trim, of average height and unimposing mien. Both were energetic combat infantry leaders who loved roaming the battlefields. Had he chosen a business career, Petraeus, with keen political instincts, would have been a CEO making millions. Mattis, less comfortable in social circles, would have made an excellent college football coach, happily exhorting his players while intently studying the field of contact. Both saw their mission as shaping the economic and political conditions of the new Iraq. Both understood this was the role of the CPA. Neither cared about the dividing line. Both viewed the CPA as part of the problem. Like Petraeus, Mattis told his battalions to restart government and restore services.

In Hillah, 100 miles south of Baghdad—home of the Hanging Gardens of Babylon, one of the Seven Wonders of the Ancient World—the anti-coalition Shiite cleric Moqtada al-Sadr exhorted his followers to protest the American presence. Faced with an unruly mob, Lt. Col. John Mayer took off his helmet and armored vest and strode into their midst with an interpreter, shouting, Is this the thanks you give to the soldiers who removed Saddam's boot from your neck? Abashed, the crowd dispersed. The next day, the city council asked Mayer to sit with them.

In Karbala, a city revered by the Shiites, Lt. Col. Matt Lopez organized the elders, appointed officials based on a show of hands in meetings outside city hall, solicited donations and gifts from the States, and settled disputes by holding court once a week. Upon hearing that his battalion was leaving, the council sent a protest letter to Mattis and elected Lopez the mayor.

Battalion 1-7 went to Najaf, the holy city where the Grand Ayatollah Ali al-Sistani and the Howza council of religious elders lived; 1-7 was a high-morale, tightly bonded unit that at the start of the war had seized the "Crown Jewel"—Iraq's major oil pumping station—and ended their march to Baghdad with a wild firefight on the grounds of Baghdad University. Arriving in Najaf in early May, the battalion commander, Lt. Col. Chris Conlin, conferred with the political and religious party leaders. Each time he received money, bulldozers, or cranes for a project, he appointed Iraqis as managers.

In late July, Sadr organized a protest, busing in 5,000 supporters to demand that the Americans leave. Shouting and pushing their way down the main street, the protesters angered the local residents. Screams about American "devils" and a "sissy" city council were met by vendors cursing "beggars" and "Iranian puppets." Sadr was seen as a troublemaking outsider, while Conlin had warm relations with the religious leaders and the city council. A poll taken in the city showed an astonishing 90 percent approved of the American presence.

After consulting with clerics representing Sistani, Conlin decided to hold elections for mayor and city council, confident Sadr's standing would diminish when his candidate was crushed. Conlin envisioned a council empowered with legitimacy, authority, and funds provided from the $9.8 billion in Iraqi funds controlled by the CPA.

"I thumbed through my *Small Wars Manual*, 1939 edition," Conlin told me. "I found the instructions in Chapter 14—'Supervision of Elections.' So we sat down with the Iraqis and planned an election."

The Joint Task Force enthusiastically endorsed the plan. If Conlin succeeded, the JTF would send his procedures and lessons to the other battalions. Within three months, sixty elections would be held in eighteen provinces. Lieutenant General Conway flew with Conlin to Baghdad to brief Ambassador Bremer.

"Bremer sent word he didn't have time to meet with General Conway," Conlin said. "His Excellency sent down an 'elections expert' to tell us we were out of our league. Then the 'expert' abruptly left because Bremer wanted to see him. It was insulting."

That night the word went out over the classified military Internet—Bremer will decide when, where, and how any election will be held. Sadr, wanted for murder under an Iraqi warrant, remained free to preach sedition because the CPA and the JTF couldn't agree on how to arrest him. The military stood down their plan for local elections.

"Baghdad-centric CPA kept all control," Conlin said. "In Najaf, Sadr wouldn't have been elected dogcatcher. CPA, though, worried the wrong guy might get elected. Guess what? By the time they got around to national elections, Sadr and the wrong guys were organized—and they won."

The CPA could make legitimate arguments against local elections. But the peremptory dismissal of military commanders held in high regard by the Shiites, who kept the CPA at arm's length, was unfortunate. There were press critiques that Petraeus was trying to buy his way out of a problem, while the Marines were trying to vote their way out of Iraq, indicating that sources within the CPA were unhappy with U.S. generals meddling in political matters.

In the summer of 2003, though, there was no gainsaying the genuine popularity of the American battalion commanders like Lopez, Mayer, and Conlin. The "dim-witted grunts" wanted to hand Iraq back to Iraqis. Local elections, coupled with funding for local projects and patronage, would have empowered what Petraeus called "local stakeholders" in the provinces, Sunni and Shiite. It was a road not taken.

IGNORING THE IRAQI ARMY

Forty miles east of Najaf, in the sprawling industrial city of Diwaniyah, Lt. Col. Pat Malay and Battalion 3-5 faced a different problem in July of 2003. The CPA had decided to pay a lump-sum severance to those in the disbanded military. Tens of thousands had poured into the city, swamping the Iraqi disbursing office.

Malay, a strict disciplinarian, stepped in to impose order, Marine-style. On the city's outskirts, he found an abandoned warehouse with a parking lot 200 yards long, cluttered with junk. Inside a day, the marines pushed, plowed, and shoveled the detritus off the hardtop, which they then marked off with chalk lines, separated by a few rows of barbed wire. At the far end they slapped together a row of plywood offices with wide windows on one side.

The Marines moved in Iraqi officials, together with three shifts of women cashiers and a mound of U.S. dollars. This lured money-changers insisting on absurd rates of exchange for Iraqi dinars. Knowing the Iraqi soldiers would be ripped off, Malay dispatched his squads in Humvees stuffed with millions of U.S. dollars. Once they returned from bases in Baghdad and other provinces with pallets of dinars, Malay announced to the Iraqi soldiers that he was open for business.

Want your money? Line up on the chalk lines, single file, no shoving or you're sent to the rear of the line. Once at the teller window, show your ID, take your cash, and go home.

No armed American policed a single line. Two sniper teams stood on the roof of the warehouse, visible to all. In three weeks, they had to shoot two men. One, turned away after showing a fake ID, had threatened those who were jeering him with a grenade. The other was a robber who held up a former soldier and tried to escape across an open field, while the outraged soldier screamed at the top of his lungs.

In the third week, a Spanish battalion, due to replace the Marines, took over for a practice run, while Malay observed from inside the factory. Nervous young Spaniards in fresh uniforms and polished boots stood beside the chalk lines, yelling senseless orders at the rough-looking Iraqi men. The horde of former soldiers swayed uneasily. More yelling, more aimless pushing back and forth. The Iraqis had no place to go. No one was giving up his place in line. They weren't leaving without their money. Some picked up rocks. The Spaniards backed away, gesturing with their rifles.

Malay had seen enough. He ran out, followed by a squad of marines. "Okay, good job, okay," he said to the Spanish colonel. "That's enough for today. Thank you. *Gracias.*"

As the relieved Spaniards walked back to their waiting trucks, Malay faced the thousands of Iraqis. "Put down those stones," he yelled, while an interpreter shouted in Arabic. "That's not how veterans behave. What's the matter with you, scaring those nice young men?"

The Iraqis hesitated. Here was a crusty old colonel with pure white hair—no helmet, no armored vest, pistol in holster—reprimanding them, soldier to soldier. He carried authority.

"Straighten out that line," he yelled, walking along as though inspecting recruits on a parade deck. "Shape up. No more foolishness."

The Iraqis tossed aside the rocks and got back in line. Malay called headquarters, recommending the Spaniards not take over until he finished paying 80,000 Iraqi soldiers, plus 17,000 day laborers. Mattis drove down to take a look around and Malay walked with him among the thousands of Iraqis. Seeing Mattis's two stars, the soldiers stood erect when Mattis looked at them.

"We have our pick of the litter, General," Malay said. "Special Forces, rifle battalions, commandos—you say the word and their officers will have them standing tall tomorrow. We can select the best for our own Iraqi Army."

"Not our call," Mattis said. "CPA determines what to do about the Iraqi Army."

After being snubbed by Bremer, Conway was chagrined that the CPA had brushed aside his plan for bringing back the Iraqi Army. "The thing that did not happen in our plan," he later told an interviewer, "was to take advantage of the Iraqi army—based upon some early decisions made by the CPA. . . . I have every confidence we could have called them [the Iraqi soldiers] back into service. Absolutely."

DISUNITY OF EFFORT

The president had bestowed plenipotentiary power on Bremer. He wanted to be in charge, and the president had sent him there to be in charge.

The military, however, didn't work for Bremer, who had no military background or close connections with the commanders. He wasn't invited into the military briefings to listen to their frank appraisals or to review their careful staff work. Instead the CPA was viewed, in Mattis's words, as "a weight around the neck of the military . . . rather than having representatives in each battalion, it provides episodic and contradictory guidance at the operational level and glacial procedures for providing money."

Inside a unified military chain of command, Conlin's local elections in Najaf would have proceeded. Petraeus would have received the funds to develop stakeholders. As for Malay's proposal to bring back former soldiers, reconstituting the Iraqi Army would have been the new Marine mission. Conditions were stable enough; not a single marine had been killed. But Bremer, not Abizaid, was in charge of developing a new army. So Abizaid let the 40,000 marines—viewed as an expeditionary rather than an occupation force—go home.

The U.S. military was fond of saying that civilian and military tasks can be smoothly integrated through "unity of effort." This tautology (no one advocates "disunity of effort") avoided the central issue. The CPA wasn't just separate from the military; it was at odds with it.

TWO

DESCENT INTO CHAOS

SEPTEMBER–DECEMBER 2003

DENYING THE INSURGENCY

The Marines went home in September, having found the Shiite community in the south hospitable. In Karbala, the city council had tried to elect a Marine battalion commander its mayor. In 2003, the criminal activities of Shiite militias and the malign influence of Iran had not yet emerged.

By contrast, in the Sunni Triangle to the north, the insurgency worsened throughout the fall. General Eric K. Shinseki, the chief of staff of the Army, told Congress in February of 2003 that he estimated "several hundred thousand" soldiers were needed to occupy Iraq. In the fall of 2003, there were 150,000 coalition soldiers—plus 90,000 contractor personnel not shown on the rolls but carrying out military support duties. Perhaps 240,000 were not equivalent to "several hundred thousand." But adding more American soldiers would not have made a major difference unless they operated with Iraqi forces under an enlightened counterinsurgency strategy—which did not exist at the time.

Abizaid opposed sending more American troops to Iraq, arguing that he lacked not troops but rather intelligence about where the enemy was hiding. Indeed, more Americans would irritate more Iraqis, leading to less intelligence. This rationale exposed the heart of the dilemma. If the Sunni population viewed the Americans as the invaders and the insurgents as the honorable resisters—the popular image across the Sunni Triangle in the fall of 2003—then the population would not provide intelligence. Nor could the Americans, as counterinsurgency doctrine prescribed, offer the population protection and receive information in exchange. The Americans were the invaders, and there was no Iraqi government.

Once the Sunni officer corps and Baathist officeholders were disbarred, an insurgency of some magnitude was inevitable. The Sunni city closest to Baghdad was Fallujah, thirty-five miles to the west. Thousands of Baathist officers and intelligence apparatchiks fled there as Baghdad collapsed in April of 2003. When the 82nd Airborne Division occupied the city at the end of the month, there was a tragic confrontation with a mob that ended in the killings of two dozen men, women, and children. The 82nd was hastily replaced by a battalion from the combat-seasoned U.S. 3rd Infantry Division that was solicitous of the residents' concerns, withdrawing its armor to avoid disrupting traffic.

The presence of the American forces acting with restraint did not stop the growth of the insurgency, because the Americans didn't have Iraqis working with them. In the congested market area called the Jolan, the Americans daily walked right by the cafés where the insurgency was being plotted.

Left on their own, the American soldiers didn't know who was an insurgent and who was a farmer. Rarely was an Iraqi both. During the Vietnam era, Hollywood had created a myth about the farmer who hoes by day and shoots by night. A real farmer is too tired to do both. Combat is not a pickup game. The Viet Cong fighters lived in the bush and exacted a price in rice from the surrounding villages.

Iraq was somewhat different. The insurgents did not have to rely upon intimidation to get food. A common joke under Saddam was "You pretend to work, and the regime pretends to pay you." Pay consisted of free electricity, subsidized fuel, and free monthly sacks of grain and rice. This deal continued under the CPA, resulting in hundreds of thousands of unemployed men who didn't have to work to subsist. They could join the Shiite militia or the Sunni insurgency full-time and still be fed. They lived at home, hung out at the local mosque, joined the local gang, indulged in all sorts of fancies as the Humvees cruised by, and eagerly grabbed their rifles and ran out whenever shooting started.

The Iraqi intelligence service had been disbanded. The CIA had lists of those at the top, like the fifty-two unfortunates in the deck of cards.

They stood out, and would be hunted down. But what of all the street gangs that were sprouting up? It takes years to build up human networks and sift out how much you can trust agents and informers on a city-by-city basis. The Americans had some lists and conducted serial raids at night. That was a hit-and-miss affair because Iraqi addresses were notoriously inaccurate. There was no numbering system. Soldiers rushed into the wrong house, where the frightened occupants pointed to another house, where the same frustrating procedure would repeat itself.

A strategic contradiction plagued the counterinsurgent effort. On the one hand, Abizaid's belief that American soldiers were an antibody in the Iraqi culture meant our soldiers had to be removed as soon as possible, an imperative that dovetailed with Rumsfeld's goal. On the other hand, an insurgency grew when there was no government presence among the population. Since the CPA was the only government and the local Iraqi police and soldiers sympathized with the insurgents, not placing American soldiers on the streets guaranteed the growth of the insurgency.

Lieutenant General Sanchez resolved the contradiction by concluding that no insurgency existed. At the end of September, he told a press conference, "I don't think I've got any indication that it [resistance to the occupation] is beginning to take hold with the populace."

INADEQUATE FORCES

Supported by a president uninvolved in details, Bremer made up his own doctrine as he went along. After testifying articulately about a Marshall Plan to revitalize Iraq, he received $18 billion from Congress. He set aside $14 billion for development, mostly large infrastructure projects that contributed few funds for reducing unemployment. Backed by a JTF that saw no indication of resistance, resources for security were limited to $3.3 billion, or 18 percent of the total request.

Bremer explained in his memoir that he had "three red lines" for creating the new Iraq: 1) a written constitution before elections; 2) an uncorrupt police force attentive to civil rights; and 3) an army that would play no role in internal affairs. Steve Casteel, the senior police adviser, explained the rationale: "It's as simple as, when have you ever seen the police lead a coup? If you build a strong police force, you have a republic. If you build a strong military, you have a banana republic."

Having disposed of history in two sentences, the CPA retreated into the womb of the Green Zone, a fortified palace compound in the center of Baghdad. The CPA and JTF envisioned putting 85,000 trained police on the streets within a year, a ratio of 3 cops per 1,000 citizens. In New York City, the ratio is 5 per 1,000. On paper, 1,500 retired police from the United States and Europe were to be the trainers. By October, twenty-four police trainers had shown up in the Green Zone. Two retired cops were dispatched to Anbar, a province the size of Wyoming where tribal Sunnis in a dozen cities were launching 200 attacks a month. The math worked out to one police adviser per one million Iraqis.

Washington's bureaucratic politics were no more sensible. Condoleezza Rice, concerned that both Rumsfeld and Bremer went their independent ways, persuaded the president to let her establish the Iraqi Stabilization Group within her National Security Council staff. She brought into the White House Ambassador Robert Blackwill, known for his quick intellect and sharp elbows.

By October of 2005, the Pentagon was seriously upset at the CPA for the small size and slow training of the police and the new Iraqi Army. Abizaid ordered Sanchez to use the American divisions to train Iraqi battalions recruited locally, called the ICDC, or Iraqi Civil Defense Corps. The Iraqi Army being trained by the CPA for border defense cost ten times more than the ICDC force Abizaid wanted for counterinsurgency. When I discussed the security situation with Secretary Rumsfeld at the Pentagon in November, he was enthusiastic about expanding the ICDC at a greatly accelerated rate. Deputy Secretary of Defense Paul D. Wolfowitz constantly nagged Bremer to support the ICDC. Bremer responded by referring to the Pentagon as a "six-thousand-mile screwdriver"—and by dripping out funds through a spigot.

In the absence of local Iraqi soldiers in units like the ICDC, it was impossible to withdraw the American soldiers without conceding the population to the insurgents. Nevertheless, the president's goal was to reduce U.S. forces from 131,000 to 100,000 by the following April, and in the meantime to pull back into large bases to reduce vulnerability. Maj. Gen. Raymond Odierno, commanding the 4th Infantry Division north of Baghdad, later told me, "For the first eighteen months of the war, I believed Secretary Rumsfeld's vision [of a quick exit] made sense. It was only later that I questioned it." Alarmed by the shrinking number of American soldiers on the streets, Bremer and Ambassador Blackwill, visiting from the National Security Council in November, complained to Sanchez. He testily informed them that he took his orders from General Abizaid, not from civilians.

Inside the cities, fewer American patrols meant that the marketplaces and the streets were left in the control of insurgent gangs. An excellent highway system allowed insurgents to drive sixty kilometers, conduct an attack, and return safely home, avoiding the well-known government checkpoints. In the countryside, coalition foot patrols wandered across the vast terrain for days and never encountered an insurgent.

As lethality and momentum increased on the enemy side, force protection on the coalition side morphed from a constraint into its own mission. Minimizing American casualties became an objective that further reduced the patrol activities of American soldiers. Higher headquarters restricted movement beyond fortified cantonments to a minimum of four armored Humvees and twenty soldiers. This meant a platoon could mount about one patrol a day.

Senator John McCain of Arizona estimated that, out of 130,000 coalition troops, "at any time there's 30,000 on patrol." On TV talk shows and in press releases, McCain claimed that the number, which amounted to about 1,500 patrols, was woefully inadequate. "I made public statements about the need for more troops," he said. "I talked to Dr. Rice. I talked with Secretary Rumsfeld."

Compared to prior insurgencies, McCain was correct about the inadequate number of troops. When the White House did not respond to his concerns, he turned up the heat. "It will require the president's deep involvement in his administration's decision-making in Iraq," McCain said. "As Lincoln and Truman demonstrated, American presidents cannot always leave decisions on matters of supreme national interest to their subordinates."

In December, a scruffy and lonely Saddam Hussein was tracked down and hauled out of a roughshod underground shelter. Bremer rushed before the television cameras to triumphantly proclaim, "Ladies and gentlemen, we got him!"

Circumstances recommended more modesty. Saddam and his regime had faded. While Baathists were still doling out money to rebels, the Salafist religious extremists among the Sunnis were providing the unifying rhetoric so critical to an insurgency. Sunni tribal leaders were keeping their distance, not wanting to incur the wrath of the imams. The coalition leaders were less observant, with the exception of the CIA station chief, whose warnings were not heeded.

GETTING TOUGH

In the late fall of 2003, Ramadi, the capital of Anbar Province, sixty miles west of Baghdad, was functioning economically and politically.

The highway through the center of the city of 400,000 residents and 40,000 buildings was clogged with cars, their rusted-out exhaust mufflers emitting clouds of noxious smoke. I had walked through crowds of Iraqis queued up outside the Government Center seeking contracts, medical care, job interviews, resolution of disputes, and news of missing relatives. Inside, American soldiers sat alongside Iraqi office workers listening to complaints, offering reassurances, and entering data on computer spreadsheets. American diplomats in SUVs drove to work each day from their trailers at the nearby military base called Blue Diamond. The nearby open-air market was packed with men wandering idly amidst stalls selling meats, vegetables, clothes, and basic consumer goods. Real estate prices were up. Believing an armored vest sent the wrong signal, the diplomat Keith Mines wore a pressed shirt and tie to his daily meetings with the sheiks.

In early November, however, a surface-to-air rocket brought down a Chinook helicopter in the Ramadi-to-Fallujah corridor. Sixteen soldiers on board were killed. Abizaid flew into Ramadi and told a gathering of fifty tribal sheiks that he would not tolerate the escalating violence. If they couldn't control their tribesmen, his soldiers would take drastic measures. More and more, Abizaid was taking operational control, brushing by the inept Sanchez to deal directly with matters on the ground.

The sheiks protested to Abizaid that the young men weren't listening to them. Saddam had reduced the landholdings of the sheiks and the war had curtailed their smuggling operations. No longer a source of money or jobs, the sheiks relied on tradition, smuggling, and shared values to persuade their followers. Even during their heyday, the direct authority of the sheiks was limited. Sir John Bagot Glubb, the legendary British officer who created the Arab Legion, began his career in Ramadi in 1922. "The Arab tribe," he wrote, "is so democratic as to be almost entirely lacking in discipline. The ordinary tribal shaikh has no power to enforce compliance with his decisions."

Maj. Gen. Charles H. Swannack, commanding the 82nd, told the sheiks that he wasn't going to tolerate the attacks against his paratroopers, which had increased from twelve a day in October to twenty a day in November. The JTF initiated Operation Iron Hammer, a get-tough (or tougher) approach to quelling the insurgency. Attack aircraft with thousand-pound bombs were directed at insurgent hideouts and arms caches, the wives of insurgents were detained for questioning, and uncooperative villages were sealed off with barbed wire.

THE FIRST SUNNI TRIBAL OFFER

The CPA representative in Anbar accepted the need for a serious military response to the increasing attacks but worried that force alone would never be enough if there wasn't a parallel political process that led to power sharing. Keith Mines was a foreign service officer who had served as a major in the Army Special Forces in Latin America. He worked out of a trailer on the 82nd's base, comfortable around his fellow soldiers. He was a diplomat who spoke their language and could handle an M16.

After four months in Anbar, Mines sent a forceful memo to CPA headquarters in Baghdad. "We have disenfranchised and marginalized the Sunnis," he wrote. "The insurgency will grow unless we change course and empower their leaders. We need to gather the leaders from each province and put them in one tent to reach an agreement about national reconciliation, like the Loya Jirga."

In 2002, Mines had attended Afghanistan's loya jirga—literally, tribal council—at which the warlords and province chiefs had agreed to share power to avoid a civil war. Elections, albeit imperfect, followed nine months later and since then Afghanistan had wobbled along, beset with problems but not descending into tribal warfare. A loya jirga in Iraq was sure to raise concerns with the Shiites, who intended to seize full power as the majority via a national election. Rumsfeld endorsed the loya jirga, but the CPA, organizing its own tightly controlled caucus system for eventual power sharing, rejected Mines's proposal. A loya jirga was simply too uncontrollable for Bremer's taste.

Mines, supported by General Swannack, scaled back his concept. At least, he argued, empower the Anbar sheiks who have come forward. General Abizaid had berated them for a lack of leadership. Now Sheik Bizea Gaaoud was offering a force of several hundred tribesmen, if the United States would pay and arm them, let them guard their tribal lands, and back them up. Again the CPA refused, arguing that creating a Sunni militia—or any militia—undermined a unified Iraq. "The Coalition Provisional Authority deliberately side-lined the tribes in 2003," the counterinsurgency expert David Kilcullen wrote, "in order to focus on building a 'modern' democratic state in Iraq, which we equated with a non-tribal state." In his memoir, CIA director George Tenet described how Bremer scuttled the CIA program to work with the Sunni sheiks, referring to them as the "CIA's old pals." The Sunni tribes were on their own. The coalition offered them nothing. They could accept that, or join the insurgency.

STORM CLOUDS AT HOME

By December of 2003, the president's approval rating for handling Iraq had dropped to 50 percent. Antiwar protesters heckled administration officials at public gatherings. Deputy Secretary of Defense Paul Wolfowitz, a prominent neoconservative intellectual who had strongly advocated overthrowing Saddam, was a favorite target. Appearing in Manhattan at an event sponsored by *The New Yorker,* Tom Ricks of *The Washington Post* reported that Wolfowitz was greeted with shouts of "War Criminal!," "Murderer!," and "Nazi!"—notwithstanding that Wolfowitz had lost most of his extended family in the Holocaust.

THREE

A NEAR COLLAPSE

ASSESSMENT WITHOUT CHANGE

Rumsfeld and Abizaid knew they had a big problem. Quietly they put together a small team with on-the-ground experience, led by Maj. Gen. Karl Ikenberry, a strategic planner known for being evenhanded. Their charter was to assess the security situation and the development of Iraqi forces. Neither the JTF nor the CPA was enthusiastic about this intrusion from higher headquarters.

After visiting all the divisions, the team submitted its report in February of 2004. All sixteen U.S. battalions interviewed stated that security conditions were worsening. While five U.S. divisions were running two-week rudimentary classroom courses for policemen, the instructors simply shook their heads when asked to evaluate the results.

Yet at the same time, Wolfowitz, making a brief stop in Baghdad, was told the 1st Armored Division was pulling out of the city. From a peak of sixty operating bases, Thom Shanker of *The New York Times* reported, the division was on a glide path to pull back to six bases outside the city, plus guarding the Green Zone. Baghdad was turned over to 8,000 police with scant training, no command structure, and leadership unknown to the Americans.

The Iraqi military was as hapless as the police. The CPA insisted the Iraqi Army, still in basic training, be set aside for border patrol. As for the forty fledgling ICDC battalions, they were orphans without any support or leaders above the battalion level. The American division commanders didn't believe the ICDC would last a week on their own. They weren't the Americans' ticket out of the country.

The mission of the JTF was to provide security until the Iraqis could take over; the CPA had the authority for developing Iraq's armed forces. Although an insurgency was primarily political, it was also war, and the CPA had no military competence. To General Ikenberry, a professional planner, assigning responsibility to one staff and authority to another invited failure.

As a member of the team, I discussed with Ikenberry two options to correct the situation. The first was to place the CPA under the military command in Iraq. In Vietnam, I had patrolled with a Combined Action Platoon of fifteen marines in a village with 5,000 Vietnamese. Based on that experience, I joined with Sir Robert Thompson, the British counterinsurgency expert, to advise Ambassador Robert Komer, the White House coordinator for the civilian side of the counterinsurgency effort in South Vietnam.

The situation in Vietnam in 1966 resembled that in Iraq at the end of 2003. In Vietnam, the resources for rural security were managed by civilians working directly for the U.S. ambassador. However, the ambassador's interests and skills were diplomatic. And while the State Department, the Agency for International Development, and the CIA all liked controlling their own separate bins of resources, security in the countryside was eroding. The U.S. military was standoffish, viewing pacification as the embassy's business, not theirs.

In 1968, President Lyndon B. Johnson unified the commands, appointing Ambassador Komer as the civilian deputy in the military chain of command. The civilian personnel didn't change. The district and province advisers reported through the civilian deputy for pacification to General Creighton Abrams. He then judged how both American and Vietnamese forces were performing, and adjusted as he saw fit. Abrams also determined the size of the local forces. In his excellent book, *A Better War*, the historian Lewis Sorley described how unity of command under Abrams led to dramatic improvements in the counterinsurgency struggle. That lesson applied to Iraq. (See Appendix A on counterinsurgency organization in Vietnam.)

Ikenberry decided it would be too traumatic to pick up the CPA and plop it under the JTF, which hadn't distinguished itself. That left a second option: relieve the CPA of the strategy, training, and funding of the Iraqi security forces. If the president was holding the U.S. military responsible for security, then he should give it the authority to carry out that responsibility.

Ikenberry told Bremer that this would be his recommendation. To soften the impact, Rumsfeld later sent Bremer a draft of the shift in command authority, hoping Bremer would make the changes himself. When there was no response, Rumsfeld sent a signed memo in March of 2004. It wasn't until Bremer left Iraq three months later that the change took place.

EMERGENCE OF THE EXTREMISTS

The Baathists had instigated the insurgency. John McLaughlin, the respected deputy director of the CIA, estimated that up to 90 percent of the full-time insurgents were led or somehow directed by loyalists to the former Baath Party. Then in February of 2004, the leadership of the insurgency showed virulent change.

On February 12, General Abizaid visited the ICDC and police headquarters in Fallujah, signaling how security was passing to local control. He intended to walk down the main street, but that was canceled when insurgents opened fire on the headquarters. Abizaid flew back to his headquarters in Qatar, 300 miles south of Iraq, where he told reporters the attack was of little consequence and did not change his plans. "We are taking our hands off the control," he said. "It is their country."

The next day, insurgents again attacked the police headquarters while the American troops were in their large base three miles outside the city. The insurgents attacked room to room, shouting, "God is great!" They opened cell doors, freed a hundred prisoners, and drove away, after killing twenty-three policemen and ICDC soldiers. It was the most brazen Sunni-versus-Sunni attack in the Iraqi war, the harbinger of a shift in the leadership of the insurgency that was to break the spirit of the Sunni tribes in Anbar.

The attack marked the emergence of al Qaeda in Iraq, or AQI. While the Jordanian-born terrorist Musab Zarqawi was in Iraq before March of 2003, the American invasion resulted in the monthly infusion of about 60 to 100 al Qaeda–type extremists from Saudi Arabia, Sudan, Syria, and other countries. Fallujah, long tolerant of Wahhabi imams with radical views, was a magnet for these foreigners.

After the police in Fallujah fell apart, the ICDC retreated into a compound outside the city and no one would tell the Americans where the imam Abdullah al-Janabi and other extremist leaders were hiding.

Fallujah was emblematic of the plight of the Sunnis, who saw themselves as disenfranchised, occupied by heavy-handed Americans who had given power to the Shiites. The Baathist administrators had disappeared, replaced by shadowy former officers who urged rebellion and seemed to welcome the rise of terrorists like Zarqawi and radical clergy like Janabi preaching a brand of political Islam that was short on hope and long on hate.

THE APRIL UPRISING

Generals Conway and Mattis were taking the Marines into Anbar in late March of 2004, replacing the 82nd. Sanchez greeted them with an upbeat message. "We've made significant progress in Anbar Province," he assured them.

"General Sanchez treated the insurgency like a broken arm," Brig. Gen. Joseph Dunford, chief of staff of the Marine division, told me. "Fix Baghdad, and later move on to Anbar. An insurgency is a cancer. You can't treat it later. Beneath the surface, Anbar was out of control. We had no idea how deeply the insurgents had burrowed in."

Mattis planned a two-pronged counterinsurgency campaign. On the one hand, Marines would partner with local Sunni police and ICDC battalions to attack the insurgents and take control block by block in cities like Fallujah. On the other hand, conditions assumed to be fueling the insurgency—unemployment and the rough American tactics of raids and sweeps—would be mitigated by economic projects and new tactics. Mattis invited veterans from the Combined Action Platoons in Vietnam to address his battalion commanders, explaining how to partner with local soldiers and police. He sent a letter to his 22,000 Marines. "Act with restraint and keep your honor clean," he wrote. Marines, Mattis decided, would enter cities like Fallujah in light-colored uniforms to signal they were a new force with a new attitude.

A Marine battalion commander sent an op-ed to *The New York Times,* chiding American units for employing excessive firepower. "For every reported military success," Lt. Col. Sam Mundy wrote, "there are also reports of Sunni Iraqis who are angered by tactics like knocking down doors of houses and shops, demolishing buildings, flattening palm groves, firing artillery in civilian neighborhoods and isolating large segments of the population with barbed wire fences."

Many in the Army were stung by the criticism. Mattis tried to tamp down their anger by rescinding the order about the distinguishing uniforms. Conway and Mattis didn't deny, though, that their approach rejected raids in favor of slowly clearing a city, then standing up Iraqi forces to hold it while trying to stimulate the economy.

The strategy never made it out of the starting blocks. Less than a week after the Marines took over, the military occupation of Iraq began to fall apart. On March 29, four American contractors from Blackwater USA were ambushed and killed on the main street in Fallujah. Mobs then burned and dismembered their bodies and hung the black corpses from a trestle bridge. The ghoulish pictures flashed around the world. An angry President Bush ordered the city seized, overriding Abizaid's recommendation to proceed with a deliberate plan worked out by the marines on the ground. Conway was ordered to commence the assault.

"By attacking frontally," Conway said, "we unified the city against us."

Bremer trumped the president's impetuosity by ordering the arrest of one of Sadr's top deputies. Sadr struck back by calling for rebellion by his militia—the JAM, or Jesh al Mahdi (Army of Mahdi). When Conlin set out to humiliate Sadr by holding elections in July of 2003, JAM members organized into fighting units numbered under 1,000; by April of 2004, aided by Iranian funding and advice, the JAM had swelled to 6,000 in fighting units.

JAM cohorts rampaged through the streets of Najaf, Hit or Kut, and Sadr City. In Fallujah, pickup squads of Sunni youths were battling American battalions, while Sunni and Shiite gangs alike in sedans and pickups were racing along the highways shooting at convoys. Al Jazeera ran videos of a series of beheadings orchestrated by Zarqawi to demoralize viewers in the West. At the same time, Al Jazeera and other Arab television networks graphically depicted the American military as the Mongol hordes of Genghis Khan. American reporters such as Tony Perry of the *Los Angeles Times* and Darrin Mortenson of the *North County Times* wrote detailed descriptions of what was actually happening, but to no avail. The Al Jazeera narrative prevailed in Iraq and across the Middle East.

The discombobulated American hierarchy had ignited a full-scale rebellion in early April of 2004. Shiite shop owners grabbed their rifles and rushed into the street to attack an Iraqi battalion en route to Fallujah. The battalion mutinied against the orders of its advisers and raced back to base. Across the Sunni Triangle, in Baghdad and in Shiite cities, soldiers in the new Iraqi Army and police shed their uniforms and fled. In Anbar, 80 percent of the Iraqi soldiers deserted; in Baghdad, 50 percent; in Baquba, Tikrit, Karbala, Najaf, and Kut, over 30 percent. Police desertion rates were even higher.

A year of unilateral American rule had set up the expectation that Americans would do all the fighting as well as the governing. The Iraqis had no stake in their country. Yet the chairman of the Joint Chiefs of Staff, Gen. Richard Myers, characterized the uprising as "a symptom of the success that we're having here in Iraq."

April of 2004 marked the nadir of the invasion of Iraq. In the second week in April, Col. Michael Groen, the top intelligence officer in Anbar Province, swept his hand across a huge wall map in his operations center and told me, "It's a jihad wildfire, spreading mosque to mosque from the Syrian border to Baghdad." Inside the Green Zone, food rationing loomed a few days away, and plans for evacuation had begun.

Abizaid called Conway for a candid appraisal.

"What the hell's going on, Jim?" Abizaid asked. Maj. Gen. Charles Swannack, commanding the 82nd, had claimed Iraqi security forces were in control and running Anbar Province. Sanchez had assured both men that security was improving. Conway responded that the JTF had badly misjudged the insurgency. The JTF had to scramble to avoid losing control of Iraq.

Lacking a reserve, Sanchez ordered Maj. Gen. Martin Dempsey to turn around his 1st Armored Division, which was en route to Kuwait on the way home. In a series of maneuvers that exceeded the logistics feats of the famed Red Ball Express in World War II, Dempsey wheeled his armor around and systematically drove Sadr's gangs from one city after another. Twice Dempsey had Sadr cornered, but according to Sanchez, Bremer persuaded Bush to let Sadr stay free, fearing that his arrest or death would inflame the Shiites. After Bremer assured Sadr in late April that the intent was not to kill him, Sadr slunk off unharmed and his Jesh al Mahdi militia dispersed to fight another day. Bremer said his plan for dealing with Sadr in late April was based on President Lincoln's "anaconda strategy," which squeezed the Confederacy in 1864–1865. The problem with the analogy was that Sadr was the snake.

While Dempsey was beating back Sadr's gangs, Mattis relieved the pressure on Baghdad and opened the critical route from the south by pulling his 7th Regiment out of western Anbar. Task Force Ripper—4,000 Marines mounted in 500 armored vehicles—swept 200 miles of highways west and south of Baghdad, and the attacks that had cut off the supplies to Baghdad ceased. It was one thing for Sunni youths to careen down a highway in a pickup truck with best buddies, shooting wildly at plodding truck convoys. That excitement turned to fear when Humvees lurking in culverts opened up with .50-caliber machine guns, followed minutes later by tanks that had been hiding nearby.

Senator McCain went on television to blast Rumsfeld. "It's not an accident that this [April] was the bloodiest month of the war," he said, calling Rumsfeld's planning "inadequate" and demanding more American troops be sent to Iraq.

The chairman of the Joint Chiefs of Staff viewed it differently.

"No, this was not an uprising. This was not a popular resistance against the coalition," General Myers told reporters in Baghdad. "He [Rumsfeld] has never, to my knowledge, ever denied or even set a troop strength limit."

Told that the president had received no request for additional troops, Senator McCain snapped back, "These decisions have to be made at the highest level." He went on to point out that presidents often made decisions at odds with their generals. The generals were subordinates; the president was the commander-in-chief.

Inside Fallujah, Mattis attacked from the north with one battalion, while another battalion attacked from the south—1,600 grunts taking on a city of 300,000. During the northern battle, Capt. Doug Zembiec led fifty marines across a graveyard to set up a forward position in an abandoned house. Within an hour, hundreds of Iraqi fighters, armed with AKs, swarmed the house. The marines fought their way back across the tombstones, with Lt. Ben Wagner holding LCpl. Aaron Austin in his arms, chest-to-chest, the blood from Austin's bullet wound sopping both their uniforms. Twice Austin slipped from Wagner's grasp. Each time Wagner gathered him up and stumbled along, muttering, "You're going to make it, Devil Dog, you're going to make it."

Austin died on the medevac helicopter. Zembiec was the last man to leave the graveyard. A few days later, standing beside a cardboard marker for Austin at the edge of the graveyard, he said to me, "I pray, I mean, for my men, not for something selfish like myself or winning the lottery." It was impossible to sleep at Zembiec's forward position. All night, the Marines taunted the insurgents by playing hard rock bands like Guns N' Roses at ear-splitting decibels, while the imams reciprocated with screechy music from their minarets. Slayer, the AC-130 gunship with thermal-imaging gun sights, throbbed overhead, sounding like a washing machine filled with tin pots, occasionally unleashing a burp of 40mm shells that ripped apart some poor bastard who thought he was invisible in the dark. Winning hearts and minds was not part of the Fallujah battle.

To the south, Lt. Josh Glover, radio call sign Red Cloud, and his platoon raced to a remote farm where a Black Hawk helicopter had been shot down, arriving after the crew had been picked up by another chopper. Returning to the main road by the only donkey path, they ran a gauntlet of fire that shot out all the tires on their nine Humvees. They sped along the hard top on metal rims, sparks pluming behind them, frantically trying to stanch the blood pouring from PFC Noah Boye's leg. They pulled into an aid station at the outskirts of the city, where the corpsmen treated the wounds of eight marines and prepared them for evacuation. Boye succumbed before the helicopters arrived.

Told an amtrac—a box-shaped vehicle that carries a dozen troops— had taken a wrong turn inside the city and was under attack, Red Cloud swept the blood and spent brass from his Humvees, loaded fresh ammunition, and raced into the city. Marines on a rooftop outpost pointed to a column of black smoke in the distance. "The trac's been hit!" a marine shouted down.

Red Cloud and his forty-seven marines drove forward of the front lines, turned down a side street, and bumped into 100 insurgents gathered to attack the smoking amtrac. Both sides were equally surprised. A furious melee broke out. The trac was like a wounded stag, and the insurgents weren't about to give up their prize. Their aim was poor, though, and many, carrying AKs without stocks, sprayed the air with what the troops called "the death blossom," wildly shooting without looking. As the marines methodically shot them, the insurgents broke, retreating into houses, shooting and shouting curses. Red Cloud dashed to the burning amtrac, arriving too late to save Cpl. Kevin Kolm, whose father and grandfather had served as marines, who was trapped inside.

Battlefields are primordial. Before the guns open up, tenseness pulses in the air. It's like stepping outside just before a thunderstorm. The civilians sense it and get off the streets. When the firing starts, it's almost comical to watch sergeants and lieutenants gesturing wildly, swinging their bodies in a primitive dance to direct their men, who can't hear a thing. Troops move at top speed once they hear rounds cracking so close they know someone is aiming at *them,* not just throwing rounds downrange. Advancing a block or two, you see the bodies. Wounded marines lie propped against walls out of the line of fire, corpsmen tightening bloody tourniquets while waiting for a Humvee to rush up. Luckless civilians lie crumpled in the streets and in cars. Someone will bury them when the battle swirls by. Enemy in civilian clothes can be seen fleetingly, turkey-necking around corners or foolishly sprinting across a street. Some stumble and trip under the fusillade and lie still. Others are grabbed by comrades, dragged around a corner, and not seen again. So it goes street after street, block after block.

On the third day of the fight, Mattis brought in a third battalion to attack from the east. Battalion 3-4, combat-seasoned from a series of fights the year before during the march to Baghdad, put two rifle companies on line and methodically advanced street by street. Cpl. Daniel Amaya, who wanted to be a comic in a Las Vegas show, assaulted a fortified house. When he was killed, his squad backed off and burned the house. LCpl. Torrey Gray died shielding his buddy from machine gun fire. Lt. Oscar Jimenez, the "old man" of the battalion, died bringing up the supply column.

Under attack from three directions, the morale of the city's defenders broke. Their cell phone conversations sounded panicked and senseless. Cars and taxis carrying Iraqi fighters were driving aimlessly down back alleys, shying away from the sound of the guns. As the defenses crumbled, I watched as Lt. Col. Bryan McCoy, commanding Battalion 3-4, told Mattis he would be across the city in a day, two at the most. He had the momentum.

Progress on the battlefield, though, was irrelevant. Fallujah had become a political symbol. Al Jazeera had portrayed the battle as a slaughter of the innocents. Abizaid agreed with Bremer to order a twenty-four-hour unilateral cease-fire to allay the anger in Iraq. According to then–undersecretary of defense Douglas Feith, Rumsfeld asked what would happen if the Iraqis demanded a longer cease-fire.

"I recommend no extension," Abizaid said, "unless there's a strong reason for one."

As a result of that indecision, for three weeks the Marines were frozen in place while battles like Zembiec's flared along the lines.

Toward the end of April, Abizaid finally recommended to President Bush that the Marines complete the attack against Fallujah. The Iraqi Governing Council—a dozen Iraqis appointed by Bremer who lacked decision-making power and popular credibility—threatened to quit if that happened. Bremer recommended against the attack, and the president agreed.

The descriptions of the televideo conferences with the president in the memoirs of Bremer, Feith, and Sanchez depict disorder, bellicose rhetoric, and inchoate hand-wringing, with Bremer insisting the insurgency will grow if Fallujah is seized, yet saying the city must eventually be taken—a belief shared by Abizaid. The televideo links between Washington and Baghdad substituted spontaneous gossip for careful staff work. Bremer later told me he believed the seizure of Fallujah would take another seven to ten days; Mattis estimated one to two days. But neither Mattis nor Conway—the commanders on the ground—was included in the videoconferences. It is sad to read Feith's account of White House meetings during the Fallujah battle, in which America's top leaders debated about Iraqi politics while they pulled the rug out from under the thousands of troops they had ordered to take the city. At one point, Feith quotes Abizaid as saying, "We shouldn't be focused on retaking all of Fallujah." It was as if the owners of a football team, sitting up in their skybox, decided how to play the game without asking the coach on the sidelines.

I was in Mattis's small convoy, which was the last to pull out of the city. The insurgents had shot at Abizaid three months earlier on the same street. Maybe they'd be foolish enough to do it again, breaking the politically imposed cease-fire. Mattis was testy, and the marines were edgy. Put bluntly, they were hoping for a fight. All that blood spilled. The frustration had bubbled over in Mattis, who in a high-level meeting had blurted out Napoleon's epigram to a field marshal, "If you're going to take Vienna, then by God, sir, take it!"

Mattis had McCoy's battalion hidden behind berms outside the city. If the fight erupted again, they would pounce. "Remember, Bryan, you're to take only the Government Center," Mattis had warned McCoy, who was prone to attack, attack, and reattack. "I don't want you to roar by me on your way to the Euphrates. If they attack, we clear this shit hole block by block."

While Mattis prepared his small force, there was a large explosion deeper in the city. A few minutes later, a nondescipt four-door sedan drove down the empty highway and turned in at the Marine position. As McCoy's men shot out the radiator and tires, four bearded occupants spilled out and flung themselves belly-down, arms above their heads. One shouted in English. He was a brave or nutty CIA officer who had driven into the city with three Iraqi informants to scout Mattis's route. He said an insurgent had just blown himself up setting an IED. Aside from that idiot, the CIA officer said, the insurgents were hanging back, under orders to lie low.

His report proved correct. The insurgents held their fire and watched Mattis and his angry marines drive away, deprived of their last chance to seize Fallujah. Austin, Boye, Kolm, Amaya, Gray, Jimenez . . . all for naught.

The presidential order to attack Fallujah had been intemperate; the consequences of calling off the attack midway were worse. If you hesitate, if you second-guess your mission midway through an attack, the enemy gives you no credit for being open-minded. You don't fight for a tie. Teenagers with rifles don't argue about geopolitics. You emerge from battle the winner or loser.

A few old Iraqi generals went into the city, claiming they could work things out. The time of the Baathists had passed, though. The young insurgents and the terrorists under Zarqawi weren't about to relinquish power. Safe inside the city, Zarqawi increased his campaign of kidnappings, suicide bombings, and beheadings. The balance among the insurgent leaders tilted. Up-and-coming insurgent leaders wrapped themselves in religiosity, or at least did not speak out against the al Qaeda pathology that infected Zarqawi and the others who declared all Shiites were heretics deserving death. The morale and recruiting base of the extremists soared.

Gen. Richard Myers, U.S. Air Force, the chairman of the Joint Chiefs of Staff, defended the pullout. "This is the right way to do it," he said. "We need to know when to use force. We need to know when to back off." Myers had been a superb pilot.

On the other hand, Abizaid, like Bremer, believed the Marines would probably have to attack Fallujah again. The next fight would be much harder.

SHAME SEEN GLOBALLY

The body blows of relinquishing Fallujah and letting Sadr walk free were followed by a serious bloody nose for America. For six months, Sanchez, the JTF staff, and the Pentagon had been investigating charges of prisoner mistreatment at the Abu Ghraib prison, west of Baghdad. They did nothing to prepare the public or Congress. At the end of April, pictures taken by one of the abusive guards burst across print and television networks around the globe. The images of sexual degradation and sadistic mental torture suggested an America that treated Arabs with contempt. Pictures of a hooded man with wires dangling from his wrists and pyramids of naked bodies were shown over and over. One squad of sadists and weak-minded followers had altered the image of America.

Abu Ghraib illustrated the power of the digital world. We first glimpsed it in the horrifying pictures of the collapse of the Twin Towers on September 11, 2001, repeated so often they became seared into our memories. Al Jazeera added to the effect by playing videos of terrorists sawing off heads in Fallujah in April of 2004—again providing indelible images. Abu Ghraib showed the full effect of the ubiquitous digital camera as a tool for the global media in May of 2004. Without that grotesque picture of the hooded man, Abu Ghraib would have been a scandal rather than a global event.

Abu Ghraib was blown far out of proportion to the severity of the crime. The Iraqi prisoners were degraded, but not killed. In World War II, prisoners were frequently killed. According to the historian Stephen Ambrose, "no courts-martial were ever convened for men charged with shooting prisoners. It is a subject everyone agreed should not be discussed, and no records were kept. . . . I've interviewed well over 1,000 combat veterans. . . . Perhaps as many as one-third . . . related incidents where they saw other GIs shooting unarmed German prisoners." Ken Burns devoted less than one minute in his six-hour documentary, *The War,* to an interview where a veteran recounted how German prisoners were killed.

The scales of justice we used to judge ourselves in 1945 were weighted differently than in Iraq. In the past sixty years, our societal values have become more sensitive, as defined by the swift expression of shock or revulsion, perhaps tinged with hypocrisy. With each election, we have become more divisive and critical of each other. It was to be expected that Democrats would seize on Abu Ghraib as a hammer to pummel the administration. The reaction to Abu Ghraib, though, exceeded partisan politics. In a paroxysm of angst, the Senate rent its garments and apologized to the world.

The criminal abuses at Abu Ghraib were committed by one motley squad—a sergeant, three privates, and four corporals. This small band of misfits lacked basic training, basic morality, and basic leadership. A few colonels and one brigadier general were relieved of command and disgraced, while seven low-level soldiers were sent to prison.

Abu Ghraib infuriated the senators because they understood the negative effect on public opinion, even as some of them were stoking that feeling. National morale is critical to the prosecution of any war. The strategist, like the politician, must react quickly to the unanticipated event that threatens his stature or his plan. The president was both the nation's chief politician and the war's chief strategist. The question was how he would respond.

Several presidents had fired their secretaries of defense. Robert Strange McNamara was this country's worst secretary of defense, because he did not believe in the mission he was sending troops to die for. President Johnson relieved him in 1967. In 1976, President Gerald Ford, in a ham-handed effort to shore up his election race against Governor Jimmy Carter, dismissed Secretary James R. Schlesinger. In 1992, President Bill Clinton dismissed Secretary of Defense Les Aspin after American soldiers were ambushed in Somalia.

Neither Sanchez, the Joint Task Force commander, nor Rumsfeld resigned. Rumsfeld had already decided to replace the bollixed Sanchez by sending him to a senior command in Germany. When Rumsfeld twice offered his own resignation, he was retained by a president unable to distinguish between personal loyalty and wartime duty. Mr. Bush attributed Abu Ghraib to the "disgraceful conduct by a few American troops." Although the president did not hold the secretary of defense accountable, that did not gainsay the principle of accountability.

The import of Abu Ghraib outweighed the contributions of any civil servant, even had Rumsfeld not already antagonized many in the Senate. "Mr. Rumsfeld wanted the war over quickly," a four-star general told me. "He set a tone at Abu Ghraib by insisting on information from prisoners. He did not hold himself accountable. Don't get me wrong. I still listen to him and I obey." You don't have to like your boss to perform as a loyal subordinate. Still, when you believe in your heart he should have stepped down, that corrodes candid discussion and problem solving. Although Rumsfeld never wavered in his intent to prevail in Iraq, from May of 2004 onward he was damaged goods. He had lost the moral authority to lead.

Due to Fallujah and Abu Ghraib, the approval rating of the president's handling of Iraq plummeted in one month from 50 percent to 40 percent. In May, Mr. Bush made a major address, claiming that "we're making security a shared responsibility in Fallujah. . . . Our soldiers and Marines will . . . conduct joint patrols with Iraqis." Nothing of the sort was happening. The president laid out a goal of 35,000 Iraqi soldiers, while holding out the hope that the U.S. presence would be reduced in the near future. He did not explain how 35,000 Iraqi soldiers could replace 138,000 American soldiers. It was baffling who had given the president such bad military advice.

SOVEREIGNTY WITHOUT REASONABLE CONTROLS

Throughout the spring of 2004, the Shiites insisted on swift elections that they knew they would win. They believed President George H. W. Bush had encouraged them to revolt in 1991, after the Iraqi Army was expelled from Kuwait. After Saddam used tanks and helicopters to crush them, many Shiites harbored a deep suspicion that America would again mislead or trick them. After convoluted negotiations in-

volving the United Nations, and British, American, and Iraqi (principally Kurdish and Shiite) leaders, Bremer announced a firm timetable.
By June, sovereignty would be returned to Iraq via an appointed Interim Government. In January of 2005, a national election would be
held to determine an interim National Assembly that would draft a
constitution and select an acting government. In October of 2005, the
nation would vote on the constitution. If it passed, then in December of
2005 there would be another national election to choose a permanent
government.

The election process satisfied the Kurds and the Shiites, who were
confident in their solidarity, while further antagonizing the Sunnis.
Some Sunnis objected because they could not possibly organize when
they couldn't even drive to work. Most Sunnis feared the wrath of the
insurgents if they did vote and practically all were antagonistic about a
process intended to give power to the majority—the Shiites.

President Bush saw it quite differently. Addressing the Army War
College in May of 2004, he shifted the rationale for the war from removing the Saddam regime to bringing democracy to the Middle East.

"I sent American troops to Iraq to make its people free," he said,
adding that the Iraqis should install a government that reflected their
own culture and values. He clung to the belief that an election and an
Iraqi government would reduce the insurgency and improve security by
unifying the country. "Mankind has an innate thirst for freedom and
self-rule," the president said.

While it was not clear how elections would reduce the distrust between Sunni and Shiite, it was predictable that the electoral labyrinth
would be a military nightmare. At a minimum, the voting schedule in-
sured that three times in one year the U.S. military would have to focus
upon voter protection, a mission that in itself yielded no longer-term
security. The timetable also meant that the U.S. military would have to
work with three separate Iraqi governments in less than three years,
with three different ministers directing the police and the army.

Worse still, the focus on the technicalities of the electoral process
masked the most critical military error—losing control over the leadership of the Iraqi security forces. The unstated axiom underlying counterinsurgency doctrine is that foreign forces must intervene because the
indigenous forces have failed due to poor leadership. The American—
and British—military knew from experience that quelling an insurgency is far more difficult when the indigenous military and police,
having made a mess of things, continue to select their own leaders for
their own purposes.

Once sovereignty was restored, the American and coalition forces would retain operational control over the provinces until conditions permitted Iraqi forces to assume control on a province by province basis. The Iraqis would determine their own promotions and leadership positions. No senior American military official asked for a National Security Council meeting to recommend a process that would restore sovereignty while reposing authority in the American military to select the Iraqi security leaders until Iraq was capable of ensuring its own security. After all, Iraq could not exist as a state without Americans dying to protect it.

President Bush may have ruled against such a recommendation. But the Joint Chiefs of Staff and the Central Command erred greatly in not raising the issue for a full discussion.

At the end of June, Ambassador Bremer gave back Iraqi sovereignty to an interim government. His term had expired. The Coalition Provisional Authority under his leadership had been caught between two stools, operating with the instincts of a benevolent, all-knowing conqueror but without sound administrators or a sensible plan for providing the people with security, basic services, and local rule.

Bremer was strong-willed enough to rule along the lines of a nineteenth-century British plenipotentiary. But he wasn't given that power. Eventually the United Nations and the White House reined in his preferred political blueprint, while the military ignored him. Bremer's chief of staff was retired Marine Lt. Gen. Jeffrey Oster, a seasoned professional who strongly defended Bremer. "He did his best. He never stopped working," Oster said. "Sanchez and his military staff wouldn't share. I was astonished and tried to put a stop to that."

As Bremer put the finishing touches on the transfer of sovereignty, the U.S. military was satisfied that the Multi-National Force, commanded by an American, would keep control over the nascent Iraqi Army and over operations, and eventually transfer control on a province-by-province basis by mutual consent. The U.S. military proposed no voice in determining Iraqi promotions and posts. As a result, over the next five years, the Iraqi forces developed erratically, to the frustration of thousands of advisers.

The president had given Bremer wide latitude. The notion, though, that power bequeathed is power obeyed proved pernicious when applied to Iraq. Bremer tried to rule without a functioning bureaucracy. He banished the Baathists who ran the government and dissolved the army that provided security.

The Kurds swiftly organized themselves. The Sunnis, deprived of their military and Baathist leaders, turned to the mosques for guidance. Imams stoked the growing resentment of rough treatment from American forces. Islamic extremists found sympathy when they called for jihad. The lone diplomat in Anbar, Keith Mines, in vain proposed a loya jurga to provide the tribal sheiks with a stake in the new Iraq. Deprived of local allies, the Americans fought alone in the Sunni Triangle.

On the Shiite side, the exiles brought back by the Bush administration concentrated on palace intrigue, while religious leaders focused on elections to cement Shiite quasireligious rule. Sadr and other anticoalition leaders harnessed the resentment of the dispossessed by blaming the coalition for all ills. American division commanders like Petraeus and Mattis, and battalion commanders like Mayer and Malay, instinctively understood the need to provide resources to local leaders to build constituencies and win swift local elections. Instead, the coalition chose a top-down approach, delaying all elections until the 2005 rollout of a list-based national election, which was boycotted by the Sunnis.

From the start, the top-down approach toward politics deprived local secular leaders of resources, leverage, and constituents, thus assuring extremists on both the Sunni and Shiite sides with a large supply of foot soldiers.

Ambassador Peter W. Galbraith, a champion of the Kurdish cause and longtime observer of the Middle East, offered an analysis of the first year of the American occupation: "His [Bremer's] biggest error, however, was to think he knew best. He was in charge of Iraq, but could not accept the obvious: that Iraqis knew much more about their country than he would ever know."

Lest his plane be shot down, Bremer employed elaborate decoys to unceremoniously decamp from Baghdad at the end of June. His stealth departure symbolized America's misfortunes since Saddam's statue fell in Firdos Square in April of 2003. Americans had swept into Baghdad as liberators, and a year later the president's personal envoy had to sneak out of town.

The invasion had given freedom to the Shiites and Kurds, while disenfranchising the Sunnis. Imagine if, by a sudden maneuver, the Union Army had captured Richmond in 1862. Many white southerners, not having tasted defeat, would have turned to guerrilla war. But in 1865, when Jefferson Davis, the president of the Confederacy, suggested resorting to guerrilla warfare after Gen. Robert E. Lee surrendered at Appomattox, Lee firmly rejected the notion. After four years of grueling destruction, Lee said, our people have suffered enough. Lee well understood what Gen. William Tecumseh Sherman and the Union Army would do to defeat an insurgency.

Like Richmond in 1862, the Sunni Triangle had not suffered the destruction of war. The swift invasion had not touched the Sunnis. Before a person can be rehabilitated, he must acknowledge his wrongdoing or the hopelessness of persisting with his past ways. The Sunnis did neither. They felt they were the aggrieved party. The American Army, while heavy-handed at times, was by historical standards restrained, making mistakes that encouraged the rebels while not imposing the draconian tactics that had suppressed many prior insurgencies.

FOUR

WAR

JULY–DECEMBER 2004

THE NEW TEAM PLANS

Ayad Allawi, the interim prime minister of the new Iraq, was dealt a poor hand that he played with poorer skill. Before he slipped out of the country, Bremer declared Iraq to be once again a sovereign nation. Pending an election in January, the United Nations, the United States, and Britain had worked out a slate of appointees to act as temporary caretakers. Allawi was a former doctor who lived in London, where he directed an expatriate anti-Saddam political action group. A favorite of the CIA and of conservatives in the Bush administration, Allawi was seen as a tough-minded secularist who wanted to play to the middle, appealing to both Sunnis and Shiites on the basis of restoring services, ensuring security, and projecting a nonsectarian, technically competent government.

He was a lame duck from the day he took office. Because his cabinet with twenty-six ministerial posts was chosen for him and had no loyalty toward him, Allawi was unable to dispense patronage and build a following. Allawi didn't know the first names of half the members of his own cabinet. The minister of interior filled the top police posts with cronies and Shiite militia leaders, and the minister of defense proved to be a world-class thief.

Allawi came into the appointed office thinking he could be the first *elected* prime minister in Iraq. He intended to govern from the center, projecting himself as a firm but reasonable authoritarian figure. With the big American stick behind him, he could talk softly to the insurgents and persuade them to cut deals. He planned to emerge as the peacemaker, appealing to Sunni and Shiite alike, no man to cross, but someone who kept his word. With good reason to distrust his cabinet, he confided principally in the new American ambassador and four-star general.

Ambassador John Negroponte, a polished diplomat, had taken over from Bremer. The CPA, without changing offices, was functioning as part of the embassy staff. National Security Presidential Directive 36 designated to Negroponte, as chief of mission, many of the CPA's prior responsibilities, with the organization and training of Iraqi security forces assigned to the U.S. military. With stints in Vietnam and in Honduras during the contra wars in the 1980s, Negroponte was comfortable dealing with governments in crisis and the American military during wartime. President Bush had sent him to Baghdad to work alongside Gen. George W. Casey, who had been handpicked by Rumsfeld to relieve the hapless Lieutenant General Sanchez.

Casey was a quiet, thorough infantry officer. His father, a major general, was commanding the 1st Air Cavalry Division when he died in a helicopter crash along the Cambodian border in 1970, the highest-ranking American killed during the Vietnam War. George Casey was a senior at Georgetown University at the time. He had been close to his dad, who loved competing with his two sons in golf, tennis, running, whatever. George went into the Army after college because he wanted to lead a platoon, and ended up staying as a career. He caught Rumsfeld's eye when, as the Army's deputy chief of staff, he disagreed when he thought Rumsfeld was wrong and set forth his arguments with calm logic.

Casey and Abizaid had agreed on a central principle: Reduce the American presence and insist that the Iraqis deal with the insurgency— a view Rumsfeld heartily endorsed. As a first step, Casey met frequently with Negroponte in Washington. When they arrived in Baghdad, they had a plan worked out and immediately issued a joint military-embassy mission statement. To show they would work as a team and put aside past antagonisms, they set up adjoining offices in the baroque palace in the Green Zone where Bremer had worked.

Casey's title was commander of the Multi-National Force—Iraq, or MNF-I. Casey focused on strategy and relations with the Iraqis, while operational matters were handled by Lt. Gen. Thomas Metz, commander of the Multi-National Force—Corps, or MNF-C. Practically speaking, there was substantial overlap in the roles, especially during crises.

Petraeus was promoted to three stars and returned to direct the training of the Iraqi Army. When he found that three divisions were being trained to defend the borders, he went to Prime Minister Allawi, recommending that the mission be immediately changed to fighting the insurgency. Allawi agreed.

That proved the easy part. The U.S. military had not envisioned disbanding an army in May, only to be ordered later to put together a new one. The Special Forces—the best trainers—had been pulled off to undertake "direct action" against—meaning find and eliminate—the senior leadership of the insurgency. Bremer had hired American contractors to do the job of training the new Iraqi Army, but that hadn't worked out well.

Casey and Negroponte determined that they faced four main tasks, or "lines of operation." The first was security, obviously an MNF-I responsibility. The embassy took the lead in the next two—governance (Iraqi politics) and economic development. Both MNF-I and the embassy pitched in with the fourth task, called "strategic communications," aimed at driving a wedge between the insurgents and the Sunni population.

When Gen. Maurice Challe took command of the French forces in Algeria in 1959, he discovered that his predecessor had divided the country into seventy-five sectors and, according to the historian Alistair Horne, "there were 75 ways of making war"—without any overall strategy. Inheriting a similar condition in Iraq from the hapless Sanchez, Casey ordered a campaign plan to unify the military effort.

The American Army excelled at such top-down efforts. The Army was a guild where everyone started at the bottom and received reports from bosses who changed every year, ensuring promotion based on merit and not on cronyism. As officers and noncommissioned officers proceeded up the ranks, they absorbed the Army's procedures and ways of thinking. Casey's staff passed ideas back and forth, coordinated with diplomats, coalition partners, and the CIA, and put together a "red team" to find holes in their approach.

"I had two objectives," Casey told me. "The first was to instill a philosophy of counterinsurgency. Our army was built for kinetics—shooting the enemy and winning battles. In Iraq, that wasn't the way to go. Second, we had to partner with the ambassador and the embassy, not fight with them. I gave the guidance and let the colonels write the plans and assessments."

The staff was proud of the result, and Casey issued the first "MNF-I Campaign Plan" in early August of 2004. The plan had two tracks: developing Iraqi security forces and quelling the insurgency. One method for doing that was to organize a constabulary force similar to those in Spain and Italy—a supra–National Guard for internal security. The American Army's last experience in constabulary warfare had been in the Philippines in 1898. Since then, wars had been state against state, often on a giant scale—World War I, World War II, Korea, Desert Storm in 1991, and Operation Iraqi Freedom in 2003. Even in Vietnam, the Army had fought along conventional lines in search and destroy operations. Thus the second method—structuring the Iraqi Army along conventional American Army lines—had a built-in training base inside the U.S. Army. Because American soldiers understood their own system, by taking a mirror-image approach they believed they could quickly rebuild the Iraqi Army.

The Iraqi ICDC or National Guard battalions had collapsed in April, it was believed, because they were orphans—ill-trained collections of 400 former soldiers expected to fight against their own tribes. That experiment had failed. In the new Iraqi Army, battalions would report to brigades, and brigades to divisions. No unit would stand alone. Most of the initial volunteers were Shiites who expected to serve in their home provinces.

With his usual optimism and energy, Petraeus set about the task. The campaign plan directed that the training of the Iraqi Army should "focus on building quality, not quantity." At the time, somewhat ruefully, Petraeus told me, "You don't grow battalion commanders or command sergeants major in a year or two." It was a phrase I would hear repeated, year after year.

The plan's second track was subduing the insurgents, described as a loose amalgam of about 10,000 Sunni Arab "rejectionists" led by former Baathists. The main effort—a key military phrase that sets priorities—was to "neutralize" the rejectionists by controlling fifteen key cities by the end of 2004. "Neutralize" was a vacuous verb. Did it mean the insurgents were to be killed or arrested, or co-opted, or simply driven out of the cities? Did "control" mean to win the cooperation of the residents, or to keep them under guard?

More baffling still, according to Bob Woodward, the journalist granted extraordinary access by the White House, General Abizaid had concluded that "we've got a really bad situation over here [in Iraq]. Can't win it militarily." That Delphic phrase became the mantra of the generals. At the least, it absolved them if Iraq fell apart. It also contradicted the goal of the campaign plan, which was to neutralize the insurgents. If the military could not accomplish that mission, why was it the main effort?

The colonels who wrote the plan understood conventional battlefields but had not fought insurgents. They consulted analysts who had studied the insurgency in Vietnam, but hadn't fought there. Without a means of understanding what was happening on the ground, the plan lacked an objective reporting system to measure progress or the lack thereof. In a conventional war, the front lines measured progress. In Vietnam, measuring progress by counting the number of enemy killed had proved fruitless. The military refused to use it as a measure in Iraq, but did not propose another measure. This absence of clear goals and measures would bedevil the military effort for years.

The campaign plan of August 2004 was the work of both military officers and the diplomats responsible for managing the politics. It was a joint document signed by Ambassador Negroponte and General Casey. Rumsfeld had selected Casey and the two had extended discussions that Casey did not share with his staff. Nonetheless, the goal of finishing the job in eighteen months was the consensus view of the senior military staff in Baghdad, endorsed by Rumsfeld and the Joint Chiefs of Staff in Washington.

"I didn't noodle," Casey told me. "You can't run a huge institution as one man. The staffs collected the data and fielded the questions from the field. We reviewed the campaign plan and reassessed every six months."

The plan envisioned coalition forces gradually falling back to large bases and providing "coalition support in extremis." By the end of 2005, the Iraqis were to achieve "self-reliance," enabling U.S. forces to leave the country in 2006.

While structured and logical, the plan was a theory. As General George S. Patton observed, "Victory in the next war will depend on execution, not plans."

THE NEW TEAM MEETS REALITY

In the summer of 2004, the Sunni insurgency gathered steam. At first, things were deceptively quiet. Abizaid had put out the word that U.S. troops should support the transition to a sovereign Iraqi government by taking a low profile. In early July, a Marine spokesman, Col. J. T. Coleman, confidently told Dexter Filkins of *The New York Times* that "Fallujah is moving ever so slowly in the right direction."

In fact, the Americans were being isolated from the population. Abdullah Janabi, the chief imam in Fallujah, became chairman of an insurgent council that imposed the sharia code of Islamic fundamentalism, including whippings for women who wore lipstick and death for anyone suspected of working for the invaders. A campaign of murder and intimidation began. Every day, American soldiers found Iraqi corpses, arms bound behind their backs, in the ditches along the main highways. Drivers, seeing Americans carrying away Iraqi bodies, spread the message: Stay away from the Americans. The number of contractors showing up for work at Marine division headquarters dropped from sixty in early June to zero by late July.

Prime Minister Allawi, who had studied medicine and never served in the military, didn't grasp the gravity of the deteriorating security situation. Instead, within a few weeks of taking office, he left on a tour of neighboring Arab states. It seemed a rite of passage for all Iraqis appointed to high positions to escape for several weeks from the oppressive heat and danger of their nation. In Allawi's case, he reaped no benefits. Replacing Americans with Arab forces was not an option. Saudi Arabia pampered the Wahhabist Sunni sect, which railed against Shiites as heretics. The Saudi regime viewed Shiite power in Iraq as a danger to its stability. The populations of Egypt and Jordan loathed the American occupation, as was the case throughout the Middle East. Syria, ever the louche dodge, was permitting suicide bombers to slip across its borders and follow what U.S. intelligence called "the ratline" down the Euphrates River valley. The Arab League was antagonistic, haughtily declaring that Arab troops couldn't cooperate while Americans were occupying an Arab state.

Allawi returned empty-handed from his tour to find the insurgents' M & I—Murder and Intimidation—campaign in full swing. By midsummer, there was no functioning government in Anbar and other parts of the Sunni Triangle. The American troops called Fallujah "the bomb factory." Zarqawi and the terrorists had set up safe houses where they beheaded prisoners, taped snuff videos for Al Jazeera to broadcast, stuffed explosives into cars, and dispatched Sunni zealots to slaughter innocent Shiites. Sunni residents looked on Zarqawi's band with a mixture of admiration and fear. The foreigners made common cause with local imams who wanted to be on the winning side. Zarqawi appointed Janabi his spiritual adviser and chose as his chief military lieutenant Omar Hadid, a former intelligence operative who was courageous in battle and who casually cut the legs off anyone accused of collaboration.

"Not one man in a hundred," Mattis said, "will stand up to a real killer. It's ruthlessness that cows people."

The Marines were hit by suicide bombers on the roads and by rocket attacks from inside Fallujah. Thirty miles north, up the road in Ramadi, every American post was struck every day by small arms fire or mortar shells. You're not supposed to count kills, but almost every rifleman does. As the attacks mounted, inside the platoons a competition increased; no one wanted to be rotated home before scoring a clear kill. Iraqi teenagers with AKs were sneaking up to Marine outposts, intent on taking a few shots and running away, not knowing that better-trained Americans were lying behind sandbags with the telescopic sights on their rifles zeroed in, dripping sweat and scarcely moving hour by hour, hoping, just hoping, they were on duty when the next attack came.

Mattis was so angry he called a meeting outside Fallujah of the imams and ranted at them, asking how men of religion could incite worshippers to rush out to their deaths. "They're kids," he burst out as he angrily left the meeting. "Untrained, undisciplined teenagers. They don't stand a chance."

Nothing changed. The attacks kept coming. The battle lines had been drawn. "The tribes only saw us as the enemy," Mattis said. "I needed the real enemy [the extremists] to make mistakes [by killing tribal members] and expose themselves for what they were."

In 2004, that didn't happen. Every time the Americans launched a raid, bursting into a house to make an arrest—sometimes a genuine insurgent, sometimes not—their actions fueled anger and reinforced the Salafist message that Americans were infidel invaders intent on installing a repressive Shiite regime. In Ramadi, a Shiite mosque was burned and gutted, a sure sign that the Salafist radicals were on the offensive. Shiites and Kurds were driven from Haditha, Hit, and other cities west of Baghdad and from the villages to the south of the capital. In Samarra, north of Baghdad, Sunni insurgents drove the Shiites from the city after the police fled, forcing American troops from Tikrit to race to the rescue.

The obvious solution was to employ more Iraqi forces, at least for static or simple defensive tasks. Mattis approached Brigadier General Fahad, who commanded about 3,000 soldiers in National Guard battalions scattered uselessly across Anbar Province. Mattis offered to transport the soldiers to Taji, a large base that Petraeus was using for training. He would ensure they returned safely. Fahad refused. Sunni soldiers would stay in Sunni cities. This was a refrain often heard in insurgent circles, and Mattis warned Fahad that he was keeping bad company.

Still, Mattis had expected the rebuff and had a counterproposal ready. All right, he said, how about if we join forces? I'll move my marines in among your soldiers. His plan was to drive a wedge between the insurgents and the residents by partnering American squads with local Iraqi soldiers who knew the insurgents by face. The Marines had done this in Vietnam, placing squads in 100 villages to train and patrol with local forces comprised of farmers. The Combined Action Platoon, or CAP, program, as it was called, had been successful. Although the fighting was hard, 70 percent of CAP marines extended when their one-year tours came to an end. In the villages and hamlets, they patrolled on their own—no formations or first sergeants yelling at them—and they had earned the respect of the villagers. No CAP village was ever retaken by the Viet Cong guerrillas.

Mattis and Fahad agreed to test the CAP concept with the 506th Iraqi Battalion stationed at Habbaniyah, a town on the main road connecting Fallujah and Ramadi.

Mattis sent Colonel Dunford to Habbaniyah to meet with Brigadier General Khadar, who commanded two National Guard battalions in the area. Khadar resisted, complaining that he didn't want tanks shooting up residential blocks. No tanks, Dunford said, only squads who will fight the insurgents with rifles. My jundis (soldiers) have bad equipment, Khadar said. We will ask General Petraeus to send you new equipment, Dunford said. Finally, Khadar admitted the truth. I will not permit Americans near my battalions, he said. If I do, my jundis will be killed when they go home, along with their families.

The Combined Action Platoon plan failed because the real government with a monopoly on the employment of street-level violence was the insurgents. The same condition was true in Samarra and Baquba, north and east of Baghdad. When Mattis arrested a top insurgent, Baghdad ordered the man's release. The orders from Baghdad in the summer of 2004 were clear: "Keep the noise down out there." Allawi was convinced he could negotiate a political deal with the insurgents, and he didn't want Americans mucking that up by simultaneously working a military deal aimed at identifying and killing them.

This placed Casey in a tough spot. Allawi was negotiating from weakness. He had nothing concrete to offer. He did not control government positions, money, or jobs. His ministries didn't answer to him. The Iraqi forces out in the Sunni Triangle were Sunni. They stayed alive by tolerating or abetting the insurgents, and above all by not collaborating with the American forces. Allawi hosted secret meetings, some in the Green Zone, with representatives of the insurgents, even as 5,000 Kurdish residents were driven from Fallujah and thousands of Shiites fled from Samarra. The sectarian cleansing had begun.

Casey visited every American battalion to get an on-scene assessment. I met with him in Ramadi in August, where the 760 marines in Battalion 2-4 had taken 31 killed and 284 wounded. The insurgents controlled the streets, no contractor dared show up for work, and the local Iraqi forces hid in their compounds. Fighting up and down the streets was constant. Mattis and Casey viewed the sniper battles from an observation tower. In a discussion later, I told Casey what appeared most bothersome was an inability to name one Iraqi officer who was leading from the front (see Appendix B). Casey said the Iraqis had to stand up. "It's your country, now fight for it" was how he put it.

The battalion commander, Lt. Col. Paul Kennedy, responded that at least the provincial governor, guarded by an American platoon, was standing up. But a week later, the governor's sons were kidnapped and the governor went on Al Jazeera, tearfully apologizing for betraying Islam. After his sons were released, he fled to Jordan.

Colonel Dunford was disturbed that U.S. commanders were not candid enough. "General Casey wanted local control by the end of 2004. When he made his rounds [visiting the battalions] in August," Dunford said, "some Marine and Army commanders told him yes, it could be done. That was crazy!"

It was crazy but understandable. The military "can do" spirit conflicted with candor. The commanders didn't want to tell a four-star general that a mission could not be accomplished. U.S. forces by their presence alone could ensure a small bit of local control. But that was better than zero control by the local Iraqi forces. In the spring and summer of 2004, I embedded with more than a dozen U.S. battalions and their attitudes were much the same: The Iraqi police in blue shirts and black trousers acted as the sentries for the insurgents, while the Iraqi soldiers ran away.

In July of 2004, Petraeus suggested that I spend some time with an Iraqi battalion that had mutinied during the April uprising. When I arrived at their sector in south Baghdad, I was greeted by Maj. David Lane, the senior adviser. He explained that in April the 700-man battalion was driving to Fallujah on a crowded two-lane road lined with ramshackle shops, with hundreds of unemployed men lounging about. When someone fired at one of the unarmored trucks, the driver slowed down and then leaped from the cab. The truck banged harmlessly into a guardrail, stopping all traffic. Hundreds of soldiers leaped out and began firing in all directions, the Iraqi death blossom. The merchants and bystanders grabbed their AKs and fired back. Few died in the panicked melee because nobody knew how to aim. The Iraqi battalion commander helped the advisers safely extract the battalion and return to base. Then the commander and two of his company commanders joined with 200 jundis who declared that they had quit. They put down their weapons and went home. Iraq has no laws or punishment for desertion.

"Iraq has a peasant army," Lane said, "like the European armies in the eighteenth century. A hundred men—a company—will follow one good leader down the street. A second company will run after the first, to fall in behind that same leader. But if you don't have a few good leaders, forget it."

It had taken Lane and his advisers three months to reshape the battalion. Petraeus had rewarded their efforts by giving them a quiet patrol zone of about one square kilometer. They were left by themselves. A few blocks away, American soldiers were doing the patrolling, separate from the distrusted jundis. Local control did not mean control by local forces.

The standard counterinsurgency technique for controlling populated areas was called the oil spot. The idea was to flood a few key villages with first-rate troops, flushing out the guerrillas. Local leaders were then encouraged to come forward. Some money for local improvements was given out. Once there were local leaders, hometown police were recruited. Most of the first-rate troops then moved on, like an oil spot spreading outward.

The practicality of the oil spot depended upon terrain as much as the quality of the local forces. The theory sprang from the Malaya and Vietnam experiences, where the guerrillas walked and carried their supplies on their backs. Once pushed out of a village, the guerrillas fled into the bush, that sprawling tangle of undergrowth and small trees, sometimes several kilometers deep, that marks the dividing line between cultivated fields and triple-canopy jungle. Getting back to the original village or moving into another village was a serious chore for guerrillas on foot. They had to hike for several hours in a single file of at least a dozen men. Smaller units could not defend themselves. Laden with rifles, ammo, and food, they had to move at night, avoiding open fields. Every night's move required planning rallying points and escape routes. The nightmare for the guerrillas was to sneak back inside an oil spot zone during darkness, bump into a local patrol, get tangled up in a firefight, and be stuck in the open when the government forces swarmed in at daylight.

In 2004, no American division could apply the oil spot strategy. There weren't any local Sunni forces that would work reliably with the occupiers. The roads remained open, allowing the insurgents to drive back in after the Americans swept by. Iraq, with a superb highway system, millions of unregistered cars, and no means of checking identification, was the world's first vehicle-based guerrilla movement. In the April battle in Ramadi, more than 100 insurgents drove into town, picked up their caches of weapons, left their cars at getaway points, ran down the back alleys, and launched their attack. When not massing for such large attacks, the insurgents employed the shoot and scoot tactic. It took only a few minutes to set up a mortar tube, pop off a few rounds, and drive away.

SADR REDUX

Moqtada Sadr revolted a second time in August. He was now a serious player with a plan, while the Iranians were supporting him with money, political advice, and weapons. Intending to emerge as the leader of a nationalistic Shiite Islamic movement, Sadr had set up his headquarters in Najaf, home to the Ayatollah Sistani and the religious council. The provincial governor told Ann Scott Tyson of *The Christian Science Monitor* that eighty Iranian Republican Guards were embedded with Sadr's troops, training them in the use of antiaircraft guns.

When fighting broke out, Allawi, a Shiite, told Casey he was determined to arrest Sadr in Najaf and defeat his militia there, once and for all. Najaf was not to be a sanctuary. Casey sent his reserve, the 11th Marine Expeditionary Unit, and the 2nd Battalion of the 7th Cavalry Regiment to destroy the Jesh al Mahdi, the JAM. Sadr responded by seizing the shrine of the Imam Ali, a revered site visited by millions of the faithful and bordered by a vast cemetery dotted with tens of thousands of crypts and headstones. In 120-degree heat, the American soldiers pushed slowly forward day by day, fighting among the resting places of the dead, careful not to damage the shrine from which Sadr's followers fired mortars and machine guns. Some Americans fought with intravenous needles taped against their forearms, leaving the lines after a few exhausting hours to lie on stretchers to absorb quarts of saline solution, and then returning to the fight. To combat the snipers, some from Iran, firing down from the top floors of the tourist hotels outside the shrines, Casey called in dozens of countersnipers from the Special Operations Command.

As had happened in Fallujah in April, the Arab press sided with the rebels. Shiite politicians who had urged Allawi to crush Sadr denounced the violence. One of the Interim Government's two appointed vice presidents, Ibrahim al-Jaafari, called on the Americans to leave Najaf. Jaafari, who wanted to replace Allawi as prime minister, typified the fecklessness of Iraqi political leaders who wanted something done, wouldn't do it themselves, and then complained regardless of what happened.

Sistani, who was in London, decided that the battle was endangering both the integrity of the shrine and the unity of the Shiite political movement. He decided to return and save Sadr. "Allawi said we had to get Sadr, who was hiding in the shrine, before Sistani could rescue him," Casey told me. "The Iraqi defense minister claimed Iraqi forces could do it. I told him they'd get creamed and the shrine would be destroyed. They weren't ready to go, and Sistani was on his way back."

Casey ordered a twenty-four-hour crash course for the Iraqis, to be followed by an assault after U.S. Special Forces, not Iraqis, breached the defenses. The Mahdi Army was reeling, low on ammunition, disorganized and demoralized.

That plan came apart the next day when Sistani drove in a ceremonial processional into the city and negotiated privately with Sadr. Allawi's hands were tied. Any further fighting jeopardized the lives of Sistani and his senior clerics and would collapse the Interim Government. In a bold move, Sistani had reestablished his dominance over Shiite politics and had set limits on the actions of the government. Allawi had miscalculated in believing that the Shiite political order would stand with him to eliminate the vulpine power of the renegade Sadr. Instead, the Shiite parties chose the expedient advantage of a temporarily unified Shiite slate for the upcoming national elections. Allawi lost standing among Shiites because he hadn't prevailed as the nation's leader and among Sunnis because he had caved under Shiite pressure.

Casey and the Americans were the biggest losers. The overthrow of Saddam and the blunders thereafter had alienated the nine million Sunnis and provoked the Sunni insurgency. The three million Kurds and eighteen million Shiites, however, had viewed the Americans as liberators. Not one American had been killed in the Shiite south during the summer of 2003. One year later, by not finishing Sadr in either the

April or August battles, the Americans faced a malignant Shiite insurgency aided by Iran that would grow more dangerous year after year.

THE FIERCEST BATTLE

By the beginning of September, the fighting in Najaf had fizzled out. In the States, the presidential race was in full swing. Polls indicated that only 40 percent of Americans approved of how President Bush was handling Iraq. Bush countered by conflating Iraq with the larger "Global War on Terror" that included the incessant hunt for Osama bin Laden, the ongoing war in Afghanistan, the train bombings in Madrid that had killed 122 Spaniards, and the weird warnings from the Department of Homeland Security in Washington that the country was either in Condition Orange or Condition Amber. Out of this jumble of images, Mr. Bush distilled a simple message: You're safer with me in the White House. His Democratic rival, Senator John Kerry of Massachusetts, failed to project a clear, forceful message of his own. He said he was in favor of the Iraqi war, and then against it; he supported the troops, but voted to cut off funding for the war. Kerry was unable to gain traction from the unpopularity of the Iraqi war.

Inside Iraq, Casey was pressing Allawi to act. Both Samarra to the north of Baghdad and Fallujah to the west were controlled by the insurgents, jeopardizing the countrywide elections scheduled by year's end. The minister of interior had claimed that his personal tribal ties, combined with undercover work by the special police, could break the insurgent grip on Samarra, but it hadn't happened. Finally, Casey sent in a regiment from the 1st Infantry Division, and in a week of fighting over 100 insurgents were killed and the city settled down for a while.

Samarra was a warm-up for Fallujah, the fiercest battle of the war. With Zarqawi's ruthless gang lurking in the background, the insurgent council inside Fallujah had rejected Allawi's peace offers. Most of the city's 300,000 residents fled the city as about 2,000 fighters dug in to repel the American assault. Zarqawi left the defenses up to his military commander, Hadid, who was advised by several Chechens who said the Russians they fought at Grozny didn't dare to leave their tanks to search room by room. Hadid encouraged his men to hide in small groups inside the 30,000 concrete buildings, using back alleys to duck around the American tanks and swarm in from the side. Americans, like the Russians, would fight only from their tanks.

A week after President Bush's reelection, Casey had assembled five

Marine battalions and three Army armored battalions to encircle and attack the city. Interspersed among the 10,000 American troops were 1,000 Iraqi soldiers in two battalions, adding an Iraqi flavor to the mix. Half of the American soldiers serving in Iraq at the time were National Guard or reserve forces. The assault forces, though, were America's shock troops—the Marines.

The Marines had annually practiced seizing houses in exercises called MOUT, or Military Operations in Urban Terrain, and they knew Fallujah. Unmanned Aerial Vehicles with video cameras had flown hundreds of missions, plotting the lairs of the insurgents by watching as bodies were dumped out of cars, and then following the cars back to houses that were marked on detailed maps.

"We rehearsed our squeegee tactic over and over," Lt. Col. Pat Malay, commanding an assault battalion, said. "Two companies would advance over a frontage of three blocks, staying abreast and checking out every house. That scrubs the heavy dirt off the windshield. My third company follows in trace, checking every room a second time. That wipes the windshield clean."

On the eve of the assault, a sergeant major reminded the Marines of their history—how their forefathers had crawled over the razor-sharp reefs at Peleliu in 1944, shot their way down the streets of Seoul in 1950, and driven 10,000 North Vietnamese regulars from the walled citadel of Hue City in 1968. By instilling tradition one more time, the sergeant major was reminding them that others had overcome hard obstacles. They weren't the first to face a fanatical enemy, and they were expected to win. To loosen up his troops, Lt. Col. Willie Buhl lightened up the mood by staging mock gladiator fights, complete with wooden swords and obstinate donkeys pulling wooden carts with the word "chariot" printed on cardboard signs.

The assault began at night under a cold drizzle and swirled on for weeks. Zarqawi and Janabi sneaked away, passing through the lines dressed as women. Hadid stayed with his men. True to form, they attacked in small groups, relying on Adidas sneakers and local knowledge to scamper from one alley to the next, seeking unguarded seams. The marines, bulky and slow in their armor, advanced stolidly. Each battalion had a different style, a few moving rapidly through their assigned sectors, only to be shot at from the rear and have to retrace their steps. Eventually all employed Malay's squeegee tactic, doing exactly what the insurgents believed Americans would never do—leaving their armor and searching methodically house after house, room after room.

The basic tactic was called the stack. A dozen marines in a squad lined up outside the courtyard wall and shouted and stomped, hoping any insurgents inside would fire prematurely. Usually they didn't. The marines then breached the outer iron gate, ran across the tiny patch of grass, and flattened themselves along the wall next to the front door. On signal, the door would be smashed in and four marines would rush into the front room, each pointing his rifle toward a different corner, each betting his life that none of the others would freeze or not shoot quickly enough.

In the course of three weeks, 100 squads searched 30,000 buildings. In one eight-day period, Lima Company of Battalion 3-1 had twenty-five fights inside houses, killing sixty insurgents while losing five marines. In three days, the thirty-eight marines in 1st Platoon of Lima Company engaged in sixteen firefights, losing three killed and twelve wounded and evacuated, while killing thirty-eight of the enemy.

———

Sooner or later, every squad bumped into jihadists lurking in ambush. Imagine the scene. You are tired, sweaty, filthy. You've been at it day after day, with four hours' sleep, running down hallways, kicking in doors, rushing in, sweeping the beam of the flashlight on your rifle into the far corners, jerking open closet doors, checking under the bed, yelling "Clear!," stepping back into the corridor, and edging along the wall to the next door. You push open the door and rush in, pivoting to cover your sector when there's a flash and the firing hammers your ears. You can't hear a thing and it's way too late to think. The jihadist rounds go high—the death blossom—and your M4 is suddenly steady. It had been bucking slightly as you jerked and squeezed through your thirty rounds, not even knowing you were shooting. Trained instinct. In the dark you slap home a fresh magazine. Everyone's been shooting. The cordite's thick in the air. It's hard to breathe, let alone see.

"Out! Out!" Your fire team leader is screaming in your face, his hand grabbing your armored vest and dragging you toward the door. You lurch into the corridor, back against the wall, and count bodies. Four. All out. The team leader already has a grenade in his hand, shaking it violently to get your attention. You nod, as do the others. He pulls the pin, plucks off the safety cap, and chucks it underhand into the smoky room.

"Frag out!" You didn't need to be told. You're already hunkered down. The explosion is dull. Maybe the grenade rolled under the bed or your hearing is still screwed up. A second grenade is lobbed in. Another cloud of dust and smoke rolls out of the room. You have that gritty, yucky taste of gunpowder in your mouth and you're convinced your teeth are black. You reach over your shoulder and take a suck from your CamelBak, swishing the water and spitting it out. Your mouth tastes like iron and your ears are ringing. You look over at your team leader, who is taking a smoke. His mouth is as numb as yours. He can't feel the nicotine.

You call it in over the ICOM radio taped with Velcro to your left shoulder. Your squad leader and lieutenant come in and you all wait while the dust settles. No noise from the room. Again you take your place in the stack. Again you rush in, first man firing a few fast bursts. Flashlight beams sweep in all directions, then converge on two jihadists with AKs and ammo vests sprawled at angles impossible for live men. One has a thick beard and half a throat; the other has no jaw. You check for booby traps, police up their weapons, walk into the courtyard, and pitch them into the street for the idling tank to crush them. You take out your can and spray-paint an X—house searched—and a 2—two bodies inside—on the courtyard wall. The squad leader points to the next house and you get back in the stack. Ten more houses to go before it's too dark to search.

Bursting into one house, Cpl. Rafael Peralta was shot. As he fell, four marines in the stack rushed forward to protect him. From an overhead balcony, an insurgent pitched a grenade into their midst. Peralta grabbed it and tucked it under his stomach, absorbing the explosion, giving his life to save his comrades. A tough squad leader, Peralta had a funny side and spent hours teaching his two sisters how to salsa.

A few days later, President Bush called Peralta's mother. Not wanting to be late for her housecleaning job, she asked him to call back. No problem. When he called again, she hadn't finished cleaning. Could he call back? No problem. Mr. Bush called a third time to speak to the mother of a marine nominated for the Medal of Honor.

In Fallujah the fighting continued day after day. In the back room of a house at the southern end of the city, a jihadist with wild black hair shot and killed Cpl. Travis Desiato, then hurled a grenade at Cpl. Timothy Connors, knocking him to the dirt floor. When Connors regained consciousness, he charged back down the corridor. Grenades and bullets flew back and forth. When it was over, Omar Hadid, the leader of the insurgents, lay sprawled among other jihadists, riddled with bullets.

In a house a few blocks to the north, 1st Sgt. Brad Kasal batted aside the barrel of an AK and shot an insurgent in the face, kicking off a four-hour battle. Shot numerous times, Kasal shielded a fellow marine on the blood-slick floor while Lt. Jesse Grapes threw down protective fire. Once all were rescued and safe outside, Grapes blew to bits the house and the tough Chechens barricaded inside. One marine died and eleven were wounded inside the House from Hell.

Near the Blackwater Bridge, named for the four contractors whose mutilated parts had dangled there in April, a jihadist leaped out of a closet at Cpt. Drew McNulty. The two crashed to the floor, with McNulty stabbing him to death. Several days later, a careless lieutenant neglected to employ the proper stack technique and walked into an ambush inside an upscale house. Shot in the arms and shoulders and unable to reload, Cpl. Christopher Adlesperger staggered out of the house, picked up a fresh M4, and rushed back into the fight, while the lieutenant hesitated. McNulty ran up, pulled out his marines, including five dead, and ran repeated air strikes on the house until Lieutenant Colonel Malay grasped his shoulder and said, "Drew, that's enough."

In the industrial junkyards of east Fallujah, SSgt. David Bellavia, an Army reservist, saw two of his commanders shot down, then rushed into a house and chased the jihadists from room to room. A one-man wrecking crew, Bellavia killed six insurgents, using his rifle, his pistol, and his helmet.

It wasn't any picnic out on the streets either. Every window in the city had been blown out, leaving thousands of hiding places for snipers who snapped off quick shots and slipped out a back door. By the third day, the Marines had learned to "enter every room with a boom" and to advance alongside the tanks, pointing out suspicious houses. As I moved with Malay through his sector in late November, we stopped to talk with a tank commander. Guray Ishmael Castillo told me he fired 2,700 machine gun rounds and seventeen main tank gun shells each day.

"My tank was hit by six or seven RPGs but they bounced off," Castillo said. "We keep going, day after day. The grunts give me the sign, and I'd let loose. So far, I've fired 175 main tank rounds. They cost the taxpayer $1,000 apiece. A hundred seventy-five thousand bucks!" Only the Marines, who take a perverse pride in operating on a penny-pinching budget, would comment on tax dollars in the middle of a battle.

The fighting inside Fallujah gradually—and temporarily—petered out in December. The assault had taken the lives of 70 Americans, with another 609 wounded. More than 2,000 insurgents were killed or captured, along with 18,000 buildings damaged or destroyed. From the beginning of the struggle in the spring of 2003 to its occupation at the end of 2004, 151 Americans died in Fallujah.

Toward the end of the battle, I was standing in a blasted section of the ancient Jolan district, where Zembiec had fought in April. I asked Lieutenant Colonel Ali, who commanded an Iraqi battalion, why Zarqawi had run away and not fought to the death, as he had vowed to do. An American squad was walking by on the street, their faces grimy and weapons at the ready, warily scanning the shot-out buildings. The colonel gestured at them.

"You Americans," the colonel said, "are the strongest tribe."

FIGHTING WITH INSUFFICIENT TROOPS

Fallujah was the most ferocious battle of the war. There were more than 200 fights *inside* concrete rooms against jihadists determined to kill an American and die a martyr. *Two hundred.* That's more than all the fights by all the police SWAT teams in the States in the past three decades—and against suicidal zealots armed with grenades and automatic weapons.

Editors and producers decided what the public saw and read. We read about flawed presidents and refractory generals, but didn't read about heroes. Scant coverage was given to acts of valor like Connors's struggle against Hadid, McNulty's ferocity, and Bellavia's RoboCop-on-steroids style. These men were not victims. They were warriors. Hadid had a solid operational plan. His mistake was underestimating the American fighting man.

He was not alone in making mistakes. A few months before the battle began, Generals Conway and Mattis finished their tours and returned to the States. Conway was replaced by Lt. Gen. John F. Sattler. As the fighting ebbed in late November, Sattler told the press that "we have broken the back of the insurgency . . . across the country, this is going to make it very hard for them to operate."

No assessment could have been further from reality. The general had mistaken tactical valor for strategic wisdom. Courageous American soldiers could hold the insurgency in check, but not break its back. Iraqi forces had to assume the burden of providing security, and they were years from being able to do so.

The year 2004 was the high-water mark for the Sunni insurgency. Midway through the November battle for Fallujah, the insurgents popped up in downtown Mosul. As the police abandoned their posts, the guerrillas burned the voting stations prepared for the January election and fled when American soldiers drove up from Kirkuk. When the Americans rushed to one city, the insurgents drove to another. In September, it had been Samarra's turn. In November, it was Mosul's turn.

Casey had 150,000 American troops. The basic maneuver element was the combat arms battalion, numbering between 700 and 1,000 soldiers. With fifty battalions, Casey's multinational force was occupying eighteen cities, keeping open 1,000 miles of highway, and holding the megalopolis of Baghdad. On paper there were 80,000 trained Iraqi soldiers and police. Most, however, were stationed in the Shiite south. Those in Baghdad and the Sunni Triangle were unreliable.

The size of the task was staggering. In east Baghdad, for instance, the 1st Battalion of the 64th Armored Regiment in the 1st Cavalry Division had 710 American soldiers amidst 1.6 million Iraqis. Each day, 1-64 sent out seven patrols to sweep the highways for IEDs, a mission called route security. That left enough soldiers to hold one meeting a day with the Iraqis, plus ten four-hour patrols. There were too few American soldiers. In a U.S. city of 1.6 million, the police conduct *one thousand* patrols a day. In addition to Baghdad, Casey dispatched units to seventeen other cities to prepare for the January elections. This meant one or two battalions—1,500 soldiers—per city, with populations of 200,000 to 350,000.

Opposing them were about 10,000 insurgents who could drive where they wanted and operated in small cells of ten to twenty, many related by extended family and most belonging to a tribe that provided shelter. Each cell launched an attack once every week or two, and then lay low for a while. The campaign plan called for "neutralizing" those insurgents. That had proven as difficult as catching water bugs. You stomped on Fallujah and they squirted to Mosul. The cumulative effect was 550 attacks a week, up from 200 at the beginning of the year.

In April, Lieutenant General Sanchez had told the press that "there has never ever been any direction from my higher headquarters that forbade us or kept us from asking for additional forces." Bremer had recommended more troops several times. Mattis told Wolfowitz on two visits that more troops were needed. There were typewritten notes from a commanders' conference attended by Abizaid citing a request from Mattis for another brigade. Before the second battle for Fallujah, the division commander said there weren't enough troops in Anbar Province. Senator Joseph Biden (D-DE) recounted that as he hopped on a helicopter at Fallujah in late November a senior general shouted in his ear, "If anyone tells you we don't need more troops, he's lying."

CHANGES IN WASHINGTON

Having won reelection, President Bush announced his team for the next four years. Secretary of State Colin Powell was leaving. Iraq was the critical event of George W. Bush's presidency and Powell, luke-warm about the wisdom of the war, had never been included in Bush's inner circle of advisers, and State had not been a major player in Iraq. Condoleezza Rice was moving from national security adviser to the top job at State, replacing Powell. At the NSC, she had not organized a process that systematically coordinated State, CIA, and the Pentagon. Rumsfeld frequently bypassed or ignored the NSC process. Rice al-lowed Bremer to bypass Rumsfeld. State never advanced a clear posi-tion. Rice never demanded clarity. The foolishness about Fallujah in April and the failure to arrest Sadr in April and again in August showed what happened on the battlefield when the process in Washington was ad hoc.

At the Pentagon, Rumsfeld did not use his power consistently, pre-ferring to hop in and out of Iraqi issues. His deputy, Wolfowitz, was more focused. By October of 2003, both men were convinced Bremer was moving too slowly to build Iraqi security forces, but Rumsfeld did not put his muscle behind his deputy's efforts to accelerate the effort.

Democrats, liberals, and critics in the media singled out Wolfowitz as the standard-bearer for the neoconservative movement, which had burned brightly when Bush assumed office and flickered out when the Iraqi war dragged on. Wolfowitz was damaged goods. In 1967, Presi-dent Johnson eased out Secretary of Defense McNamara, who had mis-managed the Vietnam War, by appointing him president of the World Bank. Bush gave Wolfowitz the same appointment and moved him out of the administration.

To the surprise of many inside and outside government, Rumsfeld stayed on. He hectored rather than led, peppering his staff and the mil-itary with sharp, terse notes written on the margins of the reports they sent to him. While his queries were usually on the mark, his style was that of a counterpuncher, conceding the offense to others. He hadn't reined in Bremer. He remained aloof from the Iraqi electoral porridge, even though its interminable length assured that American troops would remain involved for years—precisely what Rumsfeld opposed. His focus was on reducing American casualties and bringing the troops home as quickly as possible, while at the same time prevailing in Iraq.

The contradiction between his two goals of getting out quickly ver-sus winning was glaring. "The U.S. military doesn't do nation building," he said. But in Iraq, that's precisely what the U.S. military was doing. Bremer realistically summed up the American effort as "a long-term project of nation-building, like it or not." Rumsfeld did not like it, but he hadn't found a way out.

A BAD YEAR COMES TO AN END

Casey, his staff, and the division commanders knew they faced a big problem as 2004 drew to a close. The first draft of Casey's end-of-year assessment, called a "Campaign Progress Review," contained the sentence, "The outcome is in doubt." Casey decided to delete that sentence because it was a political judgment. According to the mantra that an insurgency is 80 percent political, judging outcomes was the proper role for the ambassador, not the general.

So instead of admitting "the outcome is in doubt," the review concluded that "the insurgency was intensifying."

INADEQUATE MEANS

2005

POLITICAL FANTASY

President Bush was impatient with anything that smacked of negative thinking. He was relying on the Iraqi election to turn the tide. That Iraq would emerge as a stable democracy was based on a transcendental principle firmly believed by the president, not on a practical strategy that matched resources to policy goals.

A few weeks earlier, Bush had awarded the Medal of Freedom, America's highest nonmilitary honor, to General Franks, Ambassador Bremer, and Director Tenet, who accepted it reluctantly after losing faith in the administration and resigning as director of the CIA. The search for WMD, weapons of mass destruction, had proved fruitless, knocking out the chief rationale for the war, and Tenet had been tagged with the error. The ceremony rewarded loyalty to the president rather than national achievement, smacking of self-justification for the principals in a mismanaged war far from won.

Still, the president exuded self-confidence. From a low of 40 percent, public approval of his handling of Iraq had rebounded to 50 percent, mainly due to American bravery during the Fallujah fight. On January 20, Bush delivered a soaring inaugural speech, proclaiming that it was America's duty to aid the cause of freedom around the world. "It is the policy of the United States to seek and support the growth of democratic movements and institutions in every nation and culture, with the ultimate goal of ending tyranny in our world."

If uttered by most politicians, such rhetoric would be dismissed as boilerplate. For President Bush, the words were a cherished belief and a means of turning attention away from the absence of WMD and onto the Iraqi elections only a few days away. In the president's Manichaean view, the innate goodness of man would shine through if allowed to vote. America's concept of liberal democracy would be copied by Iraq. The instrumentalities, modalities, and compromises that marked the fitful, grinding emergence of Western democracies counted for less than the principle of casting a vote. Faith was a more powerful tool than reason.

That was bleak news for the interim prime minister, Ayad Allawi, who called the administration's rush to elections "flawed and senseless." Politics is all about who gets what and why, and Allawi could do nothing for anybody. He was discredited among Sunnis after the assault on Fallujah and blamed by Shiites for a lack of electricity, fuel, drinking water, and everything else that was going wrong. The only hope for his nonsectarian party at the polls was American aid. The CIA was prepared to provide financial and organizational help to offset the $11 million a week Iran was spending to elect its favorite Shiite blocs. Presidents from Harry Truman through Richard Nixon had provided such clandestine cash infusions in many nations, including in Europe and Latin America. Allawi represented the best hope for electing a nonsectarian Iraqi government.

According to columnist David Ignatius, however, Representative Nancy Pelosi (D-CA) and Dr. Condoleezza Rice agreed that aiding Allawi violated the true spirit of free elections. President Bush supported that view. America would not interfere, no matter how much money Iran spent on its Shiite candidates. Allawi sank like a rock at the polls.

The Iraqi election at the end of January 2005 proceeded smoothly. The American battalion commanders had done an excellent job of providing an outer security screen, and the Iraqi police and soldiers knew what guard posts and stations to man. The insurgents, without a central command authority, responded with no large-scale organized violence. There were forty-four deaths in nine separate attacks against polling stations across the country. Over eight million voters went to the polls, many proudly posing with purple index fingers held aloft to show they had indeed voted.

President Bush was delighted and the American national press was generous in its praise.

Americans wanted to believe their sacrifices had been for a good cause. Once they grasped the significance of the results, though, they were considerably more reserved. "The elections had, to some degree, the opposite effect of what we had hoped for," General Petraeus later said. "Because of the voting along sectarian divides, it did not unify the country as much as we had hoped."

Prodded by U.N. advisers, Bremer had approved a process for voting for national party lists rather than for representatives from local districts and provinces. This permitted Sistani to gather the Shiite parties under one umbrella—the United Iraqi Alliance—which included the Supreme Council for Islamic Revolution in Iraq (SCIRI), the Dawa Party, and Sadr's representatives. As the spiritual leader of the Shiites, Ayatollah Sistani preached that the roles of government and of Shiite Islam were indivisible; the state protected the religion, its precepts, and its followers. From the Shiite mosques, the word went out to vote for the UIA.

So the election amounted to a sectarian census. The Shiite majority voted for the Shiite slate, resulting in a cabinet and a National Assembly that owed everything to national religious parties and nothing to provincial and local constituencies. The UIA captured 148 of the 275 seats in the National Assembly and the Kurds 75 seats, while Allawi's nonsectarian party ran a distant third, capturing 40 seats.

The elections ushered in a tyranny of the majority. The United States had bestowed on Iraq a democracy founded on majority sectarian rule and dedicated to the proposition of intolerance. For centuries, the Sunni minority had oppressed the Shiite majority. Now the Shiites were poised to repay in kind while America stood guard.

THE HIDDEN HAND OF CORRUPTION

In Baghdad, the Iraqi politicians were bickering over plum posts. They did not worry about security; the Americans provided them with comfortable houses, meeting halls, schools, and twenty-four-hour protection inside the Green Zone. A dispirited Allawi presided over ministries where officials were scurrying to curry favor with the new power elite. Arguments about who got what and how to divide the spoils of office went on for months.

The stakes were huge. Revenues from oil exports exceeded $1 billion a month. Although the incoming finance minister had a sterling reputation, once monies were disbursed to the ministries, there were no systems or audit procedures in place to detect, let alone deter, massive theft. These were Iraqi monies that could be stolen without fear of imprisonment by the Americans.

Over three decades of rule, Saddam had institutionalized corruption. In nations without the patrimony of oil, each generation must produce salable outputs to exist. Since politicians must persuade thousands of businessmen and farmers to part with some of their earnings, they have to deliver something in return. Conversely, taxpayers are outraged if their money is stolen. Iraqi politicians were not constrained by any such social contract. When they took office, the Americans provided the security and oil provided the opportunity for self-enrichment. Money was there for the taking.

For months, rumors had swirled around Baghdad about officials at the Ministry of Defense demanding kickbacks for weapons purchases. In December of 2004, an American weapons dealer, Dale Stoffel, sought payment for $25 million in refurbished equipment. The ministry told him the money had been transferred to a mysterious Lebanese middleman for payment. Stoffel made the mistake of complaining to Senator Rick Santorum (R-PA) and to the Pentagon. At a meeting outside Baghdad, ministry officials agreed to pay him. When Stoffel and another American contractor drove out of the base, a truck crashed into them. Two men walked up to the damaged vehicle, shot them to death, took Stoffel's laptop computer, and drove away.

Twenty-five million dollars was small change. The official in charge of procurement for the Iraqi military, Ziad Qattan, had told the *Los Angeles Times,* "Before, I sold water, flowers, shoes, cars—but not weapons. We didn't know anything about weapons." Qattan parlayed his street hawker skills into a partnership with Hazem Shaalan, the defense minister and his comptroller, who previously had sold shoes. Together they transferred $1 billion from the Defense Ministry and flew to Lebanon with hundreds of millions in cash to buy arms.

In return, Iraq received from Poland and Egypt junk weapons— helicopters that couldn't fly, armor that didn't stop bullets, and AK-47s that didn't fire. Qattan and Shaalan later fled Iraq for countries without extradition agreements, including Poland. Lt. Gen. Martin Dempsey, the deputy commander at CentCom, told me it appeared Shaalan personally made off with $200 million in cash. Iraqi officials called it "the largest theft in history."

Americans complained about the lack of "capacity," meaning that the Shiite officials lacked education and administrative skills. The causes of incompetence ran deeper. One annual index of 180 countries placed Iraq as the world's third most corrupt country. Corruption impeded the delivery of pay, food, fuel, and weapons to the Iraqi soldiers; it invited the padding of payroll lists; it engendered suspicions, disloyalty, and cliques; it affected morale and performance. Few clean hands led to many blind eyes.

Lt. Col. Kevin Farrell, commanding an Army battalion in Baghdad, worked alongside Iraqi units in 2004 and 2005. "Corruption was rampant," he said. "Every time a soldier wanted to go on leave, he would, of course, pay his commander to allow him to go. . . . For the Iraqi mindset . . . he is not doing his duty [for his family] if he doesn't take that cut."

Much of it was invisible to American officials because it involved money disbursed through Iraqi channels. General Casey said it was rare to find conclusive proof. "We put together solid evidence against only a handful," Casey told me. "Their system gave them a lot of crooks as ministers."

The Nobel Prize–winning economist Professor Roger Myerson offered an explanation about when corruption works and does not work to support a state. Chiang Kai-shek's government in China in 1949 is cited in U.S. counterinsurgency theory as an example of how corruption corrodes a regime, leading to victory by the guerrillas. Not so, Myerson argued. "The problem was that highly connected government agents took profits from their positions without providing the governance and services that were expected of them." Chiang failed as a leader because he did not ensure that his subordinates were rewarded only when they performed their jobs correctly. When they were rewarded even while failing, those failures became the insurgents' gains, spreading the perception that Chiang's rule was doomed and motivating his subordinates to steal more while they could. They did nothing to prevent the collapse they had engineered by their own ineptitude. Conversely, the British in India in the 1860s granted local authority as a property right to landlords called zamindars. Thus permitted to tax and benefit, the zamindar bureaucracy ruthlessly stamped out any anti-British movements because a rebellion would mean the end of their livelihoods.

In Iraq, once the Baath Party and the Iraqi Army were disbanded, there was no bureaucracy, no matter how corrupt, to provide services and security in return for a paycheck. When the Saddam regime fell, there were paid shills, not national leaders, waiting in the wings. Ayad Allawi was paid by the CIA; Ahmed Chalabi, convicted in absentia of bank fraud in Jordan, was paid by the Pentagon; Moqtada Sadr was paid by Iran. Appointed and elected officials expected payoffs, not sac-

rifice. It was misleading of President Bush and General Abizaid to extol
Iraqi leaders, and it was calumny to compare them to America's
Founding Fathers.

What Cuba, Saudi Arabia, Nigeria, and Russia shared in common
were apparatchiks who understood they had to do their jobs to get
paid. Although it offended the U.S. military to know that many Iraqi
officers and high officials were thieves, the behavior of many countries
demonstrated that a corrupt state could provide security and services
for the people.

The dilemma the American military never resolved was reconciling
its ethics with the behavior of those it put in power. The American military creed banishes thieves. It is an American axiom that a good leader
cannot exploit his troops. Yet that is exactly what happened throughout the ranks of the Iraqi military and American advisers never pro-
mulgated a uniform set of rules for addressing corruption.

Col. Juan Ayala, after serving as the senior adviser to the 1st Iraqi
Division, wrote:

> Corruption exists. The Iraqis know that we know. They know we
> would never condone it or report it if we saw it. Never overt, the rank
> and file complain about it. . . . It can't be viewed through American
> eyes. It has been part of life since the sands of Mesopotamia. . . .
> Seeking corruption would distract mission focus, severely strain sen-
> sitive personal relations and, worse, compromise our force protec-
> tion posture [meaning there would be retaliation].

General Abizaid strongly disagreed with the colonel. Testifying before the Senate, Abizaid said, "Corruption in this part of the world is
one of the great corrosive influences that causes extremism to flourish."
Yet the senior generals never issued clear guidelines, leaving a generation of American advisers not knowing how to deal with the sleaze and
corruption they routinely encountered.

CHANGING MILITARY STRATEGY

In 2004, the coalition had fought its way to the elections by conventional offensive operations. Fallujah was the last stand-up battle of the
insurgency. After the Marines searched house by house, finding and
killing 1,800 insurgents, including Chechens, never again would the insurgents choose to stand and fight.

However, Zarqawi and the al Qaeda movement had emerged by the end of 2004 in the guise of mujahidin, or holy warriors, and were followed or at least left alone by the other Sunni resistance groups. The IED became the chief means of attacking the Americans, while the suicide murderer, in a car laden with explosives, emerged as Zarqawi's method of slaughtering Shiites to provoke a civil war. Zarqawi had released a letter warning Sunnis that "Shiism is the looming danger and the true challenge. They are the enemy. Beware of them. Fight them. By God, they lie." Once the country was divided, Zarqawi would establish thirteenth-century caliphates in Sunni areas.

Unable to prevent the January election, the insurgents urged a Sunni boycott. Eight percent of Sunnis and 70 percent of Shiites went to the polls. In Baghdad, 78 percent of the voters were Shiite. In Anbar, only 2 percent of Sunnis voted.

The Sunni boycott notwithstanding, the main event in 2005 was the election of a sovereign government. That posed three courses of action for the coalition forces: 1) continue offensive operations against the insurgents; 2) clear and hold the Sunni Triangle and Baghdad; or 3) transition to the Iraqis the responsibility to hold the Triangle.

Casey ruled out offensive operations. In late November of 2004, with gunfire echoing from the side streets, he had stood on Fallujah's main road. Directly ahead lay the Blackwater Bridge, where a marine had written on a girder: "This is for the murders of the four American contractors." The "this" was the destruction that Casey saw all around him—blackened streets littered with burnt-out cars, empty shells that crunched underfoot, fronts sheered off apartment buildings revealing smashed bedrooms and sagging kitchens with dripping pipes, metal gratings of storefronts peeled back like sardine cans, bodies of insurgents bled out and shrunken, flies buzzing around, the rotting, cloying smell of human decay.

Offensive operations like Fallujah, Casey decided, weren't the solution. American battalions swept through Sunni cities like large snowplows, unable to clear the side streets and alleys. Snowplows don't change the weather. Thousands of insurgents had died, but as many had taken their place.

The second option, then, was for the coalition forces to conduct counterinsurgency—COIN—operations. Classic COIN doctrine called for American forces to hold the Sunni cities after they had cleared them. This alternative carried considerable baggage. With images from the escalating battles in 2004 still fresh in their minds, the Sunnis looked upon the Americans as infidel invaders. To hold the Sunni Triangle would require substantially more American troops, a request not welcomed by Abizaid, Rumsfeld, or the Joint Chiefs in Washington.

That left the third option: transition security responsibility to Iraqis. Politics was central to an insurgency. After a year under Bremer and months under Allawi's appointed rule, a freely chosen Iraqi government was now poised to step forward and vindicate President Bush's eschatological faith in democracy.

Casey chose the transition strategy. The main effort was to build the Iraqi forces. The goal, as Lt. Gen. John R. Vines, the new corps commander, put it, was "rapid progress in training and preparing Iraqis to assume responsibility for security in every province." The strategy was not the "victory" that President Bush talked about. American units would not be the primary counterinsurgent force; instead, they would put Iraqis in the lead and pull back. Casey estimated it would take years, perhaps a decade, before the insurgency was defeated. Until that happened, Iraqi forces only had to be good enough to keep the insurgency from fracturing Iraq and prevent the takfiris—Sunni extremists—from operating freely.

The strategy was a hope posing as a plan.

A DUBIOUS IRAQI ARMY

I had stayed with two Iraqi battalions for several days during the November–December battle in Fallujah. As long as Americans were alongside them, usually in the lead, the jundis had fought fairly well. They weren't tested in the toughest sections or left on their own, though, and their advisers had doubts about the Iraqi Army as a viable system.

The organization charged with developing the Iraqi Army as a system had the aptly awkward-sounding title of Multi-National Security Transition Command—Iraq, or MNSTC-I. General Petraeus commanded a pickup staff. The staff's qualifications, including combat or counterinsurgency skills, were scant. It had been thirty years since the Army had undertaken such a mission.

The trainers were learning at the same time as the trainees. The goal called for eighty Iraqi battalions organized into eight divisions. Half of the divisions, however, were recruited under the promise that they would not leave their home provinces, meaning a majority of the Iraqi Army, from the time of recruitment, was out of the main fight.

Progress was erratic. The improvement of Iraqi units depended upon the competence of their leaders, the dedication of their American trainers, and the support provided by nearby American units. These three factors aligned properly about a third of the time.

Iraqi Leadership

As the Fallujah battle drew to a close, I had walked through the ruins of the Jolan district, past the warehouse where Zarqawi had beheaded Nicholas Berg, the young California civilian. Al Jazeera had repeatedly played the gruesome videotape that Zarqawi had distributed to terrorize American and Iraqi soldiers alike. The jundis in the Shiite battalion I was accompanying on patrol had a cocky air, mocking the takfiris (the Sunni extremists who proclaim death to all Shiites as heretics). But they wouldn't give me their last names, explaining that takfiris read the Internet and would track down their families. The imams left in Fallujah, they said, were still preaching jihad. When the patrol ended, they asked their adviser, Capt. Ken Gardner, to call the nearest Marine company to send over their evening chow.

"They rely on us too much," Gardner said. "These jundis are Shiites. They shit inside homes to show disrespect and scribble on walls stuff like 'We kill all Sunnis.' It's empty bragging. They know who controls the streets. They put on civilian clothes to hide when they go on leave. They're not ready for prime time yet. Their own officers don't look out for them, or discipline them."

Too often the Iraqi officers simply didn't care. In early 2005, for 10 percent of a battalion to quit each month wasn't unusual. When the 18th Battalion of the Iraqi 5th Division was ordered to Fallujah in mid-December—after the battle—many of its 700 soldiers did not return from leave. When ordered to get on the trucks, 200 more walked out the gate, including the battalion commander.

American Advisers

The American advisers, with fewer than 3,000 in the field in early 2005, fell into two camps. Some saw their primary role as advising on planning and staff procedures, leaving it to the Iraqis to carry out operations. Others actively engaged side by side in combat, advising by example and sharing the dangers equally.

When the Iraqi officers cared and the American advisers operated alongside them, security improved rapidly. In Tikrit, I joined Capt. Jason Deel of the 4th Infantry Division for a night patrol with his combined platoon. It was similar to the Combined Action Platoon I patrolled with in

Vietnam. Inside the base—a palace on a cliff along the Tigris—thirty Iraqis and eight U.S. soldiers slept on cots in separate rooms but shared a command center that consisted of a few military radios, a TV with DVD player, dozens of magazines, a wall map, a blackboard, and a refrigerator. With a piece of chalk, Deel sketched the patrol route, rally points, and formation. An Iraqi lieutenant, Uday Nofan, then did the same.

When we stepped off, the Americans and Iraqis fell into their familiar patrol positions. For the next several hours, we moved up and down the dark streets. We passed packs of snarling, half-wild dogs and paused at several unlit houses, where Nofan opened the courtyard gate, knocked at the door, and talked in low murmurs.

"Nofan has a few informers," Deel said. "We stop at a lot of houses at night. No one knows which houses are his sources."

On the main street, Deel pointed out recent IED bombings—a deep gouge in the curb near a kebab stand, shattered cement next to an Internet café, a small hole in the macadam, a storefront with smashed windows.

"Since we got out of our Humvees and partnered with these jundis, we don't get hit anymore," Deel said. "The IED is their weapon. During the middle of the day, when there's traffic moving, a car will drop one like a turd, right through the floorboards, and keep on moving. Bam! Some poor civilian is hit. Nice guys, huh?"

When I met with Capt. Eric Navarro, who was advising an Iraqi battalion in Baghdad, he was skeptical about the rate of improvement. When he wasn't supervising, the Iraqi officers let basic tasks, like cleaning weapons and posting guards, slide. Lackadaisical tactics that could get you killed, like walking directly up to strange cars, recurred time and again. Navarro could give no direct orders or relieve anyone for incompetence or endangering the unit.

Many advisers posted on their bulletin boards the quote from Colonel T. E. Lawrence, the fabled Arabist: Better the Arabs do it tolerably than you do it perfectly. It is their war. Help them, don't try to win it for them. Wise words—if America was willing to keep advisers in Iraq for a decade.

American Support

How American units interpreted the mission of transitioning to Iraqi security forces varied tremendously across Iraq. Some instinctively reached out to help the local forces. In 2004, I visited with Lt. Col. Dominic Caraccilo, commander of the 2nd Battalion of the 503rd Airborne, in Kirkuk, a city of more than a million Kurds and Arabs. While avoiding the 503rd's heavily defended base, the insurgents had attacked the Magreb police station in the heart of Kirkuk four times. On his own hook, Caraccilo went to the police chief, Abdul Tarhan, and proposed stationing an American platoon inside the station.

Although Iraqi officials in Baghdad, Fallujah, and elsewhere had rejected American offers to move into the police precinct houses, Tarhan enthusiastically accepted Caraccilo's offer. Within a few weeks, the paratroopers were patrolling the streets jointly with Magreb's 200 policemen.

But Caraccilo stood out because he was the exception. At the start of 2005, there was no discernible overall pattern to the American support for Iraqi forces. Few American units took as their primary mission Casey's admonition to transition from controlling the battlefield to helping the Iraqis take the lead. Most U.S. units were still operating separately, hunting insurgents they could not identify.

ANBAR ON ITS OWN

The size of North Carolina, Anbar Province stretched from Baghdad across lush river valleys and arid desert to the borders of Saudi Arabia, Jordan, and Syria. The Euphrates River wended its way southeast for 200 miles to the outskirts of Baghdad. Anbar was a tough land inhabited by 1.2 to 2 million Sunnis, most belonging to tribes. Industry, education, and toleration were in scant supply. Over the centuries, hardscrabble cities like Qaim, Haditha, and Fallujah had grown up along the trade route down the river. The cities, offering supplies and sympathizers, provided an ideal ratline for foreign takfiris eager to defend Islam against the infidels and heretic Shiites.

Although Anbar was the setting for almost half of the fighting and dying in Iraq and the sanctuary for the foreign fighters, the province in 2005 had 20 percent of the coalition forces and 5 percent of the Iraqi Army. Petraeus had agreed to train on a priority basis 1,000 former soldiers from the Habbaniyah area. But the Sunni recruits refused to leave the province, or fight alongside Americans and have their own people turn against them. The Shiite battalions stationed near Baghdad didn't want to come to Anbar and be shot at. It was difficult to follow Casey's order to transition to Iraqi forces when there weren't any.

"In a counterinsurgency, generals have three tasks—determine the mission, set priorities, and allocate resources," Colonel Dunford, who spent twenty-two months in Anbar, explained. "Anbar was the heart of the insurgency. But we were the economy of force. By 2005, I was beating the bushes for troops."

About fifty sheiks met with Dunford. They had seen the destruction in Fallujah and feared what was coming. Abdullah Janabi, the zealot adviser to Zarqawi, was skulking in the Habbaniyah area, somewhere between Ramadi and Fallujah, wearing an explosive-laden vest with a suicide switch, cursing the infidels. The takfiris were burrowing into Ramadi, where no contractor would work for the coalition. The few gas stations and schools had closed. The Marines refused to withdraw from the Government Center downtown, driving the latest in a line of short-term governors to and from work in an armored column. Daily the insurgents fired at the center and daily the Marines returned a volume of fire, gradually smashing up the city.

The sheiks offered a deal in March of 2005. They wanted arms and ammunition, plus vehicles. They would protect their turfs with a tribal force of roughly 5,000 men. They would agree to boundaries and point out the takfiris. That would stop the IED attacks along the main roads.

Dunford refused. You have an elected national government, he said, with a new army. Send your tribal sons to Taji (north of Baghdad). Asked if he could promise they would return to their tribal areas, Dunford said no. There was an elected government and no need for another militia. The days of the tribes were over.

For a second time, the Sunni sheiks of Anbar had been rebuffed. The Anbar tribes would not be permitted to take up arms in their own defense, regardless of whether one called it a mini–loya jirga, as the diplomat Keith Mines did in 2003, or warlordism, or federalism, or a militia. The answer remained no.

Instead, the Marines began Operation River Blitz, the first in a series intended to drive the foreign fighters from the cities along the Euphrates. Casualties during River Blitz were light. The insurgents melted away as the American armor approached.

"We can hold it [a city] easily for as long as we are here," Maj. Mike Miller, a company commander in Battalion 1-23, said after the operation. "But we can't make any promises beyond when we leave. So I can understand that locals are reluctant to get involved."

The snowplows were again clearing the streets.

SHIFTING DIPLOMATIC COURSE

Appearing on CNN at the end of March 2005, General Abizaid said, "We've gone from a primarily military environment to a primarily political one. And that's a very encouraging sign." In a convolution of roles, the military was citing politics as the primary reason to believe security was improving.

After five months of wrangling, the officials of the appointed Interim Government were replaced in May by the elected transitional government, which was to rule for a year, and then be replaced in yet another election. The prime ministership went to Ibrahim al-Jaafari of the Dawa Party, which had an impeccable Shiite pedigree of opposition to Saddam and the Baathists. Jaafari was a solid Islamist who could be relied upon to purge the relatively few former Baathists and secularists Allawi had managed to bring into his interim government. The Ministry of Interior, in charge of the police, was turned over to Bayan Jabar of the SCIRI party. SCIRI's militia, called the Badr Corps, was better organized than Sadr's rival Mahdi Army and more entrenched in southern Iraq. Sadr, rewarded with the Ministries of Health, Transportation, and Housing, used them as a power base to strengthen his militia. If his militia could gain control of Baghdad, he could impose a shadow government, like Hezbollah in Lebanon.

The United Iraq Alliance's overarching goal in 2005 was to consolidate Shiite power as the governing force in Iraq. This conflicted head-on with the American goal of acting as the midwife to deliver reconciliation between Shiites and Sunnis. While the extremists had to be killed, political compromise was the preferred means to persuade the large majority of the Sunni insurgents to cease fighting.

From the start, Prime Minister Jaafari wasn't cut out to be a leader. He'd talk for an hour and conclude where he had begun. He was incapable of reaching a conclusion. Power passed into the hands of the ministries, many of which pursued a vigorous anti-Sunni agenda. The Ministry of Interior was a snake pit, and Sadrists in the Ministry of Health abetted the killings of Sunnis who entered the hospitals.

Iraqi governance and politics were the responsibility of the State Department. In June, Ambassador Negroponte was replaced by Ambassador Zalmay Khalilzad, who had served in Afghanistan, was fluent in Farsi, and familiar with Iraqi politics. Where Negroponte had been low-key and hands-off, Khalilzad relished rushing in. He tried to curb the instincts of Jaafari's government by championing Sunni inclusion, summed up in the word "reconciliation."

As had been the case with Negroponte, Casey worked collegially with Khalilzad. They shared adjoining offices and talked several times a day. The problem lay in execution. Khalilzad and his diplomats were expected to maintain constant oversight and pressure on the prime minister's office, on the National Assembly, and on a dozen key ministries that ignored direct orders from their own prime minister.

"I'd walk out of the morning meeting with Casey and Khalilzad with a dozen taskers," Maj. Gen. Timothy Donovan, Casey's chief of staff, said. "I had ten generals and six major staff sections to call on. Khalilzad had three deputies. Three. He had no bench. Plus, Khalilzad loved to negotiate. That was what he did for a living—go to meetings, jawbone Iraqis, and kibitz with Washington. His staff didn't have the depth or the talent to execute assignments."

During Bremer's tenure, the U.S. military developed a disrespect, bordering on disdain, for the civilian staffs charged with rebuilding the nation of Iraq. During the tenures of Negroponte and Khalilzad, who were not arrogant or condescending, personal relations at the top were cordial. Still, the military as an institution saw no appreciable change on the ground. Generals had to bang on the desks of State Department officials to get money or projects moving. Gradually, the military's low regard for the rest of the U.S. government—the CIA excepted—transcended personalities and became systemic, almost mythical.

A BIT OF THE BUBBLY

Whether chastened by the ferocity of the Fallujah assault or thrown off stride by failing to disrupt the January election, the insurgents had attacked with less frequency in the winter of 2005. This resulted in a series of buoyant statements by senior military officers in the early spring. General Abizaid was optimistic, testifying before the Senate that the insurgency was weakening: "Voting in Iraq, the political process . . . have driven those numbers [of insurgents] down . . . the Iraqi security forces I think in 2005 will take on the majority of the tasks."

If the key task was confronting the insurgents on the streets, the data weren't as encouraging as the official statements. The weekly number of attacks exceeded 600, well above the average in 2004. General Petraeus, in charge of training the Iraqis, was supportive but cautious. While pointing to a steady increase in the numbers and capabilities of Iraqi forces, he warned that there was a "huge amount of work to be done" before they could stand on their own.

Maj. Gen. Joseph F. Weber, the chief of staff for Casey's command, said that the strategy for transitioning to Iraqi forces was "becoming a reality." As anecdotal evidence, he cited seeing "squared away" Iraqi soldiers on the highway that connected the Green Zone with Casey's headquarters on sprawling Camp Victory. When he was leaving Iraq at the end of his tour, Lt. Gen. John Sattler, the commander in Anbar, said, "I've never been more optimistic. . . . The Iraqi security forces are capable, well led and confident."

General Abizaid agreed. "I don't think the terrorists are growing in the region. . . . I think it's [the insurgency] receding," he told *The News-Hour* in early March. "Building the Iraqi security forces is a phenomenal success."

Interviews with dozens of advisers, though, pointed to basic problems. Older Iraqi officers came from a culture where rank conferred privilege rather than responsibility, the enlisted men weren't treated with respect, supplies were terrible, and support from the ministries nonexistent. Discipline was erratic and the jundis were given one week a month home leave, disrupting the continuity of training and operations. The wounded were sent to hospitals resembling those during the Civil War, and the families of those killed in action frequently received no compensation from the government.

The U.S. military and the American press differed about context—which story was selected to be written—rather than the facts inside the story itself. As Iraq dragged on, the skepticism of the press increased. The military had not established consistent benchmarks. Instead, the war was assessed by military judgments that varied from day to day.

"General Abizaid was frustrating to read," a senior White House counselor said. "He's Yin and Yang. One day he tells the president things are good, and the next day he says the opposite."

The nature of the war—small attacks by hundreds of uncoordinated gangs and tribes—was frustrating to any analytic effort. Given high ambiguity amidst violence and turbulence, the intuition of a military commander was no better than that of an experienced reporter. Had the press accepted the evaluations of the generals at face value, the war was basically won in 2003 (according to Rumsfeld and Sanchez), in 2004 (according to Sattler), and in 2005 (according to Abizaid).

Casey's Campaign Review, in June of 2005, specified the "center of gravity" for winning the war was public opinion in the States, where approval of the president's handling of Iraq had dropped to 38 percent.

Maj. Gen. Peter W. Chiarelli, the commander of the 1st Cavalry Division, stationed in east Baghdad from mid-2004 to mid-2005, wrote an influential article arguing that Iraq had changed the nature of war. Chiarelli wrote that U.S. military staffs and headquarters had to "achieve a capacity equally weighted" to five Lines of Operation—

combat, training Iraqi forces, providing services, promoting governance, and economic development.

Chiarelli cited a decrease in attacks on American forces in Sadr City
in 2004 after sewers were installed, asserting that attacks by Sadr's Jesh
al Mahdi would not last if progress was made in all LOOs. The concept
was a startling change, placing the military in the forefront of reconstruction missions traditionally filled by State, AID, and other civilian
agencies.

Chiarelli argued that "a direct correlation existed between the level
of local infrastructure status, unemployment figures and attacks on US
soldiers. The findings were an epiphany to the task force." That finding
was sobering, since economic conditions were terrible throughout all
of Iraq, not just Sadr City. If governance, services, and the economy
had to be fixed before attacks on Americans decreased, the United
States was in for a very long war. The idea of paying attention to underlying conditions and not just to military matters, however, seemed
convincing. As a framework for daily briefings, the Lines of Operation—combat, training, services, governance, and economics—became
standard throughout the divisions for the remainder of the war.

The campaign plan's priorities for 2005 were Baghdad and Mosul.
Yet Anbar accounted for 40 percent of the fighting, far higher than any
other locale. The objective was to partner an American battalion with
every Iraqi battalion. But in Anbar, the Marines were conducting unilateral offensive operations. The campaign goal was to transition responsibility to Iraqi forces and reduce the visibility of U.S. forces,
consolidating to a few bases by the end of 2005. The reports expressed
"optimism on the progress of Iraqi Security Forces." The intent was for
most coalition forces to be out of Iraq by the end of 2006. There was
no discussion in the plan about sectarianism or the performance of the
Iraqi government.

These goals were extraordinarily ambitious. Casey visited four battalions every week and met with every combat arms battalion. He trav-
eled only with his aide and, not forgetting his Ranger training, went
out on patrols. On one occasion, he was walking through a bustling
market in Baghdad when Iraqi police stopped the patrol. They said the
market was off limits—per orders from the coalition. "I am the coalition," he said, motioning to the squad to proceed. At other times, I saw
him huddling with soldiers. I asked him how he could be in touch with
his subordinates and yet receive staff reports that were a fantasy.

"From January through June [2005]," Casey said, "my energy was consumed on getting our commanders to support the Iraqi forces. It took months to sell that idea to my generals. Our Army—senior and junior commanders—are kinetic. They want to get out and destroy the enemy. The optimistic reports? I called them framework ops—patrolling the LOCs [Lines of Communication, or highways], guarding bases, et cetera. The statistics show thousands of patrols, but so what? Once the battalion commanders thought they knew what the division commanders wanted, because it was what I was pushing, that's what they reported."

SEARCHING FOR GROUND TRUTH

To determine what was happening on the ground, in the summer of 2005 Casey ordered Col. William Hix, a key adviser, and Kalev Sepp, a retired Special Forces operative, to visit battalions across the country and analyze what was working and failing. Their report, entitled "A Survey of COIN [counterinsurgency] Practices," was widely circulated. The successful techniques reflected traditional COIN doctrine: Focus on the population's security and needs, gather intelligence from the population, employ advisers down to the platoon level, establish a secure area and expand from there, and put the police in the lead, with the military in support. Eyebrows were raised about employing the police, because in most areas the police were worthless and untrustworthy. As a model, though, the list of successful practices seemed reasonable enough.

The list of unsuccessful practices was more controversial. The authors included among them: killing the enemy rather than engaging with the population, conducting battalion-sized operations as the norm, operating from large bases, and building the Iraqi Army in the image of the American Army. All four actions were common across the theater. In fact, the campaign plan called for consolidating into large bases.

"The move onto the super-FOBs [Forward Operating Bases] evolved out of General Abizaid's perception that we needed to be out of sight," Sepp told me. "The loggies [logisticians] argued endlessly for a few large bases instead of many outposts. That lessened the IED hits and maximized the ease of resupply. They had the numbers to back them up. Gradually the small FOBs were closed. The one- and two-stars [generals] didn't argue back about how to deploy to win the war."

The FOBs were self-contained cities with basketball courts, gyms, movie theaters, Internet connections, snack bars, pizza parlors, video games, and beds instead of cots. The centerpieces were the DIFACs, or dining facilities. The term "mess hall" was inappropriate for dining rooms that offered salad bars, three main courses, sandwiches with all the fixings, omelets made to order, pies, cakes, cookies, and five flavors of ice cream. A corporal once asked a crusty colonel why the food was so much better than on bases back in the States. "Because the allowance is $4 a meal back there," the colonel said, "and $34 a meal over here. That's why you're spoiled."

Life on a FOB was addictive. As habits formed, patrols became predictable, leaving after breakfast, dropping in for lunch, and returning for the evening meal. The work cycles resembled those at state police barracks. Every platoon knew its routine. The troops called it "commuting to work."

Patrolling from FOBs affected security in the provinces. North of Baghdad, for instance, a battalion was pulled out of Samarra, always a difficult city.

"Every few months, we pushed a task force down from Tikrit, twenty miles north of Samarra," Lt. Col. Steve Miska, a battalion operations officer, said. "When we advanced down the streets with our Bradleys, the muj [insurgents] would spray and scoot, staying about a block in front of us. Occasionally we'd see one sprinting across the street or aiming in with an RPG, and we'd pop him. We'd clear the city, pull back to the FOB in Tikrit and they'd sneak back in. It made no tactical sense."

To the east, in Diyala Province, the pullback to the FOBs had a similar result. "In December of '05 we swapped out a brigade and built up a FOB outside Baquba," Capt. Phil Carter, an adviser, said. "Immediately Sunni insurgents pressed into the city. The Iraqi forces, mostly Shiites, were driving to the Iranian border, loading up weapons for their militia buddies, driving back through Baquba, and dropping the weapons off in Baghdad. Without American soldiers, security deteriorated."

Casey established a counterinsurgency school in Taji, thirty miles north of Baghdad, and insisted that all incoming battalion comman ders and many staff officers attend a two-week indoctrination course before reporting to their units. He listened when his staff warned him not to be Westmoreland, referring to William C. Westmoreland, the four-star Army general who stubbornly pursued search and destroy operations in Vietnam, leaving the villagers under the control of the Viet Cong guerrillas. Casey gave the same lecture to every incoming battalion commander—Iraq is counterinsurgency. It's all about bringing security to the people. The contradiction between moving onto the FOBs and living among the people was not resolved.

Casey shifted command of the advisers from the training command to the corps commander. Each U.S. division was assigned a counterpart Iraqi unit, and was responsible for assisting in training as well as supporting the advisers, or MiTTs (Military Transition Teams). The intent was to impress upon the divisions—also called MSCs or Major Subordinate Commands—that the main effort was to transition to an Iraqi lead.

There were growing pains. "The MSCs were the warfighters," Col. Bradford Parsons, the senior adviser to the Iraqi 5th Division, said. "They saw it [assisting the Iraqi forces] as a threat drawing down on resources they had. . . . Now they not only had to play the combatant role, but they also had to be the support arm for the adviser teams. . . . I don't think it was well received."

The main tool for the transition mission was joint operations under American supervision. As the Iraqi units improved, the Americans stepped into the background, although the Iraqi battalions continued to require American support for fuel, ammunition, spare parts, and the logistics necessary to fight. Beginning in 2005, the 101st Airborne, operating from FOB Speicher in Tikrit, gradually turned over forty battle sectors to Iraqi battalions.

Instability, however, in cities like Fallujah and Baquba—as well as Baghdad—showed that battalions and insurgents could occupy the same neighborhoods. A well-trained battalion could defend its base, go on patrol, return to base, and not control what happened on the streets when the patrol wasn't there. Col. Dominic Caraccilo believed in the transition mission, but was concerned about confusing proficiency in a few tactics with providing security. The fighting and violence had not diminished. "What was unclear," Caraccilo later wrote, "was how the day-to-day actions would unfold so the [American] soldiers partnering with Iraqi counterparts at the lowest level could recognize progress."

Establishing a training command and ordering American battalions to partner with Iraqi battalions and their adviser teams were the two most significant organizational decisions in the war. It would be years before the results were satisfactory. It takes about three months to instill a habit of, say, exercising or dieting. Most people later put on much of the weight they shed while motivated. In a few short weeks in 2003, the social and military order of Iraq had been overthrown. In a few short months in 2005, the Iraqi battalions supposedly learned how to emulate American soldiers. Whether the habits would persist was an open question. You can't change military culture in a few months, and the Iraqi security forces were a mess.

Partnering assumed an osmotic proficiency in Iraqi battalions due to association for a few hours a day with American battalions. Yet the American officers weren't naive. They knew the security problem was systemic. They deplored the lack of Iraqi military leaders and the Iraqi politicians who were foisting corrosive sectarianism.

The American military ethos, however, emphasized overcoming obstacles to accomplish any mission. When the outcome was most in doubt—the Normandy landing, Iwo Jima, Hue City—resolve emerged as the determining factor. If the mission called for an Iraqi Army emerging quickly, that would happen. The "can do" spirit accepted nothing else.

"In August of '05," Kalev Sepp, the counterinsurgency expert, said, "Colonel Hix and I visited the battalion commanders. Each said his Iraqi battalion would be ready inside twelve months. It was the same with the advisers—things were terrible when they got there, and good when they were leaving. Not a single battalion commander told us the mission could not be accomplished."

At the same time, Casey had set up an evaluation system for measuring the proficiency of the Iraqi battalions. In November, he told the Senate that only one Iraqi battalion was capable of fighting independent of American support.

The result was a Multi-National Force Campaign Plan for 2005 of dizzying optimism. It assumed Iraqi forces could take responsibility for security within a year. The plan concluded with the twin goals of "reducing visibility of Coalition forces to a QRF [Quick Reaction Force] by 1 Dec 05 . . . and being in overwatch outside Iraq by the end of 2006."

WIDESCALE FIGHTING

2005

EVERYONE'S FAVORITE SUCCESS STORY

Colonel H. R. McMaster comes across as an affable commander with a quick sense of humor. He also writes with a razor. His book *Dereliction of Duty* sharply criticized the senior generals during the Vietnam War for not telling their civilian bosses what was militarily possible and what was impossible. In May of 2005, Casey sent McMaster and the 3rd ACR (Armored Cavalry Regiment) to the city of Tal Afar, 200 miles north of Baghdad. The troublesome insurgents in the area were accounting for 10 percent of all attacks countrywide and threatening Mosul, fifty miles to the east. Casey wanted the area cleaned up.

The 200,000 inhabitants of Tal Afar were 75 percent Turkoman Shiite and 25 percent Turkoman Sunni. In the fall of 2004, coalition and Iraqi forces had swept through the city, leaving behind a sectarian Shiite police chief who fired all Sunni policemen and holed up in the Shiite section of the city, from where he launched raids that antagonized the Sunnis. The Sunni terrorists moved in to use Tal Afar as a supply base, pointing to the police chief as an example of why the government in Baghdad was the enemy.

McMaster spent three months closing in on Tal Afar, employing cordon and search operations to squeeze the insurgents out of the surrounding villages and becoming acquainted with the eighty-three tribes that lived in the area. In three villages, 116 insurgents were arrested. Insurgent attacks dropped from six per day in May to three per day in August. Inside Tal Afar, the tactics of the takfiris became more brutal. Schoolteachers were told not to go to work. In their place, men with fifth-grade educations held classes for schoolchildren in how to rig IEDs. As had happened in Fallujah the previous fall, the extremists leaped to the conclusion that they were being betrayed. A city councilman was pulled from his car and shot thirty times in front of his screaming family. A child was killed and a grenade placed under the body. Beheadings became common.

In September, after enclosing Tal Afar inside a thick dirt berm that restricted traffic to a few checkpoints, McMaster rolled into the city with an overwhelming force of 5,000 Iraqi and 3,800 American soldiers. Three hundred insurgents were quickly killed or captured. When the fighting ceased, Lt. Col. Chris Hickey, McMaster's chief operational deputy, set up thirty combat outposts manned by Americans and Iraqis. In a city of fifteen square kilometers, there was an outpost every five or six city blocks.

Captain Niel Smith of the 2nd Battalion, 37th Armored Regiment, was assigned a neighborhood of 5,000 Sunnis called Sa'ad, where 70 percent of the houses were abandoned. His first step was to cordon off the area and, together with Iraqi soldiers, search every house. In eight hours, 500 males were paraded through a schoolroom where several masked informants sat behind a screen. About thirty men—or 5 percent of the military-aged males—were arrested.

Smith then moved a platoon of thirty-six soldiers into a patrol outpost called Dwarf, a house protected by layers of sandbags and coils of barbed wire. Four days later, two of the children who played on the street walked to the gate, looked up at the soldier on guard, pulled back the wire, and turned to run away. A small car screeched out of a side street and headed for the opening, as the guard shouted a warning and opened up with his 240 Golf machine gun. When the bullets shattered the windshield and killed the driver, the car caught in the wire and jerked to a stop.

"Fire in the hole!" the guard instinctively screamed. The warning sent all the soldiers flat on their stomachs before the car blew up, collapsing the courtyard wall and shattering the windows on the surrounding houses.

No American was killed and Smith continued patrolling from Dwarf, four squad-sized foot patrols a day of two hours each, up and down the streets. Over the next thirty days, the platoon spent twenty-two days inside the outpost, four days on guard duty back at the battalion FOB, and four days on the FOB when they could relax.

"On a fifteen-month tour, you have to rotate and give your guys a break," Smith said. "Soldiers don't stress out as much as they dehumanize. They don't look on the Iraqis as human beings, especially when we're not rolling up any bad guys."

The soldiers were hit by five IEDs and two mortar attacks, losing one killed and five wounded in the thirty-six-man platoon.

"I was out there with them. They were asking, Does the boss know what he's doing?" Smith said. "The hardest thing as the leader was persuading my soldiers to keep going out when no one else was taking casualties and we're getting no results."

Patrolling in the same sector were Iraqi soldiers. They weren't arresting anybody, but they had reported no serious casualties.

"The jundis were better at spotting the IEDs," Smith said. "Their advisers had taught them good TTPs [Tactics, Techniques, and Procedures], but not COIN. They were just like us."

After a month of patrolling by themselves, Smith's soldiers were joined by fifty Iraqi police, who moved in next door. Most were Shiites who lived in the southern sector of the city, and many knew the neighborhood, its back alleys and hiding places. Inside a week, they had uncovered three weapons caches, while the Iraqi soldiers looked on resentfully. To break down jealousies, Smith started running patrols with jundis, police, and his own soldiers. The police lectured the jundis and soldiers, explaining that the insurgents putting in the IEDs didn't live in Sa'ad. Showing off their superior knowledge, they brought Smith to a ravine on the north end of the neighborhood. They cross here at night, the police said. Set up a barrier.

Smith strung concertina wire through a kilometer of scraggly bushes, garbage, and human feces, thinking it was a waste of time. Everyone knew that barriers had to be covered by armed sentinels. Over the next two weeks, there were no IED attacks in Sa'ad. Smith wasn't fighting enemy soldiers. The insurgent gangs weren't about to cut through barbed wire, sneak in, set up an IED, ambush a patrol, and try to escape through the same small hole.

Within a month, Sunni families were returning to their homes, which represented 90 percent of their worldly capital. Smith's battalion commander, Lt. Col. Teehan, provided him with "walking-around" money to help with repairs. Smith and a local sheik inspected houses, then handed over between $200 and $500. Other sheiks returned and they held a meeting, electing by a show of hands a Sunni to serve as

Sa'ad's mukhtar, or leader. He was given $60,000 in U.S. military funds for reconstruction projects, solidifying his power. The neighborhood to the north, where the IED gang was holed up, asked the mukhtar for Smith's soldiers, offering any house they wanted.

"I've read all about how we Americans are an antibody," Smith said. "I reject the antibody premise. It was not my experience. When we fell back to the über-FOBs and went to commuter COIN, we ceded the cities to the thugs."

McMaster's real success was not clearing and holding the city by setting up outposts like Smith's; it was overcoming the sectarian feud. By force of will, he dominated the scene. "H. R. [McMaster] is a real hardhead," Casey told me. "Once he gets a concept, he won't be shaken loose." McMaster succeeded in removing the malign Shiite police chief and his 133 handpicked deputies and replacing them with a balanced force of 1,700 policemen. He pried loose U.S. funds to be doled out by a joint Shiite-Sunni city council. Both the city leaders, who gained power through control of the purse, and the population, who gained security and services, had an incentive to oppose those who supported a return of the takfiris.

It wasn't, though, what McMaster had done. He was just one leader. Smith didn't even work for McMaster. It was what the American Army as a system had done. In the months and years after McMaster left, security in Tal Afar remained precarious as a succession of American units struggled to prevent the Ministry of Interior from appointing officials selected for their sectarian and militia ties. Therein lay the irony. In COIN theory, the government knows it must win the support of the people. In Tal Afar, the U.S. military was forcing the government in Baghdad to support the people.

President Bush, Secretary Rumsfeld, and General Casey lauded Tal Afar. No analysis was done, however, to determine how many troops were needed to apply the Tal Afar model on a countrywide basis, or whether the gains would continue without persistent American presence. Tal Afar was the star that shone bright, alone and alien.

M&I PREVAILS

While in Tal Afar the goal was to restore civility between the majority Shiites and minority Sunnis, in Anbar there was no civility and no Shiites. Seen on a map, the Sunni Triangle was delineated by the Tigris and Euphrates Rivers, forming a V that almost touched at Baghdad. The Tigris wended straight south from Mosul, while the Euphrates meandered in from western Anbar along a string of isolated cities that increased in size near Baghdad.

These two river valleys provided a haven for terrorists and foreign fighters coming from Syria. By mid-2005, the takfiris were seizing the leadership of the insurgency. Although few in numbers, their ferocity and ruthlessness were unmatched. The far larger tribal resistance groups that were resisting the Americans fell into line.

On the other side, the American military was wooing the resistance groups. Casey had persuaded Khalilzad to overrule his diplomats and allow the military to negotiate with insurgent groups. Casey then called the leader of a Sunni political party, using a cell phone number traced back to Zarqawi. Through an interpreter, Casey told the frightened politician, who knew he was facing a long prison sentence, that the link to Zarqawi would not be revealed and he would remain free. In return, he would set up meetings in Jordan with resistance groups. The politician happily agreed.

"We started a dance with the insurgents," Casey told me. "They were willing to talk. After all, we were the guys killing them."

Casey anticipated no formal breakthrough. Only the Iraqi government could do that and Jaafari opposed the contacts, although he couldn't prove they were ongoing. Casey was convinced that Army and Marine generals would gradually convince the insurgents that aligning with the American military was a better deal than sticking with the takfiris who were killing the sheiks.

In the meantime, the extremists were extending their control, even infiltrating back into Fallujah, where they had been soundly defeated in 2004. Residents returning to the shattered city found that a berm had been thrown up around the city, limiting traffic to a few entry points. All weapons were banned. Each male resident was required to carry a biometric identification card showing his picture, fingerprints, and iris scan. The intent was to seal out the insurgents.

In December, I had accompanied Lt. Col. Pat Malay through the bulrushes and muck along the Euphrates on the outskirts of shattered Fallujah. "Those fuckers are coming back," Malay said as he whacked aside the reeds. "They have a ratline somewhere, and I'm going to find it."

He didn't find it that day, and eventually Malay and I both returned to the States. In September of 2005, I went back to see how things were going in Fallujah. I caught a helo ride with Casey, who was flying out to order the Marine generals to stop the flow of foreign fighters from Syria down the Euphrates.

"It's slow going," Casey said. "Changing governments three times

[Bremer-Allawi-Jaafari] in fourteen months was ridiculous. At least Allawi was secular. Jaafari was both sectarian and weak. The Iraqi human infrastructure was poor. No matter what happens, there's a huge role ahead for the U.S. as the guiding hand."

Inside Fallujah, Lt. Col. Joe L'Etoile, commanding Battalion 2-7, met me at the landing pad. It was my sixth visit to the city. This was L'Etoile's second "pump," or deployment, to Iraq. On his prior tour, he had worked as Mattis's chief operations officer, a post usually held by a more senior officer. L'Etoile knew how to lead and how to frame the larger picture. Half of his 1,000-man battalion had at least one prior pump. Marine units served for seven months, went home for seven, and then came back again. Army units served for twelve to fifteen months, then usually had a year off before returning. Soldiers disliked their tour length, while the marines liked theirs.

From the landing pad, L'Etoile drove west out of the city on Route Boston and into the lush farmlands along the Euphrates. A narrow two-lane strip of blacktop, Boston had been hit by IEDs so often that it was closed to military traffic. L'Etoile drove slowly, explaining that several days ago a roadside bomb had killed Pfc. Romano Romero, nineteen, of Long Beach, California. He was the 160th American to die in Fallujah.

In response, L'Etoile had considered cutting down all the trees along the road, so the insurgents couldn't creep up. But clearing acres of trees would deprive thousands of farmers of shaded pastureland for their livestock. Instead, he sent four squads into the farmlands on ninety-six-hour patrols. They scoured the palm groves and checked farms and back roads for hide sites. At night, they moved into the bush; they got up in the morning and moved out, startling farmers accustomed to seeing Americans only on the roads.

L'Etoile had just gotten a call from a patrol leader. SSgt. Gordon Van Schoik had been searching a farm near where Romero had been killed when he noticed that the cars on Route Boston were slowing down and then driving away at high speed. The marines sneaked up through a palm grove and surprised two insurgents digging a hole under the hardtop. They shot both of them and, in the mud of a nearby culvert, found a cache of a dozen artillery shells.

"They don't expect us to come in at them from the farms," Van Schoik said.

It was a cat-and-mouse game. Firefights had become rare in the Fallujah area. IEDs had become the main challenge, accounting for 65 percent of the American casualties in Fallujah and across Iraq. Nothing was more frustrating to a combat unit than being hit with IEDs without being able to strike back. Eliminating the IED team that had probably killed Private First Class Romero provided motivation for more patrolling. Each day, the battalion averaged seventeen foot patrols inside and outside the city, plus twelve mounted patrols and random "cordon and knocks" at farms and city residences. In Malaya, there were twenty soldiers and policemen per 1,000 civilians. In Fallujah, portions of two American and three Iraqi battalions occupied the city, providing a similar ratio. But to extend that ratio throughout Anbar would require twice as many American and three times as many Iraqi battalions as were assigned to the province.

Next to the checkpoint was a registration center with several hundred males lined up to be issued the ID cards. An interpreter complained to L'Etoile that he simply couldn't process a line that seemed to grow every day.

"Biometric cards are a good idea with no follow-through," L'Etoile said. "Most Iraqis have fake IDs and marines have no way of knowing when they stop a guy. We have to hold the guy four days while Baghdad runs a check. So if we find a guy with no biometric ID, we drive him out of town and make him walk home."

A few blocks to the south along the river, L'Etoile stopped to chat with Lieutenant Colonel Karousal, who commanded the Iraqi battalion L'Etoile was responsible for mentoring as a "partner." Karousal's small bedroom, with a cot, table, refrigerator, DVD player, twelve-inch color TV, wall maps, and an air-conditioning unit in the one window, doubled as his office. It was too cramped for a table. L'Etoile sat on the cot while Karousal went over the day's events.

Two Iraqi contractors who had agreed to fix up the police station had been shot and killed, he said. He had lost two jundis to an IED and one informer had been assassinated. He knew who did it, but he found nothing in his home to show he was an irahibeen (terrorist). Karousal went on to rant about Americans and "human rights," complaining that L'Etoile wouldn't let him take care of the matter.

"Karousal's squared away," L'Etoile said later. "I take care of his logistics. No need to cut our patrolling in half to have my marines patrol with his jundis. This is a Shiite battalion. They haven't broken through to these people."

———

After spending several days with L'Etoile in southern Fallujah, I switched over to an advisory team in northern Fallujah to observe how the Iraqi soldiers were operating. The thirteen-man MiTT—Military Transition Team—occupied a three-story villa a block away from where I had stayed with Capt. Doug Zembiec during the April 2004 battle. Zembiec was a wild man, terrific in a firefight and brimming with enthusiasm. Lt. Col. Jim MacVarish, the forty-two-year-old MiTT commander, radiated the same enthusiasm. A reservist who taught physics at a boarding school in Massachusetts, he wanted to hear about the prior fights. We walked over to the house where Zembiec had fought and had scarcely returned inside the wire when we heard a dull *crump!*

"What'cha got?" MacVarish barked over his handheld radio.

"RPG," Gunnery Sgt. Nathaniel Hill, thirty-seven, of Chicago replied over the radio. "The shooter's between your post and mine."

MacVarish and his team rushed south a few hundred meters and linked up with Hill, who was accompanied by Iraqi soldiers. The neighborhood was a tangle of trails and dirt roads meandering among palm groves and dozens of shoddy, one-story houses, each surrounded by sturdy square cement walls.

"The back blast was right outside our wire," Hill said, pointing at a house a stone's throw away.

A jundi held down the outer coil of barbed wire, and a dozen Iraqis and their advisers crossed a grassy field littered with the trunks of trees felled during the November battle. As they closed on the suspect house, Hill glanced at the sole palm tree left standing, then laughed. Embedded ten feet up was an unexploded rocket-propelled grenade, the aluminum tail fins glistening.

"The muj hit the only protection we had," Hill said.

The company commander, Capt. Khodar Juwad, banged on a rusty door and a skinny middle-aged man peeked out. Juwad asked a few questions, and then moved on.

"He saw nothing," Juwad said. "He is very frightened."

"I'd be frightened too," Hill said. "Muj comes into my backyard and takes a shot at the jundis. If the old man squeals, he's dead. If he doesn't, the jundis give him a rough time."

The jundis walked warily down the dusty trails, talking briefly to residents anxious to be elsewhere. A man in a yellow shirt vaguely described a black-clad figure running down the street. Maybe he got on a bicycle. Juwad thanked him and told him to move on.

Juwad's battalion covered the Jolan, in northwest Fallujah, a twisting labyrinth of alleys and cluttered shops. The Jolan had been the headquarters for Zarqawi. The jundis—almost all Shiite—were under no illusions about the attitudes of the Sunni residents of the Jolan.

After a fruitless search, MacVarish returned to his villa. A Kurdish family lived in the two-story house next door. Usually the children were playing in the driveway. Tonight there were none.

"Where're the kids?" MacVarish asked the sergeant major of the Iraqi battalion.

"The irahibeen just killed the father at his work downtown," the sergeant major said. "The family is packing to leave."

The irahibeen had broken the legs of the dead man's brother five days earlier, warning them to get out of Fallujah. They hadn't left fast enough.

"We'll get the family out of this shit hole and send the widow some rent money," an angry MacVarish said. "We'll tell our comptroller we need the house for security."

The next morning, MacVarish decided to go into the Jolan to show he was not intimidated. Juwad agreed. Their target was an old torture house terrorists were suspected of revisiting. When the Marines had seized the city, they found cell blocks, chains screwed into ceilings, blood-splattered walls, al Qaeda flags and pamphlets, and mutilated corpses inside seventeen houses.

In four vehicles, the Iraqi platoon raced down the back streets and screeched to a stop in front of a house with a distinct balustrade. A frightened man opened the iron door, while passersby disappeared into their houses. No, the man said, he did not own the house. It was empty, so he had moved in.

The jundis moved on to the next house. A large man in a white dish-dasha opened the door and the interpreter for the adviser team, Ahmed Brahim, twenty, questioned him. Brahim, a Shiite, had joined the Iraqi Army when he was thirteen. Somehow, in April of 2003, he had latched on to a U.S. battalion. A born linguist, he had remained with the Americans for the next thirty months. Brahim considered himself an American. He lived with the advisers, shared the danger and the laughter, and believed MacVarish could do no wrong. Brahim peppered the man in the dishdasha with a barrage of fast questions.

Across the street, workmen were placing scaffolding on a new brick house that would not look out of place in a middle-class neighborhood in Palm Springs. Brahim pointed at it.

"This guy's giving me the usual Fallujah jive," Brahim said. "Says the Marines destroyed that house. It wasn't used for torture. This is a fine neighborhood. The Marines are the problem."

Shown a computer picture of the house standing after the battle, the man shrugged. Shown next a picture of a dead man in the cell with his legs cut off, the man shrugged.

"Time to move," Brahim said. "This guy's lied to us long enough. Anyone tells us anything, he'll die."

Brahim walked down the street.

"They're all the same," he said. "They know who controls the Jolan. They hate Iraqi soldiers as much as marines. We're Shiites, outsiders. I feel it every day in their eyes."

As the patrol hopped back into their Humvees, three young schoolgirls were walking up the street. When they drew near the torture house, they clung to one another and hastened by.

———

In two weeks in September of 2005, nine men had been killed in Fallujah: one American, two insurgents, three jundis, two Iraqi contractors, and one civilian. Five IEDs had been found and another three had exploded.

By the standards of prior wars, the number was modest. By peacetime standards, the toll was stunning. The insurgency had not been broken. Fallujah wasn't just abnormal; in the fall of 2005, Fallujah remained the signature success of the irahibeen Murder and Intimidation campaign.

ARMING A SUNNI TRIBE

Cracks were beginning to show, though. A few evenings later, L'Etoile swung by the advisers' outpost to pick me up. "I think I've got a deal," he said, "to get some Sunni tribes into the fight. Some sheiks want a private meeting. Let's go."

Here we went again. The old rope-a-dope. The tribes wanted to protect themselves. No deal. Either they agreed to Baghdad's terms or nothing. The governments of both Allawi and Jaafari agreed they would not arm a tribal militia that was Sunni.

L'Etoile knew that. He also knew the coalition was less rigid. To the consternation of the Shiite political parties, the CIA was developing an Iraqi intelligence service under former general Shawani, a crafty old Baathist. Shawani had recommended the two former generals who tried to pacify Fallujah in May of 2004. When that failed, as recompense he sent a rump Sunni force of former soldiers to patrol with the hard-pressed Marines. They performed well until the family of their commander was kidnapped and mysteriously returned. Thereafter, the commander issued confusing orders and performance deteriorated along with morale. Although he lived on an American base, the commander and his intelligence officer were assassinated en route to some shadowy meeting. No one knew which side killed them. After that, his force was gradually dismantled.

The CIA believed Shawani was the genuine article—a skilled intelligence operator. His contacts among insurgent and tribal leaders were extensive. He kept feeding tantalizing tidbits to Casey about insurgent chiefs in Jordan who didn't trust the Iraqi government and viewed American diplomats as bringing little to the table. They wanted to talk to American military officers. They had power and the insurgents knew who they were. By mid-2005, Ambassador Khalilzad was persuaded and signaled the go-ahead to Casey. Soon staff officers were shuttling back and forth to Jordan. Having served on senior staffs, L'Etoile knew the game being played and the high command was tolerant of his extracurricular initiatives.

We drove west on Route Michigan, passing the mural of Suleiman al-Fitikian, the proud commander of a local battalion who told the Marines he would clean up Fallujah without their help. Zarqawi and the city's leading imam, Abdullah Janabi, had poured boiling water over Suleiman before beating him to death. The Marines painted his portrait superimposed on the Iraqi flag on a large concrete block and warned that snipers would kill anyone who defaced it.

Once across the Euphrates, the drivers turned off the Humvee lights and zigzagged through dirt paths along the riverbank. Thick courtyard walls lined every street and the Humvees had to twist through bushes and around palm trees. Through their night vision goggles, the drivers saw armed Iraqis on rooftops and in doorways.

They drove inside the gates of a large compound. Leaving a few marines standing guard, L'Etoile walked across a well-lit expanse of close-cropped lawn that separated twin villas. Colorful rugs were spread about. On the porch of one villa sat a small BMW roadster wrapped in a dust cover. Two sheiks greeted L'Etoile.

Sheik Ibrahim was reed-thin, a constant smoker in his late sixties who said little. Sheik Talib, fiftyish and of ample girth, engaged in pleasantries for several minutes before getting down to business.

"One of the Farhan brothers is out of jail," Talib said. "I saw him in the market last week."

L'Etoile was not happy with the news. It had taken months to arrest several Iraqis implicated in the murder of Suleiman. Now one of them had been released.

"Last Tuesday, a suicide bomber tried to kill my older brother,

Sheik Khamis," Talib continued. "My son died in the attack. Why? Because our tribe is against the takfiris. They are crazy."

After being quoted in *The New York Times* and *The Washington Post* earlier in the war, Sheik Khamis Hasnawi, a candid and respected elder in the Abu Eisa tribe, had dropped from sight. L'Etoile waited. The sheiks wanted revenge and they would finger someone.

"Two insurgents are feuding," Talib said. "Omar Hamady of the Albugutna tribe placed a bomb on the road at the farm of Khasem Muhna of the Ju Ara tribe. He wanted you to arrest Muhna."

L'Etoile's translator, Darawan Faris, pulled out a photomap for the sheiks to study. Faris, a native of Baghdad and a fan of the Tampa Bay Buccaneers, had applied for American citizenship after serving for two years with the Americans. After palavering for several minutes, the sheiks pointed to a house on the map and drew a sketch of the farm.

"They will try to kill us again," Ibrahim said. "A bomber will blow us up at night."

L'Etoile looked around. A car bomb would smash the compound to bits. "We have patrols," he said.

"No, we want you to stay away," Ibrahim said. "Our sons and nephews live here. Give us a piece of paper for weapons."

When L'Etoile asked how many gun permits were needed, the sheiks said 100, maybe 200. Too many, L'Etoile said. Eventually they settled on fifty. The sheiks asked for one more thing—a special pass for Sheik Khamis. It was dangerous to wait in the long lines entering the city.

"He will have a purple card like mine," L'Etoile said. "He will never wait in a line again."

The two sheiks nodded and waited. Faris whispered to L'Etoile.

"We thank you for Omar Hamady," L'Etoile said. "It must be difficult bringing food to your tribe out here. We captured a bongo truck last week. We could drive it out here and leave it."

The sheiks nodded and invited L'Etoile to stay for a meal of chicken and saffron-flavored rice. After eating, L'Etoile thanked his hosts and drove back to base.

"They agreed to fifty weapons permits," he said. "That means the enemy isn't numerous—and the sheiks know who they are."

I asked if the tribes were turning against al Qaeda in Iraq.

"I'm no expert on tribal politics," L'Etoile said. "This Abu Eisa group has a reputation of being reasonable. I look at it tactically. They have a strong defensive position on the river. I'm allowing weapons. After the suicide bombing, no stranger will get in there again."

"That bit about not wanting the sheik to wait in line," Sgt. Maj. Michael Barrett said, "reminded me of Sonny in *The Godfather* waiting at the toll booth and getting shot."

Later, Faris, the translator, picked up on the analogy to the Mafia. Like many of the translators with American battalions, Faris was cynical about grand concepts for dealing with the insurgency.

"Here in Fallujah we're up against hard guys," he said. "Those guys aren't going to change because of elections. They're feared. They like power. Even if we [Americans] offered construction jobs, paying better money, they'd never take it. Never. They're killers, gunmen. That's what they are, and that's how they see themselves."

Since Suleiman had been tortured to death in August of 2004, several Sunni leaders had stepped forward to say: This is my city; it does not belong to the takfiris. Each was gunned down. Two Marine and three Iraqi battalions kept plugging away with the military tactics they knew—patrols, cordons, electronic intercepts, knock and search. These techniques were the same as McMaster's, except in Tal Afar there were twenty-nine outposts compared to nineteen in Fallujah.

The basic difference was not technique; instead, it was the attitude of the population whose city had been destroyed and whose Taliban-like rulers had vowed to return. Unlike Tal Afar, there were no Shiite neighbors proposing compromises. The Abu Eisa tribe had cut a quiet deal with the Americans to bear arms. But that was for self-defense, not to hunt down the takfiris.

"L'Etoile wasn't unique," Colonel Dunford said. "In the spring of 2005, I met with dozens of sheiks. They were shaken up by what we had done in Fallujah. They said they'd fight on our side, but refused to go through the government in Baghdad. In 2005, we weren't willing to accept that deal."

American officers were continuously hopping across the Jordanian border to meet with self-styled insurgent leaders like Sheik Majid al-Gaoud, a cousin of the governor of Anbar. Contacts sputtered on, but no American general had the authority or backing to propose radical changes to the status quo. Either the tribes joined with the Baghdad government on its terms, or the tribes stayed out in the cold.

DOLLARS REJECTED

The heart of the insurgency was the Ramadi–Habbaniyah–Fallujah corridor, a thirty-mile swath of villages anchored by Ramadi to the north and Fallujah to the south, with the farmlands of Habbaniyah between the two cities offering ideal concealment. Two main highways and a maze of dirt roads provided safe movement for the takfiris, who played off twenty-eight tribes against each other while murdering those sheiks who spoke out.

In April of 2004, Fallujah had gained worldwide attention, while in the provincial capital of Ramadi an equally fierce fight raged. For four days, the battle swirled up and down the main streets and alleyways, inside a cemetery, outside the soccer stadium, in the marketplaces and along the riverbanks. Marine Battalion 2-4 took 16 killed and over 100 wounded. Dead insurgents were loaded in trucks and taken to the hospital to be claimed by relatives. Others were left in piles by the side of the road.

When Fallujah was seized in November of 2004, one group of insurgents fled to Mosul, while another group, led by Abdullah Janabi, drove up the road to Ramadi. Colonel Dunford met with the local sheiks, who assured him they would drive out the takfiris. Instead, attacks upon coalition convoys increased, closing the highway between Habbaniyah and Ramadi.

"It's hard to get an informer to accuse anyone in open court. And you can forget hard evidence. Only the idiots keep incriminating stuff in their homes. A guy shoots, drops his AK, and walks away," Maj. Benjamin Busch, a civil affairs officer, said. "When we do send them away, they come back. It's a revolving door."

The sheiks insisted unemployment caused the disaffection of their young men. When I visited Ramadi for the fourth time in mid-September of 2005, development was at a standstill. Since the beginning of the year, forty-seven contractors had begun projects. By August, five had been killed and thirty others had fled the city. Six projects had been completed, and four contractors—all suspected as fronting for insurgent groups—were still working.

One contractor had bid $70,000 to fill a dozen potholes. Busch estimated that the work should cost $5,000. The contractor protested that he had to buy his own cement trucks. No one would rent a truck to go to Ramadi. He had to hire guards who insisted on driving their own vehicles. He paid local officials for "licenses" and paid the sheik who said he owned the street. The insurgents demanded their cut. His work crew refused to stay overnight in the city, choosing a four-hour round-trip from Baghdad that cut the actual workday to three hours. Hence, $70,000 for a $5,000 job.

Determined to complete at least one job, Busch agreed, stationing a tank at each end of the street to guard the work detail. On the second day, three men walked under the barrel of a tank gun, spoke to the workers filling in a hole, and left. Minutes later, the workers packed up their shovels and drove out of town.

"Insurgents, terrorists, tribal leaders, officials, and the vast criminal element key on to any contract work as deserving to be fleeced," Busch said. "The contractors have to manipulate the local politicians, criminals, and insurgents. Make a wrong step and you're dead. I pay middlemen so the contractors can say they're not taking American money."

In 1965, President Lyndon Johnson believed he could win over the Viet Cong guerrillas by offering construction projects of a vast scale. The Viet Cong, like al Qaeda in Iraq, had responded by killing anyone who accepted a job.

WHACK-A-MOLE

The situation was worse in the Upper Euphrates valley. North of Ramadi, there were no Iraqi forces at all. In cities like Haditha, Hit, and Husaybah, the insurgents ruled, plain and simple. Having decided the 12,000 Sunnis in the National Guard battalions in Anbar were untrustworthy, by the spring of 2005 Baghdad had stopped paying their salaries. The 60th Iraqi Brigade and the 500th and 501st Battalions ceased to exist. That left 3,200 marines and soldiers to patrol thousands of square miles.

Western Anbar, or AO (Area of Operations) Denver, encompassed 7,000 square miles of riverbeds and farmlands and 23,000 square miles of scrub desert. The population of 400,000 was scattered in a half dozen midsized towns and across thousands of farms and villages. An estimated 60 to 100 foreign fighters crossed the 120-mile border with Syria each month and made their way down the Upper Euphrates. U.S. commanders believed these foreign fighters were the catalysts causing the M&I campaigns and suicide bombings from Ramadi to Baghdad. Casey wanted that ratline cut.

Col. Stephen Davis commanded the 2nd Marine Regiment, comprised of four 800-man battalions spread over 30,000 square miles in western Anbar. He embarked on a series of operations called the Upper Euphrates Campaign.

"The goal is not to seize territory," he told the Associated Press. "This is about going in and finding the insurgents."

Iraqi civilians told the marines that they should either come and stay, or don't come at all, because reprisals began once the Americans left. Week after week, month after month, a battalion or more of troops gathered and struck at a city or farm complex along the 200-mile, serpentine Euphrates valley. Their eponymous names described their purpose: Dagger, Sword, Spear, Quick Strike, Iron Fist, Steel Curtain, Iron Hammer. In Vietnam, such operations were called search and destroy. The Euphrates operations were hit and leave, hard combat with no smiles for the people.

Fifteen of eighteen marines interviewed in 1st Platoon, Kilo Company, though, told me they preferred the offensive operations to counterinsurgency. "We'd get on line during the Euphrates ops and go at it," Cpl. Robert Montgomery said. "There was us versus them on the other side of the FLOT [Forward Line of Troops]. It was cleaner than this counterinsurgency shit."

In mid-June, 1st Platoon was searching a section of houses when a bearded man in a white dishdasha walked out into the street. "No ali baba," he said, pointing to his house. "No ali baba."

"We thought he was ballsy," Cpl. Michael Nemis said. "He didn't want us breaking up his house, so he tells us there are no muj there. We decided to take a look anyways."

The marines lined up in their normal stack, pitched in a flash-bang grenade to shock anyone in hiding behind the door, and rushed into the vestibule. All clear. The bearded man followed the marines into his house. As LCpl. Adam Crumpler, carrying the Squad Automatic Weapon, or SAW, turned toward the stairway, the man shouted in Arabic and ran out the back door. Crumpler started after him, only to be grabbed by LCpl. Patrick Mitchum. "Not your role!" Mitchum yelled. A fusillade of tracer rounds lashed them from the stairway. Crumpler fell, mortally wounded. Bullets struck the back of Mitchum's armored vest, failing to penetrate.

As the other two marines in the hallway dove for cover, two insurgents rushed down the stairs, firing wildly. Both were clean-shaven, wearing brown shirts, armored vests, and camouflage trousers. They grabbed the SAW and ran out the back door.

From the roof next door, Cpl. Michael Nemis looked down and saw an Iraqi soldier in a brown shirt crouched against a wall, looking toward a thicket of reeds where the man in the dishdasha had fled. Nemis was confused. There were a few Iraqi soldiers with the platoon as semi-translators, but they had stayed back in the street. This man was a stranger.

The man moved cautiously along the wall, carrying the SAW by its strap. That was all Nemis needed to see. He put a burst into the man's legs. As he fell, Cpl. Paul Torocco ran out of the house and pumped four rounds into his head. The other insurgent tried to run across the street and was hit numerous times. The man in the dishdasha escaped. Crumpler's body was respectfully placed in a Humvee for transportation to a helipad and the platoon continued down the street.

With 17 percent of the U.S. forces, the Marines were accounting for 29 percent of the fatalities in Iraq. The Marines were shock troops, and the Upper Euphrates was head-on combat. As the sweeps continued, thirteen of the eighteen marines in 1st Platoon shot one or more insurgents. Attitudes hardened. In August, fourteen marines were killed near Haditha when their amtrac hit a gigantic buried mine. Also near Haditha, six marines in a sniper team were wiped out and the insurgents circulated a grisly video of the bodies. The Marines responded by launching Operation Quick Strike.

So it went, back and forth. The Marines swept into Haditha three times. "You're going to have this constant need to go back and clean it up again," Lt. Col. Lionel Urquhart, a battalion commander in the Haditha area, said. "Is that a good way of doing business? I'm not going to say that." The Marines moved through the city of Hit, thirty miles north of Ramadi. When they left, the police chief was assassinated. In Baghdad, an Iraqi spokesman told the Los Angeles Times, "We don't have any security presence anywhere past Hit."

Offensive sallies followed by a rest period on a FOB contradicted the basic counterinsurgency precept of holding the populated areas. American forces were supposed to set the conditions for transitioning security to Iraqi forces. Only there weren't any Iraqi forces.

Senator Joseph Biden went on television and protested the strategy. "We leave these marines in a very, very tight spot," he said on CBS. "There are too few troops in a place that needs a heck of a lot more security." The marines on the ground agreed. "It's the truth," Maj. Jeff Eichholz, a battalion executive officer, told USA Today. "We don't have the forces here to leave marines back in every city." The troops called it "Whack-a-Mole," a popular carnival game.

It wasn't until late August that there was a logistics base north of Ramadi to supply troops stretched out over 150 miles to the border. Once he had a base, Colonel Davis asked for another 1,000 troops. He was determined to shut down the Syrian border before the end of 2005. Offensive operations continued for the next three months, causing senior officers in Baghdad to wonder if the marines after seizing Fallujah had opted for stand-up fights rather than counterinsurgency.

"This is not a hearts and minds battle," Davis told The New York Times. "This is a fight for survival."

The offensive operations didn't seem to be accomplishing much. The enemy was still slipping through. In October and November, there were as many American fatalities in the Lower Euphrates, including Ramadi and Fallujah, as in the Upper Euphrates campaigns, while the number of bombings causing multiple fatalities—a key indicator of the activity level of foreign fighters—dipped for a few months, and then shot up again.

"We tallied insurgents killed as victory," Lt. Col. Thomas Hobbs, a regimental staff officer, said. "We targeted insurgent cells, versus separating the people from the insurgents."

By December, after an operation called Steel Curtain, Davis had reached the Syrian border 210 miles northwest of Baghdad. Stretching over six months, the Upper Euphrates Campaign had required 121 convoys trekking 41,000 miles to sustain four battalions in a dozen operations. The final battle was fought for control of Husaybah, a city of 100,000 on the Euphrates at the Syrian border in the district of Al Qaim. The desert tribes were surly and uncooperative, angered by the barricades along the border that prevented normal commerce and smuggling. Foreign fighters in civilian cars drove freely along a hundred back roads, indistinguishable to helicopter pilots and sentries in observation posts. Roadside bombs and sniper attacks occurred daily.

In the fall of 2005, Lt. Col. Dale Alford pounced on the city. As in Fallujah in November of 2004, al Qaeda in Iraq knew the attack was coming and had dug trench lines and tank traps, hid ammunition in a series of houses, and practiced how they would fall back, lure the Americans in, and attack their flanks. Alford disrupted that scheme when he feinted an attack from the east, then swung Battalion 3-6 through the desert and swept in from the west. The al Qaeda fighters were caught facing the wrong way. The battalion battled the insurgents block by block and drove most of them from Husaybah.

The stage seemed set for another Fallujah, with the insurgents employing a slow, steady Murder and Intimidation campaign to control the population while the isolated Americans drove up and down the streets. Instead, Alford and his Iraqi counterpart, Colonel Razaq, divided Husaybah and the adjoining farmlands into thirteen sectors and assigned a joint company of about seventy Americans and forty jundis to each sector. They ate MREs, chickens, and sheep. They slept on cots in sandbagged outposts, without showers or toilets. Patrolling was constant, with the jundis constantly questioning the local residents.

Sheik Kurdi, an elder in the Abu Mahal tribe, met with Alford, explaining that the al Qaeda–led extremists had muscled in on the "trading" across the border. If Alford promised to stay and to give some key police posts to his tribe, Kurdi would provide 400 tribesmen for the police force, and hundreds more for the army—if they could stay in the Qaim district. Done, Alford replied.

"Colonel Razaq was a real fighter," Alford said. "Sheik Kurdi brought the tribe. He's an interesting guy. Loves to talk about our Revolutionary War and the Civil War."

When Razaq left, the new Iraqi brigade commander was selected from the Abu Mahal tribe, giving them control of the police, the army, and the city council. Tribesmen without uniforms called the Desert Protectors wandered the streets and farmlands, reporting any groups of strangers. By the winter of 2006, fighting along the Syrian border had petered out.

Casey spent a day walking through Husaybah with Alford, questioning how he had routed al Qaeda and gained the loyalty of a tribe. "Alford was the best battalion commander I had," Casey said.

Casey persuaded Jaafari to fly to Ramadi, where he promised the beleaguered provincial governor that he would send thousands of soldiers, Sunni as well as Shiite. At the end of 2005, there were 16,000 Iraqi soldiers and police officers in Anbar, as compared to 2,500 at the beginning of the year. The number was sufficient to place some American and Iraqi forces in every city, although there were police only inside Fallujah and Qaim, and a handful of government officials only in Ramadi. Qaim was the first breakthrough in Anbar, the first place where an entire tribe turned against al Qaeda.

"Because we were so remote," Alford said, "once we had the backing of the tribe, al Qaeda couldn't blend in. They had to leave or die. The Abu Mahal were pissed, though, that they didn't get any credit or funds from Ramadi."

BAGHDAD—A TALE OF TWO CITIES

Inside Baghdad, the goal of turning control over to the Iraqis proceeded in 2005 according to plan. Six American battalions moved inside two main FOBs in east Baghdad—Rustamyah and Loyalty—while adviser teams lived on four smaller FOBs. In west Baghdad, five battalions operated from the vast headquarters called Victory and from FOB Falcon, a few miles farther south. "Once we moved onto Falcon," Maj. Adam Cobb of the 82nd Airborne said, "there was less patrolling than before."

Almost every American patrol inside the city was mounted. Four

Humvees were the minimum number permitted to leave a FOB. If an IED disabled one Humvee, that left two to set up a defense while the crew of the third attended to the casualties. A battalion might deploy sixty Humvees a day for four to six hours. Altogether, at any given time the eleven American battalions were running about sixty-five mounted patrols on Baghdad's 10,000 streets, a preposterously small number. The U.S. military had, practically speaking, turned over Baghdad to Iraqi control.

Inside Baghdad, there were fourteen Main Supply Routes, or MSRs, half running north–south and half east–west. Most were main highways and only a few were restricted to military-only traffic. Humvees and trucks were constantly shuttling back and forth. A few of the roads, such as Route Irish running from the airport to the west to the Green Zone along the Tigris in the heart of the city, were consistently dangerous.

The incessant procession of inviting targets inside Baghdad drew between thirty and thirty-five attacks a day, mostly a few inaccurate shots. Often, though, an IED would kill or wound some soldiers. Everyone shared the same risk. There were no rear lines on the highways.

To get supplies through, the logisticians planned like the coaching staff of a professional football team, studying the tendencies of the opposition and plotting counters. They tracked the type, day, and time of each attack. After Friday mosque services, many Sunni insurgent and Shiite militia groups met to plan their week's activities. Saturday and Sunday generally saw light attacks because munitions were still being moved into position. Wednesday and Thursdays were the heaviest days. In the cool months, the early afternoon was most dangerous; in the hot months, attacks picked up in the evening.

Maj. Henry Groulx commanded a transportation company in the 101st that logged over 100,000 miles and 1,000 missions from FOBs Falcon and Rustamyah in 2005. Despite many attacks, only six of his drivers were wounded. He compared his operations center to a NASCAR pit stop. His watch section knew how long it took any size convoy to get to a FOB, unload, and get back. They watched the civilian traffic patterns and checked in with choppers overhead for updates. They graphed when the gangs in different sectors liked to operate, and sent out the trucks at odd times.

"Two A.M. or two P.M. makes no difference to our paychecks," Groulx said. "Combat arms soldiers used to say, 'In the rear with the gear.' Not in this war. Any explosion in my sector, it's my company that rolls the QRF [Quick Reaction Force] inside ten minutes. We haul back the damaged trucks and we evacuate the wounded. We're one team out here."

The Iraqis had deployed their own version of one team. In June of 2005, the minister of interior, Bayan Jabar, launched Operation Lightning, which placed his sectarian Public Order Battalions in the same neighborhoods as Iraqi Army battalions. This undercut the Iraqi Army, whose officers knew they were being spied upon.

At the end of August, when twenty-two men were found shot in southeast Baghdad, the minister of defense, Saadoun al-Dulaimi, accused the minister of interior of ineptitude. A few days later, a vast throng of Shiite pilgrims was crossing the Bridge of Imams on the Tigris in north Baghdad when panic set in. In the resulting stampede, over 1,000 worshippers were crushed, asphyxiated, or drowned. The Iraqi Army had failed to enforce basic safety measures. Although he retained his post, Dulaimi lost all influence.

In mid-September, in the Shiite district of Kadhimiyah bordering the Bridge of Imams, an al Qaeda car bomb killed 112 people and injured 160. Later that day, Zarqawi released an audiotape declaring war on all Shiites. After that, no one inside the Iraqi government was going to complain about the Public Order Battalions.

Not until mid-October did Casey finally wrest control over the police advisory effort from State Department bureaucrats. Even then, the MOI threw up bureaucratic roadblocks to prevent American advisers from embedding with police units. The reason became obvious in November when an American company, acting on a tip, broke into an MOI compound and discovered a hidden prison holding 170 malnourished Sunnis, many with bruises and welts from repeated beatings.

The episode ignited a political firestorm, with Sunni politicians appealing to Jordan, Saudi Arabia, and the Arab League for an international investigation. The deputy minister of interior responded by holding a press conference to deny that the prisoners were Sunni. When Casey confronted Jabar and demanded that he fire those responsible, the interior minister shrugged off the matter. "Uh, that's how Iraqis are," he said. Furious, Casey went to Prime Minister Jaafari and told him that Jabar was implicated. Jaafari expressed mild surprise and took no action. Jabar remained the minister of interior.

"We didn't have the MOI penetrated enough," Casey told me, "to know in 2005 the extent of the problem with their toleration or cooperation with the militias."

By year's end, intelligence reports estimated that up to 90 percent of the police in east Baghdad, which included Sadr City, were colluding with the Badr Corps or Mahdi militias.

ELECTORAL STASIS

The autonomic American faith in a written constitution impelled Ambassador Khalilzad to devote enormous energy to pushing through an Iraqi version. The drafting committee was controlled by Shiites who inserted language designed to devolve power, including oil revenues and rights, to regional blocs. This rewarded the Kurds with oil in the north and the Shiites with oil in the south. When the Sunnis balked, Khalilzad brokered a compromise agreement that the constitution could be amended by referendum at a later date. In mid-October of 2005, Iraqis went to the polls and voted predictably along sectarian lines, with 96 percent of the Sunnis who bothered to vote opposed, and the Kurds and Shiites overwhelmingly in favor. The constitution emerged as another impediment to national unity, with the Sunnis determined to amend it and the Kurds claiming it allowed them to sell oil rights to foreign corporations.

In mid-December, Iraqis went to the polls for the third time in twelve months to elect a parliament that would sit for four years. Unlike in the previous January, the Sunnis participated in modest numbers. The Shiite coalition won 50 percent of the seats, the Kurds and Sunnis taking about 20 percent each. The Shiite bloc promptly began maneuvering to prevent any significant Sunni role in the government.

Unfazed, President Bush called 2005 "a year of strong progress . . . three sets of elections in Iraq [is an] amazing moment in the history of liberty." General Abizaid joined in cheering the flawed process, drawing on his favorite malapropos comparison to America's founding years. "When compared to our own political experience in forming a new republic," Abizaid said, "Iraq's political progress in 2005 is impressive."

SEVEN

CONTRADICTORY GOALS

2005

NO MILITARY TIPPING POINTS

In March, Marine Lt. Gen. John Sattler had said, "I think in the west [Anbar], we have broken the back of the insurgency." Only the Qaim district along the Syrian border was under control. The Upper Euphrates Campaign had come and gone without any Iraqi forces to leave behind. In hard areas like Fallujah, when the Americans did stay, the takfiris lived down the street and assassinations continued. The police didn't arrest local insurgents. Ramadi was under siege. Overall, Anbar continued at year's end to account for 20 percent of the coalition's forces level and 40 percent of its fatalities.

While Baghdad remained the central focus, U.S. forces had moved to the periphery in the city. Suicide murderers continued to exact a gruesome toll. Protecting neighborhoods was left to incompetent police, with Jaafari and the minister of interior resisting Casey's proposal to put American advisers in the precinct houses.

In Casey's concept, Iraqis, not Americans, would hold the populated areas. This put a premium on advisers. Yet the advisory effort received only 10 percent of the coalition manpower and resources. Petraeus had gone home, replaced by Maj. Gen. Marty Dempsey, in charge of Iraqi training. He set out to force the ministries to support the Iraqis in the field.

Counterinsurgency existed as a slogan, but without changing the operational style of American battalions. In 2005, the battalions continued to do what they knew best: sweeps, mounted patrols, and targeted raids at night.

These offensive operations put a lid on the growth of the insurgency. The military analyst Anthony Cordesman concluded that "there were not signs that the struggle is being won or lost. . . . There have, as yet, been no decisive trends and no tipping points."

Casey's staff, on the other hand, detected encouraging trends. Spinning the focal lens on a kaleidoscope of turbulent conditions, the staff wrote an assessment concluding that 2005 provided "clear grounds for optimism." By year's end, Casey had reduced U.S. forces from 155,000 to 133,000, while other coalition forces dropped from 25,000 to 20,000. Over the next year, the corps staff projected that the number of coalition bases countrywide would decrease from eighty-one to forty-six, with "no plans for enduring bases."

Most important, Casey's staff predicted that "87 Iraqi battalions will own their own battle space as of July 2006," with Iraqi security forces having expanded from 142,000 to 232,000. Rumsfeld's favorite rubric was the ever-increasing number of Iraqi forces. This concealed two underlying weaknesses. First, most Iraqi forces were deployed in the Shiite south, where the insurgency was nonexistent. The Iraqi command was too weak politically to shift forces north to meet the threat. Second, Iraqi units were trained in the American image. The pace of the Iraqi gains in counterinsurgency achieved by "partnering" with American units was exaggerated. In Sunni areas, Iraqi and American soldiers alike were an occupying force, too strong for the insurgents to attack directly but too blunt an instrument to dismantle the insurgency.

The assessment warned that the steady loss of support in the States—the approval of the president's handling of Iraq dropped to 35 percent in November—jeopardized the mission. A Democratic congressman, John P. Murtha of Pennsylvania, had stood on the House floor and tearfully shouted, "Our military has done everything that has been asked of them. It is time to bring them home." The press lionized him.

In Baghdad, Casey's staff acknowledged the downward spiral of support back home. But the staff chose to emphasize the elections in Iraq, citing a quote from *The Washington Post* about "the most democratic poll in the history of the Arab Middle East." The elections, in the judgment of Casey's staff, cast a salubrious glow over Iraq's discord, offering "the opportunity to separate the terrorists from the population."

In other words, the 2005 campaign plan declared success based upon what was assumed to happen in 2006, when an Iraqi Army would stand on its own feet and an Iraqi government (the third in eighteen months) would reconcile with the Sunni population.

POLITICAL DETERIORATION

Since taking command, Casey had moved decisively to deploy a new Iraqi army. When American generals strode into a room in their scutate armor, looking like knights from the fifteenth century, they exuded command authority. They weren't trained diplomats; they didn't hide their dislike for the corrupt and the cowardly and they could not abide the venal and the dodgy. Sooner or later, their judgments had an effect because they backed it up by their own conduct. Iraqi military leaders of all ranks were fired or shifted due to moral pressure by American officers. The process wasn't rapid, and it lacked a legal authority that should have been insisted upon when sovereignty was handed back in 2004. Nevertheless, the American military was prodding and shaping the Iraqi military.

"We got Iraqi officers fired," Casey said. "Happened all the time. Why should we tolerate bad military leaders?"

This attitude was not true of our diplomats, whose main business was maintaining stable relations with cantankerous countries. The diplomatic culture emphasized negotiations and compromise based on mutual interests, not moral suasion and judgments about leadership qualifications. The diplomats didn't approach the dystrophic Iraqi ministries with the moral authority or outrage necessary to demand the removal of harmful officials.

At the same time, the Iraqi government went its own mischievous and disruptive way, packing the police with Shiite militia. Iraqi ministries routinely spent only a fraction of their authorized budgets. Twenty-three percent of Iraqis lived on less than one dollar a day, and 27 percent of the children were undernourished. Most of the $21 billion in reconstruction projects funded by the U.S. Congress had gone to international corporations, providing jobs to only 2 percent of the Iraqi labor market and leaving 40 percent of the workforce underemployed or unemployed.

TWO STRATEGIES, ONE PRESIDENT

In December of 2005, Casey's staff conducted an end-of-year assessment. A recent poll had indicated that 82 percent of Iraqis opposed the long-term presence of coalition forces. Casey met with his division commanders.

"All the commanders agreed with an assessment by Maj. Gen. Rusty Finley," Maj. Gen. Timothy Donovan, Casey's chief of staff, said, "that the presence of American soldiers out on the streets was a large part of the problem."

This cultural judgment about American unacceptability in an Islamic country was debatable. More than 40,000 American and European soldiers had been occupying Afghanistan for five years, despite dire warnings that Afghanis drove out all foreigners. In Iraq, in Karbala in 2003, the city council had tried to elect an American battalion commander as mayor. More recently, the mayor of Tal Afar had written a letter requesting that American soldiers remain in his city. Even in Fallujah, the powerful Abu Eisa tribe wanted Lieutenant Colonel L'Etoile to stay with them.

The point in 2005, though, wasn't just the accuracy of the judgment about Iraqi intolerance to American soldiers. Rather, it was the agreement among the top generals. General Myers, the chairman of the Joint Chiefs, retired in September, having for two years consistently supported Abizaid's view that American soldiers were an antibody in an Arab culture. Rumsfeld was in agreement, announcing a drawdown of U.S. forces, with "a smaller footprint to avoid antagonism and dependence." The secretary of defense, the chairman of the Joint Chiefs, the head of Central Command, and the top generals in Iraq were all telling President Bush the same thing.

Both Abizaid and Rumsfeld used the analogy of riding a bicycle. Sooner or later, you had to take off the training wheels, remove the hand from the seat, and let the new rider fall a few times. In other words, as American forces pulled out, the Iraqis would fall on their face a few times, or never learn how to ride the bike. Risk happens.

The opposing strategy, advocated by Kissinger and Rice, was to achieve victory before withdrawal. Kissinger, a close adviser to Bush, opposed Casey's plan to withdraw 30,000 troops after the December elections, arguing that this would whet the insatiable congressional appetite for more withdrawals. "Victory over the insurgency," Kissinger wrote in an influential op-ed in *The Washington Post,* "is the only meaningful exit strategy."

Like the generals, the White House knew that the Iraqis, if forced to do more, ran the risk of falling apart. Jaafari had failed, condoning an increase in sectarianism and alienating the Sunnis. The Ministry of Interior was a snake pit, the local police in Baghdad were feckless, and the Public Order Battalions were sponsoring anti-Sunni death squads. The only bright spots were the Iraqi battalions that performed satisfactorily—given American advisers, American logistical support, and American units nearby.

Under these conditions, pursuing victory without substantial risk required that American soldiers clear and then hold the Sunni cities. That meant committing American forces in larger numbers for an indefinite amount of time. Secretary Rice endorsed this clear and hold strategy unequivocally, saying that "our political-military strategy has to be to clear, hold, and build: to clear areas from insurgent control, to hold them securely, and to build durable, national Iraqi institutions."

Rumsfeld reacted with consternation, both because the secretary of state was enunciating military strategy and also laying out a long-term commitment that he opposed. From the start of his tenure in 2001, Rumsfeld had stated clearly that his goal was a light, agile force, with speed and flexibility replacing weight and mass. As the czar of what was called a military "transformation," he had appointed a retired admiral who espoused swift battles by forces that were connected to one another via the Internet. This approach had the tongue-twisting label of "network-centric warfare." In other words, rely on high technology to find the enemy's central nervous system and destroy it with a devastating combination of weapons. What was then to be done with a country whose government and armed forces had been shattered was left unaddressed.

Because he spoke Arabic, had attended Harvard, and wore four stars, Abizaid was the intellectual guru of the antibody theory. Inside the military, his judgment was heeded. "Reducing the size and visibility of the coalition forces in Iraq," he said, "is a part of our counterinsurgency strategy." That contradicted the counterinsurgency doctrine of protecting or separating the population from the insurgents who live among them. You can't be pulling the force back to FOBs—Rumsfeld's strategy—if that same force is to hold the Sunni cities while building durable Iraqi institutions—Rice's strategy.

Political rhetoric obscured the contradiction between the two strategies: Were American forces coming in larger numbers to ensure victory, or going home while accepting risk? When Rumsfeld said, "Our exit strategy is victory," he managed to get on both sides of the issue. Bush seemed to favor the Casey strategy in a speech at Annapolis, when he said, "As they [the Iraqi forces] stand up, we stand down." A few weeks later, he reversed field, saying, "We will never accept anything less than complete victory." Casey too had muddied the waters at a Pentagon press conference by saying, "We do have enough force" in Anbar, despite the Whack-a-Mole character of a dozen sweep and leave operations in six months. Vice President Dick Cheney finessed the debate by observing that the insurgency was in its "last throes," thus implying neither more forces nor more time were needed.

Senator John McCain was having none of it. "Too often we've been told," he said on *Meet the Press,* "that we're at a turning point. What the American people should have been told and should be told . . . [is] it's long; it's hard; it's tough."

Casey agreed with the point, but disagreed about the mission.

"Senator McCain pressed me frequently to increase the number of our troops," Casey told me. "I explained that from February of 2005 through the end of 2006, my mission was to transition responsibility to the Iraqis. I had enough forces to do that. I did not have enough for doing COIN ourselves. I saw in Bosnia that we kept doing it for them, and they didn't do it for themselves."

The president and secretary of state were proceeding from a different frame of reference than the military commander.

The roles of Myers and Abizaid were to provide expert oversight and flag for the president the chasm between his views and those of Casey. General Myers, though, was out of his depth at the Pentagon. Not understanding the nature of the war, he went along with Rumsfeld and Abizaid, served his time, and accomplished nothing. As the theater commander, Abizaid had abdicated his oversight role from the start by leaping over the hapless Sanchez to deal directly with Iraqis, rather than replacing Sanchez. He became operationally committed, rather than detached. After Casey took over, the philosophical agreement between the two about the mission—transition and get out—mitigated against dispassionate risk assessment. In his Operations Division in Qatar, Abizaid only had a few officers monitoring Iraq. When a staff officer recommended that the size of the Iraq section be increased, Abizaid denied the request. "I have Casey," he said. "His staff provides the information we need."

Myers and Abizaid failed to flag two high risks. First, the advisers did not believe the Iraqi forces would be ready inside a year, as the campaign plan projected. Second, Rice and the Pentagon, civilians and military alike, were in basic disagreement. The difference between the two objectives—transition to the Iraqis leading with high risk or reduce risk by undertaking counterinsurgency operations with Americans in the lead—was obvious, as Casey's remark to McCain had made clear. Rice had a theory; Abizaid and Casey had the forces. They were headed in different directions.

Transitioning responsibility was not the same as ensuring victory. Within the military, risk management was bungled. To use business terms, Casey was the chief executive officer; Myers and Abizaid were overseeing the effort as members of the board of trustees. On a corporate board, they would be charged with monitoring risk to ensure that the CEO did not run too large a gamble. The CEOs of Citibank and Merrill Lynch lost tens of billions of dollars when they ran excessive risks because their boards had not provided proper oversight. Similarly, Casey was running a high risk that the Iraqis would fail, and the National Security Council in Washington—the corporate board—did not address the risk.

The president, whom McCain described as "not intellectually curious" and Senator Carl Levin (D-MI) referred to as "intellectually lazy," did not resolve the contradiction. He talked of a victory that eschewed risk, while the military pursued a transition that increased risk.

EIGHT

THE SECOND WAR BEGINS

2006

THE SETTING

Electricity output was up. Insurgent attacks had dropped. The flow of foreign fighters had been disrupted. Insurgents in Jordan were willing to talk. Four elections in twenty months had gone off without a hitch. Ambassador Khalilzad had agreed that governance and economic development were the responsibility of the State Department. At the end of January 2006, President Bush went on television to declare, "I am confident in our plan for victory."

Casey did not have a plan for victory. He planned to turn the ongoing war over to the Iraqis and get U.S. forces out. Over the past year, the Iraqi forces had expanded from 114,000 to 214,000, and U.S. battalions had partnered with sixty-five Iraqi battalions.

The partnering had not resulted in major gains because Iraq was, in the words of Maj. Rory Quinn, a company commander, "a police war." Iraqi battalions, predominantly Shiite, had proven less effective than Americans in detaining insurgents. The police were still inept. "By law, [U.S.] soldiers were not supposed to work with police," Keith Mines, the diplomat and former Special Forces officer, explained. "In Iraq, some military units broke that rule because it had to be done. But always in the background was the understanding that it should be done by civilian police trainers, as we did in the Balkans."

Nothing resembling the robust police program in the Balkans ever emerged in Iraq. Instead, in October of 2005 an exasperated American military wrested control over the police from the State Department. Two thousand six was designated the Year of the Police. Lt. Gen. Marty Dempsey pointed out the problem.

"The police have been neglected for three years," Dempsey told me. "They have deep roots in the Shiite militia. Our advisers spend 150 contact hours with the Ministry of Defense, and six hours a week with the police in the Ministry of Interior."

Yet in Baghdad, without U.S. partnering, the police were the major force, with the U.S. battalions having pulled back to eight FOBs. "The biggest difference in Baghdad from two to three years ago," Thomas Ricks of *The Washington Post* wrote, "is the nearly total absence of U.S. troops on its streets."

The first blow to the optimism occurred on the political front. The Shiite bloc had once again won the most seats in the Assembly. Jaafari was elected to a four-year term, with Sadr's supporters all voting for him and providing the one-vote margin of victory over a secular economist from the SCIRI party. Led by Khalilzad and firmly supported by numerous intelligence sources, the Americans had concluded that Iraq would fall apart if Jaafari remained as prime minister. He tolerated the growth of the militias, did nothing to stop the death squads operating out of the Ministry of Interior, and permitted the systematic exclusion of Sunni districts from basic services. The Sunnis, Kurds, and secularists in the Assembly were united in opposing him.

President Bush had not funneled financial aid to help Ayad Allawi in the first election of a prime minister, because that would have interfered with "true democracy." This time, Bush decided there were limits to playing by purely democratic rules, stating that he "doesn't want, doesn't support, doesn't accept" Jaafari's retention of the post of prime minister. With surprising tenacity, though, Jaafari clung to office for months, adding stasis to a dysfunctional government. "The constitutional election didn't turn out to be a unifying document," Casey told me, "because the men in the government were sectarian. From February through April, Jaafari only worried about getting himself reelected. The government just drifted."

THE SHIITE MILITIAS ATTACK

On February 22, al Qaeda blew up the al-Askariya Golden Mosque in Samarra, a sacred Shiite shrine. With that sacrilege, the Jordanian-born terrorist Zarqawi succeeded in touching off the civil war he had murdered so many thousands to consummate. Urged on by Sadr, impassioned militiamen leaped into cars, vans, and minitrucks and sped out of Sadr City in east Baghdad to ransack Sunni neighborhoods and mosques. Both Sadr's Jesh al Mahdi and the Badr Corps militia launched attacks.

"I went to Jaafari and demanded a tough curfew," Casey said. "He refused to allow me to shut down the city, saying the Shiites needed to vent. It took the White House, Zal [Khalilzad], and me two whole days to bring enough pressure on Jaafari to order a curfew."

The chief lair of JAM was Sadr City, a six-square-mile rectangle in northeast Baghdad containing between one and two million impoverished Shiites, separated on its southwestern edge from the rest of Baghdad by the Army Canal. A handful of bridges provided choke points separating Sadr City from Baghdad proper. Under Saddam's old contingency plans, restive Shiites could be bottled up by a few tanks.

The day after the Golden Mosque was bombed, carloads of Jesh al Mahdi militiamen crossed the bridges from Sadr City, honking horns, shooting in the air, and screaming at cars to get out of their way. Elements of the 2nd Battalion, 2nd Brigade, 6th Iraqi Division, responsible for east Baghdad, responded, accompanied by the senior adviser, Maj. Bo Davenport, thirty-eight, from Clarksville, Tennessee. Davenport had served in Bosnia and was on his second tour as an infantryman in Iraq.

In their small pickup trucks, the Iraqi soldiers were intimidated by the JAM gang members who were banging AKs on the sides of their cars and pointing RPGs, shouting at the soldiers to let them pass. Davenport, a burly former football player, was unfazed. A few months earlier, he had shot an RPG gunner under similar circumstances.

"My jundis had two 240 Golfs [machine guns] aimed in," Davenport said. "A guy with an RPG has to get out in the open to shoot. I told my guys we could light them up anytime we chose."

As long as the Iraqi soldiers blocked the end of the bridge, the JAM gangs were bottled up. Instead of shooting, the two sides got into a screaming match that ended when Capt. Muhamed Eba was ordered to return to base with his company. Eba was called into the brigade commander's office. "How dare you let the Jesh al Mahdi into the city," the colonel yelled, while holding up a telephone so the Iraqi general at the other end could hear him. "Your duty was to arrest them!"

The colonel then called a JAM leader. "Captain Eba should never have interfered with your men," the colonel shouted into the phone. "It

was all a mistake. I have him in my office now. It won't happen again."
Eba's identity was now known, putting his family at risk if he didn't go
along.

Unchecked by the Iraqi Army, the JAM gangs drove in packs of four
to ten cars, cruising through Sunni neighborhoods to snatch the un-
wary, shoot randomly at houses, and speed away. Al Qaeda struck
back the next day on what was called the Brick Factory Road, a few
miles south of Sadr City. Men in police uniforms stopped a dozen cars
at a checkpoint and machine-gunned all the occupants, killing forty-
five Shiites. Two days later, JAM retaliated. A lengthy caravan of JAM
toughs left Sadr City and drove south through the Shiite enclave of Jisr
Diyala to the Sunni district of Salman Pak on the east bank of the
Tigris. As the Sunnis hid in their homes, the JAM took over the
mosque, hoisted the green Shiite flag, and slapped posters of Moqtada
Sadr on the stalls in the markets.

When the local American commander, Lt. Col. Brian Winski, arrived, the Iraqi commander of the Public Order Brigade—later called
the National Police—told him there was no mission requiring American troops. The Ministry of Interior was working things out with JAM
leaders. A few days later, the National Police in Salman Pak were hit by
120mm heavy mortar shells fired from Arab Jabour, the al Qaeda
stronghold on the west bank of the Tigris. Responding to a call for
help, Winski sent down snipers and a mortar team that caught the
enemy in the open the next night and destroyed the heavy mortar. Over
the next week, Winski watched as the murky alliances between JAM
and the National Police on one side and Sunni residents and al Qaeda
on the other resulted in nightly firefights, mortar attacks, and the burn-
ings of isolated farms.

In the third week in March, the fight escalated. Al Qaeda infiltrated
the town market in Salman Pak and ambushed a National Police patrol
at twilight, killing a lieutenant colonel. The brigade commander,
Brigadier General Nabil, retaliated by imprisoning 150 local Sunnis,
because no one had warned about the ambush. Although Army adviser
Lt. Col. Chuck Van Heusen secured their release and insisted on a new
brigade commander, the civil war was raging like an underground coal
fire. The American battalion commander, Winski, had 700 soldiers to
patrol 12,000 square kilometers and keep the peace between 500,000
Sunnis and Shiites. Every place the Americans weren't, a fight or a
burning broke out. Although both al Qaeda and JAM gangs placed
some IEDs to kill Americans, the two sides were focused mainly on
each other.

Since the bombing at Samarra, sectarian executions in Baghdad had jumped to over 200 a week. Across the city, Casey only had seven combat battalions like Winski's. Inside the city, there were only 7,200 American soldiers, conducting fewer than 100 patrols a day during February. Iraqi forces, not Americans, were supposed to be patrolling Baghdad, and they weren't doing the job.

THE FIRST EFFORT TO PREVENT CIVIL WAR

In mid-March, Casey kicked off Operation Scales of Justice, committing three U.S. brigades to Baghdad to bolster the 22,000 city police and 10,000 National Police. Jaafari promised to commit 11,000 Iraqi soldiers, but fewer than 2,000 showed up. While sending American soldiers back into the city, Casey did not change his focus. The Americans were supposed to be in support of the Iraqi forces, not doing the job for them. American soldiers would not move into neighborhoods and hold city blocks indefinitely in order to protect the local population. The Americans would move through, engaging anyone who shot at them. Iraqi police would then move in behind the Americans and subdue a lesser threat, thus bringing security to the population.

The flaw in the concept was not recognizing the ineptitude and connivance of the police.

"We didn't know how bad it [the collusion] was," Casey told me, "between the police and the militia death squads because we weren't permitted to deploy U.S. advisers into police stations until '06. Allawi didn't want it and neither did Jaafari. Once I knew, by March, I changed my strategic plan to say the biggest threat is sectarian violence—Iraqi versus Iraqi."

Ambassador Khalilzad agreed and in April they issued a joint campaign plan stating that "the fundamental conflict is among ethnic and sectarian groups." The plan noted that the two elections and the constitutional referendum in 2005 had strengthened, not weakened, the bonds of sectarian identity. Only four months earlier, the coalition had strongly praised the same elections. In addition to acknowledging a civil war and basic flaw in the electoral process, the plan focused on weak Iraqi governance and stressed that reconciliation was imperative.

No concrete prescription for overcoming these political ills was put forward. CentCom still wanted a smaller coalition—meaning U.S. military—presence, while Iraq didn't even have a functioning prime minister. The U.S. military viewed the State Department with great skepticism. Khalilzad was doing his best to bring about accommodation between the government and the Sunnis, despite being the object of snide remarks by spoiled Shiite politicians. If the solution to the security problem was political and not military, though, then the diplomats who had accepted the political mission had failed.

The same was true on the economic side. When diplomats testified before Congress, they praised the $22 billion appropriated for Iraqi reconstruction as "the largest since the Marshall Plan." Yet few civilians from Washington were seen on the streets of Fallujah, Ramadi, or Baghdad, where battalion commanders toiled daily with few funds.

As Operation Scales of Justice commenced, Lt. Gen. Peter Chiarelli, commander of the Multi-National Corps under Casey, which was responsible for operations, laid particular emphasis upon sewers, electricity, and employment. As he explained a few months later, "This is a different war than we fought two or three years ago, a different war than the United States has ever fought. We're not fighting large formations. We're fighting an enemy that blends into the population, an enemy that has no fixed numbers. . . . I can help the Iraqi government make sure that fresh, potable water works, that sewage systems work, that electricity works. . . . If we can have the people in Iraq believe that their life is getting better in those four or five areas, it will make Iraq a much more secure country."

There were three times more Shiites than Sunnis. It was doubtful the Shiite-dominated government would give preferential treatment or job quotas to the Sunnis. Instead of accepting Chiarelli's offer to help, the government was shutting down electricity and health clinics in Sunni districts. While Baghdad was being torn apart by violence, the provincial and city councils, in league with militias intent on driving the Sunnis out of the city, had refused to meet with the U.S. military commanders. Although surveys of prisoners indicated that one in three joined the insurgency for money, Casey was skeptical about driving down unemployment. "The economy would never be ready," he said. The laudable goal of development would take decades to achieve.

A belief in economic determinism was an instinctive American response to an insurgency. In 1966, President Johnson had offered Ho Chi Minh, whose guerrillas also blended into the population, a development project on the scale of the Tennessee Valley Authority. When that failed, LBJ met in Hawaii with the South Vietnamese leaders, challenging them to provide employment to woo away the peasants fighting for the Viet Cong. "I want to see improvements," he said. "I want to see you nail that coon hide to the wall."

It hadn't worked out well for President Johnson. Ho Chi Minh was not impressed by the bribe and the South Vietnamese government lacked the resources and the model, even if it had the desire (which it did not), to restructure a subsistence agricultural economy. There is scant evidence that the root cause of insurgencies is poverty. If so, most of the world would have been in rebellion for most of history. There are many impoverished countries without insurgencies and many countries rich in natural resources with insurgencies. The communist dogma stressing economic determinism collapsed with the Berlin Wall.

A robust employment program funded by the United States was impossible. In Iraq, there were five million unemployed Shiite and Sunni men. If provided jobs at only $300 a month, that would require $18 billion a year donated by U.S. taxpayers to a country whose oil revenues were being stolen with government connivance on a colossal scale. The U.S. Congress would not authorize that, and the Iraqi Assembly would not authorize funding that ignored the Shiites in favor of the Sunnis.

Regardless of theory, Chiarelli was frustrated by State and USAID's inaction. The billions of U.S. dollars appropriated weren't reaching the street level. State offered Provincial Reconstruction Teams to be embedded with U.S. brigades.

Rumsfeld was cool to the idea. Embedded PRTs seemed a step toward a longer involvement. By definition, economic development never ended in any country and did not necessarily win the right hearts and minds. Still, even a slight improvement by State was better than none. Supported by Casey, Chiarelli eventually talked Rumsfeld into approving the embedded PRTs, although it would be months before State could organize and send them.

Secretary of State Rice, during the 2000 election campaign as Bush's foreign policy adviser, had written, "The president must remember that the military is a special instrument. It is lethal, and it is meant to be. It is not a civilian police force. It is not a political referee. And it is most certainly not designed to build a civilian society." Yet because the State Department had not stepped forward in Iraq, the U.S. military was a police force and a political referee—and was building a civilian society. It rankled the generals that, as Casey put it, "We are not organized as a country for twenty-first-century war. The rest of government is in terrible shape."

At the same time, the military still had to defeat three separate enemies—Shiite death squads, al Qaeda terrorists, and Sunni resistance groups that didn't quite know what they were resisting. Al Qaeda seemed to hold Anbar Province in a death grip. In Baghdad, Operation

Scales of Justice had begun without a plan for radically reshaping or replacing the police, whose miserable performance had permitted the growth of JAM and the death squads that threatened civil war.

THE COIN BOOSTER CLUB

When the military took on governance as well as security tasks, it confused itself. No one serving in Iraq had fought in Vietnam, where area security had been gradually established. In Iraq, a sensible doctrine that combined providing security for the population, hunting down the insurgents, and ensuring local governance and basic services was lacking. To fill the gap, Casey had instituted a counterinsurgency school north of Baghdad and required all incoming commanders to attend a two-week course.

Back in the States, Petraeus was commanding the Combined Arms Center in Fort Leavenworth, Kansas, while Mattis was head of the Marine Corps Combat Development Command in Quantico, Virginia. Petraeus suggested that their two staffs work together to write a counterinsurgency manual. The new manual would provide a general approach to counterinsurgency.

"There are two kinds of generals," Mattis said. "Either the staff briefs the general, who then decides what to do, or the general briefs the staff, who then implement what he has directed. A general's challenge is to define in operational terms the type of war he's fighting. I call that designing."

Published at the end of 2006, *Counterinsurgency Field Manual 3–24* was the most academically influential field manual in military history. While the prime readership was intended to be battalion commanders, it was difficult to find more than a few who had read the entire document. At 150,000 words, the *FM* was as long as two books. This was the normal palimpsest expected from two enormous staffs (Army and Marine) charged with researching a century of warfare and deriving axioms about the interactions among politics, security, government services, economic development, ideologies, and insurgencies. Part sociology and part catechism, the *FM* stressed honorable behavior, based on the premise that a population—if provided security, respect, government services, and economic opportunity—will cease to support an insurgency.

Applied to Iraq, some points in the *FM* were vexatious. First, the *FM* criticized "the natural tendency to create forces in the U.S.'s image. That is a mistake." But Generals Casey and Petraeus had designed the

Iraqi Army in the mirror image of the American Army. While the *FM* said indigenous forces "should move, equip and organize like insurgents," the Iraqi Army stayed on the defensive inside bases and checkpoints.

The *FM* suggested the proper focus should be upon police forces. But in Iraq, due to bureaucratic hurdles, the police were ignored. Left to their own devices, the police became the tool of the Shiite militias that almost wrecked Iraq and Casey.

Second, the *FM* defined COIN as "a competition to mobilize popular support," requiring the government to provide a "single narrative to organize the people's experience" and serve as the rallying cry to defeat the insurgents. In Iraq, the insurgents incessantly chanted "Allahu akbar," or "God is great," thus tying Islam to their cause. On the government side, two narratives were in conflict. The Sunni narrative stressed disenfranchisement, while the Shiites stressed consolidating their dominance so that Sunni Baathism could never rise again. The Americans stressed a narrative of reconciliation that the government and insurgents ignored.

Iraq was sui generis in that there were three separate insurgent groups. The al Qaeda terrorists killed to establish a caliphate; the Sunni tribes, claiming to be a national resistance, killed to establish local control; and the Shiite death squads killed to drive out the Sunnis. Reconciliation was the only narrative that could avoid a Thirty Years War, and yet the fractious government installed by Americans could not reach such a compromise in 2006.

Regardless of inconsistencies between the theory of COIN and the realities of Iraq, the manual's basic message—treat the people with respect—was of enormous importance in modifying the behavior and attitudes of young Americans who had volunteered to be grunts and had been trained to shoot and kill. Indeed, so justly proud were the infantry of their prowess that they often referred to others as POGs, or Persons Other than Grunts. An infantryman can be tough, too tough. The *FM* didn't tell the commanders how to adjust the attitudes of their warriors. It did tell them they had to be the designers who defined what they expected their troops to do.

The COIN academy in Iraq had been teaching similar precepts for a year. What distinguished the field manual was the scope and ambition of Petraeus's outreach. Midway through the writing, Mattis moved to another job and Petraeus carried on. The *FM* was the brainchild of Petraeus and demonstrated his inclusiveness. To write the manual, he had pulled together a first-rate team that combined intellect with command experience. Lt. Col. John Nagl was an operations officer in Hab-baniyah and earlier had written a book on counterinsurgency that was praised by Casey. Col. Peter Mansoor had graduated first in his class at West Point. Lt. Col. David Kilcullen was a former Australian Army of-ficer who had studied several insurgencies. Retired Col. Conrad Crane had a world-class reputation as a counterinsurgency analyst.

When the team finished a first draft in February of 2006, Petraeus co-sponsored with Harvard University a symposium at Fort Leaven-worth to review each chapter. Over a hundred academics, diplomats, and journalists participated. Those with hard-won experience on the ground groused that the *FM* finessed the blood and the mud by pre-senting war as a branch of sociology. Much like a bowdlerized version of Plato's *Republic,* the COIN manual argued that the host nation fighting an insurgency could prevail by applying utopian socialist prin-ciples—attend to the needs of the people, provide just governance, and so on. That raised the question why, if the host nation had such princi-ples, American forces were needed in the first place, and if it did not have such principles, how Americans could implant such ideals when they were only advisers, without the authority to order radical reforms.

With counterinsurgency presented as behavioral science, however, the manual gained supporters in unlikely quarters. Liberals could find little to criticize in a document that scarcely mentioned police, let alone military, tactics—although whether they would support the war was another matter. A Harvard professor praised it in *The New York Times Book Review*—certainly a first for a military manual. Most football commentators had played the game; most counterinsurgency commen-tators had never faced an insurgent or advised a unit under fire. Coun-terinsurgency became an intellectual pop fad, attracting military and civilian authors who had never tasted the grit from a grenade, or walked down a road at night braced for the inevitable hit, or heard metal gates clang as neighbors sounded a warning to insurgents.

Walking the streets in the destitute city of Hit in northern Anbar, a battalion commander, Col. Frank McKenzie, dismissed many of the theories advanced by military strategists as "elegant irrelevance," ar-guing that the centerpiece of combating an insurgency remained the routine foot patrol.

"I think that sometimes the American military was seduced," he told *The Washington Post*. "We were intellectually seduced by guys who promise a solution to everything."

The *COIN FM* wasn't a standard field manual a platoon comman-der could study for techniques to organize a local council, develop intelligence, arrest insurgents, or patrol the streets. While the manual didn't tell him how to do his job, it did explain that he was a guest in a country where people deserved to be treated with the same respect as at home. Shooting wildly in response to an attack or trashing a home provoked anger and a desire for revenge. If he acted as a bully, he was recruiting for the insurgents.

The counterinsurgency manual was valuable as a proselytizing document. The erosion of support in the States was providing the insurgents in Iraq with their best hope of winning. While the Pentagon, State Department, and White House fretted about losing public support, Petraeus reached out to gain support.

GENERAL NAGGING

The positive attitude of Petraeus contrasted with the negative whining by retired generals about Rumsfeld's managerial style. In mid-April, *Time* magazine ran a piece by retired Lt. Gen. Greg Newbold, who urged active duty generals to speak out against Rumsfeld. "The Pentagon's military leaders," Newbold wrote, "acted timidly when their voices were urgently needed." *The New York Times* ran an op-ed by another retired general who railed against Rumsfeld, demanding his resignation. *Slate* magazine quoted Gen. Tony Zinni, an iconic combat leader, as suggesting that, had a few generals gone public in 2003, "President Bush would have had a harder time rallying political support for the invasion." More retired generals piled on, receiving lavish press coverage.

Slate magazine captioned the critiques as "the revolt against Rumsfeld." At first blush, this seemed to be tough stuff. A revolt implied a grave constitutional crisis. While nothing that dramatic was envisioned, indignant resignations by active duty generals, as urged by retired generals writing op-eds, would badly shake public support for the war effort.

To the credit of the military, the supposed "revolt" was short-lived. Like ambassadors, doctors, and senators, general officers belong to a small club that in retirement use their rank on their letterheads. Their stature confers the benefit of popular respect, lucrative positions on corporate boards doing business with the Pentagon, and the obligation of probity. The generals—active duty and retired alike—lived up to that obligation, closing ranks in disapproval of such op-eds. It was one thing to resign when you cannot in good conscience carry out your duties—a path not one of the retired generals had personally chosen—

and quite another to demand the resignation of duly appointed civilian superiors. Why stop with the secretary of defense? Why shouldn't generals demand the resignation of the president, or of a senator or congressman who voted the wrong way?

Mattis referred to "bloviating generals," while Dempsey blasted what he called "retired general courage." Concerned about precedent, Senator McCain, a harsh critic of Rumsfeld, refused to endorse the retired generals' position, saying, "The president has the right and earned the right as the president of the United States to appoint his team."

Rumsfeld was the official singled out for the most public criticism. He was constantly hectoring the military for withdrawals, a goal that should have gained him support among liberals and Democrats. At the same time, he refused to acknowledge mistakes and projected a know-it-all, flippant arrogance, delighting in intellectual hand-to-hand combat about proper grammar with reporters.

His managerial style was not to give a direct order, but instead to pester and needle until he worked the military around. Rigorously logical, Rumsfeld had the debater's skill for reducing complex arguments to quick syllogisms. Not for him was the old saw that command in war was an art form. The formidable Rumsfeld demanded a clear causality between a recommendation and an expected result. This placed the top generals—Abizaid and Casey—at an insurmountable disadvantage. Both espoused the dogma that an increase in American troops generated as much opposition as it suppressed. If more Americans only kept a lid on a cauldron of violence, why prolong the day when the Iraqis had to accept responsibility for their own country? Casey's staff observed that when he returned from meetings with Rumsfeld in Washington, he was quieter than usual, but he never debriefed his staff on what he had been told in confidence, or what verbal direction he had received. A bureaucratic master, Rumsfeld left few tracks in the snow.

THE PHONY WAR

Late spring of 2006 was a strange time in Iraq. On the surface, it seemed that things might just work out, enabling U.S. troops to gradually withdraw. After blocking the formation of a new government for four months while thousands died, the inept and selfish Prime Minister Jaafari stepped down. Inside the al-Faw Palace in Camp Liberty in west Baghdad, Casey's staff projected a "steady as you go" attitude. "It's all about them," Casey insisted, meaning that the Iraqis had to take charge of their own affairs. Casey's staff calculated that in April there were

400 patrols a day by U.S. forces on Baghdad's streets, a fourfold increase since February, plus 700 patrols by the Iraqi Army or police. In practical terms, the total was still a small fraction of the daily police patrols in U.S. cities.

Operation Scales of Justice seemed to be making slow progress in halting sectarian violence, with a slight downtrend in attacks against civilians. Maj. Gen. Rick Lynch, the spokesperson for the coalition, told reporters that the coalition wasn't aware of large numbers of forced population movements. Of sixteen incidents reported, only four were confirmed by investigations. The coalition hadn't been asked to resettle displaced persons.

On Baghdad's streets, the mood was different. In late April, I accompanied Major Davenport and Lt. Yarub Altawee on small-sized patrols through miles of east Baghdad. Altawee, twenty-six, liked to wander in and out of the shops along bustling Palestine Street, an upscale shopping area, asking, "How's business?" In the late afternoons, the street was jammed with cars, men, children, and women, many in chic, Western-style clothes. The small stalls displayed a profusion of brightly colored goods and trinkets.

Palestine Street bisected Baghdad south of Sadr City, and it was up and down this boulevard that the Shiite militias had raced in cars and pickup trucks at the end of February. There was little sense of apprehension when a patrol of eight Iraqi and American soldiers walked down the crowded sidewalk, politely sharing the space with the shoppers. Both the shoppers and storekeepers were glad to see the soldiers, and didn't try to pretend otherwise. No one ducked away or refused to answer questions—the common response I had received for years in Anbar.

In shop after shop—it seemed every fourth shop was selling cell phones—Altawee and his commander, Captain Eba, received the same voluble reply. The economy was okay, the storekeepers said, but security was terrible. The shoppers rushed home before sunset. Every shop closed before early evening, traditionally the prime shopping time in the warmth of late spring. You didn't know where a bomb would go off. And robbers were walking into shops, pointing guns, and walking out with the cash, or kidnapping the owner for ransom. Some robbers wore police uniforms. Distrust of the police was mentioned in shop after shop.

For hours, the patrol meandered through the city, from fashionable Palestine Street, to the Sunni suburb of Adamiya, through the mixed district of Babnal and into hardscrabble Fadhal, where raw sewage ran down mud alleyways too narrow for vehicles.

Lieutenant Altawee stopped before a long table blocking half the street. Sitting on rickety wooden stools and broken chairs were a dozen Sunni men with weathered faces, too poor to afford tea, idly passing the time. They stared at the soldiers, smiling and asking us to join them. "Iraqi soldiers, yes! American soldiers, yes!" an older man burst out in English. "Police, no!"

Tall buildings with bullet pockmarks in the concrete and tiny rusted balconies draped with laundry loomed tight on both sides. Heavy wooden doors, centuries old, barred entrance to tiny hovels in the alleys.

"Fadhal has a mean reputation," Davenport said. "You don't come down here if they don't want you here. They fought the police the other night. Inflicted some serious casualties."

Residents rushed up to show us the tail fins of mortar shells, shaking their fists and pointing down the street toward a Shiite section. Amidst much applause, we continued down the fetid street, crossing a small square marred by the remnants of two charred buses.

"Happened last week," Davenport said. "Bomb killed over a dozen."

On the far side of the square, a gunner in an Iraqi Humvee fired a few desultory machine gun bursts down a side alley. Shrugging, Captain Eba said the gunner thought he saw a sniper. We walked down a wide paved street, passing vendors selling ice and chunks of lamb meat. They looked at us with blank expressions.

"This is Jesh territory," Davenport explained. "They lob mortars into Fadhal at night, and the Sunnis in Fadhal shoot back from the roofs. Jesh don't mess with us."

The patrol continued on to the Qadar district, where soldiers clustered around a Russian-style armored vehicle were guarding a large mosque traditionally used for worship by both Shiites and Sunnis.

"Sadr's militia tried to take it over," Captain Eba explained. "We got here first. They drove up, shouting and honking horns. Then they drove away. They knew they'd lose. We have the Americans."

He pointed his finger toward Davenport. As the twilight darkened, the traffic thinned out and the shopkeepers began pulling down the aluminum sidings that protected their storefronts. A group of Iraqi police drove up and got out of their cars on the other side of the mosque. They stood there, keeping their distance from the Iraqi soldiers.

"There is a civil war here," Eba said, "but no one can see it. No one is supervising the police and the Public Order Battalions. One is called the Wolf Brigade for what it does. The Mahdi militia takes revenge on anyone."

A week later, the Iraqi Army pulled back from the mosque and the Jesh al Mahdi moved in. The sectarian war was swirling around the Americans without touching them.

———

While Davenport was advising the Iraqi soldiers in the heart of the city, most of his battalion was deployed two miles to the south. The next morning, Davenport met with his commanding officer, Lt. Col. Brian Winski who was leading the 1-61 Cavalry, 506th Regimental Combat Team, 101st Air Assault Division. Winski, thirty-nine, of Milwaukee, was on his second tour. I had met him a few years earlier when he was serving on Petraeus's staff in Mosul.

After swapping notes with Davenport, Winski hopped into his Humvee for his daily patrol. The battalion, not partnered with an Iraqi unit, spent a third of its time on household chores and security, a third on mounted patrols, and a third on raids. We drove south a few miles to Salman Pak, where the Iraqi battalion commander had been killed in February. We stopped at a modest police station tucked behind the usual HESCO barriers—canvas sacks as tall as a man filled with tons of dirt to absorb the blast of car bombs.

"This station cost a million bucks, more than in the States," Winski said. "Costs are crazy. I could fix a school in 2003 for 3,500 bucks; now it's $35,000. We don't know what makes this economy tick. I get money and I spend it."

Winski pulled in to compare notes with a small advisory team. A Sunni sheik had accused the National Police of robbing and killing a farmer. Small groups of the Shiite police force were scattered throughout the town, living in houses and supposedly paying rent.

"I don't like it," Winski said. "These cops are poor Shiite kids from Sadr City occupying a rich Sunni suburb. There aren't enough of us to keep an eye on them. The advisory team is tiny. But if I post a troop [company] here, that leaves another sector uncovered."

We passed a gas station with a line of cars that stretched for a mile. Green flags fluttered from most of the houses on the road.

"There's nine gas stations for half a million people," Winski said. "No one will drop a dime to finger who controls the fuel. JAM runs the show around here."

A few weeks earlier, Winski's soldiers had stopped a black Mercedes that was driving erratically. Four men stepped out, one covered in blood. In the trunk, the soldiers found three pistols and an Iranian rifle with blood on the stock. Other cars stopped and men hopped out, screaming that the four had just murdered their friend. The soldiers accompanied the witnesses to a Sunni neighborhood where a corpse lay in the gutter. The man with blood on his hands admitted he did the shooting. An Iraqi judge released all four, saying the evidence was inconclusive.

Winski's Humvees moved slowly on patrol, allowing Iraqi drivers to pass. In most of Iraq, given the risk of a suicide bomber, all civilian cars had to stay well away from a Humvee or be shot up. Winski, a strong believer in the Petraeus approach, ran the risk daily.

"General Chiarelli ordered us to stop being so quick on the trigger," Winski said. "If you make a mess, you strengthen the insurgency. I have a simple rule for my drivers: Don't be a prick."

The Humvee bumped down a rutted macadam road next to the tranquil Diyala River in southeast Baghdad. Winski passed by a string of farms nestled under palm trees. Ahead was the trestle bridge leading from the shantytown of Jisr Diyala, the southern entrance to Baghdad. When Winski stopped in a dusty field filled with taxis, a crowd of men and boys gathered around.

"Another IED went off on the river road last night," he said through an interpreter. "You keep telling me it's outsiders. Someone saw something. My Humvees are armored. Your children are the ones who get hurt."

Men started shouting. The translator, Arnold, yelled until he restored order. Most blamed Sunni villagers who lived up the road. A few suggested Sadr's militia did it. Winski offered cash for information. The men laughed, making slicing motions across their necks.

"I don't know who's an insurgent in a crowd," Arnold said in response to a question. "Do these guys? Someone knows something. It takes many visits to learn a little."

Both sides waited for the ending: soccer balls. Winski always had some for the kids. Sure enough, Sergeant Major Fields picked out the smallest children and gave them backpacks and soccer balls. Winski had a final word before he left.

"A kid up the river road had his leg blown off. That'll be your kid one of these days."

Winski drove back along the river road, stopping when he bumped into one of his platoons and an explosive ordnance team. A few hundred feet ahead, a small green robot with a long claw was snipping the wires from an artillery shell hidden in the grass. On a video feed, Winski watched the disarming for a minute, then congratulated his men. It wasn't us, they replied. A farmer had pointed out the IED, saying his kids almost stepped on it. Winski paid him $100.

After the ordnance team blew the IED, the soldiers climbed back into their Humvees. An old man who had been watching them turned his back, lifted up his soiled white dishdasha, and mooned them. Winski and his soldiers laughed and whistled in appreciation.

The gesture captured the existential absurdity of the situation. The Americans couldn't distinguish their friends from their foes. The Shiites and the Sunnis knew who their enemies were; they just weren't certain whether the Americans were on one side or the other. The mission of the Americans was to support the development of the Iraqi forces, placing them in the lead as fast as possible. But the police in and around Baghdad were rightly feared by the Sunnis and distrusted by the Shiites, while the Iraqi Army presence was thin, episodic, and lacking in decisiveness.

When confused, moon 'em all.

ISOLATION TO THE NORTH

The same pattern of American detachment from the simmering civil war was emerging north of Baghdad. To the east of Samarra lay the restive agricultural province of Diyala, which stretched east to the Iranian border. At the end of 2005, two American brigades had rotated out of Diyala and were replaced by only one. After the Samarra bombing, an American battalion pulled out of the provincial capital of Baquba and onto FOB War Horse, leaving two American platoons inside a restive city of 300,000.

"The result was Sunnis and Shiites attacking each other," Capt. Phil Carter, an adviser to the Baquba police force, said. "We'd watch the fights from the roof of our compound. Some days, twenty or thirty people were killed. We became irrelevant."

Routine patrolling, called "presence patrols," from FOB War Horse ceased. Before an American force would sally forth, the mission had to be approved at the brigade level. This resulted in fewer casualties and less influence.

"Once we adopted a commuter mind-set," Carter said, "we became risk-averse in Diyala Province. With little leverage, we didn't have much effect. The police took their orders from a corrupt Ministry of Interior and a Shiite provincial government. We ended up trying to rein in radical Shiite police teams."

THE ISLAMIC CALIPHATE

2006

In the spring of 2006, battle lines were being drawn in Baghdad and the farmland belts to the south and north, with the Shiites having the numbers and the political protection to slowly burn and drive the Sunnis out of the capital. Death squads squirted through the gaps in the thin screen of American patrols. Murders—extra-judicial killings, or EJKs, in the opaque jargon of the coalition—were averaging twenty-five a night. Inside Baghdad, the Shiite gangs tried to avoid the American forces.

To the west of Baghdad, al Qaeda was continuing its campaign, with Anbar its epicenter. As in the prior two years, Anbar continued to be the main battleground, accounting for 45 percent of American fatalities, compared to 33 percent in Baghdad Province. Having lost overt control of Fallujah, al Qaeda had concentrated its main effort against Ramadi, the capital of Anbar. If the three steps in counterinsurgency are to clear, hold, and build, in Ramadi both al Qaeda and the Americans were battling to clear each other out of the city.

In January of 2004, I had driven into Ramadi in an unarmored SUV. By April of 2004, the mood changed abruptly. After Fallujah was besieged and Sadr revolted, about 100 former Iraqi solders sneaked into town to seize the Government Center. They bumped into several

Marine foot patrols, touching off a three-day battle. Hundreds of unemployed young men grabbed their AKs and rushed into the streets to join the fracas. The fighting verged on chaos, with marines proceeding on foot down the paved streets, supported by Humvees with .50-caliber and 40mm machine guns, while the rebels sprinted down the dirt alleyways, shooting between the buildings. Others hopped in taxicabs, careened around corners spraying rounds wildly, and sped off. Men shot from inside houses, then ran out the back doors before the marines, laboring under eighty pounds of armor, rushed through the front doors.

The marines moved forward methodically, clearing the streets. Ramadi was an obscure battle because the press was drawn to the drama of Fallujah, thirty miles to the south. But twenty-four marines died in a single three-day battle in Ramadi, and more than 200 others were wounded. No other battalion experienced a heavier single engagement in the entire war.

Crushed in frontal combat, by the summer of 2004 the insurgents had adapted to shoot and scoot tactics and persisted in launching small attacks. With the battle lines drawn, the local police quit en masse. Some insurgents came from tribes in the Habbaniyah farmland district that separated Fallujah from Ramadi, while many others lived in the city. Either way, any policeman who opposed them was singled out for death. The soldiers in the local National Guard battalion followed the example of the police and deserted. The battalion ceased to exist.

Abdullah Janabi, the imam from Fallujah who was Zarqawi's spiritual adviser, had persuaded the local insurgents to join an alliance with al Qaeda in Iraq. That changed the nature and the leadership of the fight. Al Qaeda demanded strict loyalty and executed several sheiks to make the point, prompting the middle class—doctors, teachers, administrators, engineers—to flee the city. By 2005, the Americans were the only armed forces in Ramadi on the government side. Over the course of two and a half years, four governors were killed, kidnapped, or forced from office. The population dropped from 350,000 to roughly 200,000. Ramadi bore the scars of repeated battle—shuttered storefronts, shell-pocked buildings, burnt-out cars, and raw, black splotches in the pavements from multiple explosions.

The tribes in Anbar were squeezed between the ceaseless Marine operations in the Upper Euphrates River valley and the reappearance of insurgents led by paranoid al Qaeda operatives. Urged on by Casey and Khalilzad, Defense Minister Saadoun Dulaimi had met in November with sheiks, primarily from the Samarra tribe, who requested money and arms to drive out al Qaeda and protect their own lands. Dulaimi refused their request, insisting the tribesmen join the Iraqi security forces.

Lt. Col. Robert Roggeman, commanding Battalion Task Force 2-69, described the situation in western Ramadi as a "running gunbattle," with the Americans viewed as "the outsiders, the infidels." Since the summer of 2005, ten snipers in his battalion had killed 200 insurgents, one at a range of half a mile.

A few of the tribes in the Ramadi area agreed. In January of 2006, the sheiks formed a "leadership engagement" council, promising to drive out al Qaeda. More than one hundred tribesmen, including many sons of the sheiks, showed up at an abandoned factory for processing into the police force. Among them was a suicide bomber who blew himself and fifty-seven others to bits. Al Qaeda distributed to the mosques a list condemning nine sheiks on the council. Inside a month, seven were killed, crushing the spirit of the tribes. The leadership engagement council dissolved.

The fighting was fiercest around the Government Center in the heart of the city. In early 2006, every patrol took sniper fire within two hours of leaving base. Improvised explosive devices were strewn along all the main streets. On an average day, the operations center of the 800-man battalion tracked eighty-five suspected IED locations. Explosive Ordnance Demolitions teams detonated seven IEDs per day, set in by unemployed youths paid $40. When an IED was spotted, a small robot was sent forward to attach a detonation device. The insurgent triggermen liked to blow up the robots, which cost $170,000 apiece.

By the spring of 2006, nine U.S. battalions had rotated through Ramadi. The Government Center was a fortified wreck, its only inhabitants a platoon of marines manning sandbagged firing posts. The population had decreased by half and traffic jams were a long-ago dream of normal times. Ramadi, a battered shell of its former self, bore the scars of repeated battle-shuttered storefronts, shell-pocked buildings, burned-out cars, and raw, black splotches on the pavement from multiple explosions. Marines and soldiers on patrol ran across the open spots and ducked in and out of doorways.

The 3rd Battalion of the 8th Marine Regiment operated in western Ramadi and the 2nd Battalion of the 506th Army Regiment—a successor to the famed "Band of Brothers" of the 101st Air Assault Division—operated to the east. In mid-April, the insurgents attacked the guard post to the east of the Government Center. The day was overcast and drizzling, with a steady wind blowing clouds of dust that grounded the helicopters. Attacking while the Americans lacked air, the insurgents employed mortars, RPGs, and machine gun fire to pin down the sentries while maneuvering a cement truck filled with explosives through the serpentine entry to a main outpost a few hundred meters east of the Government Center. Despite being buffeted, the sentries returned fire from their sandbagged posts. After they killed the driver, the truck exploded in a blast that wrecked half the building and threw one sentry out of his tower. He scrambled back to his post and shot another insurgent before an RPG round hit the sandbags and spilled him out a second time. Again he climbed behind his machine gun and resumed firing. Once the attack was repulsed, the marines added another layer of sandbags outside the window of the governor's office a few hundred yards away.

The last thread of Iraqi government presence in Ramadi was Governor Mahmoon, who boasted that he was on good terms with the "resistance." He had survived numerous assassination attempts by al Qaeda and admitted, "It was a mistake to invite the foreigners into my city." The marines picked him up each morning at his fortified compound and escorted him to the Government Center, where he shuffled papers or talked on the phone when it was working, while the marines manned machine guns.

Lt. Col. Stephen Neary, the commanding officer of 3-8, took out the security detail that guarded the governor. "The governor always ran late," Neary said, "and asked for something. I'd bargain with him and get some good scoop."

In early May, Neary rolled into the governor's compound with six Humvees. Mahmoon was having breakfast with one of his deputies. It was a beautiful morning, the sun blazing down, temperature in the high eighties, and the governor was in fine fettle, impulsively pulling his deputy into the armored SUV for the ten-minute drive to the office. The deputy's wife followed in another car to drive him back home.

The small convoy rolled down Michigan, the main street, amidst moderate traffic. The usual small knots of men were loitering on the sidewalks, some repairing tires and working on dilapidated cars. Suddenly a shabby orange and white taxi lurched out of a side street and slammed into the side of the SUV.

The governor's car was engulfed in orange flames. A car door flew off and up like a kite, followed by a wave of thick black smoke. The concussion wave shook Neary's Humvee, two vehicles in front. He looked back and saw flames leaping through the cloud of dust.

Shit, he thought, *I've lost the governor.*

Legs, arms, sandals, torsos, and car chunks were scattered across the road. Five or six civilian vehicles were blazing, the tires and gas tanks aflame. "Suicide bomber!" Neary yelled over the radio, alerting the sentries in fixed positions on Michigan and the battalion ops center. "Big blow! Multiple cas [casualties] on governor's convoy at Justice Center!"

Gunnery Sergeant Klezarus directed his Humvee through the flames and stopped next to the stricken SUV. Klezarus grabbed the shocked governor and his bodyguard, thrust them into his Humvee, and took off for the Government Center.

Amidst the flames and screams, Neary could hear AK rounds cracking by and mortar rounds landing across the street. He called for a Quick Reaction Force to clear the nearby blocks. Sgt. Maj. Carl Gantt was loading the wounded from the governor's party into Humvees. Screaming men and women were rushing forward with wounds gushing blood, scrambling for seats. Civilian passersby with blackened skin and ripped clothes were pleading for aid.

Gantt organized the evacuation. Two Iraqis were dead and thirty wounded. Neary searched among the screaming for the deputy who had been riding with the governor. He found the charred body inside the smoldering SUV. His dazed wife, standing on the sidewalk near her undamaged car, kept asking where he was.

Each suicide bomber, small arms attack, IED explosion, or mortar attack required a spot report. The battalion had logged 1,195 spot reps in five months, or eight a day.

A routine evening patrol consisted of four armored Humvees. Gunnery Sgt. Brendan Slattery, thirty-two, of Boston, commanded a typical patrol I accompanied in early May. In the dim twilight, we rolled down an empty highway bordered by burned-out and shell-shattered buildings. Not a car or a person could be seen. Inside five minutes, a sharp *bang!*, followed by the brief chatter of a machine gun, echoed down the street. Slattery's matter-of-fact voice came over the radio inside our armored Humvee.

"One Alpha, this is Three Alpha. I've been hit by an IED at Michigan and Sunset. One cas and one damaged victor [vehicle]. Am towing it back to base."

The blast from a 120mm shell had torn the right tire off Slattery's Humvee, smashed in the steel door, and badly bruised the knee of LCpl. Jose Torres. Slattery, who already had one Purple Heart, was not hurt, but his truck was out of the fight. Our Humvee pushed up bombed-out Sunset to replace Slattery and was about to hop a curb when Cpl. William Kittell, twenty-one, yelled out, "That's not a curb. IED dead ahead!"

The insurgents had molded a square package of explosives to duplicate a loose curb block. What gave it away in the failing light were two blue wires protruding from the end. The three Humvees sat with engines idling while the drivers scanned the bombed-out buildings around us. The marines were edgy.

"The triggerman is watching us," Lt. Devin Blowes, the convoy commander, said. "He'll detonate the package. Then hit us."

The battalion was hit by an average of three IEDs a day, despite the efforts of the ordnance disposal teams. Some were detonated by large pressure plates, others by thin strips of tin that set off an electric current when pressed together by the weight of a Humvee tire or by a blasting cap connected by wires to a battery. Most common in Ramadi were concealed explosives connected to a blasting cap, a batter, and the bay station for a cell phone. A hidden spotter waited until a Humvee was abreast of the explosives, picked up the cell phone, and called the bay station, triggering the electric impulse.

Professional al Qaeda cells assembled the IEDs, some renting local houses and others operating from farms outside the city. A separate reconnaissance team selected the drop-off spots, while a moneyman recruited locals to emplace the explosives. The going rate was $40 to set in an IED, with another $60 paid if a Humvee was disabled and a $100 bonus if an American was taken away on a litter. The triggerman took up his position only after the IED was in place. Many IEDs, especially in the suburbs and farmlands, were buried and left unattended for weeks. Battalion 3-8 had the coordinates of eighty-five possible IED emplacements. Two ordnance disposal teams cleared an average of five IEDs a day, leaving at least a month's backlog of work if the insurgents quieted down (which wasn't likely).

Blowes only had to wait ten minutes before the ordnance disposal team arrived and pulled out a little robot with rubber treads attached to a cable.

"Fuckers got R2 last night," a grizzled warrant officer said. "If they get D2 here, we're out of Schlitz. Seventy-five K a pop. That's a lot of money. Why don't you guys walk to work?"

"We're lazy," Blowes said. "We want you to do the work for us."

The marines took shelter behind the Humvees as the robot trundled toward the IED that was wrapped in light-colored paper or cardboard. *BLAAM*. The street erupted in a cloud of black smoke as shards of macadam and debris whizzed by. When the dust settled, the marines cheered. D2 was intact. As the bomb disposal team reeled in the robot we proceeded down the dark road.

The three Humvees turned right to enter the market area. The pock-marked road was strewn with papers and trash, and the dark, heavy buildings with metal sheeting instead of windows were so gouged and pitted by shell holes they threatened to topple and crush us. At the far end of the street, a man scuttled from one doorway to another. When Blowes stopped the trucks, the man walked out into the road, gestured for us to come up the street, and then disappeared.

"We can't maneuver in here," Blowes said. "Back out."

"Good call," LCpl. Brian Wilson, the up-gunner manning the 40mm, said.

The Humvees cut north across Michigan onto a street wide enough to turn around in. Bursts of wild AK fire came from the right.

"Got eyes on a guy, roof left, nine o'clock," Wilson said. "It's a PID" (positive identification). He fired a five-round burst of 40mm shells that exploded on a flat roof. The Humvees skidded to a stop in front of the house. Five marines tumbled out, smashed open the metal courtyard door, burst into the house, and raced up the stairs to the roof. In the living room, a man crouched in a corner, arms around his wife, who was screaming hysterically. Excited American voices boomed down the stairs, followed by a crunching noise. A twisted television antenna tied to a board was thrown down the stairs.

"Maybe it's a signal device," a marine said.

The other marines ignored him. Snow flickered on the TV screen in the corner. The woman sobbed in terror, huddled behind a mound of cushions with her husband. There wasn't a chair in the room. The family had learned to sit beneath the windows in case a passing patrol or a nervous insurgent shot at the glow from the now disabled TV.

"He's heading for the apartments on Market Street!" LCpl. Richard Crane yelled.

Stationed outside, Crane had been watching the backyard through his night vision goggles. Cursing, three marines hopped a wall and took off in pursuit. A sharp, quick exchange of gunfire followed a few minutes later, then silence.

"Typical night," Blowes said. "That muj is long gone. Let's head to the barn."

The Humvees drove back through an upper-class neighborhood with imposing courtyard walls and a few functioning streetlights.

"Retired officers live here," Blowes said. "Used to be a safe route to take. But we got hit here last week and a civilian was killed. Al Qaeda doesn't listen to these guys anymore. They're not the big dogs."

There was a sudden commotion in an alley to the left as a faint silhouette ducked around a corner. Wilson spun his gun around too late. The Humvees drove on.

"We could never catch him on foot," Blowes said. "The muj shadow us like that. Maybe they're working up the nerve to take a shot. Maybe they get a rush fucking with us. Maybe they couldn't tell us why they do it. Who knows?"

Spot rep 1,196: two IEDs exploded, one Humvee damaged, one marine lightly wounded.

The next morning, SSgt. Christopher Winship, twenty-nine, left the base with four Humvees for another patrol downtown.

"We'll get hit in an hour or two," he said. "Depends on how long it takes them to figure out our route."

As we again drove down Michigan, the oncoming cars stopped, turned around, and drove away. Winship directed the Humvees from one street to another, changing direction abruptly, never going down the same street twice. Under a warm sun, children with backpacks were walking to school, shops were open, and a long line of cars was queued in front of the city's only working gas station.

Things seemed normal until an AK opened up and bullets whizzed by the Humvee, followed by a rocket-propelled grenade. As people scattered from the sidewalks, Winship yelled over his radio.

"COC, get off this net! You're blocking me!"

The company operations center had cut in on Winship's radio just as the firing had broken out. Frustrated, Winship directed his driver down a side street. The other Humvees followed and a minute later, half a dozen marines leaped out of their vehicles behind the building where the shooters had been hiding.

Iraqis in civilian clothes were running every which way. There was a short burst from an AK, followed by a two-round burst from an M16. Hit in the crossfire, a portly man in his mid-forties lay in a courtyard, his white dishdasha spotted bright red, a bullet hole in his right thigh.

"Corpsman up!" A corpsman ran from a Humvee and applied a tourniquet as the man winced, his eyes bulging, bewildered and pleading. His thigh was swelling like a sausage on a grill, with only a trickle of blood dripping from the bullet hole.

Another short M16 burst, two or three rounds fired by a marine covering a cross street.

"They're behind us, turkey-necking around the corner!" the marine shouted.

"Get those Humvees out of here!" Winship yelled. "Get off the street!"

The marines ran to their vehicles. The corpsman stuffed his kit into a back seat and shook his head.

"The bullet probably cut the femoral," he said. "He'll bleed to death before they get him to the hospital, or they'll amputate his leg."

The Humvees raced around a corner out of the line of fire, then slowed down. The marines scanned the houses. Nothing. Not a single person. Not one moving car. The Humvees turned back onto Michigan, where people were walking along the sidewalk and shopkeepers were tending to their wares.

"I popped one idiot who stood up on a roof to shoot at me," Winship said. "It's rare to see them pose like that, though. Slim [chance] seeing where they're firing from. Today's typical."

Spot rep 1,197: small arms fire south of Michigan, one civilian male wounded.

————

Shortly before he was killed in Ramadi in 2004, LCpl. Pedro Contreras of Jacinto City, Texas, said, "We keep pressing. The fuckers keep shooting. . . . It's fucked up. They know who we are 'cause we got uniforms. They dress like civilians."

That description was still accurate two years later. By mid-2006, most American battalions, even in remote and harsh Anbar, were partnered with an Iraqi battalion. In theory, that led to better intelligence. In fact, local residents were as reluctant to divulge information to a strange Iraqi as they were to an American.

Two Iraqi battalions had arrived in Ramadi and Lt. Col. Steven Neary, who commanded Battalion 3-8, was gradually inserting them into the fight in May of 2006.

"It'll take months before they're ready," he said. "I have them working with Barela's company."

Capt. Carlos Max Barela of Lima Company was responsible for security in west Ramadi. With no police and a few good interpreters, Barela's 145-man company patrolled a section of 600 houses and 12,000 residents. This gave Barela a terrific force advantage—ten times more, for instance, than any of Winski's companies working at the south end of Baghdad.

Barela drove and walked around his neighborhood every day, dropping off school supplies, soccer nets, and medicine. It was easy to hate Americans who acted like RoboCops, Barela explained, glowering behind their Wiley X wraparound eyeglass shield.

"We're taught to focus on killing the enemy," he said. "That's the wrong theory. How we are treating the population is isolating us from our best resource. If we can get the people to give info, we win. We can't do that by scaring them or roughing them up." Upon entering a house, Barela took off his armor and lingered for an hour or more to chat. When an elderly man complained he could not get his medicine, Barela called the battalion aid station and arranged for a drop-off. That evening, the ops center called him. A patrol had detained three Iraqis out after curfew who were asking to speak to "Captain Max." Sammy, Barela's interpreter, spoke to them on the cell phone, pulled up a photomap on a laptop, clicked on a house with the pictures of three males, and nodded at Barela. The patrol released the men.

The problem was that the interaction had occurred between the residents and the Americans, not Iraqi security forces. When residents complained that the Shiite soldiers looked at women's underwear and helped themselves to food in the houses, Barela promised to investigate. It's better if the Marines do the searches, the local men said, the jundis are gypsies.

"If you like Americans," Barela said, "why do you shoot at us?"

No, no, the residents protested, not us. It is bad men from outside. Barela laughed good-naturedly at the standard reply. Then join the army and fight them, he suggested. The army won't take Sunnis, the men replied. Barela knew the army wanted to recruit Sunnis, but it was not worth arguing. As the crowd dispersed, one man tarried. I have joined, he whispered, but my neighbors cannot know. He feared a beating, or worse. Polls consistently showed that over 80 percent of the Sunnis in Anbar considered the government illegitimate and viewed the army as a threat.

"Fear and mistrust are smothering this city," Barela said. "I tell my marines and the jundi—treat everyone with respect. On raids, knock—don't smash the door down. Don't throw suspects to the ground. If making an arrest, tell his family he's going away for a few days. Put the cuffs on outside."

Barela broke his company down into squad-sized units that moved into different houses each night, paying $20 rent. A census of each family was taken, with digital pictures of the males, where they were employed, if at all, a picture of the house and the family car, and so on. These data were entered onto a digital map so that when you clicked on a house, all the information and pictures came up. No direct questions about insurgents were asked, but all requests were entered about such matters as missing relatives, job possibilities, or stolen documents. In two months, Barela had detailed profiles on more than 1,000 residents in 400 houses.

"We don't speak Arabic," he said. "But my personal computer census gives us a shared picture. Every new tidbit goes in there."

Although the insurgents hid weapons caches throughout the city, incriminating evidence found inside a house was rare. Ten of the sixteen arrests his company had made recently were based on data gradually assembled by the census profiles. Of the 1,000 males in the census database, about sixty had disappeared in the last month. Despite snap searches in houses at three in the morning, the men were never home. Some had been kidnapped or randomly killed and their families would never learn what happened to them. They left on an errand or to go to work, and never returned. Barela estimated about forty-five were insurgents, either full-time or paid by the job. Once photographed, fingerprinted, and enrolled in the census data, they were no longer anonymous. So they packed up and left the neighborhood before someone betrayed them.

In turn, the insurgents were determined to kill him. While walking around the neighborhood, he had been shot at twice. The first was a drive-by shooting and the second was an ambush with three rocket-propelled grenades.

Barela insisted that his men return fire only if they had a positive target.

Of Barela's sixteen arrests, he was proud that fourteen had made it through the wickets and gone to jail. Like all units, Battalion 3-8 went through an elaborate process before an insurgent was imprisoned.

Sworn statements by marines acting as arresting officers—two statements, photos, and evidence tagged and bagged for each arrest—were reviewed by the battalion lawyer, Capt. Kevin J. Zimmerman. A former assistant district attorney in Nebraska, Zimmerman, thirty-one, had prosecuted 300 criminal cases before being called up as a reservist.

Seventy-five percent of his time in Iraq was spent processing detainees. In the past three weeks, he had reviewed the charges against 362 Iraqis brought in by the squads. He had dismissed about 50 percent of the charges and sent 178 forward for trial. About 25 percent were caught with IED materials, 25 percent with concealed or illegal weapons, 25 percent were "target packages," meaning Special Operations Forces had tracked them down, and the rest were miscellaneous charges.

His office was a small trailer next to a large tent that contained eight plywood cells stapled with chicken wire and guarded by a marine with a shotgun. In four cells, young men were sorting through MRE boxes, deciding what to eat. The men stood when Zimmerman entered. In two other cells, older men were lying on benches with towels across their eyes to block out the light. They peeked at Zimmerman, and then ignored him.

"Same as in the States, the hard guys know the drill," Zimmerman said. "They have their Miranda rights. I can hold them for eighteen hours and they don't have to answer any questions. We take a photo when they come in and go out. That way we avoid charges of brutality. I pay them $7 a day for their trouble and let them go, unless I have hard evidence. Barela puts together the tightest packages for me. Eventually, though, somewhere up the line in the system, most walk free."

Barela brought security and good manners. But he knew how to deal with people and he enjoyed a remarkable force ratio of one marine per eighty-two residents. In three months, about one insurgent a week was killed in his sector, the majority by snipers in a SEAL team that provided overwatch for the company.

———

In the sector next to Barela's, Kilo Company was killing one or two insurgents each day. Capt. Andrew Del Gaudio, on his second tour as Kilo's commander, believed Ramadi was a testing ground for new al Qaeda recruits and foreign fighters. Small attacks were launched daily at the pockmarked concrete walls of the Government Center. His marines would shoot back, and one or two men in civilian clothes would crumble to the ground. The insurgent recruits who ran the gauntlet and survived moved on to less hazardous duties. Del Gaudio was convinced that lurking out of the line of fire were the puppet masters who kept feeding young men into the meat grinder, waiting for the Americans to lose heart.

"This is a war here [in Ramadi], not politics," Del Gaudio said. "We're a Band-Aid on a sucking chest wound."

Ramadi had become the magnet for the rebellion, much as Fallujah had been in 2004. The flow of fighters into the city resulted in persistent clashes. In late May, a few dozen al Qaeda members actually drove through the center of the city, honking horns and shouting that Ramadi was their caliphate. They drove off before the tanks arrived. Ramadi was a war zone. Knowing they would fight every time they went downtown, the Americans had a RoboCop attitude. A senior American officer in charge of the city, who asked to remain anonymous, vented his frustration at the battle of attrition Americans alone could not win.

"I'm damned mad. Close to a hundred Americans have died in Ramadi on my watch," he said. "We need more troops to clean it out. We need Iraqi soldiers—four or five battalions of them. Secretary Rumsfeld has announced 30,000 Americans are going home. Well, send some here. I'll put them to use."

FALLUJAH—THE INTIMIDATION WAR

In 2004, the two most savage battles of the Iraqi war had raged up and down the streets and inside the 30,000 concrete buildings of hardscrabble Fallujah.

The result was a bloody urban brawl, with over 18,000 buildings damaged or destroyed. After the battle, all military-aged males were issued identification cards and an earthen berm was thrown up around the city, limiting entrance to seven checkpoints.

Over the next eighteen months, al Qaeda maintained at least a dozen small cells inside the city. When I returned in May of 2006, the city was averaging four IED explosions and shootings a week. Sixteen Iraqi soldiers, seven policemen, and five marines had been killed since January. Two Iraqi battalions provided security, together with 1,300 local police. The city council insisted the checkpoints remain. An hour's delay was preferable to a heavy return of terrorists. Due to the comparative stability, in May of 2006 there was new construction on every street.

Two Marine battalions patrolled the outskirts, while inside the city the American presence had dropped from twelve rifle companies in

2005 to one company from the 25th Marine Regiment. In May of 2006, I accompanied an evening patrol commanded by Maj. Vaughn Ward through the market to the Blackwater Bridge, and you could feel the tension.

The marines walked with wary confidence among hundreds of Sunni men clustered on the sidewalks outside small shops offering fresh vegetables, butchered lamb, cell phones, TV satellite dishes, refrigerators, generators, and a thousand types of brightly colored trinkets. Two years ago, these same shops in the souk had sold AK-47s, grenades, and machine guns. Some of the shopkeepers probably were the former arms merchants. The marines affected an insouciant air, cheerfully uttering repeated salaams while scanning the rooftops for snipers. The Iraqis responded reluctantly, replying without a smile or turning away.

Sam, the Iraqi translator, kept his pistol strap unhooked, warning that he did not like the area. Sam had worked in Fallujah for thirty months with a succession of American units and, like most translators, was cynical of his fellow Iraqis.

"Sure, you see big changes. Things are better," he said. "The Iraqi Army is here now. They're Shiites. When the Marines leave, there'll be fighting."

The shot-up buildings around us loomed menacing in the shadows. Sam warned the marines they were being watched and to stay off the center of the street. A burst of fire came from a few streets away, punctuating the ululating call to evening prayer from a nearby mosque. Ward hesitated, and then decided against rushing around in the growing dark. The patrol passed a police station surrounded by barbed wire. Several police stood outside, talking with the shopkeepers. None greeted the passing marines. Ward pointed to a blue, thin-skinned police pickup, observing that there were no bullet holes, while the Iraqi Army pickups were riddled.

"We get along great with the Iraqi Army," Ward, the company commander, said. "The police won't have anything to do with us. Any cop that helps us would get popped when he walked home. Some of them are dirty."

A few days earlier, Ward had hidden a sniper team inside a bombed-out building and then called the police to report an IED outside the building, saying marines would return to disarm it. A half hour later, a carload of insurgents drove up and parked in an alley, waiting to ambush the marines. Two were killed and two captured.

Although the police chief, Brig. Gen. Saleh Khalil, was solid, he knew he had informers in his ranks. In the past eight months, the vice chairman and the chairman of the city council had been shot and killed in the streets. Their killers were still at large. Saleh had recently arrested three terrorists from Saudi Arabia, based on a tip.

The houses were jammed up against one another. No one could live inside the city in total isolation. Someone knew something about each neighbor. Army adviser Maj. William Rummel told a story to illustrate the point. His Iraqi battalion had been tipped off about terrorists living near their command center. They had burst into a house to surprise two men in their underwear watching a porn DVD and drinking scotch. In the living room was a 60mm mortar and a stash of rocket-propelled grenades.

"The tip came from a Shiite woman married to a Sunni cop," Rummel said. "She was pissed because one guy, liquored up, pitched a grenade in her backyard and almost hurt her kids. Those punks had lived next to her for a month. There was no sense of civic duty."

General Casey had declared 2006 "the year of the police," which meant unifying the police force as a reliable tool of the elected government. How to achieve that goal when the uniformed policeman were afraid to go home at night was a huge challenge.

The day after walking through the market with the patrol, I attended a city council meeting in the heart of the city where fighting had been so common. Sure enough, as soon as I walked in, the staccato of small arms fire reverberated from outside. Marines grabbed their weapons and rushed out.

Three Iraqis lay dead in the street. LCpl. Kenneth W. Boss was patting his armored vest, looking for a bullet wound. Boss had been driving by city hall in a Humvee when a four-door maroon Opel suddenly stopped in front of him and tried to back up.

"I'm going to shake down that car," Boss said to LCpl. David Pelaez, his turret gunner. "Cover me."

Boss hopped out and approached the car. When he was two feet away, the driver pointed a pistol at him and fired through the window of the car door. Hit square in the chest, Boss fell backward thinking, *I'm dead but it doesn't hurt*. Lying on his back, he fired three bullets into the car door. Pelaez was also firing on semiautomatic, as the Humvee driver, LCpl. Omare Beury, leaped out and began shooting.

Hit repeatedly, the Iraqi driver slumped sideways as his passenger slipped out the other door, ran to a taxi stopped nearby, and jerked open the door as a shield. Struck in the head, he fell. In the fusillade, the taxi driver was also killed. Boss, a reservist who was a New York City cop, was wearing a GPS receiver strapped to the outside of his armored vest. He found the bullet lodged in the armored plate above his heart.

"That's the second time someone's looked me in the eyes and tried to kill me," Boss said. "Once in New York and now in Fallujah."

The bodies were placed in the back of a police pickup and we went back inside city hall, where sixteen Iraqi council members and three Iraqi Army officers were sitting at the conference table. Along the walls sat another dozen Iraqis and a half dozen Americans. The meeting was in Arabic, with a translator simultaneously speaking in English.

The meeting was called because 600 recruits from Fallujah had deserted the Iraqi Army at the end of training, claiming they were being sent to Baghdad rather than to Fallujah, as allegedly promised. The city's fifth mayor in four years, Sheik Dhari al-Zobaie, a voluble orator, was insisting that Sunnis replace the Shiite soldiers inside Fallujah. Let the Shiites fight the Shiites in Baghdad, he yelled, I'm not sending my boys to be executed there. Exasperated Iraqi officers were yelling back. Round and round they went, getting nowhere.

After two hours, a foreign service officer, Kyle Westin, stood up. So extensive was his knowledge that both General Casey and Iraqi officials in Baghdad contacted Westin for updates on the politics of Fallujah.

"You all know me," Westin said. "I have remained in your city for two years because I want to see Fallujah succeed. But I was ashamed for Fallujah when the recruits threw away their uniforms. That was wrong, and you know it."

There was a moment of silence. None of the city council members argued with him. There were limits to how far they would go in berating one another.

In my notes on that day, I wrote, *Iraqis, US and Iraqi military talk easily.* That might seem pedestrian. But this was my seventh visit to Fallujah, and the first time I had heard a normal political argument. Yes, there were dead bodies outside. After all, this was still Fallujah. But in this same room, I had seen Mattis prepare for a gunfight. In previous meetings, I had seen men glaring at each other as enemies, meeting under uneasy truces destined to collapse. I had heard vigorous denials that there was a single terrorist or foreign fighter in Fallujah.

These men had deep differences. But they no longer disagreed about who was their common enemy. Mayor Dhari had recently fought off three attackers. Al Qaeda in Iraq had gone too far and killed too many in Fallujah.

The next morning, I was talking with Corporal Boss when there was a loud explosion outside. We rushed out to a scene of carnage. Hundreds of civilians had lined up in response to a recruiting offer by the police. A suicide bomber had joined the line and blown fourteen of his fellow Arabs to smithereens. Some police were loading bodies into their pickup trucks, while others walked about with plastic bags, picking up fragments. A water truck was summoned to wash away the blood.

The police declined the marines' offer of assistance. Then small arms fire broke out down an alley and the police reconsidered. When the marines rushed forward, the shooting stopped.

The marines drove away, discussing among themselves the irony. On several occasions, police stopped civilian traffic before an IED went off near a Humvee, or warned pedestrians to steer clear before snipers shot at Americans, or had taken away the bodies of insurgents. They obviously were on good terms with local insurgent gangs. Yet others— likely al Qaeda—killed them. The marines wanted the police to take a clear stand against all insurgents, which they would not do even as they were being killed.

The next day, a bevy of Iraqi and American generals flew in from Baghdad. The mayor welcomed them by declaring that Fallujah's residents dared not travel to Baghdad. The checkpoints manned by police in Baghdad called anyone from Fallujah a "Saddamist." Everyone was afraid of the police. The mayor himself would not risk the trip. The only solution, he said, was to recruit an army battalion from inside the city, separate from the predominantly Shiite battalions. He wanted Sunnis guarding Sunni neighborhoods in Fallujah.

Lt. Gen. Maseer al-Qdeidi, from the Ministry of Defense, patiently explained that Iraq needed a Shiite-Sunni army, not separate militias. Lt. Gen. Peter Chiarelli reminded the mayor that the "Fallujah Brigade" in 2004 had been a disaster, with the extremists taking over. Lt. Gen. Martin Dempsey, who commanded the training in Iraq, said that sectarian armies would tear apart the country and leave Fallujah with no support. As they were leaving, an Iraqi general asked if I had written the book on the Fallujah battles. I said I had. "Fallujans," he said with a smile, "thick as bricks."

Col. Larry Nicholson, commanding the Marine regiment, had given Dhari a cell phone that the mayor used to call at all hours, as often asking for advice as for materials. A week earlier, Dhari had called to say with a flourish that he was a member of the resistance, indicating he wasn't an American lapdog.

Nicholson was unimpressed with political posturing. Dhari had done little to stop the suicide bombers or to support his own beleagured police.

"So what are you resisting?" Nicholson responded. "The support we give you in Baghdad? The new water plant? The security we bring? Our division motto is *No Better Friend, No Worse Enemy*. In Fallujah's case, Mr. Mayor, we're your only friend. So work with us to improve security and living conditions because sooner or later, we're leaving."

After the meeting with the generals from Baghdad broke up, the mayor turned to his confidants—Westin and Nicholson. How'd I do? he asked. Terrible, they replied, you overplayed your hand. You'd better get those deserters back, if you want to be a player. Get on board the train; don't stand in front of it. The mayor said he'd consider it. Westin left the meeting skeptical.

"The mayor's message to the Americans is—leave, but not yet," Westin said. "Americans are the city's lifeline. Out here, Ambassador Khalilzad is called the attorney for the Sunnis."

Fallujah was a cauldron of politics, with no military solution. Before he was assassinated, Sheik Abbas, a respected imam in Fallujah, had said roughly the same thing to me. "You must take care of Anbar to stop the terrorism," Abbas said, meaning the Americans had to keep pressure on Baghdad to reach an accord.

A few weeks later, Mayor Dhari called Nicholson at three in the morning to say goodbye. The continuous threats of assassination had gotten to his family. He was leaving before dawn for Syria. Around the same time, Sheik Osama Jadaan from the Qaim district, visiting in Baghdad to organize resistance to al Qaeda, was gunned down in the streets.

In the spring of 2006, the extremists had the upper hand in Anbar and the Sunnis were being driven out of Baghdad.

TEN

HADITHA: EXPLOSION ON THE HOME FRONT

2006

On May 17, 2006, a bombastic politician rushed before the cameras on Capitol Hill to accuse marines of cold-blooded murder in Haditha, unleashing a torrent of scurrilous speculation by a hyperbolic press. A panel of foreign policy experts ranked the 2006 Samarra mosque bombing as the worst setback in the Iraq War. Haditha ranked as the second worst. Al Qaeda was responsible for Samarra; the press and politicians, sacrificing balance for sensationalism, were responsible for distorting and deliberately exaggerating Haditha.

THE ROAD TO HADITHA

In December of 2004, I met Kilo Company, Battalion 3-1, in the shattered southern remnants of Fallujah. Lt. Jesse Grapes was justly proud of his 3rd Platoon. A few weeks earlier, a half dozen jihadists barricaded inside what Grapes called the House from Hell had poured fire on four wounded marines trapped in downstairs rooms. Instead of backing off, Grapes's men had rushed the house, smashing at doors and windows and ripping off metal grates to rescue their comrades. They swarmed inside, dripping red from cuts, gouges, and bullet wounds. Blood flowed across the concrete floor, slippery as ice. It stuck like gum to their trigger fingers, pulling their aim off target as they ducked grenades that sent shrapnel ricocheting off the walls.

Sgt. Byron Norwood poked his head around a door frame. A round hit him in the head and he fell, mortally wounded. The fight swirled on until Grapes wriggled through a small window and laid down covering fire while the wounded were pulled out. Cpl. Richard Gonzalez, the platoon's "mad bomber," rushed forward with a twenty-pound satchel of C4 explosive—enough to demolish two houses. He placed it on the chest of a dead jihadist and ran outside.

The house exploded in a flash, followed by concrete chunks thudding down. A pink mist mixed with the dust and gunpowder in the air. Grapes was happy to see it. He hastily evacuated eleven wounded marines and the body of Sergeant Norwood. Three months later, President Bush invited Norwood's parents to the State of the Union address. When the president thanked them for their sacrifice, everyone applauded. Back in Camp Pendleton, the courageous platoon basked in the country's adulation. Two marines who had fought in the House from Hell were awarded the Navy Cross, the nation's second-highest medal for courage.

In the fall of 2005, Battalion 3-1 returned to Iraq with veterans of the House from Hell, together with new squad and platoon leaders. In November, the 3rd Platoon—including several of Grapes's men—engaged in a fight in Haditha in which twenty-four Iraqi civilians died. President Bush, unaware that this was Norwood's unit, said, "The Marine Corps is full of honorable people . . . those who violated the law, if they did, will be punished." A year after the president had praised the 3rd Platoon, he censured it. What happened? The president, were he a reflective man, might have asked himself that question.

BACKGROUND

In March of 2004, the 3rd Battalion of the 4th Marine Regiment was sent to Haditha, a drab city of 100,000 on the Euphrates River 140 miles northwest of Baghdad. Battalion 3-4 had experienced heavy fights during the 2003 invasion and had hauled down Saddam's statue in Firdos Square, an image seen around the world. The battle-tested battalion flooded Haditha with hundreds of four-man foot patrols. Insurgents who responded with their usual shoot and scoot tactics were chased down by squads of marines. Although the mayor had been assassinated the previous summer, the insurgents were not well organized. A platoon was ordered to combine forces with the local police; Lt. Matt Danner, the platoon commander, moved his men into the police station. Joint patrols with the local police became the norm.

The Combined Action Platoon was a success. When the Marines arrived, they engaged in a dozen fights in the first month; six months later, they were down to two fights a month. As the Iraqi police gained self-confidence, they became more aggressive and effective. Danner had hit on an axiom of guerrilla warfare: Once the population decided the CAP was the strongest fighting force, information flowed to them.

Then, on March 31, four American contractors were lynched in Fallujah, ninety miles southeast of Haditha. Ordered to attack the city, General Mattis called Battalion 3-4 down to join the fight. "Some of the jundis in my Combined Action Platoon were up for the fight," Danner recalled, referring to the Iraqis who had joined forces with his platoon. "They wanted to come with us. We had lived together, fought together. I told them they had to guard Haditha and that we'd be back for them."

Danner and his men returned to Haditha in May and resumed living downtown with the police. The Americans had left once; now there was uncertainty when they would leave again. "Most of the police we lived with were local Sunnis," Danner said. "A few were tough enough to stand on their own, but 80 percent needed to know we Americans were there with them and would back them up."

In late summer, Danner's battalion rotated home, and Battalion 1-8 moved into the Haditha area. The new marines patrolled vigorously. Word of how Americans had fought in Fallujah had spread, and the insurgents avoided the new marines, targeting instead the Iraqi soldiers. "On some blocks, people would wave," Cpl. Timothy Connors, a squad leader in Battalion 1-8, said. "But mostly they ignored us, like we weren't even there. You could sense something was going on, but no one dared shoot at us." The hearts and minds of the Sunni residents had not been won over, but the insurgents did not challenge the superior force.

In October 2004, Battalion 1-8 was called away to prepare for the second battle of Fallujah. In Haditha, two weeks after the Marines left, insurgents captured the police station and executed twenty-one policemen, including the police chief. The insurgents became the de facto government. The deputy police chief gathered his family and fled to Baghdad.

"He was a good man," Danner said. "The November battle in Fallujah pulled the rug out from under the police. We left them on their own. Without moral support, they collapsed."

In March of 2005, the Marines swept through Haditha, searching door-to-door. The insurgents slipped away. When the Marines left, the insurgents returned, rounded up nineteen remaining Iraqi police, marched them to the soccer stadium, and executed them. A few days earlier, they had assassinated the new police chief and three of his family members.

The Marines responded by again stationing a battalion in the area, Battalion 3-25, a reserve unit from Ohio. The cycle of hope, followed by abandonment, followed by executions and reprisals, had worn down the population. This time the city council refused to meet with the Americans. Instead, a delegation asked that no pro-government messages be played by the local radio station. The surviving Sunni police had fled. The Associated Press quoted the American colonel in charge of the area as saying, "What I need most now is someone who can say, 'This is a good guy, and this is a bad guy.' "

In August an English newspaper, *The Guardian*, smuggled an Iraqi journalist into Haditha. He slipped out to report that the city was tightly controlled by two terrorist gangs, one answering to Zarqawi and the other to a local radical. Executions of suspected spies had become a sport to entertain the crowds. When the Americans drove by on patrol, no one would point out an insurgent.

Battalion 3-25 stayed in Haditha for seven months and suffered horrific losses. An IED killed fourteen marines in a single blast in August, the worst such explosion in the war. Efforts to recruit yet another local police force came to naught. The Americans, having failed for a year to provide a steady presence, patrolled the sullen streets alone.

THE KILLINGS

That was the environment Battalion 3-1 inherited in Haditha in the fall of 2005. After Fallujah, the veterans of the House from Hell, like other battle-scarred marines, had their own way of looking at houses.

"I don't like to say it, but after a while, when you have the rifle, and you see how the Iraqis look at you and how they live," said Corporal Connors, "then some of our guys feel superior—like the people in Haditha or Fallujah aren't quite human like us. You don't think of them the same way. That's not right, but it does happen."

On the morning of November 19, 2005, a thirteen-man squad from

3rd Platoon was driving down a main road in four Humvees. The patrol turned a corner and—*boom!*—the fourth Humvee in the column disappeared in a red flash and a thick cloud of smoke and dust. A popular lance corporal, Miguel "T.J." Terrazas, was killed—ripped apart—and two other marines were badly burned.

Back at battalion headquarters, streaming video from an Unmanned Aerial Vehicle circling overhead showed a confused situation, with marines at various locations maneuvering amid radio chatter indicating incoming fire. The remaining ten men in Terrazas's squad approached a car that had stopped nearby. The five men in the car were shot and killed, allegedly when they tried to run away. The squad leader later reported that his men took fire from a nearby house. The squad assaulted first one house, and then a second. Over the course of four hours, fourteen Iraqi men, four women, and six children were killed in three separate but related incidents.

Marine commanders from the company to the division level accepted without questions a garbled report about civilians killed in a melee. In the markets the next day, warnings flew that the Americans were retaliating for roadside bombings, and for the next several weeks IED attacks dropped off. Iraqis, including captured insurgents, kept insisting to marine officers that civilians had been executed. The marines claimed they were following the rules of engagement for clearing rooms when under fire.

The ROE stipulated the circumstances under which a soldier may employ deadly force. In the Fallujah battle, Battalion 3-1 was fighting so fiercely that reporters referred to the ROE as "Enter every room with a *boom*." But in Haditha, unlike Fallujah, there wasn't fierce fighting and there were civilians in the rooms.

General Casey ordered two investigations, one into the killings themselves and another into whether the chain of command had been negligent in determining what had happened. In March, *Time* magazine reported the killings and the ongoing investigations. The story was solid and balanced. The reporter, Tim McGirk, refrained from casting aspersions or reaching conclusions about guilt. Marine generals went to Capitol Hill in May to alert the key committees.

THE RESPONSE

After being briefed, Representative John Murtha held his world-famous press conference. "They killed innocent civilians in cold blood. They actually went into the houses and killed women and children,"

Murtha thundered. "But I will not excuse murder. And this is what happened. There's no question in my mind about it."

As a leading advocate for an immediate withdrawal from Iraq, Murtha advanced his own agenda by acting as judge and jury. Instead of cautioning restraint, other politicians opposed to the war attested to Murtha's credibility. "What I know is here is a guy who served our country," Senator Barack Obama said. "I would never second guess John Murtha . . . he's somebody who knows of which he speaks."

Murtha typified the type of politician the mainstream press ordinarily despised—a man who flouted his power, cut backroom deals, and inserted earmarks into appropriations bills that funneled hundreds of millions to special interests, while receiving campaign contributions from those interests that assured his reelection and perpetuated pork barrel politics. Murtha abused his office as chairman of the Defense Subcommittee on Appropriations by slipping into the 2009 defense bill $176 million in earmarks—a record in the House. Instead of excoriating Murtha for sleazy politics, the mainstream press deified him because it suited their purposes. By burnishing the label of "Vietnam veteran" and gushing about medals awarded for vague wounds and even vaguer acts of courage, the press enshrined Murtha, thus adding gravitas to his charge of cold-blooded murder. Haditha was presented as the totem for the moral degeneration of American youths thrust into an immoral war. "We've, frankly, been there so long that we're going to see quite a few of these [Haditha] incidents," Senator Carl Levin said.

European and American columnists gloatingly linked Haditha to My Lai. In *Newsweek* magazine, the columnist Eleanor Clift wrote her own obituary for the war: "Members of Kilo Company apparently didn't attempt to distinguish between enemies and innocents . . . killing as many as 24 civilians in cold blood. The systematic execution of civilians, including women and children, evoked memories of Vietnam, another war that had soured."

By any measure, the Americans in Iraq had been restrained in applying firepower. An article in *Foreign Affairs* estimated that American firepower inflicted nine times fewer civilian casualties in Iraq than during the Vietnam War. But such careful analysis counted for nothing. Senator Harry Reid (D-NV) chose to link Haditha to Abu Ghraib, besmirching the troops while seeming to praise them. "Raging in Iraq is an intractable war," Reid said. "Our soldiers are fighting valiantly, but we have Abu Ghraib and Haditha—where 24 or more civilians were allegedly killed by our own." Having singled out two misdeeds in three years of warfare, Reid recommended the solution: congressional hearings. "During the Clinton years, the House Government Reforms Committee issued 1,052 subpoenas," Reid said. "How many do you think they've [the Republicans] issued regarding Abu Ghraib or Haditha? Zero." While forty investigators were drawing up court-martial charges against a dozen marines, Reid's contribution as the leader of the Senate was to recommend a circus.

INDIVIDUAL CONSEQUENCES

The tactics at Haditha were a disgrace to the Marine Corps. Due to execrable leadership, a squad that had fought valiantly in Fallujah acted like a street gang, recklessly shooting and pitching grenades, failing to tend to those they had wounded and killed, heedlessly bounding among houses, entering rooms without backup, endangering themselves and civilians, and tragically killing women and children.

To any trained infantryman, the conduct was inexcusable. After a four-hour battle inside a dingy house with cement walls and dirt floors, Cpl. Timothy Connors had killed Omar Hadid, the commander of the insurgents in Fallujah. A veteran of a dozen fights inside houses, Connors was at a loss to explain Haditha. "I can't understand it," he said. "That's not how we were trained and that's not what my squad would ever do."

Inexorably, the mills of American military justice ground exceeding fine. Investigating officers with decades of command experience reviewed the evidence against each squad member and the officers above them. The tactics and the command leadership were faulted. One by one, preliminary trials roughly equivalent to grand juries proceeded, with the press reporting the testimony of each witness. What emerged was a tableau of mass confusion and chaos, not of cold-blooded calculation. Four cases proceeded to court-martial on charges that included dereliction of duty resulting in negligent homicide.

Empathy should not cloud judgment or excuse wrongdoing. To kill a child by firing blindly or, in a rage, to execute unarmed men and women is a criminal act meriting punishment and dishonor. But the world of an infantryman is unlike any other, and a soldier's motivations in battle are hard to judge from the outside looking in, despite Murtha's conclusion to the opposite.

Civilian casualties were accepted as inevitable in high-tech, standoff warfare. President Bush initiated the war in 2003 by authorizing a massive air strike against Dora Farms, outside Baghdad, because one CIA agent said Saddam was there. Civilians were injured and killed; Saddam was not there. In 2006, Israeli aircraft bombed a housing complex, because Hezbollah rockets were believed to be there. Thirty-seven children died in that bombing.

The infantryman does not stand off. The grunt must make instant, difficult choices in the heat of battle. He opens the door, enters the house, and, like Sergeant Norwood, is often posthumously praised. He must resist the sin of wrath when fighting an enemy who hides among compliant civilians. Those of higher rank must resist the sin of pride, lest they act impulsively in ordering air attacks because they are far removed from the gore of battle.

The military historian Max Boot has written, "The most important military unit in the emergence of modern states was the humble infantryman." But beginning after Vietnam, the Pentagon neglected the infantry, believing that high technology would win wars. By 2006, American forces had more combat aircraft than infantry squads, and more combat pilots than squad leaders. Of all who served our country, the humble foot soldiers sacrificed the most for the rest of us. Fully 75 percent of Army and Marine infantry leave the military after their four-year tours. They receive no pension, a tiny educational stipend, and no transferable skills.

They had each other; they were their own tribe. General Casey told me that he talked to dozens of soldiers about Haditha. "Universally," he said, "they told me, 'We hope our brothers get a fair shake.' "

All they wanted—all they took away with them after four years—was praise for their valor and service. They wanted to be able to say, "I served at Fallujah, or Mosul, or Baghdad," and be respected for their dedication. The publicity heaped on Haditha unfairly tainted that recognition.

CORPORATE ACCOUNTABILITY

General Mattis was the senior review officer. He was blunt about what he expected. "We have teams to assess incidents," he told me. "All commanders know to call on those teams immediately and to be clear about the ethical framework. No matter how provoked, a marine has to suck it up, stay friendly one minute longer and not turn into a racist. The goal is to diminish the enemy, not to recruit for him."

The Marines punished from the top down. The general in charge of the division and the regimental colonel who seemed sure to make general received letters of censure, finishing their careers. The battalion commander faced court-martial for dereliction of duty.

The larger corporate failure, though, lay at the strategic level. Haditha had degenerated due to a lack of security manpower, both American and Iraqi. In 2004 the insurgency had grown in Anbar when troops were shifted to Fallujah. The hardened veterans of Fallujah were then sent into Haditha to operate in isolation because no Iraqi forces were available. Senior commanders left our squads to fight alone for too long on what Mattis called "a morally bruising battlefield."

In a war fought to minimize casualties, there was scant interaction between the American units and the Iraqi people. Americans looked like RoboCops, often riding past in armored vehicles with bulletproof windows firmly shut. No people like an occupying army. In 2005, 60 percent of Iraqis believed the American presence was hurting rather than improving security. You can't be separate from the people and provide security for them.

The U.S. Army conducted a survey that showed 40 percent of the soldiers disliked the Iraqis and 38 percent believed they did not have to treat them with respect. (A similar survey in 1968 showed the American troops had a lower opinion of the Vietnamese.) At one time or another, most front-line units broke down doors, terrified sleeping families on raids on the wrong house, screamed at drivers to get off the road, fired randomly in response to an IED explosion, and so forth. Every squad had a few bullies who pushed Iraqis around; many platoons had moments of fear when they sprayed bullets carelessly; every company conducted sweeps that disrupted and antagonized entire neighborhoods.

Successively over the years, the frequency of such crass incidents lessened. The mark of an ethical institution is that it corrects its mistakes not because of outside pressure, but because it's the right thing to do. In General Casey's words, "Don't be kinetic." Mattis insisted all marines undergo cultural training. Lt. Gen. Chiarelli hammered on the need for restraint at checkpoints, despite the danger of a suicide bomber. As a result, shootings of Iraqi drivers dropped dramatically. Maj. Gen. Walt Gaskin, a division commander, distributed a plastic checklist to all 20,000 troops in his command. Rule #1: First, Do No Harm. The U.S. Army ran the most advanced trauma hospital in the world in Baghdad; more than half the casualties treated were Iraqis, including many with injuries unrelated to any coalition action.

PRESS ACCOUNTABILITY

The press devoted more attention, by orders of magnitude, to Haditha than to any other incident in five years of war. The press and the politicians used each other. Murtha became a household name.

Journalists are not cheerleaders. The press was called the Fourth Estate because it had a duty to report what the government would withhold. The tone and torrent of the Haditha stories, though, crossed the line. When exhaustive investigations did not support the charge of cold-blooded murder, the press slunk away—burying Haditha in one-paragraph stories. Nor, having built Murtha into an icon, did the press hold him to account for his reckless charge and self-serving political agenda. When the Marines changed tactics in Haditha, the press provided no follow-up story to provide context.

The trouble was not the military justice system. We will never know beyond a reasonable doubt what occurred. The trouble was that Haditha was used as a weapon in "the loud public debate on the deployment of the U.S. military," transforming a tragedy into a metaphor. *Time* even entitled a story "Who Will Be Punished for Haditha?"

THE EFFECT ON NATIONAL VALUES

No army fighting an insurgency ever performed with more honor and self-imposed restraint. In Iraq, the coalition imposed rules of engagement and rigors of self-criticism without parallel in a savage war where the enemy survived by hiding in civilian clothes.

There were no heroes from Iraq, because neither the press nor the administration brought them to the fore. Inside the Marine Corps, the best-known hero was 1st Sgt. Brad Kasal, seen on a thousand posters walking out of the House from Hell soaked in blood, pistol in hand. On Google, there were 700,000 returns for the query *killings at Haditha*. There were 30,000 for *Kasal*. The killings at Haditha were twenty times better known than the valor at Fallujah.

The hype lavished on Haditha showed the dark side of America in the twenty-first century. The wartime balance between errors and valor has shifted tremendously since World War II, when 161 American soldiers were executed for crimes such as rape and murder, and soldiers had to witness public hangings as a means of spreading the word. Had politicians such as Murtha and the press covered dozens of hangings with the outrage applied to Haditha, we would pay no reverence to "the greatest generation." The press and the politicians do not determine what we think, but they do determine what is presented to us to think about, and how much attention is given to a story.

The attention heaped upon Haditha should trouble our society. When a single deed of tragic negligence receives vastly more attention than a hundred deeds of valor, the country is diminished. Courage,

Aristotle wrote, is the virtue that makes all other virtues possible. We depend on volunteers to man our thin red line. By the tone of our criticisms, we can undercut our own martial resolve. If we as a nation lose heart, who will fight for us? When valor has no champion, America loses.

ELEVEN

A FLAWED ASSESSMENT

MID-2006

Iraq wasn't going well for President Bush at midyear. His approval rating on the handling of the war had sunk to 32 percent. The attacks by the Democrats were relentless. The intensity of the press stories about Haditha, combined with some other reports of murder, had shaken the public's faith in the decency of the American fighting man. That fed into a desire to bring them home rather than place them in morally wrenching situations.

Anbar, the fiercest battleground, had not improved. Ramadi was a slugfest, while assassinations plagued Fallujah. About sixty to a hundred foreign fighters and suicide volunteers were again slithering down the ratline from Syria each month, hop-scotching from city to city along the Euphrates before slipping into the farmlands southwest of Baghdad. There they would lie low until a car was packed with bombs and they were sent into the capital to murder civilians.

Baghdad, as the heart of Iraq, was a more serious problem than Anbar. Whether called a civil war or something else, most of the sectarian violence was happening in and around the city. The Shiite death squads were firebombing Sunni neighborhoods, systematically driving out the residents. Al Qaeda cells were infiltrating into the city from the west, assuring the Sunnis that they would protect them. At first it seemed that sectarian casualties and incidents—executions and bombings—had substantially decreased between April and May according to initial coalition figures. But the decrease didn't hold up when later checked by *The New York Times*. Despite Operation Scales of Justice, sectarian violence in Baghdad was five times higher than before the Samarra bombing in February.

American fatalities had averaged sixty a month in 2005. They dipped at the beginning of 2006, and then pushed past seventy in April and May. Casey explained in a memo to the secretary of defense and the president that 13 percent of the casualties occurred in the course of the thousands of daily convoys hauling food, supplies, and troops throughout Iraq. Convoys moved with the precision and protection of naval armadas on the main highways—the Main Supply Routes, or MSRs—which were constantly swept.

Seventy percent of American casualties—most caused by roadside bombs—occurred on offensive patrols in contested areas. Consolidating to fewer FOBs and moving out of urban areas did not decrease the number of casualties if Americans still went back to the neighborhoods occupied by insurgents. The soldiers would have a longer commute, but eventually be exposed to the same level of danger. Only when the Iraqi Army took the lead did American casualties decrease (by 17 percent), while Iraqi casualties increased by 25 percent. The message was clear—get the Iraqis in the lead.

The president, obviously concerned, had called for a meeting at Camp David with his top advisers in the second week in June. Joining in by televideo, Casey was cautiously upbeat, observing that "the broad strategy was about right." The week before, Zarqawi had been tracked down and killed in a farmhouse northeast of Baghdad, due to the skill of the CIA, Jordanian intelligence, and Special Operations Forces. Prior to speaking with the president, Casey had breakfast with Chiarelli and his division commanders. They told him they had enough forces to train and put the Iraqi Army in the lead, but not enough to hold Iraqi cities with U.S. troops. Casey asked if any commander objected to "offramping" from fifteen to thirteen brigades over the next several months. There were no objections. Backed by Khalilzad, Casey recommended accepting "the risk of putting the Iraqis in the lead," while gradually moving U.S. forces out of the cities once Baghdad settled down.

In view of al Qaeda's grip in Anbar and the continuous sectarian killings in Baghdad, this seemed remarkably upbeat. Casey was relying on the leadership of the new Iraqi government. After clinging to power and ignoring the deterioration in the country, Prime Minister Jaafari was forced out in April when Ayatollah Sistani turned against him. The new prime minister, Nouri al-Maliki, had been elected by one vote in the Assembly. A little-known member of the Dawa Party who had lived in Iran for twenty years, Maliki assured Casey and Khalilzad that he was a nationalist.

Under the ill-conceived U.S.-U.N. political structure, ministries were apportioned according to the proportion of votes cast for different parties. Like his two predecessors, Maliki inherited a cabinet over which he had limited control. But the Defense and Interior Ministries seemed capably led, while Maliki said he was determined to put an end to the sectarian killings in Baghdad and reach a settlement with the Sunnis.

A striking factor about the war was the openness of the U.S. military staffs. In Vietnam, General Westmoreland and his staff were accused of presenting only optimistic data and withholding the rest from both Washington and the press. In Iraq, reporters were routinely allowed to sit in on briefings. Casey was not outgoing, but he was matter-of-fact. Every morning, he and Chiarelli met with the enormous staff for what was called the BUA, or Battlefield Update Assessment. Each staff section would present PowerPoint slides filled with mind-numbing data about enemy activity, significant events, electricity and fuel consumption, Iraqi politics, and so on. The BUA was seen simultaneously at a dozen bases and agencies in the States, with the latest data widely shared.

At a Camp David meeting in June, the grim numbers were there for everyone to see: 6,000 insurgents killed and 12,000 imprisoned in the past two years. Yet the insurgency had regenerated, with its numbers estimated between 12,000 and 20,000. A war of attrition had not worked. Momentum had been lost when it had taken half a year to form a new government. The CIA was pessimistic that the new government would pull it together. In May, there had been 3,200 attacks countrywide, a record number. Murders had risen from 453 in January of 2006 to 1,422 in May. The Iraqi security forces were expected to protect the population, with the United States transitioning to support and "allowing the Iraqis to make mistakes."

After listening to Casey, Bush had lunch on June 12 with a few knowledgeable civilians from outside the administration. Eliot Cohen, a military historian with a son serving in Iraq, said it was time to look for new leadership. In past wars, presidents had gone through many generals before finding one whose leadership and vision fitted the president's desires. The president was the commander-in-chief, Cohen argued, and he should select the generals he wanted, not leave it to anyone else. Bestselling author Robert Kaplan advised that U.S. soldiers protect the population 24/7. Fred Kagan, a historian with good contacts in the Army, urged sending more troops to Baghdad.

The president was more impressed by the advice than he indicated at the time (Cohen later joined the administration and Kagan became a key adviser). That afternoon, Bush slipped away secretly and the next day showed up in Baghdad, where Maliki was being sworn in. Meeting afterward with American soldiers, Bush said, "I have come to not only thank you, but to look Prime Minister Maliki in the eyes—to determine whether or not he is as dedicated to a free Iraq as you are, and I believe he is."

The CIA employs psychoanalysts to assess when a man is lying by observing his facial expressions. It is, however, an inexact science. Some presidents, like Lincoln and Franklin Roosevelt, understood the strategic details and risks entailed in the wars they commanded. Bush disdained even reading newspapers, which provided more context and detail than did staff papers. In the White House, details were for staffs. For Bush, what counted was taking the measure of a man's character based on a short meeting, although looking into a man's eyes hadn't worked out well in evaluating Vladimir Putin.

Things didn't work out well in Baghdad either. In the first two weeks in June, there had been an average of one vehicle or suicide bomber a day, claiming two or three victims. While the president was in Baghdad on June 13, there were four car bombings that killed sixteen, plus four mortar attacks.

Operation Scales of Justice had failed to reduce the sectarian violence. The Multi-National Force staffs in Baghdad were recording 600 to 1,000 patrols a day inside the city, most being reported by Iraqi forces that could not be trusted. The 22,000 local police were at best useless and at worst complicit in the actions of the Shiite death squads. The 9,000 National Police were duplicitous. The 11,000 soldiers of the Iraqi Army were more reliable, but manned checkpoints and eschewed active patrolling.

Bases in Baghdad had shrunk from thirty-six in 2003 to eight in mid-2006, with five in support of patrolling. Eleven battalions drove to work in the city, averaging twenty-five patrols per day. By comparison, battalions in Vietnam averaged forty patrols per day, but took more casualties. The larger, mostly mounted patrols in the Baghdad environs resulted in fewer casualties, but also less presence among the people.

In mid-June, Scales of Justice ended, having been criticized for spreading inadequate forces citywide. Chiarelli promptly launched Operation Together Forward, focusing the U.S. and Iraqi soldiers in high-risk Sunni areas, with the police expected to hold the more permissive Shiite areas. Casey held a press conference, noting that this was the third corps commander and staff he had seen rotate through Iraq and stressing that the "new government of national unity" was implementing "a vigorous security plan for Baghdad," intended to extend over several months.

"I'm confident," Casey said, "that we will be able to continue to take reductions over the course of the year."

The next day, al Qaeda in Iraq launched five suicide bombing attacks inside Baghdad, killing twenty-eight Shiites. Casey shelved his plan to pull another American brigade out of Iraq.

"Maliki said the right things in taking over," Casey said. "We seemed to have his goodwill. We had gotten Zarqawi. I told the president it was looking good and that my commanders had enough [troops] for transition—but not to do it themselves. Then, holy shit!, the AQI [al Qaeda in Iraq] bombings hit. Maliki and his government were not ready to do a thing. He froze, but he wouldn't let go of the army."

The Baghdad coroner's office reported 1,600 bodies in June. A higher rate was reported in early July. Although over the past four weeks Maliki had issued eight separate policy pronouncements about the new Baghdad Security Plan, few additional Iraqi forces had flowed into the capital, despite his promises, and the advisers to the 13,000 National Police assigned to the capital were turning in highly negative assessments. Casey shelved the Multi-National Force plan to reduce from fifteen to thirteen brigades. "I'm not comfortable sending these troops home," he told General Peter Pace. (When Myers retired in late 2005, Pace became chairman of the Joint Chiefs of Staff.)

Skeptical of Maliki's sincerity, Casey reviewed the situation on July 10 with his staff, saying he did not think "the new Iraqi leadership really understood what it takes to execute this kind of comprehensive plan." He was particularly frustrated because violence was down where the United States had taken the lead in predominantly Sunni areas, while Iraqi forces, in the lead in Shiite areas, had not reined in the death squads.

Disturbed by the persistence of the violence in Baghdad, the president quietly asked General Pace for an independent assessment. As the chairman of the Joint Chiefs of Staff, Pace was the principal military adviser to the president and controlled the Joint Staff, comprised of 1,200 bright military officers accustomed to punctilious staff procedures and layers of coordination to ensure that the equities of the Army, Navy, Air Force, and Marines and the theater commanders (Europe, Africa, the Pacific, Central Command, and the like) were protected. Inside the Joint Staff, Pace put together a small study group from the four services, led by a Navy captain. Although the group included some like McMaster with hands-on experience and iconoclastic views, the group was weighted down by tendentious bureaucratic procedures that defied rapid analysis and decision making. While the Pace review proceeded at the pace of a state funeral, Baghdad continued to deteriorate.

In the States, preliminary partisan skirmishing had begun in anticipation of the midterm congressional elections to be held in November, with attention drawn to Connecticut, where Senator Joseph Lieberman, the Democratic vice presidential candidate in 2000, faced strenuous opposition from the liberal wing of his party because he supported the war. A CNN poll found that 80 percent of Democrats in his state opposed the war. President Bush invited Maliki to Washington, where in late July of 2006 he addressed a joint session of Congress, promising reconciliation with the Sunnis, honest government, services for the people, and an increase in trained Iraqi forces to replace the Americans. Democratic senators dismissed his assurances, which were reported in a ho-hum fashion by the mainstream press. Maliki left Washington having said nothing to change attitudes one way or the other.

The belts around Baghdad had virtually no presence of either U.S. or Iraqi forces. The southwest approach was the staging ground for car bombs and suicide bombers. From Arab Jabour on the Tigris west through what was called the Triangle of Death to the Abu Ghraib district adjoining Anbar Province, terrorists enjoyed a vast sanctuary. Inside Baghdad, al Qaeda disciples sneaked into Shiite neighborhoods to bomb unsuspecting civilians during the day. At night, Shiite militia groups firebombed Sunni neighborhoods, gradually extending their influence and becoming the de facto government inside the city. Maliki, though pressed by Khalilzad and Casey, refused to take decisive action against the Jesh al Mahdi. Despite that, Casey remained determined to push Maliki and his commanders into the lead, letting them make mistakes until they learned.

In mid-August, Chiarelli initiated Operation Together Forward II, with 15,000 U.S. soldiers in four brigades, plus 10,000 Iraqi soldiers and 37,000 police—at least on paper rosters or promised to deploy. Most of the National Police were pulled out of the city for retraining, and their commanders were relieved. As before, the operation proceeded with U.S. forces clearing neighborhoods and police expected to then move in and protect the residents. Two new wrinkles were Maliki's ambiguous verbal agreement to isolate Sadr City in order to restrict the death squads and the deployment of concrete barriers to restrict vehicles and reduce the blast impact of car bombs.

The initial results in August mirrored July. When the Americans moved in, violence dropped; when they moved out and were replaced by police, violence resumed. Ambassador Khalilzad wrote an op-ed in *The Wall Street Journal,* acknowledging that Iraqis were "being subjected to unacceptable levels of fear and violence" and warning that the "Battle for Baghdad will determine the future of Iraq." When Rumsfeld and Abizaid testified before the Senate regarding appropriations for Iraq, Senator McCain bore in on the secretary of defense, arguing that there weren't enough troops to curtail the violence.

The Democratic senators were unanimous in declaiming the effort as failing, repeatedly citing Lt. Gen. Chiarelli, who said, "In 29 years, I had never trained to stop a civil war." This seemed an odd statement. The Sunni resistance and al Qaeda had been fighting Americans for years, and their lairs in the city were well known, while burned-out houses marked the front lines as the Shiite death squads advanced night after night. Because the Shiite militias were moving by cars in small groups, to halt their advance did require posting U.S. soldiers twenty-four hours a day in key neighborhoods. While that tactic meant moving off the FOBs, it didn't require new training. U.S. soldiers were well trained to fight armed gangs.

In mid-spring, Congress had appointed the Iraq Study Group, comprised of twelve distinguished Americans, Democrats and Republicans, to assess alternative strategies. When several members visited Baghdad in August, according to *The New York Times Magazine,* Chiarelli told them that without more American troops, he couldn't hold the city, although why the troops already in Baghdad remained on the FOBs was not discussed. Rumsfeld insisted he had not received a request for more troops from Abizaid, Casey, or Chiarelli—and he was in constant touch with all three.

Conditions appeared equally dire in Anbar. While 33 percent of American fatalities in 2006 were in and around Baghdad, fully 45 percent occurred in Anbar. In mid-August, Maj. Gen. Richard Zilmer, the top commander in Anbar, made clear that the American mission was to support the Iraqi forces and hand the war off to them, not to win it. "If there is seen a larger role for coalition forces out here to *win* [emphasis added] that insurgency fight," Zilmer said, "then that is going to change the metrics of what we need out here. . . . We cannot win the insurgency."

The next day, Tony Snow, the president's spokesman, rebuked Zilmer, insisting that the mission from the president was indeed to win. "He has made it absolutely clear to generals that the job is to win," he said, "and the first thing you have to do is, to the best of your ability, cut through the fog of war and tell him what the situation is and what they need to get the job done."

President Bush remained committed to the Kissinger thesis—Don't yield an inch and insist on victory. The president said the goal was to win, and the generals said it was not to win. The fog of war got thicker the next day, when General Pace, the chairman of the Joint Chiefs of Staff, backed Zilmer and rejected the option of increasing U.S. forces.

"The current force [133,000] is the right size for the training mission," Pace said. "More US and coalition forces could get the job done quicker, but that would mean dependency much longer for the Iraqi armed forces and the Iraqi government."

So which was it—win by sending in more American soldiers, or withdraw Americans and put the Iraqis in the lead without winning? Due to the fog of Washington rather than the fog of war, the administration lacked a coherent military strategy.

TWELVE

AL QAEDA: MURDER AND INTIMIDATION

FALL 2006

FALLUJAH REGRESSES

In October, on my sixth trip to Fallujah, I checked in with Lt. Col. Chris Landro, who commanded the 1st Battalion of the 25th Marine Regiment. After seven months of fighting, he was cynical about claims of progress. During the summer, the new government had released 700 prisoners into the city, many of whom had fought in the battle for Fallujah. Since then, snipers had killed three marines, local informers had clammed up, and roadside bombings had increased.

"In this city, al Qaeda has a secret police and assassination squad," Landro said. "The police have no prison here in Anbar. They turn a prisoner over to us or send him to Baghdad, and Baghdad doesn't want them. We need a new model—one that doesn't let detainees come back and kill those who sent them away."

As on a prior visit, I stayed at the company outpost downtown, with Maj. Vaughn Ward. "We don't go into the market like we did when you were last here," Ward said. "They hit us from the upper stories of the buildings. We take a Humvee with a.50-caliber on every patrol, and we don't walk down the streets. Some of those pricks who were released from Cropper [a U.S. prison] can shoot."

When Ward got a tip on a cell phone about an IED, he waited until it was dark. Then he moved out with two small units, in case one was hit. We rode at a snail's pace through the deserted streets, the marines warily scoping out each trash heap through their night vision goggles while an engineer team blew the IED in place.

"We find an IED every day," Ward said. "Lost a marine to a sniper on this street last week. If we pulled out, al Qaeda would take over. We don't know who they are. It's like holding water in your hand."

Kyle Westin, the State Department diplomat who had lived in Fallujah for two years, thought the Marines were caught on a treadmill. "The status quo isn't working," he said. "Baghdad gives nothing to Anbar. The people don't have hope. The police go without pay and wear ski masks to stay alive."

Relationships with the police had steadily improved over the months, but about half the imams still railed against "infidel occupiers" in their Friday sermons at the mosques. The police and Iraqi Army blamed each other for inaction, but both avoided the most dangerous areas like the Jolan market, leaving the marines to patrol alone. If a jundi or policeman was killed, at best the grieving family received skimpy compensation. Even after two years, the marines couldn't take the final step of pulling out and turning security over to the Iraqis.

The top commander in the city, Col. Larry Nicholson, kept exhorting the city council to take a stand. "We aren't going to fight for you forever," Nicholson said. "You have to help your own police. Tell them who the irahibeen [terrorists] are."

Brave Iraqis did step forward. In February, the council chairman was killed. In June, the newspaper editor was shot in the head. The popular deputy police chief was murdered. In August, the police chief moved to a safer job in Baghdad. When Baghdad is considered safer, you know you live in a bad neighborhood. When the police arrested two men for murder in August, a judge dismissed the charges and hastily left town. In protest, half the police force walked off the job for several days. Brig. Gen. Robert Neller sent a blistering memo to the command in Baghdad, demanding a halt to the constant catch and release of insurgents.

The six entry control points to the city were flooded with thousands of people coming and going every day. Technically, all males were supposed to have iris scans and fingerprint checks. The American biometric system, though, was convoluted. A marine on patrol had no way of easily checking an ID card, and forgeries were rife.

As I did on each visit, I checked in with "Sammy J," a twenty-eight-year-old interpreter, or terp, from Baghdad (the jihadists search the Internet for the real names of translators) who had come to Fallujah in 2003 with the 82nd Airborne and had stayed with seven different U.S. battalions since. He had his own room in the barracks. Sammy occasionally got on the loudspeaker system mounted in a psyops Humvee and cursed the insurgents. Marines suggested the filthiest insults they could think of and Sammy would scream them at 140 dB.

"When I go home, I lie about how I earn money," he said. "The police would betray me. So would my neighbors. Americans are my only friends. If I went to the market here, I'd be killed. This city has an insurgent council and about six or seven groups. Only one is al Qaeda hard-core. The rest are locals. The shop owners know who they are."

Between March and September of 2006, Charlie Company detained 120 suspects. Twenty-four were sent to prison. The rest walked free due to insufficient evidence. To imprison twenty-four while releasing 700 prisoners, Colonel Nicholson said, was "outrageous." Many of those released kept their prisoner bracelets in their wallets for bragging rights when they walked through the souk.

The Marine battalion and its partner Iraqi battalion arrested about twenty a month; the police arrested seven a month. "I'll put it to you straight," Ralph Morton, a chief detective on leave from the Los Angeles Police Department to instruct the Marines, said. "No police chief in the States could keep his job with the poor arrest rates of the police in this country."

Nicholson understood their reluctance. "They have to stay alive," Nicholson said. "Kassim, the acting chief, has told his men to sleep in the barracks. You can't be a decent cop and go home at night. You'll die."

I'd known Kassim since the first battle for Fallujah in April of 2004. Tall and trim, he always wore a pressed uniform and an unthreatening expression. His men liked him and he worked at keeping good terms across the city, a trait that mildly concerned the Marines. His son, a junior officer on the force, eagerly joined the Marines on raids and Kassim unhesitatingly went after foreign terrorists—he'd just jailed four Saudis. But he seemed vague about local insurgents. I asked him about the mood in the city.

"Bad," he said.

Fear hung like a fog over the city. Everyone was waiting for someone else to lead. It was maddening. Nicholson pointed out the irony—

residents shrugged when terrorists killed his marines, yet expected the Marines to prevent terrorists from again taking over the city.

CHASING GHOSTS IN HABBANIYAH

Ramadi and Fallujah were separated by thirty miles of riverside farm-lands in the district of Habbaniyah. The effluvial richness of the Eu-phrates supported vast, flat tracts of lush undergrowth and smooth fields for easy farming. The crop fields were divided by rows of palm trees that shielded the farmhouses from prying eyes, while the irriga-tion ditches prevented the quick arrival of armored vehicles. Highway Michigan provided a straight path near the Euphrates from Fallujah to Ramadi, but had been closed for a year due to IEDs, forcing the farm-ers to make a 130-kilometer detour and tripling transportation costs. Due to soaring fuel costs, people were cutting down trees to burn when winter came.

Violence would continue to bubble in Fallujah and Ramadi as long as insurgents controlled the Habbaniyah corridor. It was standard guerrilla doctrine to slowly encircle the cities by building up strength in the surrounding belts of villages where the vegetation provided excel-lent concealment. Seventy years ago, Mao Zedong had urged guerrillas to attack the cities from the countryside. Fidel Castro glorified his march in 1960 from the Sierra Madre into downtown Havana. The major assault against Ramadi in 2004 had come from the Sofia farm-lands to the west.

Inside the cities, al Qaeda in Iraq had to be always on guard, lest someone in an adjoining apartment betray them. It was safer for the leaders, bomb makers, and top-of-the-line assassins to live in the farm-lands, making forays or suicide bombing runs into the cities after care-ful planning.

Lt. Col. Todd DesGrossiers commanded the 3rd Battalion of the 2nd Marines in Habbaniyah in the summer of 2006. I had first met him in Fallujah, where he won the Silver Star for blasting insurgents at point-blank range. In Habbaniyah, his battalion was trying to open up Route Michigan, where the shell-pocked buildings along the highway testified to years of hard fighting.

No Sunni police or Iraqi soldiers were partnered with Battalion 3-2, and few interpreters. Thirteen platoons lived in separate outposts in the villages and palm groves along thirty kilometers of highway. An out-post consisted of a two-story concrete house surrounded by barbed wire, with a generator, an outdoor shower stall, Internet connections, a refrigerator, a microwave, cots, and MREs. Each platoon sent out five foot patrols a day to control about six square kilometers.

In Kilo Company's sector, the terrain and the smells reminded me of patrolling in Vietnam, except now the grunts had to wear heavy armor as they wandered through backyards and across paddy dikes, shooing aside cows and glancing at men slaughtering sheep and women baking bread in large outdoor clay ovens. The patrol patterns were similar to Vietnam—tactically sound formations, scant talk, varying routes, desultory peeks into houses, cryptic greetings exchanged with incurious villagers.

A squad from Kilo pointed to a section of thick bulrushes. Three IEDs had been set off under the dense foliage. Finally, through a long-range telescope the marines spotted a one-armed man emerge from the weeds, dragging a long length of electrical wire that he hid in a garbage heap. He then mingled among some shoppers at a roadside market only a few yards away. A patrol ran down the road and grabbed him. Startled, he blurted out, How did you pick me out of the crowd? The marines loved telling that story.

Most rural locales in Iraq were like Habbaniyah. Every few days, some rounds would snap by, or an IED would explode. The battalion encountered six IEDs a day and had lost eight killed in the past seven weeks. Snipers were becoming more deadly, taking one shot, then remaining hidden among the buildings.

The Marines were keen on patrolling, given their small unit experience in Vietnam. In that war, though, the Viet Cong guerrillas moved as platoons, with their rifles ready. Since men tend to use the same routes, if you sent out enough patrols, sooner or later, you would cross paths with the guerrillas, and both sides would open fire. Of every 1,000 patrols in the I Corps area of South Vietnam in 1968, sixty made contact, resulting in fifteen enemy fatalities and one American fatality. The Viet Cong made a terrible mistake by fighting. They were gradually ground down. When the North Vietnamese seized the South, few Viet Cong guerrillas were left to share the prize.

Patrolling did not have the same result in Iraq. "They shadow us," Lt. Nathan Smith of Kilo Company said. "They know exactly where we are and where our unit boundaries are. Before they attack, they put on masks."

Standing outside the outpost, LCpl. Mason Jones pointed at a house across the canal. Three times inside a week, the Combat Outpost, or COP, had taken a few shots from the roof of the house. Exasperated, a fire team had sneaked across at three in the morning and rousted the owner out of bed. The man was trembling, but refused to say who occasionally took a shot from his roof. "You won't kill me," he said. "They will."

One day while patrolling with a platoon from Kilo, I wrote down the incidents that were typical of the nickel-and-dime counterinsurgency routine:

1. White station wagon with civilians hit by IED.
2. Scout-snipers engage AIF [Anti-Iraqi Forces] on far bank of Euphrates. Killed two.
3. SVIED [Suicide Vehicle IED] detonated prematurely on Michigan.
4. 120mm mortar shell found.
5. IED detonated near tank—mobility kill; tank towed away.
6. Three rounds of 82mm mortar exploded outside COP.

"They shoot, and we have no idea where the shot came from," LCpl. Robert Montgomery said. "It was cleaner on our last tour. On large sweeps, we had a forward line of troops and knew where we could fire. Our morale was higher then. Now we have all kinds of restrictions. It'll go on and on. They're [the enemy] invisible. It's hard to kill a ghost."

The Marines could not control Anbar because they could not identify the insurgents.

Warriors at one of Saddam's palaces (April 2003).

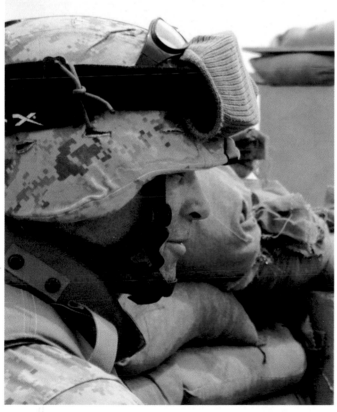

The Lion of Fallujah, Capt. Doug Zembiec, Fallujah (2004)— an American hero.

Iraqi males forced to ground outside Fallujah (April 2004).

A typical patrol in Fallujah (November 2004).

Blackwater Bridge, Fallujah (November 2004).

ABOVE: An IED as seen from inside a Humvee (below windshield wiper), Ramadi (2005). LEFT: The same IED viewed through a telescopic lens.

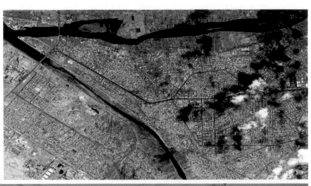

RIGHT: Ramadi
(racetrack in center).
BELOW: Why there
will never be enough
free power, Baghdad
(2006).

An apartment building in downtown Ramadi (2006).

Caring for a mortally wounded Iraqi, Ramadi (2006).

Lt. Gen. James Mattis and the author, Habbaniyah (2007).

Sheik Sattar Abu Risha in Ramadi just prior to his death (2007)—an Iraqi hero.

Police chief Farouk in Haditha with the author (2007).

The author on a burned-out Sunni block in Ghazaliyah, Baghdad (2007).
(Photograph by Chris Hondros.)

Jesh al Mahdi sentries in a Shiite neighborhood, Ghazaliyah (2007).

Deputy police chief Abdul Kareem and the author, Fallujah (2007).

Raid force from Fort Apache, Adamiyah, Baghdad (2007).

Lt. Col. Joe L'Etoile's marines in combat in the Zidon (2007).

ABOVE: Outraged survivors of a suicide bombing, Rusafa, Baghdad (2007). LEFT: Col. Ahmed Sharki and Lt. Col. William Jurney, Ramadi (2007).

"Alex," an interpreter who left Iraq to join the Marines, in Habbaniyah (2007).

Abu Abid, the insurgent leader who drove al Qaeda from Amariyah, Baghdad (2007).

In 2004, al Qaeda in Iraq began at this bloody police station wall in Fallujah (2008). LEFT: IED hit on Lt. Col. Keith Barclay's recon, Mosul (2008).

General David Petraeus
in Fallujah (2008).

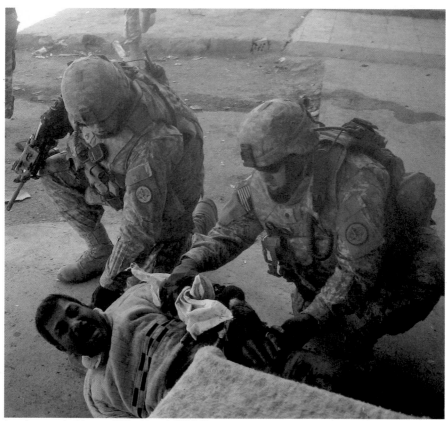

Iraqi wounded by an IED, Mosul (2008).

"Sons of Iraq" in Bayji (2008).

Lt. Col. Ken Adgie in Arab Jabour (2008).

Former insurgents, Amariyah (2008).

ABOVE: Palestine Street,
East Baghdad (2008).
LEFT: Maj. Owen West
and the author near
Baghdad (2003).

Al Qaeda in Iraq and Sunni Insurgents

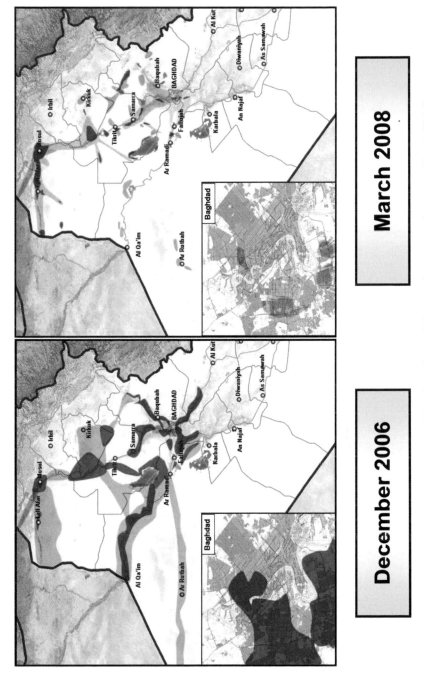

December 2006   **March 2008**

Al Qaeda in Iraq driven back (slide from General Petraeus's report to Congress, March 2008).

Provincial Iraqi Control

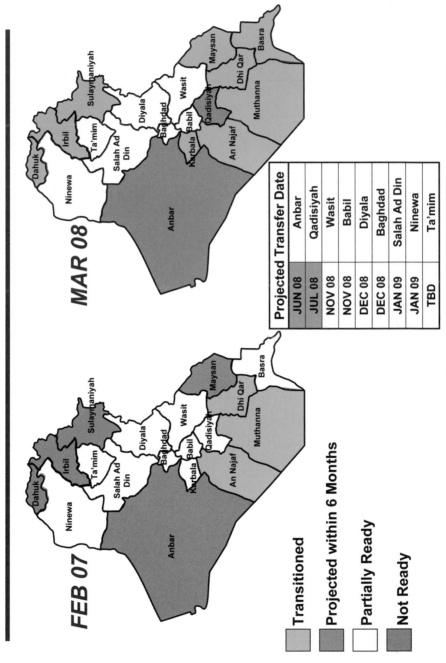

Anbar changed the complexion of the war (slide from General Petraeus's report to Congress, March 2008).

THIRTEEN

THE TURNAROUND BEGINS

FALL 2006

THE RAMADI PIVOT

In the fall of 2006, Ramadi looked like Berlin in 1945. It required an American armored convoy to get the governor to work in the morning, where he sat in a usually empty office while on the roof a .50-caliber machine gun took a daily toll of insurgents. The week before I arrived in September, the insurgents had assaulted the dingy, sandbagged Government Center. The Marines killed twenty-nine attackers, then stopped firing to allow unarmed youths to emerge from the rubble and carry off their dead.

In five visits since 2004, I had watched the American casualties climb beyond those suffered in the Fallujah battle. General Casey told me he had confidence that Col. Sean McFarland, commanding the five battalions assigned to 1st Brigade Combat Team of the 1st Armored Division, would get Ramadi under control. McFarland, who had taken over in Tal Afar from McMaster on his previous tour, was a shrewd planner. To recruit police, he had agreed to protect their families living in a tribal area northwest of the city. His energetic staff assistant, Cpt. Travis Patriquin, was meeting constantly with the sheiks. Both he and McFarland were impressed with a young, midlevel sheik named Abdul Sattar Buzaigh, also known as Abu Risha in reference to his subtribe. For eighteen months al Qaeda in Iraq—mostly Iraqis—had consolidated leadership over the Sunni insurgency by purging, in the style of Robespierre, all who questioned its authority.

In August of 2006, AQI assassinated Sheik Abu Jassim because he had urged his tribesmen to join the police. To insult the tribe, AQI dumped the body in the undergrowth, rather than return it for burial as tribal custom demanded. Sattar, whose father and two brothers had been murdered, called on the tribes to strike back. In September, McFarland and Patriquin attended a meeting of several dozen sheiks at Sattar's house a few kilometers west of Ramadi, where he proclaimed the formation of the Sawah, or Awakening Council. Media-savvy, Sattar contacted the Iraqi press in Baghdad, grandly proclaiming he had the support of twenty-five of the thirty-one tribes in Anbar, with 30,000 armed tribesmen. Sattar was expressing a hope, not a reality. Possibly six small tribes would stand with him, including the influential Sheik Fassal al-Guood, who had served as governor of the province.

McFarland had successfully organized tribes in the Tal Afar region farther to the north, and saw a similar opportunity around Ramadi. McFarland told me Sattar would help turn Ramadi around. I had heard it before. Sheiks were always promising and not delivering.

Sattar, an inspirational leader with a gift for fiery rhetoric, had vowed revenge. McFarland promised him cooperation and protected his farm compound, while quietly recruiting police from the tribes that had joined the Awakening.

Inside Ramadi, McFarland had deployed three battalions, with two more on the outskirts to cut off enemy infiltration. His intent was to employ the oil spot technique by constructing a series of combat outposts to provide local security. He suggested that, as in my prior trips, I stay downtown in the key sector assigned to Lt. Col. William Jurney, who commanded Battalion 1-6. Jurney and his battalion—the fifteenth to rotate into Ramadi—were on their second tour in Iraq.

When I stood with Jurney on the roof of the Government Center looking at shattered buildings in all directions, the view didn't inspire hope. The marines were awaiting the daily harassing attack by snipers. The battalion was averaging five small arms fights a day. Every marine had fired 700 rounds on the rifle range before deploying. There was no doubt about their marksmanship, but as Lieutenant General Chiarelli put it, "You can't kill 'em all."

The diligence of the insurgents in studying Marine tactics had impressed Jurney. The Iraqi soldiers and marines had amused themselves by building crude replicas of camera monitors and lashing them to trees, partially to deceive but also to taunt the insurgents. A week later, the insurgents left a posting on the Internet that they had cut down a camera and found nothing inside it.

Jurney was responsible for about half the city, with 585 jundis and about ninety Iraqi police on duty. Most of the police lived outside the city, protected by their own tribes. The Iraqi battalion had been there on my visit last year, but this time I heard fewer complaints about the conduct of Shiite soldiers.

Jurney was showing me through a joint security station when a fire-fight erupted down the street. A tank took a rocket hit that knocked out its electronics, but no one was seriously injured. Jurney nodded and turned his attention to his counterpart, Lt. Col. Khalied, who proudly announced that his soldiers had captured three irahibeen at a nearby TCP (Traffic Control Point). They had let 600 cars through, searching about one in eight, and had detained these three. A marine reluctantly explained that without evidence, the three would go free.

"This is your American system?" Khalied replied.

Jurney, who had a natural gift of gab with the Iraqi soldiers, explained he couldn't control what higher did with prisoners. But he could control Ramadi, and there would be no "American system." Every system, every outpost, every patrol, every operational decision would be joint—jundis, shurta (police), and marines together. When there were problems between a marine and a jundi—and there would be—the commanders would work it out together.

"In Vietnam, you worked with a Combined Action Platoon," Jurney said to me. "I have a Combined Action Battalion. People say we don't have enough troops. I say, get over it. We have more than enough Iraqis. I'm employing them side by side with my marines. We're one unit here in Ramadi."

When he got back to his own office, Jurney knelt on the floor and unfurled a large photomap. It showed four Marine positions and one small symbol of the Iraqi flag at the western end of the city—the lone police station. North of the Government Center, Jurney pointed to a broad road that looped in a prominent semicircle encompassing about fifty blocks.

"The Racetrack is the enemy's stronghold," he said, "and I'm going to own it. I'm going to constrict his freedom of movement and take the population away. Know why? Because I bring power, water, clean streets, and schools. Al Qaeda brings nothing."

I promised to come back in six months to see how far he got. Every battalion commander in Ramadi had started with a plan—all fifteen of them.

EAST OF THE SUN, WEST OF THE MOON

To look at other counterinsurgent techniques, I headed for the base at Assad, forty miles north of Ramadi. I hitched a ride in a convoy with Cpl. Benjamin Potts, twenty-two, who was driving a large truck called a 7-ton. In two months, he had logged 5,000 miles and spent twelve-hour days behind the wheel.

"I like it," he said. "I pick up tips from the old guys. They know their stuff." He pointed to a group of American truckers straight from central casting—heavyset guys with beards, ponytails, Levi's, jackets covered with patches, most chewing and spitting tobacco. Although the civilian truckers were paid $90,000, versus $18,000 for Potts, there was little friction. When the convoys were stuck overnight, the old guys shared their cabs, which had bunk beds, and pitched in to fix breakdowns.

When we rolled into Assad, after waiting half an hour for a 100-truck convoy to exit, we passed several soldiers bicycling to work from the Pizza Hut, wearing safety helmets as they pedaled past signs that warned: "Bicyclists—12 KPH [kilometers per hour]; Vehicles—24 KPH." "It's a $60 fine if you don't have a fluorescent strip on your bike," Potts said.

Welcome to life on a FOB in the middle of nowhere. On a wall map, you can cover the space from Assad to the Syrian border with the palm of your hand and you will miss nothing, because nothing is there. Assad was the supply and air base for AO (Area of Operations) Denver—a vast brown desert crisscrossed by brown wadis and a trickle of green alongside the Euphrates River. The size of South Carolina, AO Denver was, to borrow an expression from Kipling, east of the sun and west of the moon.

Controlling Denver was the responsibility of Col. Blake Crowe, who commanded four American and six Iraqi battalions, plus 2,000 police (on paper). On the ground, Crowe had to deal with half a million rebellious tribal people scattered across 33,000 square miles. When I visited Crowe and his operations officer, Lt. Col. Chris Dowling, at their headquarters, they were matter-of-fact about their mission.

"We have no judges out here, no prisons, no contact with the Baghdad government," Dowling said. "We've got tribalism, nepotism, smuggling, skimming—just like in Bosnia, and we've been there for eleven years. Our goal is to build the police. Will we succeed? We don't know what we don't know about this culture."

Dowling pointed out that in Qaim, a hundred miles northwest on the Syrian border, al Qaeda should easily have stayed in control. Yet the tribes had heaved the terrorists out.

"I don't have enough troops for the tasks out here," Crowe said. "But this isn't a shooting war; it's about police. Insurgencies grow from the bottom up. Police are locals. They know who the insurgents are. The military is a top-down organization. The colonel tells the major what to do, that sort of thing. The military is too removed, too top-down for a police war."

Most of the jundis in the 7th Division were Shiites. While Crowe wanted to recruit more Sunnis as soldiers, his first priority was building up the police.

"Plop a battalion down. Spread out the companies," Crowe said. "Recruit police, protect the people, take a census, make arrests. We understand counterinsurgency theory."

So what was the problem?

"Distances," Crowe said. "This area is huge."

THE EMERGENCE OF THE POLICE: FIRST INKLINGS

Thirty miles north of Assad, the Euphrates River meanders in a few lazy loops, creating a vast plain of fecund fields and palm groves called the Triad, named after Haditha and two smaller towns with a combined population of 85,000. The Triad was a passageway for the 100-odd foreign fighters infiltrating from Syria each month.

Baghdadi sat at the southern end of the Triad, a lonesome truck stop on a major highway around which the town of 10,000 had sprouted up, guarded by a battalion from the Iraqi 7th Division and a hundred police. In June of 2005, a dozen contractor trucks had screeched to a halt outside a small Marine outpost at the edge of the road. An Iraqi guard from the convoy stormed up to the gate, demanding ammunition to attack robbers who had just killed his brother. Given fresh weapons, he gathered up a few other Iraqis, drove off, and shot the robbers. The Marines promptly promoted Sha'ban Barzan from truck guard to police chief, with the Iraqi rank of colonel.

When I met him, he was proudly wearing the eagles that designate an American colonel. "People call me a Jew and say I work for infidels because I wear American rank," he said. "I tell them Americans do good things, takfiri [terrorists] steal, kill, and do shit. Jamil Dhahan kill that Special Forces guy. I find him and put him away."

The American advisers with me later confirmed that Jamil Dhahan, wanted for killing an American soldier, had indeed been arrested by the Baghdadi police.

"Foreign terrorists," Sha'ban said, "I kill half and put half in jail.

Go to jail six, seven months, then start again. Iraqi government send them home. I want American people to know they should stay in jail."

"Sha'ban just lost another brother. He's pissed about letting people go," Lt. Patrick Kinser, an adviser, told me. "Fifteen police recruits were gunned down outside the gate here. The poor bastards went into a restaurant for lunch. Two carloads of al Qaeda drove up, executed them, and drove off."

The police station, enclosed inside a former military camp surrounded by high walls and guard towers, had the feel of a maximum security prison. Next to the station were a soccer field, a school, and rows of town houses with air conditioners in the windows. The streets were neat, with no garbage and few cars. A few sheep and goats were wandering around the large, open fields.

"All police families live on base," Kinser said. "If they need food and haven't been paid, they stop trucks on the highway. We want them to start their own gardens. The families don't dare go to the market. A fourteen-year-old had his throat slit when he went to the market because he had been seen laughing with us Americans."

The families of the police lived in neat, 1950s-style bungalows on quiet, paved streets where the kids rode their bikes, walked a block to school, and played soccer in nearby fields. It seemed normal enough, until you looked up at the high wall with barbed wire and guard towers. They were the ones inside a prison, while the insurgents lived comfortably at home.

Pleased to have a visitor to his obscure outpost, Sha'ban exuded confidence.

"I give my police Marine rank, like corporal or sergeant," he said. "Know why? Americans stronger than takfiris. When I get all my people here, we go to town together. I recognize all takfiri. We get them."

Lieutenant Kinser explained that last year, there had been thirty-seven police in Baghdadi, and they never left the base. Now Sha'ban had 100. A few blocks away, Kinser and eight U.S. marines were living with sixty-five jundis. Another 200 police were being trained in Jordan.

"He means it," Kinser said. "Once he gets those 200 back, we're all going downtown. There'll be about 400 of us. That'll be quite a day in the market. My marines are looking forward to it. So's Sha'ban."

I hadn't expected to find such spirit at a truck stop on a road to nowhere, although the tactic made sense. Iraqis loathed patrolling. It was hard, dull, and dangerous, giving the opposition the first shot or first IED detonation. Iraqis worked gang-style, getting information on someone and rushing into a house at night with fifty guys. The more, the better. Kinser had better wait outside. When Sha'ban went through that market, he wouldn't be reading suspects their Miranda rights.

"THE RULE OF LAW"—HADITHA

From Baghdadi in late September of 2006, I caught a ride in a convoy twenty miles north to the violent city of Haditha, where the battalion commander was due to meet the police chief, after a swing through the market by the river.

"We get hit near the market every day," Capt. Matt Tracy, the company commander, told me. "So we go there every day."

Our five Humvees drove in single file past storefronts whose owners were hastily pulling down steel shutters. The street hadn't emptied of shoppers before the first shots cracked from our rear. With no room to turn, we drove on and a few seconds later someone shot at us from a palm grove off to the right. Quick as a blink, half a dozen marines tumbled out and rushed into the grove, Tracy and Lt. Col. James Donnellan, the battalion commander, among them. Wary of snipers, the marines darted from tree to tree, running through the grove. Half an hour later, they returned to their Humvees, dripping sweat from their helmets and armor. As usual, the shooters had escaped.

When we reached his combat outpost, Captain Tracy offered me a warm Coke.

"Sorry, we have no cold drinks," he said. "We had two freezers, but a prisoner died two nights ago under Iraqi police interrogation. So we shipped the body in our freezer to the States for an autopsy and investigation. Then yesterday we shot a guy running a checkpoint. He was on our wanted list, but we had to put him in our other freezer until battalion sends down an investigator. I'll use Clorox when we get our freezers back. Right now I have to deal with an angry police chief. We've been asking him how his prisoner died, and he doesn't like it."

Tracy walked outside and escorted a compact, unsmiling Lieutenant Colonel Farouk, the police chief, into his office, which consisted of a huge wall map, a cot, a desk, and a small sofa. Farouk was boiling over.

"Every American is asking how one terrorist died," he said. "We questioned him, and he died. That's all I say. You let him out of prison. He came back and betrayed my police. Their heads were tossed in the dirt in Bayji. And all you ask is how a terrorist died."

"We go by the law," Tracy said. "We have rules."

"Rules? What about nine bodies without heads? My brother's

body?" Farouk said. "My mother complains I have lost the family because I help Americans."

"Bayji's seventy kilometers away," Donnellan, the battalion commander, said. "I'll take a force there. You can come with me."

"How long?" Farouk demanded.

"Higher has to coordinate," Donnellan said. "Two or three days from now."

"The bodies will be gone by then. You investigate a dead terrorist right away. But my brother has to wait," Farouk said. "Your rules? You won't see strong police the American way for a hundred years."

CATCH AND RELEASE

Farouk had a point. Americans were building up a police force, while tearing down the basic police tools of arrest and incarceration. A source of anger among our troops in 2006 was the self-inflicted hemorrhage of catching and then releasing insurgents. Most insurgents who were captured served little or no time in jail. In prior occupations, the United States military had convened tribunals to review the records of prisoners and decide who remained imprisoned and for how long. According to Michael Frank, an Army judge advocate who served in Iraq, during the past 130 years, the U.S. military engaged in thirteen major occupations, and employed military tribunals, or courts, in all instances. In Iraq, however, U.S. and Iraqi officials decided that insurgents were criminals, to be tried according to Iraqi law. This brushed aside the fact that Iraq lacked judges, prosecutors, defense lawyers, a prison system, and a code of punishment for insurgent actions.

After the Abu Ghraib scandal, the U.S. military wanted no part of a penal system. Rumsfeld, Casey, and other senior generals set repeated end dates when all insurgents in U.S. custody would be handed over to Iraqis. In theory, the United States wanted Iraq to develop a rule of law based on a preliminary constitution that guaranteed a host of rights to anyone accused of a crime. In practice, the result was cynicism among American and Iraqi combat units. In war, uniformed enemy soldiers, once captured, are held until the war ends. In Iraq, insurgents were routinely turned loose to choose whether they would fight again.

There was a dual problem: undeserved imprisonments and undeserved releases. Ignorant of the language and culture, American soldiers in 2003–2004 repeatedly detained innocent family members and passersby. By 2006, however, they were no longer indiscriminately rounding up suspects. Instead, they had to fill out arrest forms, collect sworn affidavits, take digital pictures, and bag evidence. Each arrest package was reviewed at the battalion level, then at brigade level, and a third time at the Bucca prison in southern Iraq or at Cropper prison in Baghdad. Four out of every five suspects detained by soldiers at the battalion level were released. The one in five sent to prison remained locked up for an average of 300 days.

Of 58,000 Iraqis who were imprisoned between 2003 and the end of 2006, 43,000 were released. Iraq was a police war, not a military engagement. Between June 2004 and June 2006, 6,000 insurgents were reported killed, versus approximately 21,000 captured and sent to prison. During the same period, 20,000 were released. In early fall, the daily number of murders averaged twenty-five, versus two insurgents killed. Getting away with murder was easy.

From Secretary Rumsfeld on down, imprisoning Iraqis was viewed as a political burden to be removed as soon as possible. This led to the construction of an inadequate number of prison cells, because the process was based on political expediency.

The rate of arrests by police in the United States resulting in imprisonment for violent crime was more than twice that of U.S. soldiers in Iraq. While this was to be expected, soldiers weren't given the training for policing. Yet their arrest rates were much higher than those of Iraqi police.

The rearrest rate in 2006 was 8 percent, compared to a 67 percent recidivism rate among violent criminals in the United States. Either the hastily manned U.S. prisons were achieving a world-record reform rate of 92 percent of all inmates—even though al Qaeda members were not segregated from the other prisoners—or the insurgency was so large and U.S. and Iraqi arrest capabilities so poor that being arrested twice was highly unlikely.

One in seventy-five American males was in jail, compared to one in 450 Iraqi males, suggesting that Iraqis were six times more law-abiding. Yet the chances of a civilian being killed in Iraq were twenty-one times greater than in the United States.

Farouk, the police chief in Haditha, was on solid ground when he complained about murderers walking free.

Maj. Eric Glassie, a reservist and fifteen-year veteran in the FBI, found that his primary job as an adviser was providing the police with the essentials of life. "Farouk has thirty-five cops," Glassie said. "They have twenty-two uniforms. They share shirts and helmets. They have no running water, no TV, no pillows. We pitch in to buy them food."

In Haditha, the Iraqi Army authorized 120 jundis. Fifty were present for duty, while another fifty had quit because of poor living conditions. They had joined the police in their hometowns in the south, where they could sleep at home.

Baghdad ignored Sunni cities. Lt. Col. Norm Cooling had commanded 3-3 in Haditha for seven months, patrolling an area of 2,800 square kilometers. The battalion had lost fifteen killed and eighty-eight wounded. "We didn't have the manpower to control the MSRs [Main Supply Routes] and hold Haditha," Cooling said. "The Iraqi Army was as blind as we were. The insurgents killed anyone who spoke to us. We tried to start a police force."

Working with U.S. Army Special Forces, Cooling located Farouk, who had been the deputy police chief, and persuaded him to return in mid-2006, guaranteeing the Americans wouldn't pull out and leave him stranded. Cooling proudly brought him to the mayor, who fidgeted while signing the form to get Farouk reinstated. Marwan, an Arab-American interpreter from Tucson, chided the mayor, pointing out that the signature wasn't a real name. The mayor re-signed the document and quickly fled town. A week later, Farouk handed Marwan and Cooling papers that tied the mayor to the insurgents.

Many residents disliked Farouk, who carried a club instead of a rifle. They complained that the tribal relatives he brought with him were rough and uneducated. No one doubted his ferocity, though, and he zealously pursued tips and leads.

"Once Farouk got rolling, we sent up 400 detainees," Cooling said. "Twelve cases came before a judge. We'd send a guy away, and three months later he'd sneak back into town. This puts the troops in a very tough position. Bitterly frustrating."

Each month, the police and army adviser teams in Haditha drove 200 kilometers to Baghdad to arrange food convoys and pick up payrolls that required up to twelve signatures to be released. Donnellan shared food with the Iraqis and scraped up cots and jackets.

"Our command wants to force the Iraqi system to work," Donnellan said. "But I can't leave the police with nothing because their system ignores them."

HIGH TECH AT SQUAD LEVEL

Iraq had set aside about $8 billion for its army and police, and then didn't spend a large fraction of it. The 2006 congressional supplemental for the U.S. forces in Iraq was $90 billion. The disparity was evident on the battlefield.

Every day, aerial cameras hovered over the cities in Iraq, some mounted on Unmanned Aerial Vehicles and others on helicopters; some infrared, others streaming down video in sharp, brilliant colors. One day I was in a company operations center—shared with the Iraqis—in downtown Haditha, when Capt. Bert Lewis, the air officer, pointed at a screen showing a video feed.

"Check that dude next to the white Nissan," he said, speaking into a handset.

An operator several miles away zoomed in the UAV's camera. On the screen, we watched a man in a white dishdasha hastily scooping dirt over a boxlike package, while cars drove by without slowing down.

"FedEx delivery," Lewis said to general laughter. "I don't believe this dude." The Nissan drove away as the man finished packing dirt around the IED.

"Follow the car or the mandress?" Lewis asked.

"Nail that sucker," came a chorus of replies.

The man in the mandress looked up and down the street, then ran south. The picture tilted, then zoomed in, holding him in the center frame. A series of black numbers scrolled along the right edge, updating the GPS coordinates. The man, solidly built and in his mid-thirties, had left the road and was running along the riverbank.

A half dozen marines clustered around to watch the chase. The man could hear the high-pitched whine of the UAV, which sounded like a monster mosquito. He was running harder, back rigid, chest out, looking over his shoulder. "Look, he's doubling back." He ran down a path between houses, across a field, and back to the riverbank. After fifteen minutes, he slowed to a walk, then stopped with his hands on his knees.

"Sucking wind. Send the coordinates to the QRF."

As a Quick Reaction Force patrol closed on the GPS coordinates, the fugitive sat down in the shade of a palm tree, beckoning to someone on the river. Just as a wooden square-nosed skiff putted up, two Humvees burst out of the undergrowth. The man scrambled to his feet and raised his arms to show he had no weapon. The man in the skiff sat stock-still.

"A twofer! All right! Send a squad to bring those guys here."

The Iraqi police on duty in the op center ran out the door, hopped into a tinny pickup, and followed the two Humvees roaring off to pick up the two prisoners.

The chase was an impressive demonstration of battlefield technology. It did illustrate, though, the gap between procurement priorities and military doctrine. Iraq was a counterinsurgency. But neither the Iraqi police nor the American battalions had simple tools and training for basic police tools like taking fingerprints. The U.S. military purchased systems for war, not for police work.

QAIM: A TRIBE SWINGS OVER

From Haditha, I caught a helicopter hop to Qaim, the district that abutted Syria. Inside military circles, there were two success stories with strong parallels: Col. H. R. McMaster in Tal Afar, 180 miles north of Baghdad, and Lt. Col. Dale Alford in Qaim, 230 miles west of Baghdad. McMaster commanded a brigade of 3,500 soldiers, and Alford commanded a battalion of 750 marines.

Qaim was too remote to attract many visitors. But Casey held it out as a model because the Sunni tribe there that had turned against al Qaeda had actually prevailed. When Alford, who had partnered with the local Abu Mahal tribe, returned home in early 2006, he was replaced by Lt. Col. Nick Marano, who continued the process.

In Qaim, the Marines lived the way the Combined Action Platoons had forty years earlier. The insurgents couldn't stay in the same villages or towns because when the Americans walked by side by side with tribal members, sooner or later someone tipped them off. American casualties dropped, while the Iraqi forces gained confidence. The police chief, the Iraqi battalion commander, and the head of the city council were all members of the Abu Mahal tribe, an arrangement that gave the tribe primacy over smuggling and local services.

By October, the streets were teeming with shoppers. In empty lots, children were playing soccer. In a bustling market, the merchants were complaining about commerce, not security. The local bank, with $100,000 in dinars, had no armed guards. The American civil affairs colonel had five times more projects in Qaim than there were in any other city in Anbar.

"In Baghdad, the high command believes that if we do projects, the Iraqis will swing against the bad guys," Lt. Col. Andrew Roberto, a civic action director, said. "I told General Chiarelli that I respectfully disagreed, based on two tours. When Iraqis don't take ownership, projects don't change attitudes. You can spend years doing projects and not have Iraqis buy in. In Qaim, they took responsibility and my microfinance projects took off. I loan money and they pay it back. Qaim works."

None of the police on patrol downtown wore masks to hide their identities. In one middle-class neighborhood, the police proudly pointed out their houses and stopped for ice water. On one street corner, the balcony of a house had been demolished and the walls gouged by bullets. I asked the police if they had done that. No, they laughed, irahibeen were hiding in there with a machine gun, so we brought marines. No strangers dare to come here anymore, they said.

Dusty graffiti covered one courtyard wall. One slogan in Arabic read: "Home of a traitor who aids infidels." It was crossed out, and next to it was written: "Home of a Hero of the Abu Mahal."

Whether Qaim would remain peaceful without a Marine battalion in the district was a subject the American advisers had discussed among themselves.

"I think they can prevail—their way," Maj. Jarrod Stoutenborough, a battalion adviser, said. "There's no trust between units. Everyone wants a piece of the pie. Getting support from Baghdad is the biggest problem. If we weren't here, they'd behave differently and the press wouldn't like what they'd do."

Maj. Jason Vos, who had worked for two years with many Iraqi units and was disappointed in the performance of senior Iraqi officers, agreed.

"The older officers like the old Saddam system of little work and regular payoffs," Vos said. "The measure of a trained army is whether they behave in the new way we've taught them after we advisers leave. If we weren't here tomorrow, they'd revert to their old selves. We're ten years from a new system with roots. But they'd hold on to Qaim. Ninety percent of the insurgents come from tribes seeking to gain, and the top tribe in Qaim has swung over."

In September, Tom Ricks of *The Washington Post* reported about a classified intelligence assessment, citing al Qaeda's grip in Anbar. "AQI is the dominant organization of influence in Al Anbar, surpassing the nationalist insurgents, the Iraqi Government, and MNF [the coalition] in its ability to control the day-to-day life of the average Sunni." On the ground, the situation confirmed that, yet was more complicated. Due to murder and intimidation, Fallujah had regressed. Assassination was the chief weapon. In the farmlands and palm groves of Habbaniyah,

the Marines were fighting ghosts. Ramadi persisted as the major battleground in Iraq where firefights occurred daily. Yet even in that shattered city, the oil spot tactic was taking hold. There were four combat
outposts, with more planned. Police were showing up for duty, a sign
that the tribes once again were trying to throw out al Qaeda. In Baghdadi, Haditha, and Rawah, tough police chiefs had emerged.

Sheik Osama Jadaan from Qaim had tried to organize other
tribes, calling themselves the "Desert Protectors." Jadaan shuttled via
unmarked helicopters to the Green Zone for quiet negotiation and
frequently organized meetings in Sunni neighborhoods. Al Qaeda assassinated him in June, but that wasn't the end of it. With American
help, the Sunni movement was reaching from the Syrian border to the
streets of Baghdad. Al Qaeda in Iraq knew there was a problem coming out of the west.

The Americans had learned how to play the tribal game. They could
unleash firepower or money. They wanted nothing, except to pulverize
al Qaeda and return to their own land. The Iraqi Army, both the 1st
and 7th Divisions, was offering assurances that Sunni recruits would
serve in Anbar. The Americans had finally badgered the Ministry of Interior into allowing Sunnis to serve.

Al Qaeda in Iraq had come to prominence when they ruled Fallujah
in the summer of 2004, shoving aside the old Baathists and former
regime elements. Although led by foreigners, al Qaeda was 90 percent
Iraqi and numbered only a few thousand, certainly less than 20 percent
of those fighting against the Iraqi government and the coalition. Iraqi
military officers, police chiefs, and interpreters for the American units
consistently scoffed at al Qaeda claims of jihad and religious purity. A
few were charismatic zealots, but the rank and file was filled with criminals and opportunists motivated by money, power, and adventure.
When they were winning and the Iraqi police were running away and
the tribes were in disarray, recruiting was easy, and other resistance
movements stayed out of their way or followed their lead. Al Qaeda in
Iraq had to keep control in order to survive. Keeping control meant
killing Sunni Iraqis who disobeyed.

Anbar was a series of fierce struggles for local control. There was,
though, a huge change in the situation. In 2004, the Sunnis were fighting the Americans. In the fall of 2006, the Americans were supporting
Sunnis who were fighting other Sunnis.

FOURTEEN

THE CIVIL WAR

FALL 2006

BAGHDAD DETERIORATES

In Baghdad, the Americans were supporting an Iraqi government that had not stopped Shiites from fighting Sunnis. "The center of the problem is Baghdad," Abizaid said. "It's the area where we've got to expend the most military effort."

In early summer, Operation Together Forward had failed because Iraqi forces did not hold the areas cleared by U.S. forces. OTF II had kicked off in early August with a promise from Maliki that this time he really, really would deliver. When I visited in late September, Casey's staff had just conducted a review, concluding that "the National Police were widely discredited . . . the GoI [Government of Iraq] did not have resolve to move into Sadr City . . . and there has been no broad sustained reduction in city-wide violence."

Col. Michael Beech, commanding a brigade in the 4th Infantry Division, escorted retired four-star General Wayne Downing and me through the Sunni district of Doura, row upon row of lower- and middle-class houses, with Humvees and police checkpoints at the end of each street. Beech had deployed one American rifle company and an Iraqi police company per two mulahalas, city blocks containing 1,300 houses and about 17,000 people. At that rate, it would take 140,000 soldiers to control the city of seven million. The United States had committed 14,000. The Iraqis had 40,000 police and soldiers on the rolls in Baghdad. How many were actually patrolling was not clear.

The streets were remarkably clean because Beech had hired garbage trucks. The U.S. soldiers assigned to Baghdad had a fund of $50 million. The idea was to clear and hold an area, then provide basic services so that the people would support the government.

At the Multi-National Force operations center, the generals were briefed daily on four measures: security and transportation, economy, commerce, and governance. The tag line on the first slide read: "Restoration of services will decrease support for AIF [Anti-Iraqi Forces]." The Mahdi Army, however, took credit for the American projects in the Shiite areas, while the Sunni insecurity prevented development in Sunni neighborhoods.

Earlier in September, the Iraq Study Group had visited Baghdad. This was a group of six Democrats and six Republicans with sterling records of public service; Congress had charged the group with taking a fresh look at Iraq. When former secretary of defense William J. Perry asked Casey and Chiarelli if they could succeed with another three to five American brigades, both said no.

As a courtesy from one grunt to another, Casey had quietly arranged a trip to the battlefield for former governor Chuck Robb (D-VA), a member of the Iraq Study Group. In 1968, Robb had served as a rifle company commander on Hill 55, south of Da Nang city. He knew about snipers, mines, mortar shellings, buses blown up on the highway, village elders assassinated in their homes. Accompanied by a platoon, Robb had walked the streets of Doura, talking with the soldiers and the residents.

Their accounts of violence and distrust contradicted what the Iraqi officials, safe inside the cocoon of the Green Zone, had told him. The American soldiers had shown him the vastness of the city, compared to their few numbers. Yet none of the generals who briefed the Study Group had shown any interest in ramping up U.S. forces, and seemed to Robb to be tired and ready to run out the clock. Robb sent a memo for the record to the Study Group when they left Baghdad.

"In Iraq, we cannot afford to fail and we cannot maintain the status quo," Robb wrote. "We need right away a significant short-term surge. . . . It's time to let our military do what they're trained to do on offense. . . . It's going to cost more in the short term, just as we'll temporarily sustain higher casualty rates on the military side, but both costs and casualties will be reduced in the long run."

A few days later, several bodies were dumped on a street where he had lingered, a taunting response to the Americans who brought a VIP into the neighborhood. Doura was a hard nut. Al Qaeda gangs had moved in, grabbing and murdering the Shiites driving along the main north–south highway that abutted the district. Shiite death squads and rogue police units retaliated by prowling Doura's quiet streets, looking for a chance to sneak around the Americans and shoot a Sunni. In Doura, the restoration of services included picking up bodies in the morning.

"We've cut down the murders from a dozen a day to one or two," Beech said. "But my brigade will be moving on. The Sunnis see the insurgents, even al Qaeda, as protection from the JAM [Jesh al Mahdi] after we leave."

As Robb had done, General Downing got out of a Humvee and walked the streets with Beech, talking to residents. None offered an opinion about the garbage pickup, but most were quick to insist the Americans had to stay, seeing the police as their enemy.

"The Ministry of Interior are the killers," Maha Daoud Saeh, an electrician, said. "Our friend was walking down the street and a police car took him away. They killed him. The police shot out the transformers so we'd move out."

––––

When I met the next day with Maliki, he didn't defend the police. Instead, he blamed Ambassador Bremer. "Bremer formed the police wrong and we are paying the price," he said. "Bremer opened the door [into the police] without a filter. Now we have to take out the bad elements and retrain everyone."

I asked why he did not release the $70 million owed to Anbar Province.

"They have money," he said. "The security problem prevents it from spending."

"Why not offer money as a public gesture of reconciliation, even if they can't spend it?"

"They [the residents of Anbar] already know," Maliki said.

The American diplomats and generals I met in Baghdad in September and October were skeptical of Iraqi officials.

"Anbar is deliberately starved. No money, no jobs, no future," Chiarelli said. "What do you think all those nineteen-year-olds are going to do? You can't kill them all!"

"One school of thought is that Maliki is consolidating his Shiite base before reaching out to the Sunnis," an American lieutenant general said. "The other school is that he is consolidating his Shiite base."

A bright spot in Baghdad was the performance of the Special Operations Forces, or SOF, which included Iraqis. I accompanied Downing to a commando base in the city. The SEALs and Special Forces were happy to see Downing, who had headed the Special Operations Command and was happiest when he was among his troops. As we watched, the commando teams, who fired thousands of rounds each month in practice, flowed through the shooting rooms with choreographed ease, riddling the targets. Using a sand table and detailed photos, they rehearsed how they would take down that night's target. On the wall of their operations center, a large map of Baghdad was sprinkled with bright red pins, showing the locations of 150 previous raids.

One square chunk of the map—Sadr City—showed no pins. When Downing asked why, the commandos laughed. You'll have to ask the prime minister, they said, he's the one who's placed it off limits.

The commandos operated under the equivalent of national arrest warrants that gave them the right to pull a raid anywhere without informing a provincial governor. This greatly reduced leaks, and the teams enjoyed a success rate of over 60 percent, with more targets than they could hit. In Iraq, there were White SOF units—SEAL and Special Forces teams—that worked from bases and small outposts around the country. While they reported to the Special Operations Command, on most operations they checked in with the U.S. battalion commander who owned the battle space, and often the battalion provided an outer cordon for the SOF. The Black SOF—the highly trained Delta unit—specialized in tracking down the top-level terrorists like Zarqawi, and they were often supported by Ranger companies.

The advisers said the Iraqi commandos had no fear of al Qaeda or any other extremists. When insurgents squirted from a house at three in the morning, the Iraqi commandos ran them down. Firefights were rare. They told Downing that over about 500 raids, they had killed 100 and captured over 1,000, while losing two of their own.

When they suggested that Downing accompany them on the command chopper on the night raid, his eyes lit up. I had known Wayne for thirty-five years, and he never tired of being a grunt. A phone call extinguished that hope, though, when the colonel on the other end said, "And how do we explain it if we lose our own retired four-star?"

The next day, Downing and the military historian Col. Jeff McCausland were returning to the States. Both were pessimistic. They felt the American commanders in the fall of 2006 were tiring of pushing the rock up the hill.

————

The next morning, I checked back in with Maj. Bo Davenport, who was still advising the Iraqi battalion on the southern outskirts of Sadr City. As we had in April, with a few Iraqi and American soldiers we walked down Palestine Street. As before, the shop owners were glad to see us and quick to complain that security had gotten worse. Robbers come every afternoon, they said, usually in police uniforms.

We walked on, dropping in and out of the boutique shops. The story was drearily the same—robbers, car bombs, no trust. The jundis with us weren't scared, but they weren't engaged either. In April, they had enjoyed greeting the shoppers. There had been a bit of swagger to them. Now there were few greetings.

With three Americans and five Iraqis, all well armed, we walked for hours through the city. In the poorest Sunni slums, the men still swarmed around us, smiling and nodding—"Army good. Americans good. Police bad." In the Shiite areas, the men were standoffish, but warmed up enough to gesture up the street, shaking their fists and warning us of Sunni snipers who randomly shot at crowds. On a few corners, Iraqi soldiers sat behind machine guns, manning checkpoints.

"These fixed sites are all over, and they're worthless," Davenport said. "The bad guys know not to drive up with weapons. Sadr City's right behind us. That's where we need checkpoints. But the MOI [Ministry of Interior] won't let us near the place. Moqtada Sadr is the power out here on the streets."

We stopped to chat with Colonel Hassan, an Iraqi battalion commander. Over his office door an Arabic sign read, "No Shiia, No Sunni, All Iraqis." His deputy had been assassinated at his home a few blocks away, and Hassan never went home in uniform.

"He has a hard job," Davenport said. "He never knows whether his chain of command will back him."

THE CHICKEN MURDER

The next day, I caught up with Lt. Col. Brian Winski and the 1st Battalion, 61st Infantry Regiment. They were still patrolling a huge swath at the southern end of the city.

Earlier in September, the battalion had arrested a JAM leader hiding on the seventeenth floor of the Sheik Adnon Hospital. He worked for Hameed al-Shimari, a top Sadr aide accused of murdering Sunni patients. Acting on a tip, they returned to the hospital the next week and arrested five more JAM members. A judge released all six, while the hospital administrator went on TV to accuse the Americans of stealing a payroll of $80,000.

Around midnight on September 14, Winski led a raiding party into the scrubby town of Jisr Diyala to arrest Abu Sayef, a JAM leader. Dozens of families sleeping on roofs scurried for safety as the troops engaged fleeing targets. Sgt. David Weir was killed in a burst of enfilade fire. Sayef escaped. Two days later, he returned to the mosque and executed eleven passersby as a warning not to betray him.

A few days later I accompanied Winski back to the garbage-clogged streets where Sayef was last seen. A single line of poles carrying a hodgepodge of wires ran down each street. Winski parked his Humvee and asked a few questions. No response. A soldier picked up a crumpled paper flyer signed by the JAM. Translated, it read, "We warn the people to tell their children to stay away from those despicable Americans. . . . We are going to attack the Americans severely, wherever they are, and at any time." Dozens of Iraqi men clustered around, surprised that a mere dozen Americans had again driven down the back streets.

"We're coming back until we get Abu Sayef," Winski said.

The crowd was sullen but not hostile. Without the JAM giving orders, the Shiites didn't know how to react. I had been in Jisr Diyala in April of 2003 when Mattis lost two marines before charging on foot across the bridge into Baghdad. President Bush had to liberate the Shiites. Now a Shiite militia had killed Sergeant Weir. In response, the Americans had come back, and this time Winski wasn't bringing soccer balls.

"This isn't over," Winski said before leaving.

The next day, I was riding with Winski on his daily "battlefield circulation." From Casey on down, every American commander tried to get out every day with the soldiers. There was nothing exceptionally courageous about it; it was what commanders, American or British or Australian or Salvadoran, did. Over the radio, Winski received a report of a shooting at a nearby chicken farm. We arrived as the police were dragging two bodies off the road, the dirt sopping up the blood. The shootings had occurred less than twenty minutes ago. A tall Iraqi in a blue T-shirt was angrily pointing down a dirt road shaded by bright green bamboo thickets.

"The killers ran down there," he said through an interpreter.

An old truck with a few squawking chickens in small cages was mired in a pothole. As the dead men were purchasing the chickens, two other men had walked up, gunned them down, and tried to steal the truck. The farm was on the fault line between the Sunni village of Tuwaitha and the Shiite town of Jisr Diyala. Were the slain men Shiite or Sunni? No one seemed to know. As far as the police were concerned, the incident was closed.

"We need air support to go down there," the police major said. "Very dangerous."

Winski looked at the two dozen policemen. "I'll go first," he said, "You follow." We jounced down the road toward Tuwaitha, passing burned-out farmhouses and demolished cars and trucks.

"Mahdi ReMax," Winski said. "The Mahdi Army burns out a farm about every couple of days. A few days ago, the Sunnis ambushed the police on this road. Torched six vehicles and killed two cops. They think the police are tipping off JAM. They probably are."

The shrubbery was so thick we couldn't see two feet off the road on either side. When we came out at the river, there was less undergrowth. As we approached a farm, two men darted from a run-down house into a dense palm grove. Winski and his soldiers gave chase, but in their battle rattle they had no chance of catching up. Behind the house were open chicken coops. A teenaged boy stopped to watch the giant Americans, dripping sweat, walk back to their Humvees.

Ten minutes later, the police arrived, grabbed the boy, and slapped him around. Winski intervened as the boy begged to be let go.

"They'll cut my head off if I talk," he whimpered as the police put him into a pickup.

"Poor kid," Winski said. "Regardless of what he says, the killers will think he turned them in."

The police whooped in a victory dance before driving off with the sobbing boy and the bodies of two strangers in the bed of the truck. In five months Baghdad had descended into lawlessness, with life worth less than a one-dollar chicken.

———

On September 22, 2006—Sgt. David Thomas Weir's birthday— hundreds of his fellow troopers packed a small chapel on a base in

Baghdad to say goodbye. The ceremony was the same everywhere in Iraq—boots aligned below the rifle with fixed bayonet, dog tags dangling from the rifle grip, a memorial picture, choked elegiac goodbyes, the chaplain's simple prayer for Sergeant Weir's soul and for his wife and two-year-old son, followed by taps.

Throughout history, warrior tribes have dealt with death in different ways. The Peloponnesian hoplites celebrated the fallen warrior by poem and song. The people of the plains were the opposite; Genghis Khan forbade mention of the fallen, lest morale drop. In past American wars, because the infantry were still in the field, organized farewells were rare. Death was a family affair, with services thousands of miles from the scene.

In Iraq, death was shared inside the unit. Due to improvements in armor and medical treatment, the number of fatalities was small by historical comparison. Sooner or later, though, everyone in a rifle battalion heard the crack of an AK or was buffeted by an IED blast. Death brushed by, choosing fickly.

"In my battalion," a chaplain, who had been a Marine sergeant, told me, "a third of the troops are Protestant, a third Catholic, and a third don't believe in anything. The ones who cope poorly with death are those who have no religious faith or strong family ties."

Inside the chapel, a squad leader rose to speak about Weir's two-year-old son, Gavin, nicknamed "the colonel." At cookouts back in the States, soldiers would ask: "How's the colonel?" and Weir would beam. After the short eulogies, large men with shaved heads, bulky in their armor, briefly clasped each other. The commander of the 4th Infantry Division, Maj. Gen. James Thurman, huge as a grizzly, grasped the squad leader, who was Weir's best friend, by the shoulders in Spartan fashion, looked him in the eye, and strode out.

How many memorial ceremonies had Thurman attended—thirty, fifty, a hundred? The generals carried the human cost of Iraq. I wondered what Thurman wanted to say to Maliki about sheltering the Jesh al Mahdi.

(Battalion 1-61 did eventually capture Sayef. He was not handed over to Iraqi officials.)

A few days later, Winski drove me back to the resort town of Salman Pak, his pride and joy. How many battalion commanders have a soaring arch, a symbol of antiquity seven centuries old, sitting in their battle space? We hopped out in the market and walked among the stalls,

many fewer in number than in April. The stall keepers rebuffed our efforts to converse, turning their backs and pretending to be busy. A few
young toughs from the sectarian National Police battalion stationed in
town were sauntering across the plaza, one in a black T-shirt with a
submachine gun draped over his shoulder and his companion carrying
a Glock pistol in a low-slung holster.

As he had dozens of times, Winski opened the rear hatch of his
Humvee to take out school backpacks, soccer balls, and candy. The
children gathered around, including two cute girls younger than three,
smiling shyly. When Winski offered a backpack, a man rushed forward
and slapped the children furiously, screaming at them and dragging
them away by the hair. He struck the girls, turned them loose, and took
a step toward Winski, his lips drawn back to spit. When Winski, a big
man, stepped forward, every soldier stiffened. The man hesitated,
grabbed the sobbing children by their arms, and pulled them out of the
market.

"That miserable son of a bitch," Winski said.

———

In September, there had been 1,152 sectarian murders; in October,
there were 1,028 more. Chiarelli's staff concluded that Operation Together Forward II had failed, and pulled no punches in assessing the
reasons. Suicide car bombings continued because Iraqi forces had exercised "ineffective to non-existent control of traffic that flows into Baghdad." OTF II had not received "any support from Iraqi politicians or
religious leaders." Thurman's division was clearing neighborhoods
with no Iraqi forces to hold them. Maliki vetoed raids to arrest JAM
death squad leaders. Worse, he had not ordered the Ministry of Defense to move more battalions into Baghdad.

America had instituted a democracy in Iraq that rewarded the worst
sectarian instincts of the Shiites, who controlled the national government. The disenfranchised Sunnis gave shelter to their homegrown extremists, who slaughtered Shiites in order to provoke a civil war,
enabling al Qaeda to eventually seize power. Casey's strategy of creating a new Iraqi Army could not control the violence because Sunnis in
cities like Fallujah weren't going to tip off the Shiite jundis, and the Shiite politicians wouldn't allow the army in Baghdad to curb the militias
who were killing Sunnis. As a result, according to *New York Times* reporter Michael Gordon, Casey received a briefing in mid-October that
showed Baghdad "sliding toward chaos."

Winski was living that chaos. In his battle space, Sunnis had slaughtered Shiites in Narwan. In retaliation, the JAM took over Jisr Diyala, resulting in the death of Sergeant Weir, and seized a mosque in Salman Pak. When Sunnis in Salman Pak then ambushed and killed a colonel in the National Police, Winski's soldiers killed the ambushers to protect the NPs. So the Americans seemed to favor the ill-performing National Police, and a Sunni in Salman Pak had beaten up his tiny daughters for smiling at Winski. Outside Jisr Diyala, the JAM had burned out the Sunni farmers, one night at a time. When two men were murdered for a few chickens, no one knew whether they were Sunni or Shiite. It didn't make any difference.

FIFTEEN

BUSH WEIGHS HIS OPTIONS

FALL 2006

Since the president had asked General Pace in mid-June to review the Iraq strategy, inside the National Security Council, Meghan O'Sullivan, the Iraq desk officer, had pushed the Pentagon to send more troops. In Baghdad, the Multi-National Force had launched two more operations—Together Forward I and II. Both had failed to reduce the violence. By the fall of 2006, the NSC staff was convinced the Pentagon had to change strategy. On October 3, Stephen Hadley, the national security adviser, who had replaced Condoleezza Rice, pulled aside his deputy, J. D. Crouch, for a quiet chat in the West Wing. Hadley, a lawyer who built thorough briefs step by step, could read the president's moods. Let's try for a fresh look at what's needed in Iraq, he suggested. Crouch, a careful, understated planner who oversaw Iraqi matters on a daily basis, returned to his office and called in William Luti, a retired Navy captain who had commanded an amphibious ready group that included thousands of marines.

"The president's concerned that Iraq's not getting better," Crouch said, "and the Pentagon's not giving him alternatives. Try your hand at a briefing about a new strategy for Iraq. This is just between us."

As a special assistant to the president, Luti handled Defense programs on the NSC staff. Although Iraq wasn't his regular beat, he was comfortable with military planning and had worked for Rumsfeld. If it leaked that the NSC was meddling in military strategy, the Pentagon would be more forgiving of Luti than of other NSC staffers. Like the historian Eliot Cohen, Luti believed a wartime president was well advised to immerse himself in military strategy in order to guide and challenge his generals.

"The president is the commander-in-chief," Luti said. "He can task his own staff to analyze strategy. The Pentagon is another staff, not a separate kingdom."

During World War II, Roosevelt had altered the strategies of the twin titans, Generals George Marshall and Dwight Eisenhower—to the chagrin of both men. In contrast, President George W. Bush wore as a badge of honor his uninvolvement in military strategy. Pointing to a coffee table in the Oval Office, Bush had related to a group of generals how he had seen a picture of President Johnson peering at a photomap spread on the table, picking out bombing targets in North Vietnam. Bush assured the generals that he would never do that.

Bush had recused himself from strategy as well as tactics, although the generals had no special expertise in fighting the insurgency in Iraq. Abizaid, Casey, Chiarelli, Petraeus—none had led troops in battle against guerrillas prior to Iraq. Military doctrine had been expunged along with firsthand experience from Vietnam, a war forty years in the past. The generals were learning as the war progressed, and they disagreed with one another. While Abizaid and Casey advocated the light footprint approach, Petraeus was writing about American soldiers living among the people. While Chiarelli championed economic development, the marines in Anbar, with almost zero development funds, were slugging it out in local fights that resembled bringing law and order to Tombstone and Dodge City in the Old West. In this cauldron of intellectual ferment, there was ample room for a president to dive in with his own ideas—if he chose to do so.

Although Bush knew the strategy in Iraq was in trouble, he didn't know what to do about it. Sending in more troops was the one thing the Joint Chiefs in the Pentagon and the generals in Iraq agreed should not be done. A few hundred feet away from the Oval Office, Luti sat in his spacious office in the Old Executive Office Building, crafting a briefing entitled "Change the Dynamic in Iraq." Committing more U.S. troops, Luti wrote, would change the dynamic by committing the United States to prevail rather than to withdraw. Since the Iraqi forces weren't up to it, he recommended "a surge in US forces to secure and hold in Baghdad."

With Hadley's approval, O'Sullivan presented a similar briefing to the Iraq Review Committee, which she chaired, pressing for action.

On October 11, Bush held a press conference to express his support for Casey in ambiguous sentences. "I said: General [Casey], if you need more troops, I support you. If you're going to devise a new strategy, we're with you . . . the American people want to know: Can we win? . . . You empower your generals to make the decisions. . . . You can't fight a war from Washington. . . . It just won't work. And I trust General Casey."

Hadley interpreted the president as saying he wanted a fresh strategy, maybe requiring more troops. Casey and the Pentagon, including Rumsfeld, did not pick up on the hidden message. The president's demeanor of unshakable resolve masked his concerns from all but his closest advisers.

A few weeks earlier, Bush had invited in several outside experts on Iraq. Asked why he didn't send more troops to Iraq, he said Casey didn't want them. Told that Baghdad was deteriorating and the Marines reported that al Qaeda controlled Anbar, he dismissed the report as "one data point." The bad news from Baghdad was a "nanosecond" in history. Yet privately, the president was deeply concerned that the United States was pursuing the wrong strategy.

In October, Rumsfeld had informed the White House that Petraeus was his pick to take over for Casey. The vice president, Rumsfeld's close confidant, and the Joint Chiefs agreed. Because the NSC's Meghan O'Sullivan had known Petraeus in Baghdad in 2005, she acted as his point of contact at the NSC after his unofficial selection in November. Both of them were in touch with the field, both believed in population security, and Petraeus was quietly selecting a staff that included commanders in Iraq who agreed with his basic concept of counterinsurgency: Don't commute to work. Pace had recommended his assistant, Lt. Gen. Raymond Odierno, to replace Chiarelli as the corps commander.

At the end of October, Hadley, O'Sullivan, and Crouch spent a week in Iraq. Before leaving, there were quiet talks with Petraeus and Odierno. When Crouch visited Camp Fallujah, he sat down in a small room with a dozen marines with ranks ranging from lieutenant colonel to corporal. He asked, Are we getting our asses handed to us? Hell no, came the replies. The tribes are pissed at al Qaeda. Those assholes break the fingers of any farmer they catch smoking. When they want sex, they "marry" the good-looking women from the tribes. The sheiks are fed up. They're sending their young men into the police. Lt. Col.

Jurney's getting control of Ramadi one chunk at a time. If the tribes team with us, we only need a few more battalions. We can break al Qaeda. Crouch returned to Washington disagreeing with the common wisdom that Anbar was uncontrollable.

———

But while Anbar showed a sliver of light, conditions immediately around Baghdad were darkening. Suicide bombers consistently penetrated the city from their lairs in the farmlands to the south, while to the north the province of Diyala was spinning out of control. A farming province with thick vegetation bordering Baghdad on the northeast, Diyala had briefly received world attention in June of 2006 when Jordanian and U.S. intelligence agencies located the arch-terrorist Zarqawi in a remote farmhouse. Usually Zarqawi hid out in the Fallujah–Habbaniyah corridor west of Baghdad. After he narrowly evaded capture at a checkpoint outside Ramadi, he ducked over to a tribal hideout in Diyala, where an air strike killed him.

Sunnis from twenty-five tribes constituted more than 65 percent of Diyala's 1.2 million population and after the Iraqi 5th Division took over from the Americans in July of 2006, security disintegrated. Sunnis, pushed out of Baghdad by the death squads, sought refuge in Baquba, Diyala's capital, where some cooperated with the al Qaeda gangs in driving out the Shiites. In retaliation, Jesh al Mahdi militia forces drove up from Baghdad to attack Sunni villages. Posing as the Sunnis' defender, al Qaeda evicted Shiite farmers, taking over their houses and food supplies, and lining the main roads with IEDs. By late 2006, the drivers of fuel and food distribution trucks refused to deliver products into the province.

The Iraqi Army and police contributed to the chaos. The provincial police chief recruited his force from the Wolf Brigade, a National Police unit notorious for sponsoring death squads. Shiite militias smuggled arms from Iran through the province into Baghdad. The police hid in their barracks, occasionally launching raids to round up Sunni males indiscriminately. The Iraqi 5th Division was worse, targeting the Sunni sheiks who cooperated with Col. Brian Jones, the commander of the 3rd Brigade of the U.S. 4th Infantry Division.

As the brigade reached the end of its tour in November, a thoroughly fed-up Colonel Jones sat down with Richard Oppel of *The New York Times,* publicly accusing the police chief and the division commander, Maj. Gen. Shakir Hulail, of incompetence and sectarian perfidy.

"The U.S. Army is past the point where we say, 'Fire this guy,' " Jones said. "All we can say is, 'Hey, this guy is bad. Iraqi government, what are you going to do about it?' "

The division commander, Maj. Gen. Benjamin Mixon, backed up his brigade commander, saying General Hulail was either incompetent or complicit with the Shiite death squads. Either way, he had to be fired. Maliki's office vigorously defended the Iraqi hierarchy in Diyala and refused to fire anyone.

The disintegration of Diyala exposed the sectarian bias and callousness of the government. The streets of Baquba were deserted, except for ten corpses a day. Vengeful gangs and lack of food hardly benefited the Shiites; they were suffering as much as the Sunnis. The U.S. military, unable to change conditions by giving direct orders, had to use the press to bring pressure to bear. It was also a means for Casey to illustrate to the White House what it was like dealing with the Maliki government.

On November 4, the voters dealt the Republicans an epic defeat, electing a Democratic majority in both the Senate and the House. The election repudiated Bush and his Iraq policy. Public approval of his handling of Iraq remained a dismal 34 percent. Bush fired Rumsfeld, explaining he had decided to do so weeks earlier, but held off in order not to affect the elections. Republicans who lost close races were infuriated that Bush righteously invoked a sense of honor that transcended politics. After all, elections determined policies. By retaining the rebarbative Rumsfeld, after having decided to fire him, Bush had helped to elect Democrats who opposed his Iraq policy.

"Rumsfeld always wanted to win," Luti said. "Critics claim Rumsfeld bullied the generals to think his way. That's not what happened. Abizaid, Casey and Rumsfeld agreed with one another! The chairman of the Joint Chiefs—first Myers and later Pace—never contradicted Abizaid. I heard Rumsfeld repeatedly urge them to speak up, and they didn't."

After firing Rumsfeld, Bush invited Robert Gates, a former director of the CIA, to his ranch in Crawford, Texas, to discuss the job of secretary of defense. Gates, who had been a member of the Iraq Study Group when Robb had argued for increasing U.S. forces, told Bush that he favored a "surge."

On November 10, the president held an NSC meeting to launch a review of Iraq policy, to be chaired by Crouch, the deputy national se-

curity adviser. Crouch gave the generals leading the review inside the
Pentagon—Lt. Gens. Richard Sattler and Douglas Lute—copies of
Luti's surge paper and asked them to seriously consider it. He also argued that Anbar was inextricably linked to Baghdad. Politically, if al
Qaeda was broken in Anbar, it would signal Baghdad and all of Iraq
that al Qaeda was not invincible. Militarily, Anbar was key to inter-
dicting the western belt around Baghdad, al Qaeda's favorite infiltration route into the capital.

A few days later, the Iraq Study Group met with senior officials at
the White House. None of the officials was upbeat, with the CIA director, Michael V. Hayden, warning that the situation was falling
apart. Bob Woodward of *The Washington Post* reported that Hayden
said, "The inability of the [Iraqi] government to govern was probably
irreversible in the short term." Although al Qaeda was on the verge of
losing control in Anbar, only the front-line fighters sensed that change.
In Baghdad, the situation was deteriorating, a view shared by the generals and the Washington establishment. In November of 2006, Iraq
was like the stock market at the bottom of a bear market, with most in-
vestors selling before they lost more money and only a few willing to
buy.

After the meetings, Robb remained huddled with Hadley and
Crouch, urging that the president immediately increase the number of
U.S. forces in Iraq. Robb believed that a surge of forces to stabilize
Baghdad was key. Unless the United States demonstrated results in the
capital city, he told Hadley, he was pessimistic about the region and the
U.S. ability to influence world events. Although Hadley was noncom-
mittal, the idea of a surge was gaining important advocates.

Later that day, Hadley met with Pace to review the military's position. Layers of bureaucracy had sanded off the sharp edges of the
analysis done by Pace's review team. Instead of presenting a clear alternative, the Joint Chiefs temporized.

"Pace was clearly frustrated by his own staff process," a senior
NSC aide said. "He didn't want to overrule his own field commanders,
and the four service chiefs in Washington didn't agree on one strategy
to present as an alternative."

Sending more troops was a matter of logistics. The matter of strategy was what the troops would do that was different from what
Abizaid, Chiarelli, and Casey were doing. In private, some members of
the team reviewing the strategy called the Abizaid-Casey position "the
bag of shit strategy."

"We were saying to Maliki," one team member said, "here's a bag of shit. It's yours, so you figure out what to do with it. That's not strategy; that's waste disposal."

As a further complication, two strategies were being pursued in Iraq. Out in Anbar, where there were few FOBs and huge distances between cities, the Army and Marines were patrolling on foot to keep the Sunni insurgents out of the cities. They were blind without local police, though, and the fault line between al Qaeda and the tribes was just beginning to widen.

Unlike Anbar, in and around Baghdad, U.S. soldiers were operating from the FOBs, with less routine presence among the city's residents. In Shiite neighborhoods, JAM had control and the threat was the al Qaeda car bomb. The presence of more U.S. troops didn't seem to prevent car bombs. In Sunni neighborhoods, the Shiite police were seen as the enemy that allowed entry to the death squads. Al Qaeda offered to fight the death squads, and to kill Americans and any residents who spoke to Americans. What was the strategic purpose in surging U.S. soldiers to protect a population that didn't dare to be protected by Americans?

This wasn't openly debated. The military had not fundamentally changed its rigid pyramid rank structure since World War II. The command structure of an infantry division dates back to Napoleon. Yet the Internet had democratized the ranks, with everyone commenting on tactics and operations. Beneath Chiarelli and Casey, field commanders were communicating with Petraeus and a host of others. After two years in Iraq, O'Sullivan had come to the White House with a large e-mail address book. There was no subversive intent, but via e-mail people did know what was going on, and picked up different ideas.

For months, the Joint Staff had labored over a study that laid out three alternatives: "go big" by adding troops, "go long" by adding advisers, or "get out," which was the option endorsed by the State Department in November of 2006. The Pentagon's preference was for the sensible, middle option of adding advisers to accelerate the transition to Iraqi self-reliance, while reducing the level and visibility of U.S. forces. Abizaid supported the adviser concept. Lieutenant Colonel Alford, who had turned Qaim around, advocated reorganizing entire infantry battalions to provide a depth of advisers. Lieutenant Colonel Jurney argued that advisers greatly increased Iraqi effectiveness. Lieutenant Colonel John Nagl, an adviser to Petraeus, suggested organizing a separate "Adviser Corps." The Iraq Study Group was developing a recommendation to increase the number of advisers from 4,000 to 20,000.

Inside the NSC staff, though, the adviser option was viewed as temporizing. The Iraqi forces and their political leaders had failed. Having failed in Operations Together Forward I and II, they would probably fail again if given a third chance with more advisers. To steer the Pentagon toward increasing U.S. forces, Hadley gave Pace the NSC paper that recommended a surge, suggesting the Joint Chiefs reexamine the alternatives.

Both men gave short shrift to the State Department paper that argued America's original objectives had been achieved in Iraq. According to State, the way to "advance America's interests and preserve Iraqi independence" was to withdraw most U.S. forces and focus the remaining forces on raids against al Qaeda, leaving it to the Iraqis to sort out their sectarian differences. This approach largely echoed the sentiments of moderate Democrats.

Subsequent reports credited Rice with being the chief architect of the change in strategy. A year earlier, in testimony, she had advocated a "clear, hold, and build" approach that Rumsfeld had swiftly repudiated. At the critical moment in December, the NSC staff, not the State Department under Rice, forced the change in strategy. Rice's position was characterized by the NSC staff as the "cut losses, exit gracefully" option. In other words, get out.

General Abizaid, the theater commander, was equally out of touch with the president's thinking and the surge movement inside the NSC staff. Testifying in mid-November before the Senate, Abizaid said he "was very encouraged" and argued there were sufficient U.S. troops in Iraq, even while acknowledging that "al Anbar Province is not under control." An exasperated Senator McCain urged deploying more U.S. forces to gain control of Anbar as well as Baghdad, before the deteriorating situation forced an all-out battle like Fallujah. Casey had come around to requesting at least two more brigades. Abizaid was still holding out.

"I believe that more American forces prevent the Iraqis from doing more," Abizaid told McCain, "and from taking more responsibility for their own future."

Although they disagreed about what to do, Abizaid, Casey, the NSC, the Pentagon, and State all agreed about the problem: the feckless performance by Maliki and his government. For two years, the U.S. ambassador in Iraq had signed a series of Joint Campaign Plans with the Multi-National Force commander. State agreed it was responsible for governance and political matters. State and the military shared the same intelligence about the key malevolent Iraqi officials. The president was wringing his hands about changing military strategy, which all agreed was 20 percent of the solution. State's strategy for the political component that was 80 percent was nonexistent. State was not held accountable.

The excuse that Maliki had limited authority had worn thin. His pattern was to promise to protect all Iraqis equally when under pressure and later to renege. Believing the Iraqi Army was too close to the American Army, he had created an Office of the Commander-in-Chief inside his personal staff, so that he could direct army units without informing the Ministry of Defense.

In one instance, he dispatched an Iraqi battalion with militia members from Sadr City to carry out arrests in a nearby Sunni neighborhood. When the Iraqi battalion already in the neighborhood refused to obey the new battalion commander and seized the Shiite militia leaders, a furious Maliki intervened. Casey told him that, as Iraq's commander-in-chief, he could not break all the rules and jeopardize everything by using the army for his own sectarian objectives. Maliki's national security adviser, Mowaffak al-Rubaie, leaped in, telling Casey that he had stepped over the line in dealing with the leader of a sovereign nation. That prompted President Bush to call Maliki via televideo, saying that he backed Casey; a prime minister simply could not use his nation's army to settle personal scores. After securing the release of the Shiite militia leaders, Maliki ordered the Iraqi battalion to return to Sadr City.

"In the summer and fall of '06," Casey told me, "I wasn't in favor of bringing more U.S. troops to do the Iraqis' business for them. I told Maliki I'd pony up one more U.S. battalion for every brigade he sent— 800 U.S. for every 1,200 Iraqi soldiers. But I wanted it in writing."

The U.S. command had reason to be suspicious of Iraqi officials. The U.S. secretary of agriculture, Mike Johanns, had flown in to help the farmers. When the minister of agriculture, a lackey of Moqtada Sadr, snubbed Johanns, refusing even a five-minute meeting with him, Chiarelli boiled over. When Chiarelli clamped down in mid-October on the exit points from Sadr City, violence plummeted, only to pick up again when Maliki ordered the checkpoints along the Army Canal removed. Death squads surged out, while al Qaeda suicide bombers surged in. On November 23, more than 200 people were murdered by car bombs, the worst attack in the capital since the war began. Time and again, Maliki promised to bring more Iraqi forces into Baghdad, then never issued the orders.

"The longer we in the U.S. forces continue to bear the main burden of Iraq's security," Casey said, "it lengthens the time that the government of Iraq has to take the hard decisions about reconciliation and dealing with the militias. And the other thing is that they can continue to blame us for all of Iraq's problems, which are at base their problems."

On November 30, Bush flew to Amman, Jordan, to review with Maliki a joint agreement Casey had drawn up. In a surprise move, Maliki insisted that Iraqi forces could deal with Baghdad without any help. He proposed moving U.S. forces out of the city, while he took direct command of his army, thereby reducing the Multi-National Force role. Publicly, Bush praised Maliki, saying he deserved to have more control over his own army. Privately, he told the prime minister that Americans viewed sectarian violence, not the insurgency, as the biggest problem and weren't going to support one side in a civil war. Casey told Bush that Iraqi forces alone had proven incapable of controlling Baghdad; the concern was that the prime minister would stand aside while the death squads drove out the Sunnis. If Maliki wanted the Iraqi Army in the lead, Casey would work out a plan that did that, with U.S. soldiers and commanders in the background providing the muscle and direction.

"When Maliki took office in June," Casey told me, "I told him the biggest threats to his government were al Qaeda and the Shiite militias. He disagreed, saying the Baathists were his chief enemy. With both the Jaafari and Maliki governments, anti-Baathist emotions gradually became anti-Sunni."

Bush was well aware of Maliki's shortcomings. Just before the Amman meeting, a candid memo from Hadley to the president about Maliki had been leaked to *The New York Times*. Hadley concluded that he couldn't tell whether Maliki was a nationalist with weak leadership skills or a sectarian leader determined to treat the Sunnis as they had treated the Shiites for centuries. The leak in itself was a puzzle. Some believed it was an unauthorized effort to point out Maliki's fickleness. Others believed it strengthened the president's hand by warning Maliki that the U.S. government wasn't blind to his faults.

Either way, the Hadley memo, expressing deep doubt about the character of Iraq's top elected official, contributed to a restless public mood in the States. Bush had lost the confidence of the public as its wartime leader, and seemed proud of his poor public speaking, a defect that erased the advantage the bully pulpit conferred on any president. The Democrats were no better, relentlessly demanding withdrawal while refusing to acknowledge the disastrous consequences sure to follow.

In early December, the Iraq Study Group released its report and met with the president. Robb made his strong pitch for a surge of American forces. As he left, the president smiled broadly. "I'll take a hard look at that provision," he said. Hadley said the same.

The report contained a laundry list of seventy-nine recommendations, allowing its many critics to nitpick what they didn't like. It lacked a hard-hitting core, disappointing the liberal antiwar faction, while being dismissed by conservatives as Pollyannaish in its call for regional talks with Syria and Iran. The report's advocacy for a strong advisory effort and its openness to a surge of U.S. forces were lost in the noise. Because the White House was "not going to outsource the business of handling the war," Robb's support for a surge had been met with silence in public. Inside the White House, however, it hadn't gone unnoticed.

On December 9, Bush met with his national security team and concluded, "We've got to get the violence down so that the political process can work." The previous day, he had told his advisers that the stakes were too high to gamble on the Iraqis curbing sectarian violence on their own. The die was cast; more U.S. troops were going to Iraq. Bush called Casey, asking, "George, do you have enough troops? I'm concerned about the ramifications [on wearing out the force] of sending more troops. But I am more concerned about winning."

SIXTEEN

THE WAR TURNS

NOVEMBER 2006

THE GROUND SHIFTS IN RAMADI

In late November, Casey flew out to Ramadi, where Colonel McFarland escorted him downtown. This was a standard leadership technique dating back to Alexander the Great. Generals routinely went to the scene of combat to talk with the front-line commanders. Napoleon's staff called it the *coup d'oeil,* roughly, the eye in the telescope, which permitted the commander to grasp what was actually happening on the battlefield. The grunts in Anbar called it the "windshield tour," and it often resulted in a few dings in the windshield.

Ramadi in November was different; Casey wasn't shot at. For three months, Jurney's Combined Action Battalion had been gaining ground. Every week for twelve weeks, about 500 marines, jundis, and shurtas pushed forward another four to six blocks, searching every room in thousands of houses. Every week, a marine and an Iraqi soldier died, along with ten or twenty insurgents. Some, as in Fallujah, barricaded themselves inside rooms that were blasted apart. Most were caught on the streets or back alleys as they fired a few shots or launched a rocket-propelled grenade. Once he had cleared an area, Jurney declared it a "gated community." He blocked it off with concrete Jersey barriers, placed police at the entry points, and set up a precinct station, using as rules of thumb 100 police per station and 10,000 residents per gated community.

"Some called them combat outposts, or COPs," Jurney said. "But a COP signifies a military war. A precinct means normalcy—the police are here to stay."

In September, the police came from the rural areas, recruited by McFarland from the initial tribes that pledged loyalty to the Awakening. By their approval, the sheiks signaled that becoming a policeman was an honorable, wage-paying job. The rural tribes, though, didn't know the streets or social patterns of Ramadi, with its 40,000 buildings and 200,000 or more residents. As Jurney advanced, the insurgents fought tenaciously, sneaking back in after dark. At night, Marine squads moved into houses chosen at random, paying $20 to hide for a few hours, slipping back out before dawn. Most times before first light the insurgents knew the Marines were somewhere on the block and would fire a few random shots as a challenge, a way of saying this is still our turf.

In late October, the battalion set up a precinct on 17th Street at the west end of the Racetrack. Knowing they were being squeezed out, the insurgents called in reinforcements. For four days, over 75 percent of all the indirect fire attacks in Anbar Province was directed at the 17th Street Precinct. This in turn gave targets to countermortar radars, UAVs with video cameras, and attack helicopters. The insurgents couldn't sustain the bombardment, and the next week, Jurney launched another operation deeper into the Racetrack.

The 17th Street Precinct relieved the pressure on the Government Center. Governor Mamoon could now receive visitors and actually govern. For two years, the Marines had escorted Mamoon to and from his compound, despite numerous hits by IEDs plus a suicide bomber. Mamoon claimed sixty-three attempts on his life. Regardless of the exact number, he was brave, lucky, and determined.

After 17th Street had repulsed the first wave of attacks, Mamoon contributed 120 men from his Alwani tribe, commanded by Lieutenant Colonel Salaam, a tough leader who had served in Saddam's Special Forces. Jurney didn't care that the new police had scant formal training.

"We're in gang fights, not combat against battalions," Jurney said. "The new cops brought street smarts. This was their home turf. We didn't have to wait to get hit. We could deliver the first blow."

Salaam proved to be the real deal. When residents whispered about

a hideout or a moneyman recruiting on the street, the Marines and police immediately drove or ran to the scene. Within 400 meters of a
precinct, Jurney encouraged a "react first, ask permission later" attitude: Get out on the streets and stay there. By November, the Combined Action Battalion had expanded to five precincts and twenty
checkpoints at the entrances to the "gated communities." Projects like
fixing sewers and schools had expanded from $10,000 to $4 million.
Each precinct was rigged with loudspeakers broadcasting news, sports,
and occasional pep talks from the mayor or the governor. Every attack
and every Iraqi casualty was announced. Every suicide bombing and
assassination was reported, with Lieutenant Colonel Salaam excoriat-
ing the terrorists as cowards who killed the innocent.

Jurney and Salaam didn't try to distinguish between the misguided
and the evil. They were police, not judges. They called the enemy by
one name—terrorist or takfiri. If you ran with murderers, you died
with them. Similarly, development projects weren't a right; they were a
reward. An area that gave tips gained a school or a sewer. Stay silent
and smell the shit. No risk, no gain.

When Casey visited in November, Jurney estimated it would take
two to three more months to push another kilometer to reach his eastern boundary, establishing five more precincts and another twenty
"gated communities." McFarland, who referred to Ramadi as "the Gettysburg of the Iraqi war," told Casey he needed two battalions to accelerate the pace. Casey flew back to Baghdad, where he and Odierno
compared notes and agreed Anbar merited an increase in American
forces not because it was spiraling out of control, but because the battlefield momentum was shifting.

In a fashion typical across Anbar, McFarland's 1st Brigade Combat
Team was dealing with two distinctly different wars. Jurney had the
urban fight, and he was winning by running joint operations with
Iraqis to build police precincts across the city. McFarland encouraged
that. It mirrored what he had done in Tal Afar.

THE TRIBES FIND A LEADER

The second war was rural. South of Ramadi lay the Habbaniyah complex stretching to Fallujah, thirty miles of sullen towns and remote villages with allegiances to twenty different tribes. The east side of
Ramadi, called Sofia, was also an insurgent transit point and a staging
ground for attacks against the Government Center.

Around Thanksgiving, Sofia erupted again when al Qaeda was attacking a compound held by members of the Albu Soda tribe that had pledged to support the Awakening. At McFarland's brigade headquarters, Capt. Travis Patriquin received a phone call from the desperate defenders. McFarland had a battalion operation scheduled to kick off in an hour. He called Lt. Col. Charles Ferry, who swung his unit, the 1st Battalion of the 9th Infantry, against al Qaeda. When Bradley Fighting Vehicles appeared on the scene, the insurgents fled.

This type of swift response changed the outcome of more than one battle. With Jurney in the west and two other battalions east and south of the city, the tribes sensed the tide was changing. The Americans welcomed the increase in police recruits provided by the tribes. In six months, Ramadi alone had risen from fewer than 100 police to almost 3,000, with the mix changing from rural to urban after Mamoon came on board. More tribes, whose power was in the rural areas, joined the Awakening; this raised the question of what the tribes would do once the number of police reached the limit authorized by Baghdad.

Sattar was a man of large vision. The goals of the Awakening extended beyond providing manpower. He had commercial interests. His brother quickly expanded a small trucking business by negotiating contracts with Jurney's and other battalions for construction and rubbish removal. He had political interests. Sattar circulated a political manifesto that called for a representative democracy—and the removal of Governor Mamoon. The tribes in Anbar had largely boycotted the 2005 election. Mamoon belonged to the Iraqi Islamic Party, which reflected the Sunni urbanite class in Baghdad. Sattar wanted more power for himself and for the rural tribes.

He also wanted security on his terms. He didn't want to rely on Americans to come to his rescue. The tribes had their own leaders, weapons, and vehicles. Although many had been fighting against the Americans, they were now fighting against al Qaeda. They wanted to organize their own defense forces. After the disaster of the Fallujah Brigade in 2004, the Marines reacted negatively to the notion of a Sunni militia, disguised under any name. In 2005, the minister of defense had refused another request. The mayor of Fallujah had made a similar proposition and was repeatedly refused.

The staff of the Marine Expeditionary Force wasn't convinced Sattar had the stature to lead the older sheiks and was reluctant to alter strategy based on an unofficial, unfunded gathering called together by one man. Anbar, though, was too vast ever to be controlled by military forces if the tribes did not cooperate. For years, the Americans had been looking for a heroic leader to step forward, and Sattar did have an outsized personality. Casey saw the Awakening as the wedge to split the tribal resistance away from al Qaeda, similar to what happened in Qaim a year earlier. McFarland was a confirmed supporter of Sattar.

With an orator's gift, natural leadership skills, and a grasp of the big picture, Sattar from the first dealt with colonels and generals to hammer out conceptual agreements. He was at once sincere and relaxed. When a fierce argument broke out between his two top lieutenants, Sattar turned the rancor into laughter by turning to Jurney and saying, "Let's get these two guys to kiss—they like each other so much." According to Sterling Jensen, an American interpreter who served in Ramadi, Sattar mocked the usual Sunni rhetoric and lectured his fellow sheiks that "the coalition forces are friendly forces, not occupying forces!" He didn't believe a surge in American forces would change a thing until Sunni attitudes changed.

In explaining the insurgency, CIA director Hayden listed first those Sunnis resisting the occupation, then former Baathists, followed by criminals and al Qaeda. Sattar had a different view. Baathists were a relic. Resistance groups that couldn't explain what they were resisting were weak-minded. Al Qaeda pushed around the fearful and the weak-minded. It was time for the tribes to retake control of their lands. It came down to al Qaeda versus the tribes. Sattar merited Geoffrey Chaucer's epigram "Of his courage as any center stable."

AWAKENING

As for al Qaeda in Iraq, the source of their power—intimidation—was so commonplace that it featured in the plot line of a hundred *High Noon*–type movies. As the gang leader in one obscure western expressed it, "We've got to get this storekeeper . . . they've made a hero of him. . . . If we don't keep these people scared, they'll be taking potshots at us in every little town."

That's exactly what was starting to happen in the little towns of Anbar. Within the tribes, bands of warriors were chafing to take revenge after two years of seeing their tribesmen killed, their women "married," and their businesses shaken down for "protection." While Sattar talked, the tribes tested what they could—and could not—do at the local level.

The initial returns were mixed. In the Habbaniyah corridor south of Ramadi, the SEALs from Special Operations Forces hooked up Sheik Abu Abbas with the Iraqi and American battalions. Prone to action, Abbas believed Sattar was spending too much time talking instead of killing terrorists. Abbas claimed he could break up the al Qaeda cell that controlled the gasoline in Khalidiyah, a rough town where three marines had been recently killed. When Lieutenant Colonel DesGrossiers of Battalion 3-2 took the fingerprints of Abbas's men, several popped up as former prisoners. Abbas acknowledged that they had been insurgents. What did the Americans expect?

DesGrossiers and the Iraqi battalion commander, Lieutenant Colonel Mohamed, decided to let Abbas prove himself. A day later, two battered cars drove alongside a long line of vehicles waiting for gas. Without warning, Abbas and several toughs leaped out, grabbed two men at the pumps, and started beating them. One died of injuries. Abbas screamed that the man was a terrorist, and the other drivers agreed and applauded. DesGrossiers decided that Abbas could "take care of business" as long as the Marines could identify the tribe.

The MEF (Marine Expeditionary Force) staff responded by sending a stiff message stressing that Marine units (i.e., DesGrossiers) could not associate with "unauthorized militia-type groups." The top level hadn't decided how to deal with the Awakening. It should be connected somehow to a government in Baghdad that didn't care about Anbar. Abbas, supported by the SEALs, took a detour and approached the advisers to the Iraqi battalion, promising less rough stuff while insisting his men could identify the terrorists.

Mohamed and his adviser, Maj. Owen West, were angered by the constant sniping and rocket-propelled grenade attacks inside the small town of Khalidiyah. SSgt. Richard Blakely and Sgt. Jonathan Simpson had been killed by snipers. Simpson had joined the Marine Corps after his cousin and close friend, Cpl. Abe Simpson, was killed in the Fallujah battle in 2004.

The Iraqi battalion had come from Mosul; most of the jundis were Shiites. The insurgents had spotters on every street and whistled or banged pots whenever a patrol, day or night, tried to sneak into town. Youths would gather on corners and snicker as the Iraqi soldiers and their advisers walked by. No local dared provide information.

Abbas provided two informers who hid in an old vehicle and drove slowly through Khalidiyah, while Mohamed's jundis cordoned off the exits. In four hours, thirty-nine men were detained. The jundis lined them up and shouted questions, while the tribesmen hooted each time they heard a false response. What do you mean you don't know where the mortar is? It's buried in your backyard, stupid. Where'd you get the Mercedes? From a garbage pit?

Thirty-seven proved to be insurgents, with two on the SEALs' high-value list. Mohamed's jundis applauded and victoriously the two groups drove down Michigan, the main road, honking horns and firing AKs in the air. As luck would have it, the general commanding the Iraqi 1st Division and his senior American adviser were driving up Michigan as the tumultuous gang swept by. Some of the gang broke off from the parade route and smashed up an Internet café that hosted terrorist Web sites.

The furious division commander wanted to know who were those guys dressed in black and carrying AKs, swaggering down the street with smiling jundis. The senior adviser wanted to know what the hell was going on. Down the chain of command came another memo— American advisers and Iraqi battalion commanders were to have nothing to do with tribal gangs.

The lower level protested, pointing out that after the arrests due to the informants hidden in a van, tips were pouring in from Khalidiyah. The intimidators had fled and residents were clapping when the jundis walked by. Abbas led a patrol to the house of the sniper who had shot Blakely and Simpson. The sniper's brother was captured and Abu Muslim, the sniper, died a few nights later. The jundis detained a third man, who refused to talk and was released. He moved into a bad section called Abu Fleis, swearing to kill a jundi in revenge. A week later, his body was found in the street.

"It was IEDs, RPGs, mortars, and sniping, small stuff," West said. "We had no way of knowing who anyone was. Lt. Col. Mohamed and I walked by insurgents every day. They were laughing behind our backs. They stopped laughing when Abbas's men showed up."

After months of inconclusive shooting at night and deadly IEDs, plus three suicide bombings during the day, tribal gangs were changing the atmosphere in a rural community that had resisted control for years. Although without official recognition, the Awakening was showing it had teeth. An e-mail from a Marine adviser explained how the situation was changing:

November 30, 2006. We're getting after it, but I walk with 100 pounds of gear. If I go out without armor, I'll be relieved. My team can hump for only two hours. It's insane. A few nights ago, a squirter ran right by me. By the time I got my rifle around, he had disappeared.

This Iraqi battalion depends not on my weapon or radio, but on my ability to push the corrupt, fucked-up Iraqi system and get logistics for them. In exchange, I get them out on operations.

Last night we set up an ambush on Michigan. Assholes have gotten cocky the last few nights, shooting at our convoys like clockwork. Sure enough, our decoy convoy was hit right in front of our position. I flipped on my 14s [night vision goggles] and saw four guys outside a tree line, firing AK's from the hip. I centered my dot and fired twice.

Then the world opened up. My jundis lit up the skyline all the way to Baghdad, ripping through magazines. A truly mad moment. I was screaming to sight in on targets and they merrily ignored me. Final score: US advisers five shots, jundis 900.

The good news? The next night, a hundred jundis showed up for patrol. They all wanted to get some. Not too shabby. Our bosses—Zientec and Coates—have a rule: each adviser does two patrols a day. Be aggressive. If we go out, the jundis go out.

These tribal gangs are great to have around. After four months, I'm starting to understand the mindset here in Khaldiyah. Now that Abbas and his local tribe have rolled to our side, K-town is ripe to be controlled. Crazy, local world.

In early December, Casey asked Zilmer, the senior general in Anbar, what he needed to gain control of the province. Zilmer wanted two battalions, plus the 3,000 marines in the MEU, (Marine Expeditionary Unit) stationed on ships in the Indian Ocean. That would be a sufficient increase to occupy every population center along the Euphrates valley. No more Whack-a-Mole.

Measured by the level of violence—the key indicator used by the military and the press—in December, Anbar was, like Baghdad, in peril. That was what showed on paper. On the ground, the commanders in the fight believed Anbar had hit a tipping point. But they had no evidence to prove it; their credibility in the press was low and it would be another several months before the standard indicators showed a credible trend. In the cities of Qaim, Haditha, and Ramadi, solid local police forces were emerging, although Fallujah remained truculent. In the rural areas, Sattar's Awakening movement suggested that the tribes held the key to defeating al Qaeda in Iraq. The war had turned.

SEVENTEEN

WASHINGTON TURNS

DECEMBER 2006

In the States, Baghdad's plight far overshadowed Anbar. On December 9, Casey told Bush that he and Odierno, the new corps commander, were working on a Baghdad security plan that put Iraqis visibly in the lead. He was trying to persuade Maliki to accept the plan, which gave him a larger role. Bush met with and telephoned key Iraqi politicians, pressuring them to soften their public attacks on Maliki and give him breathing space.

Two days later, Bush called in a few outside commentators on military strategy, including retired Army Gen. Jack Keane. A gruff, sensible man held in high regard in Army circles and by Vice President Dick Cheney, Keane had been urging the Pentagon since early fall to send more troops to Baghdad. Keane presented a forceful case, followed by briefings to the NSC by the historian Fred Kagan. Kagan's detailed plan for additional forces to be deployed across Baghdad in combat outposts provided the NSC surge strategy with tactical specificity. Neither Keane nor Kagan had firsthand experience. But based on McMaster's triumph in Tal Afar, they believed success in Baghdad depended on leading with American soldiers.

Tal Afar, however, had seesawed after McMaster and McFarland left. Good American leadership and tactics were not the critical component in determining success. What distinguished, say, Qaim from

Fallujah was the attitude and the commitment of the Sunni residents. No one knew how Americans would be received in the Sunni neighborhoods of Baghdad, or whether the Jesh al Mahdi would fight them in Shiite neighborhoods.

The president had heard enough to be persuaded. Baghdad was falling apart; Iraqi forces couldn't stop the downward spiral; and the U.S. forces were insufficient in size to be the saviors. It was understood that the purpose of more American troops in Baghdad was to protect the population; whether the population would accept American protection and reciprocate by providing information remained to be seen.

Although the incoming secretary of defense, Robert Gates, believed "the situation in Iraq was deteriorating," the idea for the surge had not come from the Pentagon, the Joint Chiefs of Staff, or Abizaid, the theater commander. Nor had it come from Baghdad. On December 8, Lieutenant General Chiarelli had wrapped up his year as the corps commander in Iraq by concluding, "We have done everything militarily we possibly can . . . militarily, I can say without a doubt that we are winning." In early summer, the president had asked Pace for a fresh look at Iraq. Six months later, Bush was still nudging the military toward that fresh look.

It was Hadley and the NSC staff—Luti, O'Sullivan, and Crouch—who had orchestrated the surge by quietly gathering a consensus among insiders, especially Odierno, Pace, and Petraeus, and outsiders. Robb brought combat experience and political gravitas, while Keane added the stature of a four-star general and Kagan contributed concrete specifics.

Hadley and his staff had stabilized a foundering administration. They set the model: the NSC working as a coordinating mechanism to present to the president and the cabinet clear alternatives, including views from outside government.

On December 13, Bush and Cheney met at the Pentagon with the Joint Chiefs in the small conference room called the Tank. Gates, the incoming secretary of defense, and Rumsfeld, who was stepping down, were in attendance, as were Casey and Abizaid. All participants knew that the commander-in-chief was inclined to send more troops to Iraq. After Cheney posed questions indicating a surge was desired, the Chiefs raised three issues. First, the soldiers, marines, and their families were under terrific strain due to successive, never-ending deployments to Iraq and Afghanistan. Now more was being asked of them. Hadley had anticipated this objection and Bush was prepared to offer an enticement. The Army and Marines, he said, would be increased in size. Second, the Chiefs were fed up with the thin support from the rest of the government. Civilians from State and other agencies needed to get out of the Green Zone and join the brigades on the front lines. Done, said Bush. Third, the Chiefs doubted the sincerity of the Iraqi government. This was the crux of the issue. The Iraqi forces promised by Maliki had never shown up in Baghdad.

"I don't want one American soldier doing what an Iraqi soldier should do," Casey had said, time after time.

The president agreed. If the Iraqis saw a sliver of daylight between him and Casey, they'd agree to nothing until there was a new commander. And even then, they'd stall for several months. Casey had worked out the Baghdad Security Plan with Odierno, who was consulting with Petraeus. Bush assured the generals that he would extract a commitment to the plan from Maliki before more American troops were deployed.

In an interview fourteen months later, Bush explained his thinking about the meeting with the Joint Chiefs to Fred Barnes, a writer for *The Weekly Standard*.

"One of the most important jobs of a commander-in-chief," he said, "is to be thoughtful and sensitive about the U.S. military."

It was a patronizing remark, implying that strategy was too important to be left to generals whose feelings had to be assuaged. Although the Rumsfeld-Casey-Abizaid strategy did not comport with the president's objective, for years Bush had not challenged the contradiction. He wanted victory; they wanted to get out in theory. President Bush and Secretaries Rice and Rumsfeld opposed using the U.S. military for "nation building," and Casey agreed. Yet nation building was precisely what the president was doing in Iraq. Victory required it. The columnist Jim Hoagland concluded, "Bush bears heavy responsibility for the collapse of presidential authority on his watch. His reckless disregard of the hard work and details of governance have made followership a difficult and dangerous pursuit under him."

Strategy is the proper allocation of sufficient resources to achieve the political objective. For four years, Bush had substituted self-certitude for strategy, thereby avoiding the long hours of study the complexities of Iraq demanded. He had strong faith, saying, "I believe a gift of that Almighty to all is freedom. And I will tell you that is a principle that no one can convince me that doesn't exist." A family in Baghdad may want freedom; how American soldiers could deliver that freedom required the proper strategy. It was not a gift.

"The president's style as a CEO was deliberative, not decisive," a senior White House official said. "He would issue an order and wait until his subordinates came back with a coordinated, agreed solution. We knew in June we were in trouble in Iraq, but it took until February to get a new general in there with a new strategy. The president did the right thing, but it shouldn't have taken nine months."

When Lt. Gen. Ray Odierno became the Multi-National Force corps commander in early December, Casey told him to design a "decisive operation" to reduce the violence in Baghdad. Odierno developed what was called the Gap Strategy.

"Residents wanted security and their government couldn't provide it," Odierno told me. "This created a gap filled by al Qaeda–led insurgents on the Sunni side and JAM militia on the Shiite side."

U.S. forces, Odierno concluded, should fill the gap. This fundamentally altered the military mission. For the past year, the task had been training Iraqi forces and then transitioning responsibility to them. The Gap Strategy made American forces directly responsible for protecting the population by clearing and then holding the neighborhoods.

Odierno was determined to shake up the status quo. The American soldiers on the streets knew they were losing. Nothing shatters morale more than taking losses while persisting with combat tasks that the entire chain of command knows won't change the outcome. Once an area was cleared, Odierno said, it had to be held. No more turning over responsibility to Iraqi forces that couldn't, or wouldn't, keep control.

From Iraq, Odierno had reached back to the Army and asked, "What's the most I can have?" The answer was five more brigades spaced over five months. After the December 13 meeting with the president, Pace told Casey, who was considering two more brigades, that the Joint Chiefs were prepared to put all five in the pipeline, in case more were needed.

Despite two years of sputtering failures, Casey was still convinced he could split the tribes in Anbar away from al Qaeda. He urged Odierno to meet with Sheik Sattar from Ramadi, another in a long line of sheiks. Odierno came away impressed by Sattar's ferocity of spirit.

Shortly before Christmas, Gates visited with the commanders in Iraq to go over the plans for employing new brigades. At a Christmas party in the Pentagon, Rumsfeld bumped into Luti, the NSC staff member. "I suppose I should call you Surgio," Rumsfeld said, indicating he had known from the start about Luti recommending an increase in U.S. forces.

Casey had proposed to Maliki that they establish a joint operations center in Baghdad, commanded by an Iraqi general. Maliki agreed, but rejected the general recommended by Casey. I'm putting Lt. Gen. Abud Hashim in charge, Maliki said, provided he's nonsectarian. Casey left the meeting encouraged that Maliki wanted to avoid sectarian bias.

"Two factors controlled all we did in Iraq," Casey told me. "First, giving back sovereignty limited us in selecting good leaders. Second, deep sectarianism lurked beneath the surface. This was a compound problem, with the one affecting the other."

When Gates arrived in Baghdad just before Christmas, Casey and his commanders recommended an increase of two brigades. It was Casey's last major decision about force size. He had been in command for thirty-one months, a time span that included three Iraqi governments, three American ambassadors, and four corps commanders.

Casey was due to come home in the spring of 2007, strongly endorsed by Bush and slated by Rumsfeld and Army officials to be the next Army chief of staff. With the fervent assistance of Chiarelli, Casey had changed the attitude of the U.S. Army in Iraq from applying firepower against insurgents to treating a civilian population with respect. Bush stressed to his staff that Petraeus would be fighting the Army that Casey had shaped. The attitude that would facilitate Petraeus's essential new tactic—don't commute to work—had been fostered by Casey. Like Abizaid, though, Casey considered American soldiers too much of an irritant to protect an Arab population. So he persisted with the transition strategy even as Iraqi forces, when left on their own, failed.

"Without political backing, Casey wanted to get out," a four-star general told me on condition of anonymity. "With political backing, Petraeus wanted to win."

Casey had approved Odierno's brief to Gates about U.S. troops shifting to population protection. With a new mission, it was time for a new commander. Rumsfeld had penciled in Petraeus to take over for Casey in the spring. Canvassing the Joint Chiefs, Gates found solid support for Petraeus. Plus, Vice President Cheney had visited Petraeus while he was writing the field manual on counterinsurgency and left impressed with the general's style and grasp of substance.

The other candidate was Mattis, whom Gates also interviewed. Mattis was the favorite of former secretary of defense James Schlesinger, a confidant of Gates who had moved from directing the CIA to the Pentagon at the end of the Vietnam War and who ever since had retained a healthy respect for tough field commanders. A veteran of campaigns in Afghanistan, Baghdad, and Fallujah, Mattis commanded I MEF at its home base in California. Because most of the MEFs deployed units were in Anbar, Mattis was a regular visitor. He knew every city and practically every sheik. When he spoke with Gates, he conveyed a passion that the war could be won in a province many had written off as lost.

Gates told Mattis he had an assignment in mind for him, but that Petraeus was the right man for Iraq. In addition to being an excellent division commander, Petraeus had served a second tour in charge of Iraqi training. He knew the Iraqi leaders and the situation in Baghdad. Mattis told the secretary he agreed completely that Petraeus was the right man for the job.

While not part of the formal review of strategy, Petraeus was kept informed by O'Sullivan, Pace, and Keane. In addition, for months Petraeus had monitored the daily televideo of the Battlefield Update Assessment. The BUA was the morning hour-long brief in Baghdad prepared by a staff of hundreds for Casey and his senior commanders. Inter alia, the brief covered intelligence, politics, economics, press stories, military operations, significant actions, casualties, and upcoming events. The televideo links enabled commanders at selected posts around the world to stay abreast of trends in Iraq. It was a remarkably open way of conducting business. It's hard to imagine other government agencies or private corporations operating so transparently.

Having accepted the command in the last week in December, Petraeus put down two markers with Pace, asking that the primary mission be explicitly changed from training Iraqi forces to population security and that all five brigades, plus another division headquarters, be committed. Casey had preferred starting with two brigades, and adding the others depending on circumstances. Odierno, though, agreed with Petraeus, and Casey deferred to the incoming commander. Five brigades it would be.

On January 6, Maliki delivered a speech committing more Iraqi forces to Baghdad and promising there would be no safe havens for militias. That was the assurance the Joint Chiefs had sought. The pieces were in place: a promise from Maliki, a security plan with an Iraqi general in charge, a new U.S. commander, and an infusion of American troops.

The Pentagon recommended committing "up to five brigades," a loophole sure to invite Congress to second-guess the need for each and every brigade. When Hadley pointed that out, the president pledged all five brigades—eventually 30,000 troops. The Pentagon also wanted to leave Anbar unaddressed. Again Hadley went to the president, and again Bush added the word "Anbar" to his speech so that no could misinterpret his intent.

On January 10, President Bush addressed the nation, saying, "It is clear that we need to change our strategy in Iraq." Efforts to secure Baghdad had failed, Bush said, because there weren't enough American and Iraqi soldiers, and because the Americans had been restricted from pursuing Shiite militias. American soldiers would protect the population. A reduction in violence was expected to give Iraq's leaders time to reach political reconciliation.

What had begun in June of 2006 as a request for a review ended in February of 2007 with a new strategy and a new commander. The ninemonth process had shown a president diffident to generals even when he believed they were wrong and were not pursuing his objectives. It revealed a slow White House decision-making process overly focused on bureaucratic consensus. It also showed a president who held to his convictions and treated people with decency. No one was excluded, or reprimanded for advancing alternatives that contradicted the president's faith-based rationale for victory in Iraq.

After the fall of Baghdad in 2003, poor planning, shallow thinking, arrogance, and terrible personnel selection facilitated an extended insurgency that polarized the American public, and wrecked the Bush presidency. But when things fell apart in 2006, Bush didn't flinch. In the face of opposition from almost all quarters, he made the toughest call of his presidency, sending more troops into Iraq when the situation was deteriorating. However the particulars would work out, Bush was changing the dynamic in Iraq.

An increase in troops was not a change in mission. Petraeus added that clarity by insisting the American mission change from supporting Iraqi forces to protecting the population. The December 2006 assessment by the MNF-I staff in Baghdad agreed that "more US troops are needed." But it also warned about a "palpable waning of support for US presence." If so, who wanted to be protected by Americans? Would they be welcomed as liberators or rejected as occupiers in Sunni neighborhoods under al Qaeda control and in Shiite neighborhoods under JAM control?

It was a leap into the unknown to advance a strategy of protecting a population that might reject the Americans. Even for Petraeus, who had supreme self-confidence, it was daunting to take command on a losing battlefield with the president demanding victory, the Democratic

Party clamoring about hopelessness, and the Iraqi prime minister scheming.

"After I accepted command," Petraeus told me, "there were nights when I woke bolt-upright at three in the morning, asking—what have I done?"

By November of 2006, the will of the people—that essential ingredient in defeating an insurgency—had turned the war in favor of the coalition. The Sunni tribes had allied with the Americans to drive out the al Qaeda terrorists. The tribal resistance groups had ceased to resist the coalition. Ramadi, the symbol of al Qaeda's tenacity, was functioning for the first time as the provincial seat of government. The change in the attitude of the Sunni population and the momentum in a dozen cities had come from the bottom up, from the tribes and battalions.

Ironically, in late 2006, it seemed to those at the top in Washington that Iraq had lurched out of control. Statistics confirming the change at the bottom were months away. The president's decision to send more troops to Baghdad seemed a desperate act with little hope of success. He grasped the theory of protecting the population. But if the same attitude prevailed as in 2004, then neither Sunnis nor Shiites wanted to be "protected" by Americans. In that case, American force of arms could limit the violence but not alter the underlying attitudes causing the violence.

Instead, out of Anbar would come the Sawha, or Awakening, movement, which changed the attitude of the Sunnis. The movement crept westward in 2007, welcomed by the American soldiers sent into the neighborhoods and farmlands by the Petraeus and Odierno strategy.

EIGHTEEN

THE SUNNIS CHANGE SIDES

WINTER 2007

The year 2007 began on a rancorous note in the United States, as the ties of political civility that bind a nation frayed. On January 10, Bush gave the most important speech of his presidency, explaining why he was sending more American soldiers to fight a war most of the public believed he had mishandled. A dry exposition of the military rationale, the speech was delivered in the inspiring tones of a weatherman predicting a hurricane. The president increased the force in Iraq from fifteen to twenty-one brigades, with one brigade arriving each month from January through June. The objective was to protect the population.

The Democrats responded with defeatist denunciations that exceeded the bounds of proportionality. By near-unanimous votes, the Democrats in the House and Senate voted to cease U.S. combat operations by June of 2008 at the latest, coupled with a precipitate withdrawal of American forces. When Senator McCain called this the "Date Certain for Surrender Act," the *New York Times* editorial page retorted, "Victory is no longer an option." A *Newsweek* correspondent in Iraq wrote, "What's clear is that we're far closer to the beginning of this cycle of violence than to its end." John Burns, the *New York Times* bureau chief in Iraq, said, "Friends of mine who are Iraqi—Sunni, Shiite, Kurd—all foresee a civil war on a scale with bloodshed that would absolutely dwarf what we're seeing now." Burns, though, was unwilling to dismiss Bush's surge as hopeless.

The intensity of the desire to quit was not driven by the burden of personal loss or sacrifice. The economy was healthy, and the president had asked the country to carry no burden during the war. Fewer than one in 200 families had a close relative serving in Iraq. Thirty percent of Army generals had sons or daughters who served in Iraq; members of Congress had less than 5 percent. The loss of a single soldier brings heartbreak to a family. But, as the commandant of the Marine Corps observed, by historical standards the losses in Iraq were light. Three thousand Americans had died in Iraq, less than 5 percent of the losses in Vietnam.

While President Bush was trying to correct a mistake, the Democrats were pillorying him for adopting a new strategy. Anger led to incivility. Senator Jim Webb (D-VA), after snubbing the president at a reception in the White House, claimed in a Senate hearing that "seventy percent of the troops in Iraq believe we should be out within a year . . . a majority of the people in the military no longer support the approach of this administration." Few actions by a U.S. senator could be more divisive to unit morale and more subversive of the bedrock principle that the military must support their commander-in-chief than to cite polls about the military's support for its own mission.

Senator Hillary Clinton (D-NY) responded to the surge strategy by saying, "I hope it succeeds. . . . I have a lot of support among general officers and military experts that it's not going to work." Senator Chris Dodd (D-CT) agreed, saying, "This is a tactic in search of a strategy, in my view, and will not bring us a more stable Iraq." A few Republicans also reacted vehemently. "This speech given last night by this president," Senator Chuck Hagel (R-NE) said, "represents the most dangerous foreign policy blunder in this country since Vietnam."

At his Senate confirmation hearing in late January, Petraeus stuck rigorously to his game plan of laying out his strategy and answering every query factually, refusing to speculate on results or promise progress. He said the "situation in Iraq had deteriorated significantly" and in place of transitioning responsibility to Iraqi forces, the new mission was "making security of the population, particularly in Baghdad, and in partnership with Iraqi forces, the focus of the military effort . . . a persistent presence in these neighborhoods will be essential."

Asked in a practice session before the hearing if the United States was failing in Iraq, Petraeus had responded yes. In the hearing, he was not asked that key question and did not volunteer the response. He was prepared to go into depth about training, tactics, and force dispositions. But rather than asking him questions, most of the senators spent their time either defending his mission, or railing against the war and predicting a slide into escalating chaos.

When I met with him a few days later, he described the hearing as "an out of body experience." He was comfortable with the strategy he had designed and expressed a keen interest in the Sunni tribal movement in Anbar, adding that "it can't become separate from regular government." He said he would stop the catch and release of insurgents and simplify the rules of engagement. Since the killings at Haditha, rules had been added on top of rules. Soldiers had more rules restricting the use of force than the Beverly Hills police force.

"We need a sense by summer if we can make this work," he told me. "We've done a terrible job of IO [Information Operations]. IO means U.S. Congress and press support. I'm going to invite them out of the Green Zone with me. We owe being visible as leaders to show who we are. They can make up their own minds."

CASEY LEAVES

On February 1, the Senate held another hearing, voting 83 to 14 to confirm Casey as the chief of staff of the U.S. Army. His promotion had been in the works for months before Baghdad fell apart. Gates said he was the unanimous choice of the Joint Chiefs, and the staff of the Multi-National Force praised his management skills and thoughtfulness. McCain and several other senators objected, arguing that Casey had failed in Iraq. Senator John Sununu (R-NH) said that a lack of success in the field should not be rewarded. Certainly, the war had gone badly. Before Casey arrived, the military and the White House had jointly ordered the reluctant Marines to seize Fallujah, only to halt the attack due to political turmoil. After Zarqawi and the al Qaeda terrorists seized control of the city during the summer, one of Casey's first decisions as the new commander had been to order a full assault to retake the city. Two thousand four was a year of flailing. This was followed in 2005 by dozens of offensive operations to drive out the insurgents, who returned to the populated areas when the Americans left. In 2006, Casey focused on training Iraqi forces to take the lead, with American soldiers pulling back to Forward Operating Bases. When Shiite death squads attacked Sunnis inside the capital, the Americans weren't in the neighborhoods to prevent the slide into chaos.

"The existing strategy, the stay the course," Hadley said, "everybody agrees is not working—that's failure slow." Yet everybody in the military's top echelon had agreed to the strategy. At a meeting in October of 2005, the top generals in Iraq, including Petraeus, agreed to put Iraqi forces in the lead, later termed "rushing to failure."

Casey had consulted with his division commanders before telling the NSC in June 2006 that he needed no more troops. Casey had altered the Army's doctrine of the offensive to accommodate counterinsurgency, although the core tenet of living among the people to separate them from the insurgents had eluded him and his commanders, not least because avoiding casualties had become a military mission. In Anbar, there never was a pullback to Forward Operating Bases. In the Baghdad region, there was ample opportunity for commanders to recommend against the pullback to the FOBs. Casey didn't make those decisions alone. Raids remained a favorite staple of the battalions, although raids were an admission that the insurgents controlled the population.

Senator Carl Levin, chairman of the Armed Services Committee, defended Casey, saying, "It is not fair that General Casey be tagged with failures, massive failures which were caused by the false policies, the wrong policies, the deceptions, the ignorance, the arrogance, the cockiness of civilian leaders of this administration."

"From 2004 through 2006, we forced a schedule that demanded three elections," Casey told me. "Each time the mission of our troops had to change to protect the election. We put in three Iraqi governments, two of which were sectarian. Each time we gained momentum, another election and paralysis in the new government dropped us back. Militarily, it was debilitating."

I asked Casey what the lesson for the Army was from Iraq.

"I used to believe if we soldiers could do conventional war," Casey said, "we could do anything. That's not true. In conventional battle, we maneuver to avoid the civilian population. In future wars, we have to prevail among the people. That changes everything."

THE FIRST COP

When Petraeus took over from Casey on February 10, he sent all his troops a one-page letter about the mission. Petraeus's letter was clear and forceful. Gone were the winding, opaque sentences of the *Counterinsurgency Field Manual,* and gone too was any tone of softness. This was a message about war, sent to soldiers.

"We cannot allow mass murderers to hold the initiative," he wrote. "We must strike them relentlessly. We and our Iraqi partners must set the terms of the struggle, not our enemies. And together we must prevail . . . your commitment to service and your skill can make the difference between victory and defeat in a very tough mission." To break the cycle of violence in Baghdad, Petraeus and Odierno faced a choice: focus on al Qaeda or on the Shiite death squads. There weren't enough American troops to do both (or maybe either).

Baghdad had 457 neighborhoods in ten districts—five Shiite, three mixed, and two Sunni. The death squads were attacking from safe havens in the Shiite districts, especially Sadr City in east Baghdad and Kadhimiyah and Shula in the northwest. Throughout 2005 and early 2006, execution-style killings in Baghdad had averaged around 500 a month; most were Sunni males murdered by Shiite death squads. After the Samarra bombing, Sadr encouraged his Mahdi Army to take revenge, and from the spring of 2006 through January of 2007, the killings ranged around 1,000 a month.

So it would seem that the way to stop the cycle of violence and cut the killings in half was to go after the death squads. In mid-October of 2006, when Chiarelli had briefly controlled the entry points into Sadr City, the killings had dropped abruptly. They resumed again when Maliki ordered the barriers and American troops removed.

In December of 2006, there were 1,200 executions; in January, 950; and in February, fewer than 600. No new American troops had yet entered Baghdad. Instead, as word of the surge spread, Shiite militia leaders fled from Baghdad, correctly believing that Maliki had cut a deal to allow the greatly feared American Special Operations Forces to arrest the death squads.

However, the number murdered by al Qaeda suicide bombers suddenly increased from under 200 in 2006 to over 400 in February of 2007. Overall, the number of civilians killed remained high when the surge began, but the cause—what the military called the "accelerant"—of the cycle of violence shifted from death squads to suicide car bombers.

Described as "public enemy number one" by Petraeus, al Qaeda was locked in a death struggle with America. There was no middle ground. Within the Shiite militia ranks of the Badr Corps and the Jesh al Mahdi there was a vast middle ground. Since al Qaeda was the prime enemy of the United States and the prime cause of the cycle of violence, Petraeus directed that the first priority was to drive out al Qaeda and protect Sunni neighborhoods, while the SOF would target both death squad and al Qaeda leaders. To Odierno, this gave impetus to move against the belts around Baghdad, where al Qaeda was assembling the car bombs and dispatching the suicide murderers recruited from Saudi Arabia and other Arab countries.

A month earlier, a Special Forces raid in Taji had turned up a hand-drawn map by a senior AQI leader that showed a circle like a belt around Baghdad, indicating safe harbors where al Qaeda could manufacture IEDs and car bombs, rest, and plan the next attack against the capital.

"It reminded me of how Saddam planned to defend Baghdad," Odierno told me. "He put three Republican Guard divisions in a belt around the city, and one inside. Al Qaeda had the same pattern. We had to go after the belts and the city."

In early February, there were five U.S. brigades in Baghdad, numbering about 35,000 troops, plus about 100,000 Iraqi soldiers and police. The first two additional brigades would be applied inside Baghdad. Unlike the prior summer, this time Maliki was really delivering 6,000 additional jundis, providing them with some extra training, pay, and a fixed end date for their stay inside the city.

Over the past year, JAM had driven most of the Sunnis from east Baghdad and were attacking nightly in west Baghdad. To stop them, Odierno ordered U.S. units off the FOBs and into positions inside the city. By April, he planned to set up fifty combat outposts—COPs—and joint security stations. A COP was the fort where American, and sometimes Iraqi soldiers, ate and slept; a security station was the ops center a few blocks away where they coordinated and responded to emergencies, like a police precinct station.

Plopping COPs in the midst of violence ensured that the American soldiers would vigorously patrol. There was no driving back each evening to a massive FOB for an excellent dinner, a check for e-mails, a new DVD release, and a bunk in an air-conditioned room, guarded by disciplined Ugandans, Gurkhas, Peruvians, and other militaries that had hired on.

To protect their COP, the American soldiers had to know their neighbors. The neighboring Iraqis benefited from armed Americans constantly coming and going. The theory was that the residents were being coerced by local gangs and would rather turn against them than cooperate with them. In Sunni locales, this proved to be the case; ironically, in many Shiite locales, it didn't.

Casino was the name of the first COP in Baghdad, installed by the 2nd Brigade of the 1st Infantry Division smack on the fault line between the Sunnis and Shiites in Ghazaliyah, a district in west-central Baghdad. When I arrived on the day Petraeus took command, engineers were still emplacing a few more concrete barrier blocks.

Casino looked imposing. Sentry posts with protruding machine gun barrels dotted the roofs of three concrete houses with sandbagged doors and windows. The houses were encased inside a square barrier of 468 concrete slabs, each weighing 8,000 pounds. Outside the barrier, coils of barbed wire provided a second line of defense.

Casino was simply a few abandoned houses surrounded by concrete blocks in the middle of a formerly upscale Sunni district, block upon block of single-family, Spanish-style houses with barred windows, tall courtyard walls, stout metal gates, and sidewalks along straight streets softened by palmettos and palm trees. The entrance to every street was blocked by tree trunks and chunks of concrete. Mounds of garbage lined the sidewalks. Broken sewer lines had turned the streets into lakes of putrid black ooze the troops called "shit water."

The Sunnis were clinging to their homes, their one source of meager wealth and the one hope for normalcy again, someday. The JAM was pressing in from the north, driving them out, block by block. While the American soldiers were building Casino, the JAM gained two blocks. The soldiers had watched the refugees straggle by, night after night, carrying what they could.

The front lines were only 300 meters north of the fort, where a Sunni mosque was holding out. "We hear shooting at the mosque every night," Sgt. Sergei Marchaud said. "By the time we arrive, JAM has pulled back."

The previous night, Marchaud was leading an Iraqi-American patrol that bumped into some Sunni insurgents coming out of a house. Marchaud killed one and the jundis captured two others, along with a Russian sniper rifle with a telescopic sight.

In the morning, I accompanied Marchaud on a patrol led by Lt. Joel Rhea, an Auburn graduate recently qualified as a tank officer. With guard duty inside the COP, plus time to eat, take care of logistics, and maintain a platoon on quick-reaction status, the company averaged four patrols a day. On most streets most of the time, there was no American presence. Instead, the soldiers gave out their cell phone numbers. When the residents saw that they responded, the tips poured in.

Rhea's mission was to stand guard while a small Sunni market was razed. The market was nothing more than a dozen huts inside a concrete wall in the middle of a trash-filled lot. A few hundred meters away a two-story house in a Shiite section was serving as a police station. Although the windows weren't broken and the facade wasn't pockmarked by bullets, the police worried about snipers in the market.

It didn't take the Americans five minutes to drive to the market, where four Iraqi Humvees and two front-end tractors were idling. When the Americans dismounted, several middle-aged men emerged from the nearby houses and hesitantly approached, led by an old man wearing flipflops, a knotted bathrobe over his threadbare shirt and trousers, and a black knit cap on his bald head. Saying his name was Habo, he pointed to a large house on the corner.

"JAM. Bang, bang," Habo said. "Family gone. JAM bad."

He looked timidly at the jundis, who ignored him. When the two front-enders kicked into gear and moved to knock down the market, Habo and his Sunni neighbors pushed forward. "No, no. Snipers, bang-bang!" They pointed to a three-story house on the other side of the lot. "JAM." The market wall provided protection against JAM snipers.

Iraqi soldiers were kicking open the shops and hauling off trivial treasures of junk like electric wiring and rusty tools. "No pictures!" the jundis shouted, pushing back Chris Hondros, a photographer for Getty Images. Sergeant Marchaud rushed forward to protect Hondros, his rifle at high port. The startled jundis stopped their desultory looting and backed away.

Emboldened, the dozen-odd Sunni homeowners clustered around the Iraqi commander, Lieutenant Colonel Sabah, pleading for their market. "You help bad people," Habo scolded the Americans. After Sabah took him aside, Habo changed his mind.

"He is strong and we are weak," Habo said. "We need his protection. It's okay."

As the last wall was demolished, a woman drove up in a new sedan, sobbing and saying that two JAM members had broken into her house last night. She didn't dare go home. Lieutenant Rhea's soldiers hopped into their Humvees and followed the woman back to her home. The front door was broken, but there was no one inside. A neatly dressed man stepped out of a nearby house and approached Rhea.

"Seven JAM drove up last night and shot at my house," he said in slow, careful English. "My sons drove them off. They are from Shula. Uneducated. Here we are engineers, teachers. I am a doctor but I can't drive to my clinic. It is good Americans are here. Some Iraqi soldiers are all right, but others are not."

The distraught woman reemerged from her house, carrying a few picture albums. I'm leaving them my house, she said. But they'll kill me if I drive away alone. Rhea agreed to escort her out, turning over the sector to a fresh patrol led by Lt. Sam Cartee.

Cartee's men liked and respected him. When checking guard posts at three and four in the morning, he'd stay to chat for an hour before pushing on.

"When my platoon was on FOB Liberty," Cartee told me, "we did two four-hour patrols a day in Humvees. Now I patrol two kilometers. I know every inch."

We drove across the fault line, and entered a different world. The next street to the north belonged to the Shiites. The gutters were clean, children were walking home from school, a dozen shops displayed colorful wares, street cleaners were sweeping the sidewalks, while teenagers played soccer in the street. Three banks and four medical clinics were open, while in the Sunni area, the bank and clinic were closed. On every street corner, one or two young unarmed men were lounging as lookouts.

"JAM guys," Cartee said. "They're all over. JAM has more pull in these Shiite neighborhoods than the government. Sometimes you can't tell the difference. We get along okay, except for the assholes pushing out the Sunnis."

Cartee would stop, climb out, and call them over.

"Hey, not arresting you, not right now," Cartee would yell, through his translator. "I'm sending in a crew to repair the power lines. At the first shot, I'm pulling them out. You don't want a hot summer, you take care of those crews."

The young men nodded, not friendly and not hostile, unsure how to behave without being told. Most members of JAM had no desire or reason to fight Americans. On the streets, soldiers like Cartee rarely picked out the minority JAM special groups equipped by Iran to attack Americans. U.S. Special Operations Forces accounted for 70 percent of JAM leaders killed or arrested.

Heading back to Casino, Cartee cut down a side street where the houses had a forlorn, dusty look. The windows were shot out and hundreds of spent cartridges littered the street. The front of a wealthy, two-story house was charred black. The soldiers walked in, smelling for bodies. The air was clean. In the kitchen, the remains of a dinner curdled in a pan, while the clock ticked on the wall.

"These Sunnis were lucky," Cartee said. "Must have bolted out the back when the firebomb hit."

There was a black-and-white photo of a handsome woman in her mid-thirties, the instruction booklet for a 1982 PC, calendars from

2005 with bright pictures, a washing machine, two televisions, and a microwave. Clothes were hanging in the closets, including an Iraqi Air Force uniform with a colonel's epaulets. Toys were scattered in a bedroom. A mural of Swiss chalets in wintertime filled one wall in the living room.

"JAM will cart this stuff off," Cartee said. "Next week, a Shiite family will move in and push more Sunnis off the street—build a buffer so the original owner doesn't dare to come back. Ethnic cleansing with a profit motive. Everyone wins except the Sunni colonel."

Inside an abandoned house nearby, I found a packet of black-and-white pictures showing the progression of a handsome young man from his school days to middle age. One was taken in Egypt, with his wife and smiling daughter standing next to him. Most of the pictures showed groups of men, dressed in Western clothes, serious, stilted pictures. One, dated 1975, showed the man in a leisure suit, posing with an automatic rifle.

"He was probably Mukhabarat [secret service]. Good riddance," Nathan, an interpreter, said. "All those Baathists are gone. Jordan doesn't want them. Syria demands big money, $100,000 for a cheesy apartment. Egypt charges more. They'll never come back here."

"Nathan," a Shiite, had served with the American Army since 2003. A few times each year he sneaked back to his home in southern Iraq, changing the shape of his mustache and hair to deceive the neighbors who would report him to a militia group.

"Most wealthy Sunnis have left Baghdad," Nathan said. "Poor Sunnis have to stay."

Two men, walking by on the street, slowed down and glared at us. Neither of us was armed. When Sergeant Marchaud stepped out from around a corner, they hastened away. Who where they? Nathan shrugged. Maybe JAM. The Sunni terrorists had pulled out.

FORT APACHE

Sunni terrorists still had several bastions in the city. I caught a hop across the Tigris to a different kind of outpost. COP Apache, on the east bank of the river, was a small fort surrounded by thick concrete walls that had been featured in a documentary called *Gunner's Palace*. The 120 soldiers in Charlie Company, 1st Battalion, 26th Infantry, patrolled the Sunni district of Adamiyah. Al Qaeda held the 160,000 residents in a tight grip. There were no Iraqi soldiers or police inside the district in April of 2007.

The company had lost five killed, and the four daily patrols consisted of two Bradleys and four Humvees. On average, one patrol a day
received fire or an IED blast. Sgt. Lyle Buehler and his platoon showed
me around the district, careening down side streets at high speed to
avoid command-detonated IEDs.

In the distance was the Abu Hannifa mosque, revered by Sunnis.
The patrol headed downtown along trash-clogged Route Brewers and
drove slowly down a narrow alley between two-story buildings. This
was the spot where Spec. Ross McGinnis, nineteen, a .50-caliber gunner, had died in December. Buehler was driving at a crawl around a
tight turn when he saw in his left sideview mirror a man in a black
sweatshirt and sneakers dart behind the Humvee. He heard a *ping!* as
McGinnis, standing upright in the hatch behind his machine gun,
yelled *Grenade!*

"Where? Where?" Sgt. First Class Cedric Thomas, the truck commander sitting in the right forward seat, shouted.

"Shit, it's in the truck!" McGinnis answered.

Instead of hopping out his open hatch, he dropped into the truck
and smothered the blast with his body.

"He was the youngest in our platoon," Buehler said. "He was a
funny guy, always commenting on the local scene. He loved being the
gunner, standing up there, seeing stuff we couldn't."

Heading back to Apache, a tire blew out and the Humvee crept
along on a road beside the river.

"No way we're stopping out here to change it," Buehler said.

As we passed a row of large, deserted houses along the riverbank,
Buehler explained the danger. In late afternoon, the highway across the
bridge from west Baghdad jammed with commuters returning to the
poorer Shiite neighborhoods. Some drivers turned off onto side roads
to cut around the traffic. Sunni gangs lurking in alleys would rush out,
dragging small tree trunks to block the street, pulling guns, and checking IDs. Inevitably, some poor man was jerked out of his car and forced
into a deserted house. Buehler's platoon sometimes cruised by at dusk,
looking for a glimmer of light from a window. The soldiers had rescued
two captives who showered them with kisses, but usually they found
the bodies in the morning, most bound by wire and some with burns
and drill holes. Demands for ransom were routine, but few were reported to Buehler's company.

The next day, we careened down to the Sulak Joint Security Station,
set up on one side of a busy roundabout. Cpt. Scott Gilman sat in an
empty room, hooking up a radio. The police, all Shiite, stayed away

from Adamiyah. The head of the district council, Sheik Ghalib, he said, had recently been assassinated outside the Ministry of Energy, along with two other council members. They killed Ghalib with an axe. Believing the murders were set up by the Shiite ministry, the council had disbanded.

"We've been promised that police and jundis are coming back," Gilman said. "Check in again in a couple of months. We'll get this place functioning."

On the way back to Apache, the Humvees slowed down at one point to confirm that a body by the side of the road was dead.

"We don't pick the bodies up," Buehler said. "Someone will take him away. Not as many as there used to be. I've seen ten a day, now we're down to two or three."

The killers weren't shooting at American soldiers. The CIA estimated there were "tens of thousands" of insurgents, although not even a tiny fraction of that number was shooting at Americans. After the 2004 battles in Fallujah, Sadr City, and Najaf, Shiite militias and Sunni insurgents avoided gunfights with Americans. They struck at Americans with roadside bombs, and reserved their bullets for civilians who could not fight back.

When government leaders stand aside, it takes only a few to murder the defenseless. But what kind of person shoots down civilians? When I asked that of Col. J. B. Burton, the energetic commander of the 2nd Brigade, he made a few phone calls. I left COP Apache, bound for El Shubaralba prison on the west side of the Euphrates. Saddam had been hanged there in December of 2006, amidst jeers from guards loyal to Moqtada Sadr—a chaotic scene illustrating the sectarian incompetence of the Ministry of Interior. The exterior of one small prison building looked like a set from a Clint Eastwood movie—barbed wire twirled atop low concrete walls, a creaky iron gate, a dusty courtyard, disheveled guards, and a long row of heavy wooden doors. Two guards carried out a thin prisoner, feet wrapped in white rags, and plopped him on a rickety table. He curled his legs under him, hooked his elbows around his knees, and bent his head down. Ordered to talk, he told his story simply.

Saef Said, twenty-one, lived on Haifa Street in the middle of the city, several blocks from the Green Zone. Long a lair for terrorists, the street had erupted in December and January in battles against U.S. forces. In the midst of the fighting, for $100 a month, Saef was recruited by

Majef, thirty-five, "to protect people." The true enemy wasn't the Americans; it was those who worked with Americans. Majef pointed out Ayad Naeen, who was parking a 2004 Honda. As Naeen and his seven-year-old son walked down the crowded main street, Saef came up behind them. When Naeen looked back, Saef shot him in the face, then shot the boy in the head. He took their wallets, the car keys, and the Honda. The next week, Majef pointed out another spy, who was walking with his wife. When Saef shot him in the chest, the wife began to scream. So Saef shot her too.

Next, Majef gave Saef and a friend police uniforms. They set up a roadblock and stopped a passing bus, checking IDs and telling all Sunnis to get off. Then they robbed and shot eleven men, four women, and two children, leaving the bodies in the gutter. The international press reported fifty bodies found on Haifa Street over the course of a few days.

Still with his head down, Saef said he had killed "only twenty or thirty." He didn't know about the others. Maj. Ihmad Naeen, a stocky, grim cop, swatted Saef on the back of his head. I forgot, Saef said, we stopped another bus. Maybe there were some others.

Now a rich man on Haifa Street, Saef threw parties, with free-flowing liquor. The parties were reported, as were boasts about killing Shiites, provoking a midnight raid. Major Naeen was processing the dozen-odd semi-intoxicated Sunni men, trying to determine if they were involved in the violence plaguing Haifa Street, when he recognized the car keys to the Honda that had belonged to his brother, Ayad.

"Majef said every act by us is for God," Saef said, crying slightly. "I wish I never met him."

"You're a liar," Major Naeen said. "You wanted money. Your sister's as bad as you. We shot her. We'll hang you."

———

Iraq wasn't Rwanda, with neighbors hacking and shooting neighbors, or even the Balkans, where Petraeus told me he had seen more implacable hatred. It wasn't a true civil war; al Qaeda was murdering Shiites so that Shiites would retaliate against Sunnis. Remove al Qaeda, and you remove the primary provocation for Shiites and Sunnis fighting each other. The violence on the street level was not the apocalypse imagined by politicians in the States. Punk killers like Saef were preying on the weak, murdering those too scared to fight back.

Place a U.S. platoon in a neighborhood and murders decrease. AQI and Shiite death squads were hard to find, easy to kill. That was the core conviction American soldiers carried with them. It lent an air of confidence, even cockiness, to them.

RETURN TO CHICKEN MURDER

In 2005, Baghdad was about 40 percent Shiite, 20 percent Sunni, and 40 percent mixed neighborhoods; by February of 2007, few mixed neighborhoods had survived, with the Shiites occupying most of the city. At the southern end of the city, I was curious to see how the Sunnis had fared down in Salman Pak, where Lieutenant Colonel Winski had almost decked a man for beating his daughters. Winski's battalion had returned to the States. Capt. Bo Dennis of the 3rd Battalion of the 61st Infantry offered to take me around the battle space.

As we drove by the town of Jisr Diyala, where Sergeant Weir was killed, Dennis mentioned the mayor had been arrested for providing weapons to the JAM. Dennis was driving at ten miles an hour, constantly checking in with a gunship circling over us.

"We had 131 IEDs in January," Dennis explained. "JAM kept coming in, fighting with the Sunnis. The National Police threw in with JAM, and we had to back the police. So now we're seen as allied with the enemy."

We rolled by the chicken farm where the two men had been murdered. It was now a burned-out shell, with no one in sight. On our right was a giant earth berm Saddam had thrown up around the buildings of his Atomic Energy Ministry, itself a Potemkin village where U.N. inspectors in the 1990s had been offered chai while they pored over harmless papers written in the 1960s. Outside the berm stood a row of concrete watchtowers that added seriousness to nonexistent research.

About ten towers had recently been blasted to earth, great chunks of concrete lying in the dust. Each tower took hundred of pounds of explosives to topple. Across the river lay the badlands of Arab Jabour. Al Qaeda had come across in boats, blown the empty towers as a gesture, then rushed across Route Wild and randomly pitched satchel charges into Shiite houses in a mixed community called Jara. Since my last visit a few months earlier, the Sunni farms had been burned, the Shiite houses blasted, and the area turned into a wasteland, with the Shiites huddled inside Jisr Diyala and the Sunnis penned inside the hamlet along the river called Tuwaitha.

Beyond the crumbled towers and a few hundred meters from the river, the Humvees were blocked by deep ditches that had been dug by hand across the paths. Dennis was cool about it. He dismounted a dozen soldiers, who spread out in a skirmish line, and we proceeded on foot through the palm groves. When Dennis halted at the edge of Tuwaitha village, a few men came warily forward. Unsmiling, they offered no chai and stood resentfully in the sun and the dirt, a few women cooking over wood fires off to one side.

After a few calls on cell phones, an elder named Majid said the village sheik couldn't be found. It's dangerous if he's seen with you, Majid said, complaining that the local Iraqi Army unit was flying a Shiite flag at its fort.

He proposed that his village take over the army checkpoints. He would guarantee no takfiris came across the river from Arab Jabour with IEDs. Since that was a deal Dennis couldn't make, we left the disappointed Sunnis of Tuwaitha village and continued down Route Wild.

"Higher's decided to shoot up all the boats to cut off this side from the land of the 500-pound bombs," Dennis said, pointing across at Arab Jabour on the west bank.

A few kilometers outside Salman Pak, we bumped into an unexpected roadblock manned by Iraqi gunners on an old Russian tank. The tank commander was arguing with a National Police major.

Dennis left the two officers while they were still arguing. He was pleased the tankers weren't working for the National Police. When we drove into Salman Pak, it was obvious why. The market was deserted, a few dilapidated stalls, paper and debris whipped around by the wind, one lone produce truck with a few bags of grain. Near the mosque, a couple of National Policemen were sauntering across the street in civilian clothes.

Since I had last visited in September with Winski, the arrival of a new NP commander had been greeted with a mortar attack from Arab Jabour. Soon thereafter, eight local Sunnis were killed. When the Sunni imam insisted that a JAM gang leave the mosque where the land deeds were kept, the NP sided with JAM. The mayor left town, the bank closed, and the town doctor was kidnapped. When al Qaeda gangs sneaked into town, no Sunnis reported them.

On the way back to base, Captain Dennis stopped at a combat outpost he had set up outside Salman Pak. The COP consisted of a two-story farmhouse in an open field 200 meters off Route Wild, with thick palm groves out back stretching for two kilometers to the river.

The interpreter at the outpost, Dahm, came from Salman Pak. He wanted Dennis to provide him through the CIA with a fake Iraqi ID card and the name of an Iraqi official who would vouch for him. Then he could wander around in Salman Pak and pick up information. Dennis vetoed the idea, convinced that sooner or later Dahm would slip up and be tortured to death. "JAM and takfiri are good liars," Dahm said. "No one knows who they are. They both were there in town looking at you just now."

In February of 2007, the complexity of the local politics in Baghdad matched the scale of the violence.

If Baghdad was the anvil, Anbar was the hammer for flattening the Sunni insurgency and splintering al Qaeda. In the final month of 2006, fighting in Anbar was still heavy. Captain Patriquin, who had worked with Sattar, died in a huge IED explosion in southeast Ramadi. Also killed were Spec. Vincent Pomante and Maj. Megan McClung, a superb athlete popular among her peers and well known for organizing Anbar's first marathon.

The Marine Expeditionary Force had been slugging it out for three years, a step forward and a step back. In early February, Maj. Gen. Walt Gaskin took over as MEF commander from Maj. Gen. Rick Zilmer. As the commander of all Marine forces in the Central Command, General Mattis flew to Anbar for the ceremony and for a look around. I hitched a ride with him, and we stopped first at the old British air base at Habbaniyah, midway between Fallujah and Ramadi. Although now ashen-hued with dust, in the 1920s the air base had sparkled under the British, who planted majestic eucalyptus trees and built double-decked roofs with cisterns of water that dripped through holes in the ceiling and was vaporized by fans, thus cooling the rooms.

After months of chasing "ghosts" in Habbaniyah, Lieutenant Colonel DesGrossiers's battalion had returned home, replaced by Battalion 3-6. Lt. Col. Jim McGrath had continued the vigorous patrolling, putting a platoon in each of fourteen combat outposts. McGrath, who was constantly visiting his platoons, showed Mattis a map with the symbols of COPs spread across fifty square kilometers. Contact was light, McGrath noted, and commerce was improving, with people on the move. Be careful of assassination teams, Mattis warned, recalling an incident when a sniper team had set up in an unfinished house. The team didn't object when a construction crew showed up, asking to make repairs. The crew shot all four marines at close range. "Don't let your guard down," Mattis said. "It's detective work out here."

A few kilometers to the north, Iraqi Battalion 3-3-1 commanded by

Lieutenant Colonel Muhamed, was immersed in detective work to gain control of the town of Khalidiyah. A rabbit warren of tightly packed houses and narrow alleys, K-Town had quieted down since the tribal sheik Abu Abbas had fingered the sniper team of two brothers who had killed two Americans. Advisers Lt. Col. Robert "Ogre" McCarthy and Maj. Owen West had the police shurtas and jundis patrolling together, when the advisers were part of the patrol. Still, IEDs persisted along Route Michigan, the main highway.

West, a reservist, asked the traders at his civilian firm to contribute to the nonprofit corporation Spirit of America in order to purchase an identification device. Nicknamed Snake Eater, the handheld unit was used by police in Chicago. A suspect's photo and thumbprints were taken and sent via radio to the precinct, where they were checked against databases, with the results called back to the cop on the street within five minutes. In Khalidiyah, Snake Eater was a placebo, since it wasn't connected to a database. The insurgents didn't know that, though, and a day after it was used, sixty men left town. The jundis loved the idea of immediately identifying anyone on the street. The insurgents were terrific liars with excellent fake IDs, but fingerprints didn't lie and a database would immediately provide anyone's personal history.

The IED attacks plummeted, but the insurgents were still at large. Again, the aggressive Sheik Abbas came forward. This time he claimed to have the support of Sheik Sattar. Lieutenant Colonel Muhamed was irritated by tribesmen in black shirts and baseball caps swaggering around his battle space, where he had lost twelve jundis. Abbas walked the walk, though. In the local mosques, he posted the names of 120 men, demanding they renounce their ties with the takfiris. Within a week, over 100 had done so. As for the others, several bodies were found in the streets.

Al Qaeda lashed back, launching a two-prong attack led by a suicide bomber that almost breached the walls of Sattar's compound. When that failed, a suicide murderer drove a truck full of explosives into a mosque in Habbaniyah where the list of insurgents had been posted. Thirty-nine worshippers were killed.

By February, full-scale war was raging between al Qaeda and the Anbar tribes.

A POLICE WAR WITHOUT DETECTIVE TOOLS

The gradual swing of the Sunnis was to change the tide of the war over the course of 2007. The decision by the Sunnis to point out the takfiris hiding amongst them also deflected attention from the most glaring technical error in the war—the lack of an identification system.

If the insurgents wore uniforms, the war would have been over in a week. The absence of identification enabled the insurgents—and death squads—to survive. A basic technique found in all counterinsurgency literature, including Petraeus's field manual, was to conduct a census. An American or Iraqi soldier didn't know who lived in Khalidiyah versus Salman Pak because no census had been conducted.

Two thousand years ago, King Herod declared that all Jews had to register at their places of birth. This provided a tax roll and a means of tracking down agitators. During the rebellion in Ireland after World War I, both the Irish Republican Army and British agents stole each other's records in order to obtain names and addresses for arrests and assassinations. When the Germans occupied France in 1940, they instituted a system that forced French officials to account for every family. No one could travel without papers, which could be quickly cross-checked against the home of record.

The French brought that system to Algeria in the 1950s. Called the Dispositif de Protection Urbaine, by a system of quadrillage the city of Algiers was divided into sectors, blocks, and buildings, each with a number. A census recorded all families. A warden, usually an old and respected Arab, kept track of everyone on his block. Under threat of arrest, he was charged to report suspicious activity and strangers. The battle for Algiers in 1956 was short-lived because the Algerian rebels could not move from apartment to apartment even in the dense Arab sector. No one was anonymous. The French counterinsurgency expert David Galula cited census taking as a fundamental lesson from the Algerian war.

In Malaya from 1948 into the 1950s, the British forced the Chinese to live in strategic hamlets surrounded by barbed wire in order to cut off links with the insurgents in the jungle. Any Chinese on the roads had to show an ID that identified his hamlet. In the early 1960s, Cuba, advised by East Germany, adopted a system similar to the French quadrillage and quickly ferreted out the CIA agents trying to build a network in Havana.

In Vietnam, the CIA sponsored the census grievance program for similar purposes of identification. Hundreds of teams of enthusiastic Vietnamese youths, dressed in black pajamas, visited most of Vietnam's 2,500 villages during 1966–1967. They sang nationalistic songs, tidied up marketplaces, asked the villagers about their grievances, and then moved on, having laboriously written down the names and locations of every family. Once the district police had records of who lived where, the movement of undercover Viet Cong political agents from one hamlet to another was severely restricted.

In July of 2005, I asked a four-star general why a census, to include the addresses and fingerprints of all military-aged males, was not taken in the Sunni Triangle. "Why, that would take a year," he said, "maybe eighteen months."

American and Iraqi forces conducted more than twelve million identification checks a year. Americans could not read Arabic, however, and counterfeit IDs were commonplace and official IDs such as passports were sold over the counter. The arch-terrorist Zarqawi was stopped and let go. In the Sunni Triangle and Baghdad, the average military-aged male was stopped twice a year for an ID check. Millions of man-hours were wasted, and al Qaeda members escaped repeatedly, due to not adapting military techniques and procurement to a police war.

In a Marine Corps handbook of lessons learned by company commanders, Captain Rory Quinn recommended that all company commanders "start your own database immediately, with maps hyperlinked."

After years of prodding, in 2007 bureaucratic baby steps toward identification began. No directive, however, was ever issued to conduct a census or to give every squad leader the same technical ability as police in the States to fingerprint a suspect and in minutes get back his record. The failure to do so was the major technological mistake in the war.

FALLUJAH WAVERING

Regardless of technology, in the Habbaniyah farming valley, the tribes were identifying the terrorists and driving them out. But in Fallujah, the residents still weren't pointing out the assassins when Lieutenant General Mattis arrived in mid-February. Maj. Vaughn Ward's battalion had gone home in October, having suffered eighteen killed in the city, and the Marines turned the city over to two Iraqi battalions and the local police. Since then, two more members of the city council had been assassinated. The week Mattis arrived, only four council members out of twenty-one dared to show up for a meeting. The new mayor—the seventh I had met in four years—was a nervous young man in a new suit and tie, who took his cues from the police chief as he chaired a meeting no one wanted to attend.

Mattis sat down with the new chief, Feisal Hussain, who gave it to him straight. The 2nd Brigade commander stole and left in disgrace, Feisal, reputedly a former insurgent, said. The residents didn't trust the Shiite jundis.

I wandered over to the jail, where over 100 prisoners were packed in with barely room to lie down. Chief Feisal was obviously trying to do his job. Part of the problem was Baghdad, deputy police chief Kareem told me, which didn't want to take any more prisoners and hadn't paid some police salaries in four months. Kareem wanted the Marines back inside the city. I almost laughed, thinking back a few years to the time when the police begged the Marines *not* to enter the city.

The Iraqi Army's tactical style, much like the police, was to stay in defensive checkpoints until they had intelligence on a target that wasn't expecting them. Patrolling streets where they didn't know the residents didn't come naturally. Once the Marines weren't alongside them, they had stopped patrolling. The regimental commander, Col. Richard Simcock, agreed. We pulled out too soon, he told Mattis. I'm assigning a battalion to help the police.

Later, Mattis met with some of the marines going back into the city. "Fallujah's the most morally bruising place in Iraq," he said. "It's going to rock you when an IED goes off and there's blood and shit all over you. Hold the line. Show the people respect. We're here to win."

TACON/HANDCON WITH THE AWAKENING

At the base outside the city, Lieutenant General Odierno presided over the change of command in February of 2007. Looking at Major Generals Zilmer and Gaskin, he said, "The Marine Expeditionary Force has turned the tide in Anbar. You're close to it. Your soldiers and marines are fighting every day. But I can see the change from Baghdad. It's the opposite of the way things were eighteen months ago. The Iraqis are now in the lead, with fifty-five police stations and 9,200 police, all recruited inside Anbar."

Odierno had put his finger on the major change—the gradual emergence of the Sunni police, greatly aided by the sheiks. After exchanging a few pleasantries, Odierno flew off to Baghdad and Mattis to Ramadi, where the Awakening had started.

In Ramadi, Lieutenant Colonel Jurney escorted us to the Government Center, where the view from the roof was dramatically different from that of last September. Piles of rubble had been bulldozed away, and the broken water pipe that spread an inch of mud across the first floor had been fixed. Most surprising, we didn't have to duck sniper fire. In the background, the loudspeakers at a nearby precinct could be heard broadcasting in Arabic the day's news and community events. Jurney was moving his lines forward, installing one police precinct after another. He introduced Mattis to the police chief, Lieutenant Colonel Salaam, and while they were chatting, I caught up with Adel Abouhana.

A middle-aged Arab-American businessman from Florida, Adel had spent a year in Ramadi as chief translator and confidant to Marine commanders. Because his Qatari accent sounded like that of a Ramadi resident, the locals talked freely to him. I hadn't seen him since September, when there were seventy-five attacks a day in the city. He had recently returned from the States.

"I took leave because I'm not needed every day," he said. "The tribes, the governor, the police chief, us Americans—all working together. The war is over in this city. I can feel it."

That seemed a tad too confident. But a few hours later, the brigade commander, Col. Sean McFarland, gave Mattis an overview, showing gradual control across his battle space, with combat outposts "taking away the enemy's freedom of maneuver." McFarland credited Sheik Sattar and the Awakening with bringing in the recruits for the army and police. Sattar gave the credit back to McFarland, Jurney, and the MEF.

"The coalition is the only thing," Sattar said, "that makes the central government give anything to Anbar. We have a great relation with the U.S."

So many tribesmen were coming forward that Sattar had organized, or semi-organized, eleven Emergency Response Units. An ERU was an untrained collection of 20 to 100 members from a dozen tribes, anxious to drive out takfiris and prevent other tribes from entering their tribal areas.

McFarland advocated a tolerance for the organizational chaos created by the armed tribes. Some police chiefs and American battalion commanders would be annoyed, and there was the potential for shooting unidentified tribesmen. The benefits, McFarland argued, were much greater. IED attacks across the brigade area had dropped by 50 percent in six months, and small arms attacks were down by 40 percent. Sattar had even drawn up an eleven-point plan. In the past, the tribes had demanded a withdrawal of U.S. forces. In Sattar's plan, endorsed by the other sheiks, "an attack on the coalition is an attack on us."

Sattar wanted Governor Mamoon replaced, because he had been appointed by the Baghdad-based Iraqi Islamic Party, which didn't rep-resent the tribes. Mattis took this as an early sign of the return of normal politics. We're not allowing the Ministry of Interior to stop the Awakening by banning the tribal units, Mattis said. We're not arming a militia; they armed themselves.

"We should help the tribes kill every last one of those bastards," he said. "General Zinni [a former CentCom commander] had what he called handcon. We'll do the same thing."

"Tacon" in the military meant that one unit exercised tactical control over another unit. "Handcon" meant agreeing on operations by a handshake, which was how Zinni had dealt with the tribes in Somalia over a decade earlier. On February 10, as Petraeus took command in Baghdad, the tribes in Anbar had reached a handcon agreement with the U.S. military.

A few years earlier, Mattis had been awakened around midnight by an intelligence officer who showed him infrared images of an encampment near the Syrian border. Mattis said to bomb them and went back to sleep. The next day, amidst allegations that Americans had bombed a wedding party, an investigating officer asked Mattis how long he had deliberated. Thirty seconds, Mattis said.

A few days after he took command, Petraeus flew to Ramadi, assessed the situation, and endorsed the Awakening, assuring Sattar that Prime Minister Maliki would soon visit Anbar to congratulate the tribes. Like Mattis, Petraeus knew it when he saw it. Throwing in with the Awakening was the swiftest decision he made after taking command.

His instinctive approval resulted in the Sunni Awakening spreading from Anbar to Baghdad, and eventually that changed the war in the east.

NINETEEN

MOMENTUM

HIGH LEVEL

By mid-April, the surge was well under way and Petraeus had his team in place. A former professor at West Point, he had tapped into the scholar-soldier network to pull together a core to develop a draft campaign plan. Col. Peter Mansoor had graduated first in the West Point class of '82 and had commanded a brigade in Iraq. Col. Mark Martins was first in the class of '83, Col. William Rapp graduated fifth in his class of '84, Col. H. R. McMaster was an award-winning author, and David Kilcullen was an Australian expert on counterinsurgency. Odierno kidded that he was the anchorman. Because Petraeus's team arrived with combat command credentials and were nobody's fools about conditions, they won over the larger staffs.

In the view of Petraeus's senior staff, Rumsfeld's insistence on early withdrawal had driven Casey toward the wrong strategy. Patrolling from the FOB in a Humvee was as useful as being in a submarine. Appointing Gates was critical, because it allowed for new thinking. The surge strategy had come from the NSC. When Petraeus was interviewed before Christmas, he wholeheartedly endorsed it.

In his quest to improve performance, Petraeus organized what was called Team Phoenix to conduct combat and diplomatic missions with the tribal sheiks. Commanders in the field reasonably assumed that

Phoenix included the CIA, State, and Special Operations Forces, working under a general. Actually, the entire team comprised only three people, Capts. Ann Gildroy and Seth Moulton and Sgt. Alex Lemons. Petraeus didn't care that they were so junior. They had produced for him time and again.

Petraeus had arrived in Baghdad knowing what he wanted to accomplish. I asked him how he communicated his concept of fighting the war to 150,000 American troops who were tired of the whole thing.

"I have to convey a few big ideas everyone can grasp," Petraeus told me. "First, don't commute to the fight. Second, do everything with Iraqis as partners. Third, make life better in the neighborhoods."

He described what he called "the engine of change," which started with a unifying idea or theory, such as the counterinsurgency manual, that leaders studied and then applied. The key, he said, was encouraging feedback from the field, and then issuing "Frag-Os," or fragmental changes, to the existing campaign plan.

Petraeus's day began with a five-mile run at six in the morning and ended at ten at night. He ran his meetings on time, shifting gears and moving from one subject to the next. His staff vetted 400 incoming e-mails a day, and Petraeus personally sent or received 300, including dozens from informal informants. His staff estimated that he spent 30 percent of his time with Iraqi leaders, 30 percent in the field, 10 percent at headquarters, and a whopping 30 percent dealing with Washington, both the executive and the congressional branches.

"I get paid to feel what's going on. The staff tracks the standard stuff like the number of attacks. My job is to react to unexpected setbacks, or progress like in Anbar," he told me. "I have two audiences, Iraq and Washington. In the past eight weeks, I've had nine Codels [congressional delegations]. I welcome them, so they can see my goal is to gain to a sustainable situation. That may result in more violence and losses in the short term."

The audience in the Democratic Congress was unreceptive. Harry Reid, the majority leader in the Senate, said, "This war is lost and the surge is not accomplishing anything as indicated by the extreme violence in Iraq." Reid had broken faith with the American soldiers who believed in their mission. The press, though, gave Reid a free pass, barely mentioning his remarks.

In April of 2007, al Qaeda's suicide bombing campaign showed no sign of abating. In northern Iraq, al Qaeda detonated two truck bombs, killing eighty-three Shiites in Tal Afar, the small city touted as an ex-

ample of successful counterinsurgency. The local police retaliated with
a rampage, killing seventy Sunnis. Colonel McMaster had repeatedly
warned that the Ministry of Interior had appointed a police chief notorious for his sectarian bias. The retaliation proved McMaster correct.
The only good news was that the Iraqi Army had intervened, arresting
a dozen policemen.

If captured, the rank and file among al Qaeda gangs whined that
they had joined up only for money. The U.S. military reported this in
exculpatory terms, as if participating as a lookout or in other fringe
jobs associated with the slaughter of innocents was, well, not so bad.
The lookout said he wasn't religious and didn't care about creating a
thirteenth-century caliphate; he just went along for the money in a
country with high unemployment. After all, what's a guy to do?

While they numbered in the low thousands, the dedicated hard-core
al Qaeda, aided by thousands of paid accomplices, persisted in mass
murders to provoke a Shiite-Sunni war. Their prime weapon—the only
weapon of consequence—was the suicide murderer. Lt. Gen. Douglas
Lute, the Iraq coordinator in the White House, described the al Qaeda
suicide murderers, 90 percent foreigners, as equivalent to launching
precision cruise missile strikes every day against crowds and marketplaces.

While Odierno was encouraged by a sharp decline in U.S. casualties
in Anbar, he was concerned that casualties were increasing in the Baghdad area. With firm control over only 146 of Baghdad's 457 neighborhoods, with a pressing need to attack into the belts, especially
southwest of the city, to disrupt the suicide bombers, and with no more
troops available in addition to the five brigades already in the pipeline,
he had to extend the tour length for Army units from twelve to fifteen
months.

"It was the hardest decision I made," he told me. "I knew what I
was asking from our soldiers and their families. Operationally, it had
to be done. But I hated doing it."

Odierno's son, Tony, had lost an arm fighting in Iraq. Petraeus's son
was in the infantry, headed for the battlefield. Pace's son had served
there. Conway, the Marine Corps commandant, had a son who had
served, as had Mundy, a former commandant. The list went on and on.
The generals and their families shared in the sacrifices they were asking
of others. But the strain on the force and the families was not sustainable indefinitely.

The draft campaign plan written by Petraeus's immediate staff in
April was brutal in laying out past military mistakes, concluding that

"we wanted to hand over responsibility to a Shiite government we created as soon as possible. This was a rush to failure because the Iraqi Government couldn't provide services, counterinsurgency, or reconciliation. It is a government ridden with corruption and incompetence." Rather than again rush to failure, Petraeus was asking for yet more sacrifice from his soldiers.

What concerned the writers of the draft plan was whether others would match that sacrifice. The commitment of Maliki seemed tenuous. Khalilzad's replacement, Ambassador Ryan C. Crocker, who worked with Petraeus, was forthright with the press about the challenge.

"I think he's [Maliki] committed to being the prime minister of all of Iraq and that means making reconciliation work," Crocker said. "But it's also clear that this is very, very hard to do, given the legacy of that climate of fear. . . . If you're still looking for that—some level of your subconscious, that knock on the door in the night and then you add to it, you know, the violence and its enormously corrosive impact, it makes all this real hard."

Maliki had to overcome a lifetime of fear and loathing of the Baathists loyal to Saddam; his political power base was fragile; he had little control over the National Assembly or the ministries; he was suspicious of the Americans; and he had good reason to wonder whether the American military would abruptly leave. Against that background, Petraeus's staff was arguing that only by overcoming his instincts and reaching out could Maliki unify his country. Maliki, though, had surrounded himself with hard-line Shiites who, snug in the Green Zone, were determined to solidify Shiite control. President Bush had handed them power as the majority, and they wielded that power absolutely.

As had happened with Casey, Maliki had already clashed with Petraeus. The staff had expected it. With Maliki having set up inside his office his own Office of the Commander-in-Chief, with a sectarian general answerable only to him, head banging about the deployment of forces and American arrests of militia leaders was inevitable and would continue. Of more concern were the malign figures inside the ministries. The draft plan named them, and not so subtly suggested that, year after year, the State Department had promised to get tough, and never had.

The surge had initially been presented as a temporary increase, presumably lasting a matter of months, with the increase in security providing Maliki and the National Assembly enough comfort and breathing space to reach a top-down reconciliation with the Sunnis, cemented by legislation. By April, it was clear to Odierno that controlling the belts as well as Baghdad would take longer. On the political front, Sadr had returned to Iraq, quarreled with Maliki, and withdrew his six ministers from the cabinet. Petraeus benefited when a vengeful Maliki stopped hampering American arrests of radical JAM leaders.

With Maliki distracted, no movement in the Assembly on reconciliation legislation, and the U.S. military stretched thin, the White House tamped down expectations about Iraq. Congress was expecting in June or July an assessment from Petraeus concerning whether his mission was achievable. In late April, the White House announced that Petraeus would not return to testify until September. Since the last of the five surge brigades would not arrive until June, it would be a while before the effects of the strategy could be evaluated.

The strategy itself was highly decentralized.

"A commander can supervise the execution of his orders," Petraeus told me, "about two levels down. I know the division commanders. I see brigade commanders. But I can't get to the battalions. I use letters to all the soldiers, commanders' conferences, talks at the COIN academy, to communicate my intent."

Distinguishing what part of the operational strategy was Petraeus versus Odierno was not particularly revealing or productive. Ultimately, the responsibility lay with the senior commander. Petraeus set the mission and the intellectual framework. Odierno, as corps commander, prioritized resources, deployed the forces, and fought the battle. His biggest challenge was keeping al Qaeda off balance in the belts north and south of Baghdad by raids, while protecting the population inside Baghdad and gradually moving more American soldiers into the belts.

David Kilcullen, the Australian counterinsurgency expert on Petraeus's staff, said, "The Marines were always out on foot patrols. To them, the Petraeus strategy wasn't new. For some of the Army units around Baghdad, the strategy was quite different. It did mean patrolling on foot."

In theory, ground combat commanders took pride in not overcontrolling their subordinate units, because local conditions varied greatly and small unit initiative won battles. In reality, the generals interfered directly by imposing from the top a rigorous set of rules for force protection. To minimize friendly casualties, every soldier had to wear armor at all times and ride in convoys of four or more Humvees, among other restrictions. Detailed investigations probed the circumstances of every casualty, with court-martial or career-ending fitness reports for anyone who violated the rules.

Yet in terms of operational procedures, no corresponding set of rules or guidelines pertained. The U.S. Army and Marine Corps were so skilled at acting in accord with a clear set of conventional war fighting procedures that the ten battalions inside Fallujah during the fierce battles of 2004 suffered not a single fatality from friendly fire. But when Iraq morphed into a police war in 2005, the military did not have a set of best practices to promulgate. Eighty battalions decided on a surprisingly wide range of procedures.

The extent to which a unit adopted a friendly versus suspicious attitude toward Iraqi forces was determined by the battalion commander and the sergeant major. The crucible was how they reacted after the first horrific IED explosion that killed, burned, and maimed their soldiers or marines. If the troops believed Iraqi forces had been complicit, then the commander faced a difficult challenge in establishing a partnership.

By April, Odierno had set up thirty-one joint security stations (American and Iraqi soldiers in command centers or precinct headquarters with Iraqi police) and twenty-two combat outposts in ten districts in Baghdad. Every battalion understood the intellectual framework of counterinsurgency and the mission from General Petraeus. How they applied the tenets of counterinsurgency varied widely across the battlefield.

SURVIVAL AT FORT APACHE

In the spring of 2007, staying alive came before protecting the population for the soldiers of Charlie Company at Fort Apache on the east bank of the Tigris. Since my previous visit in the fall, another soldier had been killed, bringing the total to six. Company strength had dropped from 120 to 85 over six months. First Sgt. Kenneth Hendrix had sent to the Pentagon several letters supporting a Medal of Honor for Spec. Ross McGinnis, who had died smothering a grenade that had landed inside his Humvee. Hendrix bought DVDs and Girl Scout cookies for his soldiers and was also searching the Internet for glue to prevent the rain and sewage water that seeped and sometimes spouted through the downstairs walls of the old fort. The soldiers slept in double-decker wooden bunks with their sodden battle rattle draped at one end, as comfortable as a clammy dungeon.

The company commander, Capt. Cecil Strickland, thirty-six, of Fort

Worth, sent out six mounted platoon-sized patrols a day. Led by a Bradley Armored Vehicle with a 40mm cannon, the patrols prowled the streets of Adamiyah, the stronghold of al Qaeda in Baghdad. Strickland estimated there were 400,000 Sunnis packed into the four square kilometers assigned to Charlie Company. About one patrol a day was hit by an IED or sniper attack. Usually two Iraqi bodies were seen in trash heaps or lying in gutters. The police, all Shiite from Sadr City, refused to leave their precinct station. They arrived in civilian clothes, changed into their blue-shirted uniforms, cheerfully performed duties inside the wall, put on their civilian clothes, mixed with passersby, and made their separate ways home. The Iraqi Army, all Shiites, were willing to patrol with the Americans, but they were tough on the locals.

I joined a patrol led by Capt. Nate Waggoner. Once outside the wire, the four Humvees rolled slowly along a road by the river as if looking for bodies, a routine task. After sufficient time had elapsed for the insurgent lookouts to call over their cell phones the location of another routine patrol, Waggoner suddenly cut toward the downtown center. He was working with a Special Forces detachment that had the address of a moneyman working for al Qaeda.

The Humvees careened through the back streets and alleyways so narrow the walls nearly scraped the sides of the armored vehicles as they swerved around tight corners and gunned down straightaways.

"Have to keep the speed up. We got hit here with two IEDs yesterday," Waggoner yelled to me. "The triggermen are outsiders. They don't give a damn what happens to the locals."

On Brewer Street, the main thoroughfare, the Humvees raced by trash-clogged alleyways, past shuttered shops and unemployed crowds of unsmiling young men, skidding to a stop beside some run-down shops. A dozen soldiers and Special Forces commandos piled out, pitching gray and purple smoke grenades into the trash-strewn street.

"A sniper got one of us in the leg yesterday," the captain warned. "Stay in the doorways." The soldiers paused, eyeing a line of padlocked shops and checking their photomaps. An interpreter spoke quickly to a startled shopkeeper, who pointed at a shoe store and then disappeared into the smoke. The soldiers snapped a lock, rushed in, and rifled through the receipt drawer and several boxes of shoes, looking for a list. With a broom, they poked each wall, listening for a hollow echo. The *crack!* of a single AK round caused heads to snap around. A few soldiers patted themselves, feeling to make sure they hadn't been hit. Waggoner grinned. The soldiers shook their heads and went back to work. Nothing. No incriminating lists or receipts. In less than five minutes, they were back in their gun trucks, swerving wildly down Brewer.

We stopped in a middle-class neighborhood and knocked on a door. The patrols made about fifteen random stops a day. The portly owner showed us in, and a few soldiers went upstairs and returned with an AK-47 wrapped in white plastic covered with dirt.

"Sometimes we turn something up, like bomb-making material. We send to prison about ten a month," Waggoner said. "This guy is probably okay."

Waggoner asked why he had buried his rifle, since every house is allowed a weapon for self-defense. The man responded with a rambling story.

"Uh-uh, no sale," Waggoner said. "Have the jundis been around here?"

When the man nodded, Waggoner handed him back the rifle, shook hands, and left.

"The jundis are Shiites, many from Sadr City," Waggoner explained on the drive back to Apache. "They confiscate the AKs. So the residents hide them. We get more info and cooperation when we're on our own."

Back at Apache, Sgt. Robin Johnson, a squad leader who worked with the nearby Iraqi Army battalion, explained the situation. "When we arrived, the residents were getting pushed back by JAM militia from Sadr City. It's very sectarian here," Johnson said. "The Sunnis believe the police and half the army's cooperating with JAM. They get shot at more than we do. The al Qaeda guys go after us, but not the local Sunni militia."

The district council representative was murdered in December in a setup that involved Shiite officials. His killers were never found. In March, the new representative was shot eighteen times in broad daylight on Adamiyah's main street by Sunni gunmen.

"We've been here eight months," Johnson said. "We were just told about the three-month extension. The guys are really pissed about spending fifteen months in Adamiyah. It sucks here."

By the end of their tour, Charlie Company had suffered fourteen killed, almost all from IEDs, the form of attack that most frustrated and infuriated soldiers trained to close with and kill the enemy.

Adamiyah had replaced Ramadi as the nightmare scenario of the surge strategy. COP Apache was a fortress without a moat protecting the Americans from the population, turning benevolent counterinsurgency theory on its head. In Adamiyah, the population hadn't swung over as in Ramadi, Charlie hadn't the manpower, the oil spot tactic hadn't yet been applied, and the Iraqi police and army were too sectarian.

To prevent the easy movement of assassins and suicide bombers, Odierno had ordered long walls of concrete Jersey barriers placed throughout the city. The twelve-foot barriers reduced the blast effects of car bombs while dividing Baghdad into pockets of controllable size, the "gated communities." The Greeks, Romans, Chinese, Soviets, Israelis, and dozens of other countries had employed walls against insurgents and invaders. The British had forced the Chinese villagers in Malaya to live inside strategic hamlets surrounded by bamboo fences. Rice was strictly rationed; a villager who gave food to a guerrilla went hungry himself. In Algeria, the French imposed a punishment of collective responsibility. If the telephone poles outside a douar—hamlet— were cut down, the villagers were forced to erect new ones. If incidents continued, the villagers were driven from the douar. One million Algerians were uprooted from their douars. In Vietnam, tens of thousands of peasants were relocated from hamlets that supplied the Viet Cong with rice. The Protestant and Catholic neighborhoods in Belfast were separated by walls with massive gates that were closed when riots threatened.

In April, Odierno was proceeding to box in Adamiyah. Eventually he would provide additional American soldiers. In the meantime, the soldiers of Charlie Company, their morale dropping as they lost comrades to an unseen enemy and without sensing that the population wanted them to be there, paid the cost and held the line.

CASINO: CRACKS IN SUNNI RANKS

In contrast to Apache, across the river at COP Casino, the Sunnis in Ghazaliyah welcomed the Americans as their protectors. Relations with the Sunnis and the Shiites were improving bit by bit. Weekly the company made supply runs to provide propane and food trucks. Lt. Sam Cartee's platoon was conducting two patrols a day, the fatigue eased by the waves and smiles they received. More shops were open along the clean roads in the Shiite section, and Sunni women were tolerated in the markets where, earlier in the year, they would have been stoned.

In the Sunni sector, I drove with Lt. Cartee, of Charlie Company, 12th Regiment, 1st Cavalry Division, through raw sewage that clogged the road. It was like being in a garbage dump after a torrential rain. When we stopped near the market that Lieutenant Colonel Sabah had torn down in February, a handful of elderly Sunni peppered us with complaints. Their leader, Kais Abdullah, protested that the police had plastered posters on the road reading "Long Live the Mahdi Army." Only the Americans, he said, allow us to buy propane or food. Sabah's soldiers, he said, permitted Shiite families to move into Sunni houses, night after night.

To check, Cartee drove to the Sunni neighborhood where the air force colonel had been firebombed out of his house, leaving dinner on the table and the mural of winter in Switzerland on the wall. A timid woman answered our knock and invited us in. All the handsome furniture and the electronics in the kitchen were gone, replaced by a few rickety items. A thin young man stood quietly in the corner as we talked. On the verge of tears, the woman explained that American bombs had killed her husband and Sunni takfiris had murdered her son. She was living in a tent in a refugee center in Taji when the Jesh al Mahdi had offered this house in Ghazaliyah to her family. Her nephew had helped her to move. Cartee assured her he wasn't there to arrest her, and we left.

"Her 'nephew' is a JAM plant," Cartee said. "But I'm not in the re-settlement business. JAM's not firebombing more Sunnis. So it's live and let live."

We drove three blocks west and stopped beside a schoolyard wall. In red letters one message on the wall read, "Bush is appaling and dreaful." In blue, another read "Bush dos'nt response to American people."

And above it, in large red letters: "Hey we want you to destroy the JAM."

"Don't mind the spelling," Cartee said. "It's the sentiments that count. Take your pick."

Smiling Sunni men and boys poured into the street, insisting Cartee stay for lunch. We walked to a nearby house, where the lieutenant and his soldiers sat down on the soft sofas and took off their battle gear, obviously at ease. Sheik Hamid Muthanna Obeidi, a stocky Iraqi with thinning, close-cropped hair and a gap between his front teeth, talked while the Americans ate chicken and munched on freshly baked pita bread.

Hamid said that after Saddam was overthrown, life had been good for his tribe of 5,000. He himself sold used parts from vehicles and ran a money exchange. Then after the bombing of the Samarra mosque in 2006, the AQI came from Anbar. Few in Hamid's tribe had jobs, and the al Qaeda fighters offered money. Every night they fought the JAM coming from Shula.

"When Lieutenant Cartee came last January, the takfiris told us to fight the Americans," Hamid said. "Then they lost men and moved to Amariyah [to the south]."

Hamid had been arrested by Lieutenant Colonel Sabah, the Iraqi battalion commander, and released upon Cartee's insistence.

"Sabah is crazy," Hamid said. "His jundis are scared of him. Look what he did to my son."

A teenager shyly showed bruises on his arms. Sabah, he said, had grabbed him off the street, stuffed him into the luggage compartment of his Humvee, drove to the school, and threw him into the dirt, kicking him and shouting that anyone collaborating with the takfiris would be shot. Cartee glanced at the other American soldiers. Yet another in a series of episodes about the voluble, cocky Sabah that had gradually turned the American soldiers against him.

The Sunnis in Ghazaliyah were under attack by gangs from Shula, a tough district a few kilometers to the north. The Americans had no outpost inside Shula, a JAM stronghold. They had coordinated with Sabah to place a dozen four-ton Jersey barriers across the back roads from Shula. The day after the barriers were put in, the Americans found them dumped in mud-filled ditches. How had Iraqi cranes crossed checkpoints manned by jundis in the middle of the night?

Rumors swirled around Sabah. He had feuded with his second-in-command, Major Kassim, who was shot a dozen times in the face when he went home on leave. Captain Riadh, an intelligence officer, indiscreetly told the Americans that Sabah took a cut on the sale of furniture from Sunni houses. Riadh was shot in the head while on leave.

"Sabah hates me. All his men are afraid of him," Hamid said. "My tribe is between two jaws, JAM and al Qaeda. My friend Abu Iad went back to his house taken by Shiites and was killed. Let us arm ourselves and work with you."

Cartee said he couldn't make such a deal. He didn't rebuff Sheik Hamid, though. It was more like a promise to keep talking.

WHERE IS OUR GOVERNMENT?

When I had last seen Capt. Bo Dennis, he had been trying to keep the JAM from driving out the Sunnis in Tuwaitha, where two men had been murdered for a few chickens. A fresh surge brigade had taken over that area to the south. Dennis and his 3rd Squadron, 61st Cavalry

Regiment, were shifted north to a relatively quiet zone in east Baghdad, midway between the Tigris and Sadr City, farther to the east.

With forty soldiers, Dennis had set up Joint Security Station Destroyer in the Rusafa police station to work with 100 National Police and 200 regular police. Brig. Gen. Hussein Wahed, the affable police chief for Rusafa, estimated that altogether he supervised about 4,000 police working two twelve-hour shifts at nine police stations. The police manned eighty-nine checkpoints in an area containing about two million people.

Arrests, Hussein said, were few. Sometimes he slept in the office, but usually he felt it safe to go home. Once the front of his house had been blown up, and another time assassins tried to break in at six in the morning, Aside from those two incidents in three years, he hadn't felt particularly threatened. Perhaps Captain Dennis could improve the intelligence picture.

With Dennis, I walked down Palestine Street, where the shopkeepers said security had improved, but the concrete barriers and ban on parking had reduced the number of shoppers. Perhaps a few barriers could be moved. Of course, each merchant pointed to the barrier in front of his boutique. The interpreters, David and Slim, cautioned about reading too much into the calm atmosphere. JAM, they said, was better organized than on my previous visits. Instead of random robberies, now most storeowners paid $20 a month protection money, and homeowners paid $7 to $10 a month. In three months working with the police, they had not seen a single arrest of a terrorist, a death squad member, a robber, or a murderer. Some police were JAM leaders. The police chief had to tread carefully in disciplining any cop; he wasn't sure which one would pull out his pistol and shoot him.

Two days earlier, 160 Iraqis had been killed in a horrific bombing in a central market in Rusafa. From Palestine Street, Dennis and his squad drove to the scene of the carnage. Police at a checkpoint two blocks from the bombing warned us not to proceed because they were receiving sniper fire. We got out of the Humvees and walked in.

The large square looked like a scene from Dante's *Inferno*: a deep black hole in the macadam, twisted, burned-out shells of cars, odd bits of clothing, sandals, and shoes strewn about. The tall, gray concrete apartment buildings were gouged and pitted, windows shattered. The cries of women and children echoed across the square.

We were immediately surrounded by dozens of grief-stricken, angry men, still in shock. They confronted us, shouting and pushing up. Dennis removed his helmet and expressed his sorrow and shock at the horror, while his men posted a wary but unthreatening guard. The bitterness of the men was palpable.

But they weren't angry at us. One after another, they screamed their impotent rage.

"You Americans come here. You came," they shouted. "But where is our government? Why do they not come? Why? Who takes care of those women and children? All their men are dead. Where is our government?"

Maliki, on a state visit to Egypt, condemned the mass murders, and the erection of the concrete barriers in Adamiyah. He didn't cut short his trip. No elected or appointed official in the United States would keep his job a day if he turned his back on such a stunning tragedy. The Green Zone was a cocoon that sheltered the Iraqi politicians and ministries from the miseries of their people.

Everywhere I went throughout Baghdad in April, our soldiers were tired. "The one thing everyone from company commander on down thinks about," Major Eric Stetson said, "is getting through the fifteen-month tour. That's it."

THE OTHER WAR GOES WELL

In Baghdad, the surge strategy was just starting. In Anbar, a basic change was taking place. The Sunni population had aligned with the Americans, and tough police chiefs were taking charge.

FROM FALLUJAH TO THE ZIDON

In Fallujah, Sheiks Kamal Nazal and Najim Hamza had been assassinated, as had council member Abbas Ali Hussein. In late March, the police station at the Government Center was hit by two suicide bombers who failed to breach the walls but did detonate a van loaded with chlorine, wounding forty-seven civilians. The compound of Sheik Khamis was also hit by a chlorine attack. Khamis had aligned his Abu Eisa tribe with Sattar. The Marines interpreted the use of chlorine, which didn't prove that fatal, as a desperate effort by al Qaeda to keep the population in line and spread fear via an awestruck press. Instead, the press chose to point out the limited effect of the chlorine.

Al Qaeda—"the faceless ones"—persisted in slipping in and out of the city, despite the berm and checkpoints. The Marines and police had

confiscated 3,750 false IDs, most used by residents to fool JAM and
sectarian police on visits to Baghdad or for small crimes like claiming
unauthorized food rations. Al Qaeda sold the IDs, along with death
certificates to turn in to the Marines, who paid between $500 and
$2,500 for each accidental death from friendly fire. The aggressive po-
lice chief, Feisal, had cracked down, packing 450 into the city jails.

"It's still too dangerous in the market," Maj. Todd Sermarini, the
senior police adviser, said. "We own only half the city. The police react
to an intell tip with fifty to a hundred cops, but they won't patrol in
small teams."

Relations between the Iraqi Army and police hadn't improved since
Brig. Gen. Khalid Khadim had been relieved for padding his payroll
with 300 "ghost soldiers," and for stealing gasoline and selling weapons
on the black market to buyers suspected of belonging to Sadr's militia.
The brigade adviser, Lt. Col. James Teeples, had provided the *Financial
Times* of London with the story in order to get rid of Khadim, whose behavior had fractured trust with city officials. The police and the army
weren't aggressively patrolling or backing each other up. Where I had
walked past the Pizza Slice through the crowds in the souk to the Blackwater Bridge with Maj. Ward Vaughn, no Iraqi police now ventured.

"We pulled out of the city too soon in 2006," Maj. Gen. Walt
Gaskin said. "I sent a battalion back in to support the police."

In April of 2007, I sought out Deputy Chief Kareem for another of
our quiet chats. His younger son had been assassinated a few months
earlier while praying in a mosque. In his assessment, Fallujah could be
controlled only by building alliances.

"Al Qaeda is threatening the families of my police. This will go on
and on," he said. "You Americans must work with the tribes, sheiks,
and imams. The tribes must take away the hiding places."

Brig. Gen. John Allen was flying weekly to Amman, negotiating
with Sheik Mishan so that his tribe would gain control over the farmlands east of Fallujah. Lt. Col. Joe L'Etoile was back with Battalion
3-7 for another tour. Last year, L'Etoile had reached agreement with
Sheik Khamis and the Abu Eisa tribe to hold the west side of the city.
To the south lay 200 square kilometers of farmlands and palm groves
called the Zidon. Crisscrossed with irrigation ditches and accessible by
only two roads, the Zidon was home to the Zobai tribe, insular, restive,
and prone to hijacking along the main highway.

L'Etoile's marines were working fourteen kilometers away from the
nearest hardtop road. We arrived at an isolated farmhouse about four

in the morning outside a hamlet that hadn't changed since Nebuchad-
nezzar. Thorn bushes served as corrals for donkeys and thin cows,
chickens scurried underfoot, and women cooked in clay outdoor
ovens. The houses—some concrete and some mud—received about an
hour of electric power a day, and most of the pickup trucks looked like
they had survived demolition derbies.

The marines checked for signs. Al Qaeda enforced weird proscrip-
tions against spare tires, lipstick, ice, pickles, and cigarettes. Most
farmers took a break at dusk, smoking one cigarette after another. No
butts meant al Qaeda was near.

A few days earlier, al Qaeda left two headless bodies in the road as
a warning. The marines laughed at the intimidation effort and pushed
on, finding a house with handcuffs attached by rings to the wall, clubs,
and an electric drill. A snuff film showed men quivering after being
shot, or screaming as their thumbs were cut off. One clip showed an
electric drill boring through a man's palms. As he screamed, a metal
bolt was shoved through his hands and secured with a nut.

L'Etoile and I accompanied a squad searching through a hamlet
without running water or electricity. A fairly new pickup outside a bare
house attracted attention. The farmer pulled out one ID that showed
his picture, and another ID with the picture of a different man.

"I get it," the squad leader, Sgt. Brian Johnson, said. "He's telling us
one ID is for an al Qaeda checkpoint, and the other's for a Shiite one."

In late afternoon, we walked back to the company outpost, with the
company gunnery sergeant grumbling that al Qaeda was late in launching its daily harassing attack. While I was napping outside the farmhouse, al Qaeda opened up with a heavy caliber machine gun that hit
the farmhouse wall like a sledgehammer. L'Etoile suggested that I stay
down—good thinking—while the marines returned rounds downrange. Once a base of fire was established, a squad in full battle rattle
ran across a field and waded a ditch to close on the insurgent heavy machine gun mounted on the back of a pickup truck. The truck backed off
the embankment onto a road hidden in defilade. Half an hour later, the
sopping, exhausted squad returned to the outpost.

"We kill about two or three a week," Johnson said. "We light up
the dumb ones who stay too long."

The Zobai tribe in the Zidon supported the 1920s Brigade, a resistance group. For several months, the 1920s had refrained from striking
at Battalion 2-7. While they refused face-to-face negotiations, they
didn't set out IEDs to kill marines. Farmers would covertly point

toward culverts and bushes where they suspected bombs had been buried.

"The 1920s are knuckleheads," L'Etoile said. "They won't join Sattar's movement. They want us to kill al Qaeda for them."

A week earlier, a battalion sniper team had watched a BMW pull up to a small market. When a man got out with a pistol and started ordering people around, a marine 600 meters away shot him. Clutching his stomach, the man staggered back into the car, which sped away. With exaggerated gestures, the men in the market lit up cigarettes, some clutching their stomachs, while others laughed and waved toward the hidden sniper team. *Shoot more of the bastards!*

HABBANIYAH SLOWLY IMPROVES

By April 2007, back in the Habbaniyah corridor, the 1st Battalion of the Iraqi 3rd Brigade was getting most of the action. The mission was to flush out the hiding places in the farmlands. To do this, the battalion built a series of guard towers along the only hard-surface road leading to the river. It looked like French Indochina in the mid-1950s—a long, narrow road flanked by canals, palm groves, and dense undergrowth, with flimsy wooden watchtowers sticking up like isolated telephone poles.

In the first week in April, a dump truck drove up to one of the towers in the middle of the day, when the jundis were dozing. Half a dozen insurgents hopped out, rushing up to the single strand of barbed wire and pitching grenades at the dozing Iraqi soldiers. Only they hadn't pulled the pins on a few grenades, while others exploded too far apart to do serious damage. When the soldiers fired back at a furious rate, the truck driver tried to back up and skidded off the road. The attackers fled into the bushes, leaving behind three dead. Since then, one or another of the outposts received harassing fire every day.

The Iraqi battalion commander preferred to deploy his men in platoon strength outside the dusty town of Habbaniyah along the hardtop road where the insurgents couldn't dig in IEDs to be detonated by pressure plates, and to dispatch a combat patrol once every two days. On paper, the battalion had 400 men to secure an area of five by twelve kilometers. The advisers estimated that 220 were actually present for duty. The battalion reported ten patrols a day—by counting as a patrol any group of soldiers that left the barbed wire either at the base camp or at one of the towers for whatever reason, such as to get supplies or change the guard.

The rule among the advisers was that each of the eleven marines on the advisory team would patrol at least once, and preferably twice, a day from their combat outpost, called the O.K. Corral. This aggressiveness guaranteed friction with the Iraqi soldiers.

"Most of the Iraqi staff officers don't like us. Many paid a bribe of $700 to become lieutenants. After that, they're part of a system of kickbacks and small-time payoffs. We try to stop that," Maj. Tom Ziegler, the adviser team commander, told me. "They want us to provide supplies and make sure the ministry pays them. They don't like us giving tactical advice and prodding them to patrol. They punish any jundis who get too close to us."

Ziegler and three other marines set off on a daylight foot patrol with a dozen Iraqi soldiers through the nearby markets and farmlands. At first, the scene seemed normal—schoolchildren trooping by in small clusters, farmers in the field, a few roadside shops offering a few paltry goods, cows and sheep wandering the dirt roads. Most of the women who scurried past were wearing full black abayas that looked like tents or heavy drapes, with veils concealing their faces. The men who passed the patrol looked straight ahead and didn't exchange greetings with the soldiers.

We walked by a burned-out car pitched at an angle next to a muddy ditch. "Tower Two radioed in the car looked suspicious," Ziegler said, "so we rolled up in a Humvee. When we cut it off, the car backed up and sped off. So we lit it up. It started to burn, then *BLAM!,* it exploded. We found a spool of copper wire and two KIA in the debris. The neighbors said they were good men. . . . Right. They just liked to drive around with explosives and wire for detonators."

The patrol zigzagged down back alleys and cut across the open fields at odd angles, trying not to show a pattern or destination. The patrol leader and his second-in-command at the rear chatted back and forth on Motorola handheld radios, at one point screaming loudly.

"The insurgents are harassing them," Ziegler said. "The handhelds are terrific, but the Motorola net is uncovered. There's a lot of back and forth. Once the muj figure out our route, we'll be hit."

About ten minutes later, as we walked across an open lot, there was the sharp *crack! crack!* of an AK-47, with the rounds passing so high the advisers simply walked to the cover of a palm grove and waited. A few minutes later, a PKC machine gun let loose a long burst, followed by excited yells over the Motorola.

"The sniper's on a roof a few blocks over," Ziegler translated, as two advisers ran by us. Again, there was a furious jabbering over the

Motorola, then the Iraqi soldiers ran down the path, following the advisers. Ziegler hastened after them.

"They said marines are crazy, going the wrong way—at the enemy," Ziegler said. "The jundi won't close with these Wahhabis."

As the Iraqi soldiers and advisers cautiously entered the house where the sniper had been seen, dogs were barking furiously along the alley behind the house.

"He's running away," Ziegler said, "and I'll never organize these guys fast enough to cut him off."

Next door, a baby and several women were screaming. Ziegler and several Iraqi soldiers rushed into the courtyard to find a toddler with a bad gash on his forehead, blood covering his face. Frightened by the shooting and the soldiers, the boy had run headlong into a wall. The advisers applied a clean bandage and Ziegler offered to take the boy to the battalion aid station. When the family refused, he sent for the town doctor, who arrived in a dilapidated old car. The doctor explained he had no sutures, but was confident the wound would heal, leaving only a scar.

Once again, Ziegler offered to call for a Humvee; the father and mother could come also. The boy would be treated in their presence. There would be no scar. He would be back in a few hours, with toys for the other children.

Please, the father begged, we have talked too long. They will ask what we told you. If they don't believe us, they will kill us. Please leave now. The patrol hastily left.

"We have a long ways to go shaping up this battalion," Ziegler said. "But the other side doesn't have the strength to hold on if we keep coming in. Sooner or later, someone will drop a dime on them. If we keep up the pressure, they'll have to move out."

Performance varied tremendously among the Iraqi battalions. Some dispatched twenty patrols a day, and some five; some sat around a dozen checkpoints each day, and others kept on the move. The four companies in a battalion usually averaged only sixty soldiers present for duty, with another forty on leave, authorized or not, or simply missing. About 75 percent of the soldiers in Anbar in early 2007 came from Baghdad and the Shiite southern provinces. In the absence of a countrywide banking system, soldiers received their monthly pay of $800 and most took off for ten days each month to bring the money home and relax. They'd change into civilian clothes, slip into taxis and buses, and hope they didn't bump into an insurgent roadblock. The Iraqi Army had no formal way of punishing those who took unauthorized leave. Officers routinely withheld pay for days not worked, a habit that encouraged corruption and the abuse of authority.

If a battalion had a decent commander and two or more aggressive officers, it functioned reasonably well. If the commander was a poor or corrupt leader, or failed to encourage his company commanders to show initiative, the advisers were in for a long tour. Ziegler had drawn an average battalion.

They would send out daily security patrols around their watchtowers and base camp. They knew exactly how far north they could go with, say, twenty soldiers and three or four vehicles. Beyond that lay Albu Bali—Indian country—where snipers were sure to harass them and IEDs were buried into the shoulders of the road. When Ziegler prodded them, they would respond, provided the nearby Marine battalion sent a squad. With the farmers and the vendors at the roadside stands, the Iraqi soldiers had a lukewarm relationship, neither hostile nor friendly.

Across the Euphrates to the south, another Iraqi battalion of similar composition was more aggressive. The day Saddam Hussein was hanged, an Iraqi patrol surprised a carload of insurgents firing their AK-47s into the air in protest. Hearing the gunfire, the Iraqis and their advisers raced each other to the scene in their Humvees, where a young Iraqi turret gunner was the first to get a clear shot. He emptied his entire ammunition belt, killing all three insurgents, local toughs who had decided to show off.

After the incident, daytime small arms battles tapered. The Marine MiTT (Military Transition Team) leader and his North Dakota National Guard deputy decided to sneak out at night with four-man teams. Around midnight, the team leader, equipped with a special night vision scope, placed a three-round burst in the neck of a man with a rocket-propelled grenade launcher at 200 yards. Not to be outdone, his deputy took out a small patrol the next night and just missed an insurgent planting an IED near the perimeter.

Four kills in the course of a few weeks was unheard of in Habbaniyah. Success was contagious. The battalion commander, Lieutenant Colonel Muhammed, began sending out more and more patrols, until the battalion was averaging eighty per week, routine by American standards but sky-high in Iraqi circles. The jundis began to harass the toughs in town, pushing around and humiliating those they believed were planting the occasional IED and taking sniper shots. Shopkeepers began to whisper names. Some insurgents drifted across the river, into Ziegler's area and into Albu Bali.

Ziegler didn't act on hard intelligence as much as on rumors. Someone would provide a tip to the Iraqi soldiers, who would suggest a raid, or Ziegler's translators would turn up a lead. A MiTT depended on its translators to convey the right messages in the right tone to the Iraqi battalion. This was tricky, because translators received no extra combat pay and enticing good ones to serve in heavy combat zones like Anbar was difficult.

Ziegler's chief translator was "Alex." He had the bright smile of a happy college freshman and an open, enthusiastic manner. On patrol, he wore Marine cammies, complete with kneepads, a GPS on a wrist strap, Wiley X protective eyeglasses, and a black-dyed AK with a four-power scope purchased over the Internet for $800. He had all tracers in his thirty-round magazine and had killed two insurgents. His goal was to join the U.S. Marine Corps.

His patrolling skills were unusual, but his attachment to the U.S. military was reflective of thousands of other translators, and for the same reasons. Every combat platoon and MiTT bonds tightly, sharing common dangers and relying on each other. Translators are outcasts among Iraqis. For fear of betrayal, they cannot tell their neighbors what they do, and they can't trust the Iraqi police or soldiers, who consider them traitors or spies, or are jealous of their higher pay (a translator makes $1,100 a month). The translators bond with the American soldiers. They eat, sleep, and ride with the Americans. After six months on the line, they become part of the unit. Few have any formal language training. Hard though they try, many mangle subtle meanings or negotiations requiring careful translation. Most are like Alex, self-taught by watching TV soaps and talking with American soldiers. Alex's brother had been tortured to death by the JAM in retaliation for Alex's work for the Americans.

"People always say it's the Americans' fault," Alex told me after learning of his brother's death. "My country didn't do a fuck for me. The U.S. ruined Japan with nukes and then rebuilt it. Sunni and Shiite killers, there's no difference. Let's kick the shit out of them, then rebuild, like you did to Japan."

It was a near-universal refrain from the translators who risked all on the front lines: The American military was too gentle. The older translators, many from the States, usually rode with the battalion commanders and became their confidants. The younger ones, from the streets of Baghdad or Najaf, patrolled with the companies or the advisers. Many, like Alex, gave their first loyalty to their American comrades.

It was not reciprocated. In the four years after Saddam fled from Baghdad, over two million Iraqis fled their country. In 2006, of the 5,300 Iraqi translators working for the U.S. military, the administration granted visas to fifty. Although President Bush's mantra was that all people love freedom, he did nothing to extend a helping hand to those who had suffered the most. His administration floated on lofty rhetoric and refused to aid those to whom freedom meant fleeing for their lives.

As usual, the burden of practicing instead of preaching fell to the military. In the case of Alex, the leader of his advisory team badgered the Washington bureaucracies, while Brigadier General Allen weighed in with strong endorsing letters. Between them, they kept up a crossfire until the bureaucracies granted Alex one of the few precious visas. Alex came to the States to join the Marine Corps.

RAMADI TURNED AROUND

By April of 2007, Ramadi had advanced faster than Fallujah or the Habbaniyah farmlands. Driving down the clean streets with Jurney, followed by only one Humvee with a .50-cal, I noticed we were rarely out of sight of tall watchtowers. Flooding block after block with Marine infantry, followed by police, Jurney had advanced across the center of the city, as he had assured me eight months earlier. There were now fourteen combat outposts, or police precincts, each manned by 100 police and a Marine squad.

"I'm leaving no neighborhood uncovered," Jurney said.

Many of the leaps forward to seize a few new blocks occurred at night, when night vision goggles and GPS gave the Marines a decided advantage. Capt. Kyle Sloan's Alpha Company was typical. To gain a few more blocks north of the Racetrack, he moved four squads forward at midnight, posting into houses close enough to provide mutual fire support. Two families fled and two stayed.

During the night, nothing happened. But when the marines moved onto the streets at first light, there were bursts of AK fire, followed by two rocket-propelled grenades. In thirty seconds, one marine was down, hit in the thigh, and four insurgents lay dead in the streets. The marines heard the engines of mopeds kicking in a few blocks away.

One marine saw five individuals duck around a corner, but he didn't want to spray the building. Jurney's law was to hit what you shoot at, and 60 percent of the battalion had qualified as expert shots before deploying. Alerted by the shooting, marine snipers in the watchtowers hit three insurgents on mopeds.

That was the end of it. Alpha Company had secured two more blocks. The police moved in with the marines, set up a precinct, and began patrolling and getting to know the neighborhood. A few weeks later, Alpha company prepared to make the next leap forward.

Altogether in his zone, Jurney had deployed 700 marines, 800 police, and 300 jundis, plus 500 Iraqis who volunteered as unpaid neighborhood watch groups, pending openings for them in the police. So far, he had spent $5 million on reconstruction, paying $8 a day per laborer, hauling away mountains of trash and smoothing out six soccer fields.

Earlier in April, a suicide murderer driving a truck loaded with explosives and chlorine had struck a police post in western Ramadi, killing forty, mostly women and children. Jurney said that in response the police had increased their presence in that area.

"The population's not intimidated anymore," Jurney said. "They hate those terrorist assholes."

Jurney was showing me through a forward police station when the Iraqi precinct commander, Col. Ahmed Sharki, rushed in. His "eyes" (informants) had told him the hiding place of three takfiris with an IED, he said, pointing to a map. Jurney laughed. They both knew it was out of his battle space. Jurney suggested he turn the information over to the SEALs. Reluctantly, the precinct commander agreed and left, followed by a cluster of enthusiastic policemen.

"It's easy to get followers," Jurney said, "when you're winning. Last September, the going price for putting in an IED was forty to eighty bucks. Now it's four hundred. That tells you who's winning. The tribes have control outside the city, and the police can handle it inside. We're almost finished fighting here."

HADITHA TURNS THE CORNER

Haditha was a small town that showed big changes by the spring of 2007, eight months after my previous visit. Accompanying a squad-sized patrol, I was surprised by the number of people who were out and about. Stores and stalls were open for business. Sheep were being butchered as customers haggled for prime cuts, blood and entrails brushed into a barrel. Schoolchildren skipped around the mess, tugging at each other's backpacks. Battered tanks of propane and bottles of gasoline, tended by hopeful boys, lined the street corners. Two police in blue uniforms, armed with AKs, walked by us without masks on their faces.

"They're going to the mosque," Joseph, an interpreter from Palestine, said. "A few months ago, we'd send a squad to protect them. Now they go by themselves."

On my last visit, Capt. Matt Tracy had to use his company's freezer to ship a corpse back to the States for autopsy. The man had died in police custody and Colonel Farouk, the tough police chief, had stonewalled inquiries.

Tracy and Farouk had gone through tough days. Every patrol caught action.

The Marines had used mammoth bulldozers to throw up a dirt berm around the city, with only three entry points. They insisted everyone in any car carry a biometric ID card with fingerprints they could check against a log, strictly limiting the number of cards issued. This gave Farouk a fixed, contained population he could comb through to look for insurgents. Tracy's battalion, 2-3, suffered twenty-four killed and 230 wounded in seven months. But when they left in March, Farouk's police force was in firm control. Many said too firm.

The new battalion was manning eighteen positions—called combat outposts in Baghdad—with marines, jundis, or shurtas. We bumped into marines and armed Iraqis walking down every street. The fighting had stopped and normal life, except for the curtailment of commerce, had resumed. Lt. Col. James Bierman, commanding Battalion 3-3, encouraged me to walk anywhere with a squad and knock on any door.

Random interviews elicited similar sentiments. For instance, we knocked on one door and were graciously offered chai by middle-aged Farouk Taleb (a pseudonym) and his two sons, both in their twenties. Taleb was an engineer working at the hydroelectric plant at the giant dam at the north end of the city. His sons, both college graduates, had no jobs. Security was fine, Taleb said. Battalion 2-3 had been polite and listened to the city council. No problems with the Americans.

"After you killed those women and children a few years ago," Taleb said, "the takfiris went to the market and said you would kill everyone after an IED, just like Saddam. Everyone was very afraid, so for a while there weren't any IEDs. When people knew you wouldn't kill, they let the takfiris start again with IEDs. You brought back Farouk and stopped all cars. Okay, the takfiris left. Now Farouk should leave. He hates takfiri. He wants revenge. His Joghify tribe is uneducated. Hillbillies. Not from here. We're Biati tribe in Haditha."

Taleb was offended that Farouk's police included two who had been goat shepherds, and a lieutenant who had been a butcher and who slapped people around. His main complaint, though, was being shut in, with few driver's licenses issued, the bridges closed, and Baghdad unsafe due to Shiite militia checkpoints. As far as Taleb was concerned, the war was over, and the restrictions were stultifying commerce. Even so, fear lingered.

"Takfiri leaders are true believers," Taleb's older son said. "They will fight until they die. Without you Americans, they will come back. We need a strong leader. You Americans must stay."

Taleb was echoing the refrain I heard across the Sunni Triangle. Yes, Americans should leave—but not from my neighborhood. Ten percent of the troops in Iraq responding to a Pentagon survey in the fall of 2006 reported personally abusing Iraqi civilians. In response, Petraeus sent a letter to all his troops, saying, "We treat noncombatants and detainees with dignity and respect. While we are warriors, we are also human beings." Certainly during offensive operations, a hardening of attitude occurs. By 2007, however, the attitudes of American soldiers and marines in Iraq differed from the survey results of prior years. They were accepted among the Sunni population.

The attitude about Farouk, however, illustrated a cultural problem about a judicial system that hadn't been corrected. The Special Forces had gone to great effort to find Farouk and bring him back a year ago, when Haditha was out of control. He brought with him about a dozen hard, bitter men who slept in the same clothes for a month, rarely had a shower, and ate food slipped to them by the Marines. Now he had 135 cops on the payroll, 100 training in Jordan, and another 130 from his tribe hanging around, hoping to get on the force. A new police advisory team was trying to get Farouk to accept new methods.

Unlike in prior insurgencies, in Iraq the American military had instituted a rule of law concept that defined all insurgents as criminals who had to be tried by the sovereign country of Iraq. But not trusting the country of Iraq, the Americans kept in U.S.-controlled prisons about 20,000 alleged insurgents arrested by American units. Without referring them to the Iraqi system of justice, the American military released 5,000 prisoners in 2007. On the Iraqi side, 15,286 prisoners were released by investigative judges in 2007, and 5,363 were referred to trial, where about 50 percent would be found not guilty. The vast majority of those arrested on the streets were released.

"Our system cuts loose almost everyone Farouk arrests," Gunnery

Sgt. Eric Johnson, an adviser, said. "Iraqi police don't offer evidence, they just say someone's a terrorist. In the tribal system, a confession is all that's needed."

The advisers took pictures of every man Farouk arrested. General Petraeus had sent out a letter saying that advisers were to report to both American and Iraqi authorities any suspected instance of prisoner abuse, and inform their counterparts that they had done so. When I went to see Farouk, he smiled at the subject of advisers, saying he knew the city quite well. That night, he went on a raid with sixty of his men, without informing his advisers.

A year earlier, the police wouldn't have walked across the street unless marines were walking beside them. Concerns about commerce and the justice system marked the return of stability to a city where two years earlier al Qaeda had beheaded the police in the soccer stadium.

Back at the outpost the Americans shared with the police, I caught up with Farouk. I told him some didn't like his methods. He smiled and shrugged.

"Twenty or thirty takfiris came here at the end of '04," he said. "Chief Hassan had 400 police. The takfiris talk to this person and that, and say they are taking over. They went to Lieutenant Jaheed's house and beheaded him. They told Hassan that was the end of it. The next day, they blew him up in his house. I left for two years. Now I'm back. I know the takfiris by face. You think they tell the truth when I get them? In America, do you let killers go? No!"

There was no computer in Farouk's austere office, but he was carrying several cell phones. He tapped one of them, then put his finger to his forehead.

"This is my intelligence net," he said. "We police chiefs talk back and forth every day—Fallujah, Ramadi, Haditha, Baghdadi, Hit. We tell each other what we've heard, who's moving where."

A constant theme I heard across Iraq was the mobility of the death squads and al Qaeda. Al Qaeda didn't trek across the fields carrying all their gear on their backs. They relied on cars, moving constantly, rarely staying in the same house for more than a few days, often driving 100 kilometers between stops. In town after town and across Baghdad, barriers worked. Security came at the cost of commerce.

So, I asked Farouk, al Qaeda is hiding in the farmlands?

"Not now," Farouk said. "I'm eating with the sheiks. Lots of tribes fighting. In six months, it'll be better in Anbar."

In mid-April, Major General Gaskin sponsored a commanders' conference in Ramadi. From Baghdad, Odierno brought out the minister of
defense and a bevy of top officials to meet with the commanders of
Anbar's police and two Iraqi divisions. With the Americans sitting
along the walls, the Iraqis ran the meeting. The fault lines quickly became obvious. The Anbar police and military leaders backed each
other up in their arguments. The Ministry of Defense and the generals
serving in Anbar quarreled predictably about support from headquarters, while agreeing more had to be done. The focus of criticism was the
Ministry of Interior, which hadn't sent a senior officer, emblematic of
the lack of support for a police force short of uniforms, weapons, fuel,
and pay. The Baghdad delegation was unprepared for the torrent of
shortages quantified by Anbar's police chief, Maj. Gen. Hammad
Showka. As Showka showed PowerPoint slide after slide of require-
ments, deficiencies, and broken promises, his senior police advisers sat
in the rear, beaming and nodding.

The knotty problem was how to deal with the Awakening. Sattar
and the sheiks had not been invited to the meeting. In five months, the
tribal forces had grown to eight Emergency Response Units, or ERU
battalions, numbering about 8,000. The police chiefs didn't like how
they swaggered through towns, and the Iraqi generals didn't like how
they ignored boundaries between military units. Although concern was
raised about a Sunni militia, no official from the province or from
Baghdad recommended that the ERUs be disbanded or that Sattar's organization be reprimanded. The Awakening was recognized as al
Qaeda's enemy.

"The argument back in Washington," Brig. Gen. John Allen, who
dealt with tribal affairs, said after the meeting, "is whether the Shiite
government will compromise. A more basic argument is whether the
government is strong enough for any compromise it makes to be worth
anything. Give Anbar the money it's owed, and it'll take care of itself."

Gen. James Conway, the commandant of the Marine Corps, had
served two tours in Iraq, including the command of the Marine Expeditionary Force during the first Fallujah battle in 2004. Returning from an
April visit to Anbar, where marines accounted for 25,000 of the 35,000
U.S. troops, he said, "I think, in that area, we have turned the corner."

For years, the CIA had been pessimistic in its assessments about
Iraq. Quietly, though, the Agency had supported Casey in his stubborn

effort to split the Sunni tribal resistance from al Qaeda, providing in-termediaries, money, and air transportation. As a former Agency head, Secretary of Defense Robert Gates understood the intelligence game. He had come into office publicly neutral, even dour, about the chances for success in Iraq. He certainly was no cheerleader.

In the spring, the surge was in its beginning stages in and around Baghdad. American casualties were high. In late April, Gates flew to Camp Fallujah. After conducting a review, he told the press, "Anbar is a place where the Iraqis have decided to take control of their future and the sheiks have played a key role." In May, there were thirteen Ameri-can fatalities in Anbar and fifty-nine in the Baghdad region, a sharp re-versal from the prior three years.

The Awakening was a movement of social change sponsored by the American military. As the tribes of Anbar drove out al Qaeda, the prospects for Baghdad improved. The Awakening wouldn't stop at the border of the province.

OVERVIEW

SUMMER 2007

Petraeus's goals were to change the mission, deal with the Iraqi government, and project an image of cool competence to the troops, the enemy, and the American public. The key tasks for Odierno were to allocate twenty brigades for a year-long surge, partner with the Iraqi forces, and conduct sequential operations to accomplish the mission. Petraeus focused on strategy, while Odierno concentrated on the operations to carry out that strategy.

In January, President Bush said, "I've committed more than 20,000 additional American troops to Iraq. The vast majority of them—five brigades—will be deployed to Baghdad." Eventually the commitment rose to about 30,000 troops and six brigades. But only two brigades went into Baghdad, where four U.S. and eighteen Iraqi Army and National Police brigades were already working. Although Washington had emphasized Baghdad as the centerpiece, Petraeus and Odierno had decided to go a different way.

A corps is generally comprised of about three divisions and 90,000 soldiers; Odierno had the equivalent of five divisions and 160,000 soldiers, with another 160,000 contractors in support. As corps commander, Odierno was the highest-ranking field commander, charged with fighting the force. From the start, he looked at prevailing in Iraq, not just in Baghdad. One option was equivalent to Mohs cancer surgery—

insert the brigades into Baghdad and cut out JAM and al Qaeda cells until the violence abated.

Odierno rejected that as too narrow. Since al Qaeda was provoking the backlash of the Shiite militias that fed the cycle of violence spiraling downward into civil war, in mid-June Odierno launched a corps-level offensive called Operation Phantom Thunder. "It is an open-ended operation that will extend through the summer," he said. "We have already begun attacking the enemy from multiple directions in a way I believe he will not be able to resist. Our pursuit will be agile and relentless. Our goal is to force the enemy from positions of disadvantage while we maintain the initiative."

To disrupt the car bombing networks, 10,000 U.S. and Iraqi troops in Operation Arrowhead Ripper began clearing Diyala Province to the north of Baghdad, while to the south another 10,000 in Operation Marne Torch advanced against Salman Pak and the notorious Mahumdiya and Arab Jabour villages on the western side of the Tigris.

Diyala was tough country, hundreds of kilometers of farmland with thick vegetation and a sectarian provincial government at least partially controlled by JAM. In Diyala, in the first three weeks, sixty insurgents were killed. Another 155 were captured, but there was insufficient evidence to send most to prison. In the first week of Phantom Thunder, fifty-six battalion-level operations were launched, resulting in the imprisonment of about 200 insurgents, while over 300 IEDs were found and destroyed. The average American battalion in combat was killing about one insurgent a week and sending two or three to prison.

The Special Operations Command, not the twenty brigades commanded by Odierno, was responsible for most of the senior al Qaeda and Shiite militia leaders killed or captured in Iraq. The names and activities of SOC commandos, commanded by Lt. Gen. Stanley A. McChrystal inside Iraq, were kept secret to avoid giving information to the enemy and retaliation against families. Each day, perhaps a dozen SOC raids were carried out across Iraq, resulting in a few insurgents killed and several arrested. SOC focused on removing the top leaders and while each individual was quickly replaced, quality and job security suffered.

Measured by population displacement, the aggressors with momentum inside Baghdad were the death squads. Before February of 2007, the Sunnis were being steadily pushed out. Since then, Odierno had stymied the death squads by inserting U.S. soldiers along the sectarian fault lines, while McChrystal unleashed his commandos on nightly forays. The hunters became the hunted. The average tenure of a JAM brigade commander was less than two months. Once his name was known, within a week helicopters were landing on his roof.

"Our SpecOps [Special Operations] guys accounted for about 70 percent of the JAM arrests," Odierno said. "The pressure was constant."

A querulous Moqtada Sadr, whose synapses didn't fire normally, had antagonized Maliki by withdrawing his ministers from the cabinet in February. In retaliation, Maliki loosened the restraints on the Emergency Response Unit of the Ministry of Interior—hardened commandos who worked closely with McChrystal's units.

JAM's organization was under nightly assault, with the leaders imprisoned in American jails, where they couldn't be released by complaisant Iraqi judges. In response, many of JAM's top leaders pulled out of Baghdad and took cadres of their best fighters south to Karbala and Basra, where the pickings were easier. Those remaining in Baghdad generally ceased anti-Sunni raids that drew a response from commando units. JAM, though, kept control of the Shiite population in most districts. The Americans did not establish combat outposts in Shiite neighborhoods with orders to protect the population from JAM. That would have provoked a larger war, and the surge force didn't have the numbers to protect the Shiite population from JAM and the Sunni population from al Qaeda. Plus, it would have been politically embarrassing, if not fatal, to admit that the Iraqi government could control neither the Sunni insurgent movement nor the Shiite militias organized by its own political leaders.

The American military machine remained focused on crushing al Qaeda. Raids by a few thousand commandos could at best keep al Qaeda off balance. Even then, al Qaeda lashed back by unleashing one or two suicide bombers—90 percent of whom were not Iraqis—to murder hundreds of civilians. In the second week in July, 155 civilians were killed in a Shiite Turkoman village just outside Diyala by a suicide bomber driving a truck loaded with five tons of explosives. The only reason for such wanton slaughter was to instigate Shiite retaliation against Sunnis.

To excise al Qaeda as a metastasizing cancer required inserting hundreds of thousands of security forces that would gain the trust of the population, resulting in a host of informants. To hold an area and reassure the population that this time security forces were staying required enormous effort. Thousands of farms had to be searched after al Qaeda had fled, leaving behind hundreds of IEDs, many triggered by pressure plates and dug in by hundreds of insurgent cells. Sixty percent of the insurgents captured were illiterate and couldn't read a map, making it impossible to point out where the IEDs were, even if they had wanted to do so.

Each time American or Iraqi soldiers entered an area where al Qaeda had been uncontested, they took casualties from IEDs. Odierno and Petraeus knew this would happen and it pained them personally. In the summer, American casualties were higher than a year earlier, with a low return in terms of al Qaeda killed or imprisoned. In midsummer, Michael O'Hanlon, the respected analyst who tracked fifty different indicators for the Brookings Institution, wrote, "But an increase in these numbers [of U.S. fatalities], while clearly tragic, is difficult to interpret. If it results from harder fighting and more effective patrolling, it is at least possible that the sacrifices could result in a better security environment down the road."

One observable change was the emergence of Iraqi battalions willing to occupy neighborhoods they had avoided in 2006. Lt. Gen. Martin Dempsey, in charge of Iraqi force training, was on his second tour.

"When I was here earlier," he told me, "we were like a child's soccer game. We all chased the ball and left the field uncovered. Not now."

CHAIRMAN OF THE JOINT CHIEFS DISMISSED UNFAIRLY

In June, the dismissal of the chairman of the Joint Chiefs caught everyone by surprise. On Thursday, June 8, Gen. Peter Pace was looking forward to two more years as the chairman, his routine reappointment assured by Gates and the president. On Friday, Senator Levin, chairman of the Armed Services Committee, warned Gates that the reappointment hearing would be bruising. Many Democrats blamed Pace for being complaisant to Rumsfeld. Gates and the president decided to withdraw the nomination. Pace told his staff that he had not abandoned them in the middle of a war; he had been fired.

Like doctors, lawyers, and ambassadors, generals did not criticize each other, a courtesy they did not extend to civilian Pentagon officials. Tom Ricks of *The Washington Post* had challenged the Congress to criticize the generals, saying, "There's extreme unhappiness within the U.S. military . . . they blame their own leadership, the uniformed military, the senior generals. . . . Generals simply are not criticized. Why is the military allowed to get away with this? Because the U.S. Congress is asleep at the wheel."

As chairman, Pace had no direct authority in Iraq. Pace was not criticized by Congress, because the president abandoned him before the hearing.

The episode also reflected poorly on Gates, who as secretary of defense had assumed the detached persona of an umpire rather than a leader in war. He insisted that Iraq could turn out satisfactorily only if America overcame its partisan divide. Seen in that context, Pace was a replaceable cog in an enormous wheel. If cooperation meant throwing Pace over the side, over he went.

Achieving bipartisan harmony was an uphill struggle. Upon leaving Fallujah, where his company suffered five killed over the course of 191 attacks, Maj. Vaughn Ward was assigned to the Marine Corps liaison office on Capitol Hill. "The atmosphere on the Hill was poisonous," Ward said. "There was more love in Fallujah." A few days after Pace's nomination was pulled, Senator Harry Reid, the majority leader, returned Gates's bipartisan gesture by describing Petraeus as "out of touch" and Pace as "incompetent." Gates had sacrificed Pace without dampening the partisan divisiveness.

The president paid Pace no loyalty. One senior White House staff member said the president was fond of Pace, but irritated by his apparent passivity when change was needed in Iraq. Another staff member expressed more existential disappointment, saying, "I was stunned. Bob [Gates] and the president leaped to a hasty judgment. We'd have won that fight in Congress and been stronger for it."

Several months after Pace, who had been a platoon commander in Vietnam, had left the Pentagon, a visitor at the Vietnam Memorial found four silver stars tucked away under the marble wall, with a note expressing his love and respect. The names above the stars included those of the marines who had died serving in Pace's platoon.

There are some traditions that presidents and secretaries of defense should fight for. Standing by the chairman of the Joint Chiefs of Staff is one of them.

A SUBDUED MALIKI

Pace was determined to serve as chairman until his term expired at the end of September. Thus the administration deservedly had to go through the summer with a lame duck as the principal military adviser to the president. Petraeus was due to testify in mid-September, telling Congress whether or not he believed he could achieve his mission. Pace would step down two weeks later.

In midsummer, it appeared 20,000 soldiers had been added to 30,000 other U.S. troops already in and around Baghdad, with inconclusive results. The Pentagon acknowledged indeterminate first returns in its "Initial Benchmark Assessment Report" in mid-July. The report, mandated by congressional legislation, provided a sober assessment, concluding that Iraq showed progress in only nine of eighteen benchmarks.

On the ground, though, Petraeus could see steady progress at the local level. The number of suicide attacks and casualties from VBIEDs (Vehicle-Borne IEDs) had dropped significantly since February. "The big negative," Petraeus wrote in an e-mail in mid-July, "is lack of political reconciliation at the national level."

The big negative from the perspective of the Maliki government was Petraeus. A series of leaks by Iraqi officials accused Petraeus of being arrogant in his treatment of the prime minister. The Awakening of the Sunni tribes had spread eastward from Anbar, enthusiastically encouraged by Petraeus, who authorized U.S. battalion commanders to hire Sunnis to stand guard in their own neighborhoods. Fearing a Sunni militia, Maliki had threatened to recruit more Shiite militias. Petraeus was unmoved. The Associated Press and *The Guardian,* a British newspaper, reported that Maliki told Petraeus, "I can't deal with you anymore. I will ask for someone else to replace you."

In a videoconference, he complained to President Bush, who rebuffed him. Instead of removing Petraeus, Maliki soon found himself in danger of being replaced. In the third week in August, Senator Carl Levin visited Baghdad. After meeting with Maliki, Levin said the Iraqi government was "non-functional" and urged the Assembly to "vote the al-Maliki government out of office." Asked to comment, President Bush refused to endorse Maliki, saying instead, "If the government doesn't respond to the demands of the people, they will replace the government." Ambassador Crocker called the lack of reconciliation at the top "extremely disappointing," while General Casey said, "I heard more people talk about Maliki not making it through his full term in two days than I had heard in all of my previous time [in Iraq]."

Knowing he had overplayed his hand in challenging Petraeus, Maliki backed off. One word from Bush or one shake of the head and the Assembly would vote out Maliki, who had a talent for antagonizing even his allies. Petraeus had succeeded where Casey had failed in neutering Maliki, so that he couldn't interfere in the raids against the Shiite death squads.

He didn't have to worry about Bush, though. The president had moral and practical scruples about replacing him. "The president," a high-level White House aide said, "believes that to interfere in Iraqi politics would betray his strong belief in the sovereignty of a democratic country." Practically, the timing seemed wrong for replacing Maliki. Petraeus was due to testify within a month, and political chaos in Iraq would undercut his message.

Maliki was safe. He didn't have to push hard for a reconciliation he couldn't bring himself to fully support. Bush pursued a patronizing strategy of bucking him up by frequent video chats, while relying on Petraeus to change the dynamics on the battlefield.

TWENTY-ONE

VICTORY IN ANBAR

FALL 2007

In counterinsurgency, there is no climactic fight, no single date like D-Day to mark when the tide of battle changed. Col. Sean McFarland metaphorically called Ramadi "the Gettysburg of the Iraqi war." Ramadi, though, took years to change. Looking back, the key date was September of 2006, when Jurney started his drive across Ramadi's inner city and Sheik Sattar gathered a handful of sheiks to grandly declare the sahwa, or "awakening" of the entire Sunni population. Jurney symbolized the coming of age of counterinsurgency tactics by a generation of American battalion and company commanders, while Sattar infused leadership and hope into a tribal network that extended from Qaim to Baghdad.

Both trends took a year to mature. Iraq was a protracted series of local battles, and when I visited in August and September of 2007, the military momentum had swept from Anbar to Baghdad. Because Anbar was the Wild West, ignored both by the military coalition and the Iraqi politicians, no one expected it to provide the energy to defeat al Qaeda.

To the north and east of Ramadi stretches a vast, arid region within Anbar Province loosely called Thar Thar—a mishmash of scrubby farms, roadside stands, and tire repair shops servicing two highways leading toward Samarra to the east and Jordan to the northwest. Most of Thar Thar is rocks, dust, and ravines, dotted by stubborn palm trees that refuse to die under the blistering heat. In the summer, temperatures soar to 120 degrees. Most of the population lives near the main highway or along the shores of a large lake. Untouched by the U.S. military since the 2003 invasion, Thar Thar was al Qaeda's last refuge in Anbar.

The 13th Marine Expeditionary Unit, commanded by Col. Sam Mundy, was tasked with clearing Thar Thar, a 2,500-square-kilometer area, larger than San Diego County. In one incident, as al Qaeda fled before the oncoming marines, they strapped a man to a tractor tire, set it on fire, and rolled it down the road—warning that a similar fate awaited anyone branded an informer. Because al Qaeda had planted hundreds of IEDs and pressure mines, the marines spent five months walking every foot of the highways, removing 150 tons of explosives from houses, culverts, and buried caches and losing six marines.

The Pentagon had organized a massive task force and spent billions each year to counter the IEDs. When the Pentagon responded with electronic jammers, the insurgents switched to pressure plates. When the Pentagon deployed metal detectors, the insurgents stopped using artillery shells and instead filled plastic jugs with homemade explosives, with fertilizer readily available at any farm.

In the Thar Thar region, the insurgents had had the time to heat and remove sections of asphalt from the highways, emplace explosives, and replace the hardtop. Mundy's troops spread out in a long line and walked slowly down every main road and highway, checking every crack in the hardtop, while removing the trash and shrubbery on the sides of the road. It was hot, nerve-wracking work, with every marine knowing that sooner or later a mine would claim some of them. The insurgents reverted to command-detonated IEDs, running the wires across the fields for over a kilometer so they could get away while the marines were tracing back the wire. Copying the sniper team that terrorized the Washington, D.C., area in 2005, insurgents took shots from the trunks of cars or inside water trucks. The marines countered with snap vehicle control points the minute a shot was fired, shutting down the exit roads and searching every car.

By the end of August, the job was done and the MEU was preparing to leave this desolate place. Mundy took me along as he toured his battle space, driving 100 miles and stopping at three combat outposts. At each, I was greeted by marines from the 3rd Battalion, 1st Marine Regiment, whom I had last seen during the 2004 battle for Fallujah. It was their third rotation back into Iraq.

In the thick reeds back in the marshes, AQI had built concrete bunkers, perhaps telling each other they would fight to the death when the Americans came. Instead, they drove out of the province when the MEU advanced, leaving behind several mass graves with twenty to forty unidentified bodies, some headless, some in rotting uniforms, others hapless civilians and truck drivers whose rigs had been hijacked.

We stopped first at Combat Outpost Golden, a bleak, treeless earth redoubt with a half dozen wooden huts and a line of tents. The brown dust, fine as powder, was so thick it flowed over the top of our boots. Every step raised clouds of it, golden in the blazing sun.

"Took us a few weeks to get showers in here," Mundy said. "The marines looked like Pigpen. They'd sweat, and the dust would stick in layers. They couldn't recognize one another."

Inside a hut, we met the commander of the 2nd Brigade of the 1st Iraqi Division, which was taking over the battle space. A tall, imposing man, Brig. Gen. Ali Ghazi was a member of the Republican Guard who had fought the Americans in Kuwait in 1991. Ghazi explained that he could not possibly hold the area the marines had cleared. When Colonel Mundy left, he feared, his support would drop like a rock.

"In four years, the MOD [Ministry of Defense] has given my soldiers one uniform each. Last month, I got three hundred boots for six hundred soldiers. I'm supposed to give each soldier one boot? I drive eight hours to Baghdad to get my soldiers' pay. Last week, I drove to Basra for gas," he said. "We need water and food. Who gives it to us? Colonel Mundy. The government doesn't even know the Second Brigade is out here in the desert."

The general was voicing a universal complaint. The Iraqi battalions had improved, but it would be years before their logistics and support from the ministries and depots caught up.

"The IA [Iraqi Army] works while we're here with them," Sgt. Joseph Daniels said, while the others nodded. "We provide the water and chow. We leave, and they have no support."

We drove on to the next remote patrol base, where I talked with Sgt. Sam Severtsgaard from Northfield, Minnesota. His face had filled out since I had seen him in 2004 in Fallujah, where as a nineteen-year-old he had fought with courage that bordered on the reckless. On two occasions he rushed into close-quarters firefights with a grenade clutched in his hand, the pin pulled, scaring the hell out of everyone around him. He ended up shot in the side and the leg, and was being rehabilitated in the States in 2005 when 3-1 was sent back to Iraq. He talked his way out of the hospital and rejoined his company. Now he was back for his third, and final, seven-month tour as a squad leader.

"Three rotations to Iraq in four years is enough," he said. "I just got married, and I'm getting out to be a firefighter. The Iraqi soldiers can handle this. There's no real combat anymore. We're putting this outpost in good hands. But in three deployments, I've seen no improvement for the people. They don't even have water. They have nothing."

From there, we drove thirty kilometers to the next outpost, called Chicago. Calling it hell would be more appropriate. The temperature hovered at 115 degrees, and there were three small air-conditioned rooms for forty marines and twenty Iraqi soldiers.

I met with nine marines who had fought in Fallujah in 2004 and were now on their third tour. I remembered that one, Sgt. Derek Fetterolf, had held the record for collapsing the most enemy-occupied houses—more than fifty—with a rocket launcher called a SMAW. Fetterolf and most of the others said they believed that the Iraqi soldiers, with whom they had worked for the past month, could stand on their own.

Of the nine marines, two were staying in, three wanted to be fire-fighters, one a cop, one a customs inspector, one a veterinarian, and one wanted to drink beer and think about it. The war was over for them.

"I've seen outstanding progress in the jundis in four years," Fet-terolf said. "Like, they show up ten minutes early when they stand post with us, and they have all their shit on."

None of the marines believed that the Iraqis could hold the entire expanse that they were patrolling. Instead, the Iraqis, who tended toward the defense and checkpoints, would consolidate along the high-ways. That, the marines believed, was acceptable if the Iraqi soldiers stayed on good terms with the villagers.

Col. Ali Jasam, a battalion commander respected by the marines, explained his approach.

"The people have nothing," Ali said. "No electricity, no hospital, no fuel to get their vegetables to market. The government doesn't send its food truck up here to give out rice bags. The takfiris pay teenagers to shoot at us. When you Americans leave, some takfiris will come back. Okay, I tell the people—my jundis are not like marines. Not ed-ucated. One IED, and all my jundis shoot. Many will be hurt. The peo-ple understand."

O.K. CORRAL: FROM FIGHTING TO POLITICS

In the Habbaniyah corridor between Ramadi and Fallujah, the fighting had stopped. I visited again with Iraqi Battalion 1-3-1 at the O.K. Corral, where on my last trip a villager had refused medical aid for his in-jured son, lest the insurgents kill his family. The battalion had averaged six firefights and nine IED attacks a week in June of 2006; now some-one might take one potshot a week.

The 3rd Iraqi Brigade had more volunteers than it could use. Its 240-square-kilometer battle space, dotted with over 100 fixed check-points and outposts, was shared by 2,000 jundis, 800 shurtas, and 2,700 tribal auxiliaries. Lt. Col. Thomas Hobbs, the battalion adviser chief, was on his third tour. A nearby Marine battalion had sent a squad to help his eleven-man team. With twenty-five men, Hobbs was able to send out patrols and conduct civil affairs, such as repairing the irrigation pumps and opening up grammar schools.

With so many advisers in constant contact, Hobbs had become part of the social scene, hearing the good, the bad, and the gossip. Sattar was organizing for a political struggle to diminish the power of the Iraqi Islamic Party, which came to power through the list-based elec-tion in December of 2005. The police, whose ranks were filled by the IIP, lobbied Hobbs to disband the tribal-based Provincial Security Forces and Neighborhood Watches. Hobbs just laughed. The tribes were too valuable. He had come across the tribal gangs patrolling in the villages at night, when both the army and the police stayed in their forts.

Over a late dinner, Major Hamdi, a company commander I had known for some time, needled the advisers about the reasons for the lack of violence.

"You marines have been here three years," he said. "You were dis-ciplined, high-tech, brave. You got nowhere. You didn't have an Iraqi partner to provide intelligence. No civil affairs. No relation with the people."

Hobbs laughed as he took another piece of chicken. Most advisory teams ate dinner with the battalion staff, usually chicken or lamb over rice, with tomatoes or cucumbers and fresh pita bread.

"We do the civil affairs around here, not you," Hobbs said. "Your IO [Information Operations] with the people is terrible."

"The tribes want to get the power from the police before you leave," Hamdi said. "When my battalion leaves, they will fight for the gas and extortion."

With no fighting to occupy them, the advisers had the time and manpower to observe small details. What frustrated them was the per-vasive corruption. The battalion commander from my previous visit had moved on after Hobbs had shown the brigade commander evidence that impounded cars and caches of insurgent weapons held by the battalion were loaded onto the division's convoys headed for Baghdad, where they were sold to militias. The division was authorized 67 staff officers; 107 officers were serving on the division staff, inside a comfortable base, while Hobbs was three officers short in the battalion.

Hobbs was still seething about a recent incident. The team interpreters had told him that two jundis were raping the younger wife of a minor sheik in a nearby village. Everyone in the battalion, they said, knew about it. Hobbs asked several soldiers, who admitted they had heard the same thing. Hobbs discreetly approached the woman, who said the two soldiers had visited her six times in the past four months. They had threatened to kill her husband and burn her house if she told. A female doctor took her statement on tape, promising not to reveal her name and shame her before the community. Hobbs then went to the brigade executive officer, who refused to arrest the men, saying the woman had acted like a whore.

"I asked him what if it was his daughter," Hobbs said. "When I followed up by mentioning the press, he arrested the guys. It was like what happened with the battalion commander who sold the impounded cars—they left the area but didn't go to jail. Same happened with three cops."

In the case of the three policemen, an army patrol accompanied by two advisers was searching a house where they found a man tied to a ceiling beam, hanging upside down with his feet bloody from beating. Three policemen in the room said he was their prisoner. In the next room, a man lay strapped down, his stomach slit open. A rat scampered away when the jundis walked in. The advisers disarmed the policemen, cuffed them, and brought them back to the battalion. The man with the bloody feet said he was being held for ransom. They had broken his wife's arm when she wasn't able to pay for his release.

After extended negotiations with the local sheiks, the three were turned over to the police and left the district.

"Sheer Iraqi politics," Hobbs said. "The bastards had IIP connections. It pissed us off mightily."

With three successive Iraqi governments, the U.S. military had failed to negotiate an agreement for a joint U.S.-Iraqi board to review key positions and share authority to promote or to fire officers. The American advisers lacked leverage.

FALLUJAH LOCKED DOWN AND EMERGING

In the summer of 2003, the lone diplomat in Anbar, Keith Mines, the former Special Forces officer, had warned that the provincial police force of 900 men, who shared sixty pistols, couldn't possibly control an area the size of North Carolina. He had recommended immediately reinstating and paying 35,000 former Baathists, including 10,000 military officers, and filling half the positions on the provincial council with tribal sheiks. The annual price tag of $200 million in salaries to stabilize the province was rejected as absurdly high.

Mines, however, warned that Fallujah was the one city that couldn't be controlled. The city had spelled trouble for camel caravans in the nineteenth century, and for the reigns of the British and of Saddam in the twentieth century. In a memo to Ambassador Bremer in November of 2003, Mines concluded, "And it is the case that Fallujah has always had the reputation as the cesspool of Iraq. Saddam reportedly just left it alone. It is possible that Fallujah will remain hostile until the day we turn the problem over to a new Iraqi government."

Col. Richard Simcock, commanding the 6th Marine Regiment, sent a full battalion back into the city with a firm mission: Get control and keep it. Lt. Col. William Mullen believed his battalion, 2-6, needed a model. So he sent his executive officer, Maj. George Benson, up to Ramadi to see how Jurney had done it.

"It was the most intense week of learning in my career," Benson said. "Jurney laid out his op plans and walked me through his system. He sat me down with the sheiks, the city council, the police, the Iraqi Army, our company commanders, and our Special Ops guys. I studied how they worked together, and how Jurney orchestrated his tactics."

In June of 2007, Mullen launched Operation Alljah, short for Fallujah. The city was divided into ten precincts, each three square kilometers is size and cordoned off by concrete Jersey barriers, with one entry and one exit point. Cars were banned. One by one, each precinct was surrounded by marines and jundis. The police swarmed in and checked the IDs of every military-aged male, trucking in three large biometric machines to verify each ID on the spot.

In the first precinct hit with the swarm tactic, eleven insurgents were captured and three killed. Three cell phones were found in hiding places, yielding seventy-four names and cell numbers of contacts, many in Syria. The police chief, Feisal, sentenced to a week in jail about two dozen men with false IDs—students, storekeepers, and others who couldn't be bothered taking the time to register. The next day, a long queue formed outside the ID office at the Government Center. No one wanted to be hauled off to Feisal's jail.

The second precinct to be swarmed a week later yielded fewer suspected insurgents. The third precinct yielded none. The police stopped men at random in the city of 200,000 to 300,000, checked the location of their home precinct against where they were stopped, and if suspicious, hauled them in for further questioning. Knowing they were being squeezed and not being able to drive, al Qaeda left town.

Outside the city, al Qaeda encountered equally inhospitable conditions. Brig. Gen. John Allen, assigned to enhance cooperation with the tribes, spent half his time in Jordan meeting with sheiks who had fled Anbar to avoid assassination. One contact led to another, as Allen patiently reassured each sheik of protection, with no questions asked about past affiliations. He arranged for American doctors to take care of wounded relatives and set up helicopter and C-130 flights for sheiks who wanted to visit their clans without tipping off al Qaeda.

Sheik Khamis and the Abu Eisa tribe controlled farmlands to the west of Fallujah, and they had hated al Qaeda for years. To the east of the city lay the troublesome town of Kharma, which sat astride a main route to Baghdad. To control Kharma, the Jumaly tribe, numbering over 100,000, had to be won over. The tribal leader, Sheik Mishan, had criticized a fellow sheik, Abdullah Janabi, for supporting Zarqawi, resulting in the destruction of Fallujah. In retaliation, Janabi attacked Mishan, who fled to Jordan. Mishan's son was then kidnapped and beheaded when a ransom of $500,000 couldn't be paid.

In May and June, Allen met several times in Jordan with Mishan, promising the Marines would back his tribe if he returned and attacked al Qaeda. At the end of June, having lost another son in a roadside bombing, Mishan agreed. Allen flew the sheik to Fallujah and paid for a bodyguard from his tribe. Al Qaeda struck back by executing his niece and nine other relatives. Mishan then pledged his tribe to the Awakening, and Allen authorized the training and payment for a thousand-man tribal Provincial Security Force. Farther to the north of the city, Allen persuaded Sheik Hamid Mahanah of the Al Bouwan tribe to join the uprising.

"We needed a tribal confederation to stabilize the province," Allen said. "We pushed the sheiks to back Sattar. Maliki supported Sattar in Anbar and even in Diyala. It worked for us like it did for [Sir Edmund] Allenby and T. E. Lawrence in World War I. Al Qaeda couldn't conquer the tribes once they banded together."

To the south, the Zobai tribe in the Zidon still supported the 1920s

Brigade resistance group. The 1920s asked Sattar to join them in demanding that all foreign fighters, the Arabs with al Qaeda and the Americans, leave Anbar. Sattar told the 1920s that he'd crush them if they fought the Americans.

Four years ago, the diplomat Keith Mines had written about turning "the problem [of Fallujah] over to the new Iraqi government." Well, there was a functioning government, but it came with a hook. It was the Marines, with their motto: No worse enemy; no better friend. Fallujah residents looked not to Baghdad but to the Americans, who had destroyed their city, as their patron. If you wrote the narrative of Fallujah as a novel, publishers would reject it as implausible.

The Fallujah city council resented sheiks like Mishan, outsiders who were competing for the protection and reconstruction money provided by the Marines. The police chief, Feisal, thought the tribes were undisciplined and wanted their fighters placed under his control. As Fallujah quieted down, he even considered driving with a few dozen police and marines to Baghdad to follow up on a tip. He dropped that idea when the marines told him he was crazy.

Inside Fallujah, each of the ten precincts was manned by a Marine squad and fifty police, paid $575 a month. Five to ten foot patrols were run daily. Each precinct was authorized a Neighborhood Watch of 200 residents, with each man paid $150 a month to guard the entry and exit points. The Iraqi battalions were gradually withdrawn to outposts outside the city.

In late summer, without armor or a helmet, I walked down the streets with Maj. Todd Sermarini, the head police adviser. Katie Couric of CBS had recently visited the city, and the residents had swept the gutters and hauled away the trash before she came through with her camera crew. The residents I spoke to were proud their city had been shown on world television. CBS was big time, and the city had pulled together to show its best face.

The control measures, though, had a crushing effect on commerce. In treeless southern Fallujah, the impoverished residents baked under the late-summer sun. The mayor was trying to evict squatters who had no place to go, and the Marines were resisting him. The city council was demanding that some cars be allowed back in. Everyone complained about the lack of electricity and fuel. Fallujah was stable but terribly poor.

I had met six mayors and five city council chairmen in Fallujah. Four had been murdered and the others eventually had fled. I had known two remarkably brave leaders—Lieutenant Colonels Suleiman and Salam—who were killed. Given the perpetual threat of violence, Feisal was running the city with an iron fist. The jail was packed with 400 men, most in one large concrete room with not enough room to turn around and reeking of urine. The bad cases—the al Qaeda true believers—were packed off to the American prison at Bucca. All the others languished until an occasional judge sentenced or released them, or until Feisal decided they had learned their lesson.

The prime lesson was to avoid bad company. Once booked and fingerprinted, a suspect knew a subsequent arrest would go badly for him. Iraq's judicial system—an oxymoron—depended upon confession rather than evidence for a conviction. The police were usually acting on suspicion. Beatings sometimes extracted confessions. Most Iraqis in city jails like Fallujah were released in a few weeks or months with the message: Don't come back a second time.

When I asked the deputy police chief, Kareem, how things were going, for the first time in years he was optimistic.

"In April of 2004, the people believed al Qaeda were mujahidin—holy warriors," Kareem said. "Now we kill Qaeda and soon the people will know you Americans are good. My police wear their uniforms when they go home. Every day is better."

Al Qaeda was a minority group among the Sunni insurgents. After the tribes turned, attacks in Anbar dropped to almost zero. A large majority of the attacks hadn't been by al Qaeda in Iraq. After the Sunni resistance against Americans ceased, though, horrible violence persisted. In August, al Qaeda had committed the single most terrible slaughter of the war when four suicide bombers blew to pieces over 500 poor villagers near Mosul. In Fallujah, a suicide bomber blew up a funeral procession, while another detonated explosives mixed with chlorine in a market. It was an inside job, conducted by Fallujah residents.

Foreigners led al Qaeda, but comprised less than 4 percent of its fighters. Somehow they succeeded in inculcating hate and turning Sunnis not only against Shiites, but against their own relatives and tribal members. There weren't many zealots, but each was a walking, thinking cruise missile. It was in Fallujah that I first heard al Qaeda called "the faceless ones." When your unassuming neighbor or cousin may have agreed to blow you up, it changes how you deal with people. Feisal, whose brother had been beheaded by al Qaeda, and his police were rough because the consequence of tolerance was mass killings.

With Major Sermarini, I walked across the police compound from the overcrowded jail through the impounded car lot loaded with stripped vehicles. We paused by a corrugated tin shipping container where Feisal had planned to store the overload of prisoners, until Sermarini vehemently objected. Few would have survived the intense heat.

On the far side of the lot I walked into a small, abandoned concrete room—the makeshift kitchen where cops coming off duty had stopped for a cup of hot chai and a few biscuits. The kitchen was the birthplace of al Qaeda in Fallujah. The first wave of takfiris had attacked here in February of 2004, massacring twenty-four policemen. The whitewashed walls, gouged by heavy caliber bullets, bore the stains, blotches, and streaks of blood still vivid in an orange-brown that caught your eye. You could imagine the policemen screaming as they slid down the wall.

Feisal in Fallujah, Sha'ban in Baghdadi, Farouk in Haditha—tough cops locked in a death struggle with the faceless ones.

RAMADI EMERGES

By August of 2007, Ramadi was scarcely recognizable to a veteran of the street battles in 2005 and 2006. The rows of crumbled buildings had been bulldozed into heaps and hauled away in twelve-wheel dump trucks. The mounds of garbage and burned-out cars on the streets had gone the same way. The city was receiving power for six hours each day, shops were open, and blue-shirted police walked around without their armored vests.

Across the entire battle space of Col. John Charlton's 1st Brigade Combat Team, 12,000 Iraqi police and soldiers were partnered with 6,000 American soldiers and marines. There hadn't been a single attack in the past two months.

Maliki and the Appropriations Committee of the National Assembly had pledged to send Anbar another $120 million in 2007. Added to $100 million already received, this meant over $200 million in capital expenditures for "bricks and mortar"—fixing up a decrepit infrastructure of balky irrigation pumps, faulty water purifiers, and intermittent electric power. This was a paltry sum when compared to the $10 billion in total capital revenues the Iraqi government authorized while spending less than $5 billion and hoarding the remainder. What exasperated Senators Levin and Warner on the Armed Services Committee was that the administration proposed giving Iraq $4 billion in 2008, while the Iraq government was running a multibillion-dollar surplus and refusing to spend it. Across Iraq, bureaucracies from the ministries in Baghdad down to the districts hoarded about half the monies they were authorized, due to laziness, incompetence, political infighting, fear of accusations of corruption, and lack of trustworthy developers.

In 2007, Iraq received $41 billion in oil revenues, and ran a large surplus. Yet the country was chronically short of electric power and fuel. The subsidized cost of fuel from the refinery at Bayji, north of Baghdad, was five times less than that charged in Turkey, Syria, and Jordan, creating a vast black market with collusion among tribes, insurgents, and officials. Everyone was diverting fuel and selling it for astonishing profits. The official allocation to Anbar was forty-two fuel trucks per day; the actual deliveries were half that number. Petraeus's proposal to send armed convoys to the refinery to guard every truck was firmly vetoed by Baghdad officialdom as an affront to Iraq's sovereignty, an indicator of how pervasive and intertwined was the web of corruption.

The Council on Foreign Relations reported that between 2003 and 2006, the United States spent $30 billion on economic aid in Iraq—roughly the same amount, adjusted for inflation, as was provided to Germany from 1946 to 1952. There was little to show for it.

Microfinance loans across Anbar in 2007, lauded by economists because they rewarded initiative and self-improvement, numbered 229, at an expenditure of half a million dollars, most of which would be repaid. The program that most directly benefited the people willing to work the hardest received less than one percent of U.S. aid dollars. There were a dozen Web sites devoted to discussing and critiquing military counterinsurgency tactics, operations, and concepts. Economic development received a free pass because there wasn't a compass or a roadmap to determine what direction to follow, or how to know when to turn off the spigot.

In Anbar, James Soriano directed the Provincial Reconstruction Team. A two-year veteran of Iraq who was fluent in Arabic and had directed development projects in five countries, Soriano had a positive outlook. He planned for 2007 to spend at least $66 million in Economic Support Funds on capacity-building projects like water sanitation plants. The dozen-odd American battalions scattered across the province would each spend about $10 million in CERP (Commander's Emergency Response Program) projects. Battalion commanders valued CERP because it gave them wasta, or influence, in the local communities. They sat down with the local leaders, drew up lists of small projects, set priorities, and quickly spent the money.

"CERP rents influence for the ground commander. It doesn't change the underlying economics," Soriano said. "Saddam cut off Iraq from the global economy and sucked out the concept of free enterprise. There's no proven development model to follow for Anbar or the other seventeen provinces. Commerce requires transportation, but the cities in Anbar are locked down and there's no fuel. Still, these tribes have a self-sufficient spirit. I'm more bullish on Anbar than the rest of the country."

In early September, Governor Mamoon hosted an economic conference in Ramadi, attended by hundreds of sheiks and officials from across the province. Having benefited from the steep rise in oil prices, the Baghdad government had promised a supplemental to the province. Maliki and the Shiite ministers did not attend the meeting. Deputy Prime Minister Barham Salh, a Sunni Kurd, presided.

The real guest of honor was Sheik Sattar. With his trim beard, Sattar looked like Frank Zappa. He stood in the foyer, dressed in a white robe, gravely receiving homage from other sheiks, while Generals Odierno and Gaskin remained in the background. Salh gave a short speech, praising the Awakening and declaring that an additional $120 million had been set aside for the province.

Senator Joseph Biden, who visited Iraq frequently, then took the podium to issue a blunt warning. "The American people can't want peace more than the Iraqi people," he said. "It's encouraging to see central government assisting you in Anbar. In America we are waiting to see how extensive that cooperation will be. If it is [extensive], you can count on America to stay. If it is not, we can say goodbye now."

After the meeting, the sheiks mingled, nibbling on chicken and pita bread. Several were puzzled by Biden's lecture. They had expected to be congratulated for having thrown out al Qaeda. When I chatted with Deputy Prime Minister Salh, he was annoyed. "It took your country thirteen years," he said, "to get a constitution and a set of laws. Why are you talking defeatist?"

Sheik Sattar was more relaxed and philosophical about Biden's rebuke. When I asked him whether Americans had to constantly prod to get things done like throwing out al Qaeda, he replied, "We Iraqis convinced ourselves."

TWENTY-TWO

BAGHDAD: THE SURGE TAKES HOLD

FALL 2007

GHAZALIYAH: GAINING A DESPERATE ALLY

Sattar's Awakening spread across Iraq. Encouraged by Petraeus and Odierno, brigade commanders in and around Baghdad met with Sunni leaders. While Maliki was willing to accept local Sunnis into the police in remote Anbar, his resistance stiffened as the Awakening swirled into Baghdad. Unfazed, Petraeus authorized the brigades to reach into the Commander's Emergency Response Program and pay Sunnis to guard their neighborhoods at half the pay rate the Iraqi government allotted to policemen.

At Combat Outpost Casino in Ghazaliyah, Lieutenant Cartee had hired 300 unarmed Sunnis to stand watch alongside Iraqi soldiers. The two groups weren't friendly, but they tolerated each other. Sheik Hamid, who had first suggested the Neighborhood Watch and warned that Colonel Sabah hated him, had been arrested. Shortly afterward, in response to pressure from the American advisers, Sabah was transferred to an adjoining district.

"Things have quieted down, but Hamid is screwed," Cartee said. "I don't know if we can get him released."

Cartee had placed Raad Ali Hassan, a former colonel in the Iraqi Special Forces, in charge of the Neighborhood Watch program, called the Concerned Local Citizens. Soon, they would be registered and allowed to carry their own AKs back and forth to work.

"A year ago, there were fifty al Qaeda on these streets," Raad told me. "Now, in Ghazaliyah there's about ten guys left. They've tried three times to shoot me. I'll get them. Lieutenant Cartee is letting me bring back my own officers and forty soldiers. We'll join the police."

Cartee wasn't so sure. The Iraqi police up the street couldn't be trusted, and the battalion commander who had replaced Sabah slept in the American compound, not knowing which of his jundis might kill him, or why.

"The Sunnis have rebuilt their market," Cartee said. "It's shantytown stuff, but a step up from nothing. We've given them a few contracts—ten or twenty thousand dollars. It's a start. The government promised positions on the police force. If that doesn't happen, this is the calm before the storm."

The mission of Cartee and his soldiers was taped to the wall in the ops center of Casino. It read: "2-12 Cav conducts security ops to assist the Government of Iraq in creating a safe environment and improving the quality of life of the population."

The mission had turned topsy-turvy. The Americans were trying to improve the quality of life of Sunnis who had recently been fighting against them, while the Shiites up the street enjoyed a higher standard of living they were reluctant to share. Maliki and the National Assembly had failed for a year to pass reconciliation legislation from the top down. The U.S. Army wasn't assisting the government of Iraq to create a safe environment; it was creating that environment despite the government.

General Petraeus and Ambassador Crocker spoke of a "bottom-up" strategy. In practice, this didn't mean reconciliation between Sunni and Shiite; instead, it allowed the Sunnis to defend their neighborhoods. Concerned Local Citizens groups that could drive out al Qaeda could also repel JAM raiders. Every neighborhood was enclosed in concrete barriers that prevented armed gangs from driving in. A battle on foot favored the CLC defenders, who knew every street, alleyway, and hiding place. When the United States confronted the Soviet Union, the nuclear might of each side provided an equilibrium called Mutual Assured Destruction. At the level of local street fights, the CLC posed a similar equilibrium.

When Maliki and his minions complained that the Americans were creating a Sunni militia, Petraeus had a ready retort. Fine—incorporate the Concerned Local Citizens into the police. Since 2003, the Sunnis in the army had proven trustworthy. Once Sunnis like Colonel Raad entered the police force, the government controlled their leadership, pay, and ammunition. Sunni police couldn't fight without bullets. Sunnis inside the government tent weren't a threat.

I asked Col. J. B. Burton, whose brigade controlled Ghazaliyah and central Baghdad on the west side of the Tigris, if the Sunnis were joining the police.

"Raad says the deputy minister of interior promised him positions on the police," Colonel Burton said. "It hasn't happened. This isn't a done deal. If you want to see what Concerned Local Citizens are doing on their own, go to Amariyah."

WEST BAGHDAD: SUNNI FIGHTERS IN AMARIYAH

Amariyah was one of west Baghdad's newer neighborhoods, dating from the 1960s. The streets were laid out in straight lines by engineers, with none of the random twists and turns of the older neighborhoods nearer the city's center. A middle-class Sunni enclave, it sat astride the main highway that ran from Anbar to the west straight into downtown Baghdad. The district was only a few minutes' drive from the gigantic Forward Operating Base called Camp Liberty. In 2005, quiet Amariyah was patrolled by a single U.S. platoon that drove around during the day before returning to Liberty for an excellent evening meal and a good night's sleep.

After the bombing of the Golden Mosque in Samarra in February of 2006, bands of insurgents led by AQI infiltrated into Amariyah to stage attacks against the Shiite militias deeper inside the city. In November, Task Force 1-5 Cavalry, a mechanized unit with 600 soldiers, took over responsibility for Amariyah and adjoining locales. An Iraqi battalion was supposed to be in the lead, while the Americans supplied backup firepower. The Iraqi battalion commander quit after AQI called him, offering details of where his family lived.

The next commander's idea of counterinsurgency was to station his jundis inside four outposts along the highway, where they stopped traffic to extract petty bribes. On a map, it looked like the Iraqi battalion was living among the people. On the ground, the opposite was the case. AQI attacked the outposts with occasional RPG and mortar shells, keeping the Iraqi soldiers jittery, defensive-minded, and penned in. That left the daily patrolling to the Americans, aided by a few local translators.

As in other districts, Jersey barrriers boxed in Amariyah, sealing off all side streets and leaving only two entrances manned by Iraqi platoons. With no Iraqi forces inside the four-square-kilometer "gated community" containing 10,000 houses and 50,000 residents, clearing operations fell to the Americans, who had no network among the people. The eight imams in the district were surprisingly friendly, although not offering specific tips. Their cooperation ended in March of 2007, when roadside bombs and snipers broke up their meeting with Lt. Col. Dale Kuehl, the 1-5 Cavalry battalion commander. Within two weeks, six imams fled the district.

A Stryker battalion, sent in to help 1-5, launched a series of raids. Each Stryker, a multiwheeled armored vehicle, enabled six infantrymen to leap out and rush into a house in a quick, pinpoint strike. The problem was that no pinpoints existed. The AQI leaders in civilian clothes visited various houses during the day, making threats, demanding recruits, and stashing explosives. At night, they dispersed among hundreds of abandoned dwellings. Kuehl's battalion and the Strykers had a list of seventy-five names—and 10,000 homes to choose from. After twenty-four night raids yielded only a few suspects, the Strykers were moved to another district, while Kuehl sent his platoons deeper into Amariyah.

The problem was that the Americans, driving in Humvees on the inner roads, had no idea who among the hundreds of civilians was plotting to kill them. In six months, one soldier in 1-5 Cav had been killed. Then, in three days in May, bombs buried deep in residential streets killed five soldiers, with another five seriously wounded, and destroyed three Humvees. A week later, an enormous buried bomb killed another five Americans.

Having lost eleven soldiers, Kuehl banned all Humvees from entering Amariyah—they were too light to withstand the size of the blasts. The buried bomb campaign continued, disabling over the next several weeks eight tanks and eight Bradley Fighting Vehicles.

"I didn't have any local support, no warning of where those bombs were being buried," Kuehl said. "AQI controlled the streets and mined the key intersections."

To prevent heavy bombs from being moved in, Kuehl banned all civilian vehicles from Amariyah and emplaced more Jersey barriers. That still left, though, caches of explosives and gangs of fighters throughout the district. At the end of May, a firefight broke out at a mosque between AQI and the local insurgents who called themselves the Jesh al-Islami, or Army of Islam. A quick response by a Stryker platoon routed the AQI and a few days later Kuehl received word that a shadowy leader named Abu Abid wanted to meet.

A trim, unsmiling man in his late thirties with an air of quiet authority, Abid got directly to the point. Since moving into Amariyah sixteen months ago, AQI had routinely demanded food and in the hot months evicted the owners of houses with generators and air-conditioning. Over the past few months, they had snatched some wealthy residents, accused them of collaboration, and demanded ransoms. Last week, they had seized Abid's elderly cousin and insisted on $70,000 for his release. Abid had gathered some of his own fighters and rescued his cousin, sparking the fight.

Abid said his fighters now had to drive out all AQI, or they would be hunted down individually. If Abid's men moved unarmed, AQI would assassinate them. But if the Americans saw Abid's men with weapons, they'd shoot them. Can we work something out? Abid asked.

Kuehl proposed they join forces. The Americans asked no questions about how Abid and his 300 men happened to be handy with weapons and knew the AQI by name. If he found out that any had emplaced explosives that had killed Americans or Iraqi soldiers, he'd arrest them. His battalion had just received handheld devices called HIDE that captured fingerprints and eye retina pictures. The two American rifle companies building outposts inside the district fingerprinted Abid's men and entered them into the HIDE database. They could carry weapons and, if stopped, be immediately checked and identified.

In return, Kuehl paid each fighter $1,000 over three months, setting up a $500,000 contract via CERP. This would give the Iraqi Ministry of Interior enough time to train and pay them as legitimate police. If the ministry failed to do so, Kuehl would extend the contract indefinitely.

Inside Amariyah, Kuehl set up two austere company-sized combat outposts. Abid's neighborhood fell inside the zone of COP Bushmaster. Like several other COPs, Bushmaster was one of Saddam's old bomb shelters—squat, square structures with each room enclosed in several feet of reinforced concrete. Knowing it was an obvious site for an outpost, the AQI had fouled it by burning tires in the rooms and pitching in corpses to rot. Cav 1-5 had shoveled out each room, washed the walls with ammonia, and moved in cots and air-conditioning units. When the units broke down, Bravo Company endured, trying to sleep after midnight when the temperature dropped to 95 degrees, going without showers or decent latrines, burning their human waste twice a day.

"The smell's ripe inside Bushmaster," Capt. Brendan Gallagher, the Bravo Company commander, said. "It's a long summer."

Each day, Bravo sent out two to four patrols in platoon strength, walking down the streets accompanied by an armored vehicle with dozens of bottles of water. After two to four hours, the soldiers, weighed down by armor and gear, would be drenched and exhausted.

Abid's men, brandishing AKs and PKC machine guns and wearing street clothes and cheap track shoes like Pumas, patrolled separately. They were indistinguishable from AQI or other insurgents who hadn't switched sides. To avoid shooting them, the Americans set up patrol boundaries and talked daily by cell phone. Abid was responsible for the 10,000 residents living in his neighborhood, or mullhala. He carried three cell phones that were constantly ringing. During June and July, Abid's men engaged in over forty firefights, killing twenty-two Iraqis and leaving their bodies on the streets. When he had a tip about AQI in another mullhala, he called Gallagher. By August, Kuehl's AQI list had dropped from seventy-five to twelve. By September, attacks against Americans had stopped entirely.

In its place, friction between Abid's fighters and the Iraqi Army had grown. In Ghazaliyah, the district to the north, the persistent complaints by the senior American advisers about Lieutenant Colonel Sabah had gotten results—sort of. Sabah was promoted to full colonel and sent to command the battalion at Amariyah. Sabah told Kuehl that it was a mistake to work with insurgents like Abid. For his part, Abid loathed Sabah.

"For years, we resisted the invader," Abid told me with a trace of a smile. "The Iranians were helping the Shiites and al Qaeda came to help us. Then they started killing us. You [Americans] are okay— you're not really invaders. You rebuild schools. You're the good guys for us. Not Qaeda, not the jundis."

With vehicles banned from Amariyah, the residents had to walk outside the concrete barriers to buy food, water, and ice from vendors, and then pass by the Iraqi soldiers, mostly Shiites, to reenter. Captain Gallagher sent soldiers to the three checkpoints to prevent shakedowns, but they could stay for only a few hours at a time.

"The people are penned in like criminals," Abid said. "In five months, the government has given us nothing, no electricity, no water, no food. We're at peace here, yet Maliki says on television that Amariyah is bad. He closed our three schools. Our kids don't dare go anywhere. We have to pass by Sabah's men to get anything."

Get Sabah out of Amariyah, he told Kuehl. To show who was boss, a few days earlier Sabah had driven up unannounced to Abid's head-quarters in an abandoned school. His convoy was promptly sur-rounded by men on rooftops, pointing machine guns and rocket launchers. Forced to back off, he went to Kuehl, demanding that Abid's men be stripped of all unauthorized weapons. That man is out of con-trol, Sabah fumed. Not one American soldier or jundi has been killed since Abid took over, Kuehl said. He stays.

While I was talking with Abid, one of his cell phones rang. After a terse, short conversation, he hung up and laughed. Nicky, an inter-preter, explained that the caller was an Arab with a Saudi accent. "The Iraqi Army hates you," the Saudi had said. "It's not your fight. Take your family and leave now, or we will kill you."

"Fuck you," Abid replied.

Petraeus was dropping by in a few days to show some congressmen how well the Concerned Local Citizens program, numbering 70,000 in 120 locales, was working. Kuehl, concerned the congressmen not wit-ness a gunfight between the jundis and former insurgents, invited Abid to dinner at Bushmaster. The temperature outside was 110 degrees; in-side, it was 95 degrees, thanks to a few air conditioners wheezing puffs of humid air across a Formica table dappled with beads of sweat. Abid began the conversation by gesturing angrily with his cell phone.

"Three of my men were arrested," he said. "Sabah claimed they beat a woman and took her car and furniture."

"We just heard," Kuehl said. "Your men left our sector without telling us."

"She's the mother of an AQ guy. AQ gave her the car. How can my men load furniture into a dumpy little Toyota? Sabah's moving the fur-niture, not us. You get them released. I'll beat them, then settle with Sabah."

"Whoa! No beatings. General Petraeus is coming with congress-men," Kuehl said. "You have a global audience. People like Sabah want you to fail."

"My brother was killed by MOI [Ministry of Interior]," Abid said. "They used a drill. They're like takfiris—liars and murderers for money."

"No beatings, no bitching, or I can't pay you," Kuehl said. "Smile when the visitors are here. Say the right things, like how the Iraqi Army helps you."

"My men find the IEDs," Abid said. "Sabah takes the credit."

Kuehl nodded. An hour earlier, Abid had proudly shown him a half dozen shells and a metal cylinder filled with explosives, with a cell phone taped to the cylinder. Kuehl hastily ordered the device placed in an empty lot until a demolitions team could detonate it.

"You have to be a diplomat," Kuehl said. "I can't pay you forever. You have to get along with guys like Sabah."

During Petraeus's brief visit, Abid was restrained. The left side of his face was swollen from an impacted tooth, so he couldn't smile, even if he wanted to. When an Iraqi major tried to take credit for the turnaround in Amariyah, Kuehl told him to sit down and shut up. Petraeus, who knew what Abid had accomplished, nodded at Kuehl.

After the four-star visit, Col. J. B. Burton summarized the situation for me. Over the past ten months, his brigade had organized eighteen Concerned Local Citizens groups. With the Americans and the Iraqi Army, al Qaeda had been driven out of west Baghdad and the death squads didn't dare enter Sunni neighborhoods like Abid's. But Burton—nobody's fool—knew JAM still controlled the streets in Shiite districts like Shula and Kadhimiyah.

"We've gated in the Sunni communities. The Jersey barriers have stopped the easy movement of AQI and the death squads," he said. "Al Qaeda's grip on the Sunnis is wobbling. We've set the conditions for two critical pieces—putting Sunnis on the police force and bringing back basic services to jump-start the economy. The Iraqi government has to follow through."

Burton, who kept a list of which Iraqi officers and police deserved trust and which were dirty, was neutral in his tone and assessment of what would happen.

"My soldiers know what's happening on the streets," he said. "Al Qaeda's on the ropes, but JAM's alive and well in this city."

WEST BAGHDAD: JAM CONTROL IN THE KADHIMIYAH DISTRICT

Lieutenant Cartee at Combat Outpost Casino and Captain Sullivan and Abid at Bushmaster told me the Shiite death squads came from the Shula and Kadhimiyah districts, a few miles to the north. Kadhimiyah illustrated the cancerous growth of the Shiite militias, which by the fall of 2007 presented more of a danger in Baghdad than did the languishing al Qaeda cells.

For almost a year. Lt. Col. Steve Miska had commanded Task Force Justice located on the base in Kadhimiyah where Saddam had been hanged. Miska, who had taught at West Point, had a relaxed, coolly analytical style. His interpreter and intellectual equal was Hassan Benkato, an Arab-American from Houston. The two were inseparable, not uncommon between field commanders and their interpreters. In their Humvee, headsets connected them with the driver and the machine gunner, Specialists Brad Rodin and Nathan Neyer. Having logged 2,000 hours on the streets of Kadhimiyah, the four could finish each other's sentences and sense each other's moods, switching in a second from banter to full tactical alert.

As the site of the holiest Shiite shrine in Baghdad, Kadhimiyah received millions of pilgrims each years. A profusion of street-side vendors sold bright clothes and memorabilia, while closer to the shrine, hotels lined the roads and gold merchants competed for customers. Each year, over $100 million exchanged hands in Kadhimiyah, JAM's cash cow in Baghdad. Cars weren't allowed near the shrine, and on every side street there were JAM watchers, pointing out any strangers. Miska and Hassan were well known to the local imams and JAM leaders.

Images of the Iraqi flag had been painted on the concrete barriers lining the streets. Below a flag painting outside the base someone scrawled in Arabic, "JAM liberated Iraq." Annoyed, Miska stopped his Humvee, got out, and spray-painted over the graffiti. The next day, as his Humvee passed the barrier, an Iranian-built weapon called an EFP, or explosively formed penetrator, blew up, missing the Humvee by a few feet and injuring several passersby. Within minutes, two Iraqi ambulances had taken away the wounded. The police on a checkpoint several yards away claimed they had seen nothing suspicious.

"That EFP would have killed at least one of us," Miska said. "And any wounded American placed in those pre-stationed ambulances would never have been seen again. The reason it's quiet here is because JAM is in control, and the local police obey them. Obviously I pissed someone off."

Over the past year, Miska and Hassan had built a network of informers. But no one came forth to explain which JAM gang was trying to kill them, or why.

"It's a Mafia soap opera," Miska said. "My intelligence reports read like the Vallachi Papers. Guys from the so-called Golden JAM in Karbala check into cheap hotels up here to knock off some Sadr stooge, then leave town. The tougher kids from Shula, right next door, try to muscle in and are knocked off."

While rogue cells of JAM operated as independent killers, Sadr held sway over hundreds of thousands of Shiites. Posing as the voice of a truly independent Iraq, he copied the methods of Hezbollah, doling out social services, often paid for with U.S. funds, to gain support by demagoguery, patronage, and armed force. To unite his followers, he blamed America for the problems in Iraq. Controlling thirty of the 274 seats in the Assembly, he alternated boycotts with offers of moderation.

Since 2003, senior Americans had preached, citing Lebanon as the example, that the toleration of armed militias eventually corroded the legitimacy of any central government. Yet in ten months Miska, operating in the heart of JAM country, had received no plan, subtle or forceful, for systematically dismantling the militias that surrounded him.

There was no plan for dismantling Shiite militias because their leaders included the leaders of the sovereign state of Iraq. Maliki let the Americans take the brunt of hunting down the worst of JAM, while he held back the Iraqi Army. Petraeus and Crocker were hobbled.

On the ground, commanders like Miska coped as best they could. To work out a local solution, Miska had two tools: the American and Iraqi soldiers. The Americans routinely patrolled in Kadhimiyah, but weren't allowed within 600 meters of the shrine or other mosques, which became sanctuaries for JAM leaders. Combat outposts in Shiite areas did not lead to the cooperation of the locals. Unlike the Sunni rejection of al Qaeda, the residents and mullahs in Shiite districts had not turned against the JAM.

At the intersection between Shula and Kadhimiyah, Sgt. First Class Robert Sepulveda and a platoon of thirty soldiers from the 1st Battalion, 325th Regiment of the 82nd Airborne Division had established a combat outpost that they shared with about 100 police. The police claimed they would be killed if they worked with Americans. The paratroopers stood guard and patrolled alone, sending out two twenty-man mounted patrols a day. To keep fit, they hit the weights every night. Every soldier bench-pressed over 225 pounds, and thirteen had benched 300 pounds. When I visited with the platoon in September of 2007, they looked like a professional football team and enjoyed telling me Marine stories with an Army twist.

Most had operated from Tikrit eighteen months earlier, when action was plentiful on ops with the SpecOps, and they disliked the police work of counterinsurgency amongst a Shiite population that obeyed the JAM. They encountered some EFPs, but rarely did anyone shoot at them. "We're soldiers," Sepulveda said. "Someone shoots at us, we don't break contact. We maneuver to put them down. The JAM doesn't shoot at us."

On raids, they detained some suspects, but rarely received feedback. Their best results came from Iraqi walk-ins offering tips. The previous week, they had raided a hotel room and arrested three men. As they were led away, one muttered to the other two, "Someone betrayed us all." The paratroopers laughed. The man was their informer.

The platoon was proud of an op-ed in *The New York Times* written by seven soldiers in their battalion. "You see how well they wrote?" Sepulveda said. The authors had stressed that they were doing their duty, but concluded, based on hundreds of patrols in Shula and Kadhimiyah, "We don't believe the Iraqis have the sense of purpose or dedication to come together and resolve their sectarian differences."

Two of the authors, SSgt. Yance Gray and Sgt. Omar Mora, died three weeks later when their vehicle overturned as they drove at high speed out of Shula after completing a raid.

"Those soldiers died doing their duty," Miska said. "They gave the last measure of devotion. When they wrote their op-ed, they were telling the American people what was in their hearts. I could not be prouder of them."

THE KURDISH BATTALION IN KADHIMIYAH

While American soldiers went where they were told, the same was not true of the Iraqis. Although the American command cited the swelling number of Iraqis under arms, the number by itself did not signify greater capability. Most Iraqi soldiers and police were stationed in provinces where there was no fighting, as long as they tolerated the Shiite militias. Fewer than half of the 125 Iraqi battalions could be moved from their home provinces. Of the six additional Iraqi battalions sent into Baghdad in the spring of 2007, two were Kurdish and thus, like the Americans, did not speak Arabic.

The Kurds came willingly. For the two million Kurds in northeastern Iraq, the 2003 invasion had been a true liberation. They took full advantage of the gift. The two leading Kurdish parties stopped feuding and agreed to share power. The pesh merga militia morphed into Iraqi Army battalions, with their own leaders. The al Qaeda suicide bombers occasionally struck, but for the most part the Kurds successfully protected their own neighborhoods. Although wanting more land and revenues from the oilfields they occupied, the Kurds abided by political compromises with Baghdad and avoided provoking Turkey or antagonizing America, their benefactor. While they flew their own national flag, they did not agitate for immediate independence. Instead, knowing how to play the geopolitical game, they dispatched two battalions to Baghdad.

One battalion, assigned to Miska's sector, was given the mission of controlling the highway leading from Kadhimiyah into Shula, where there were no American outposts. After a month, the Kurdish commander, Lieutenant Colonel Shawan, was frustrated. When his soldiers searched cars, snipers shot at them from the Shula marketplace. They stopped one car and found an old Sunni man bound in the trunk. JAM militia attacked the checkpoint and the Iraqi soldiers ran away. The Ministry of Interior ordered Shawan to release the driver.

"Most of the local jundis are loyal to JAM. I sleep in the American tent," Shawan said. "We should clean out Shula, or send us home. General Falah agrees with me."

THE SHIITE POLITICIAN AND THE IRAQI GENERAL

But Brig. Gen. Falah Hassan Kanbar, commander of the 1st Brigade of the 6th Iraqi Division, had his own problem. His orders stated that he was in charge of security in west Baghdad, to include Kadhimiyah. The prior commander had connived with JAM and was posted to Basra. The Iraqi who had accused him was assassinated. When Falah took over, JAM warned him to stay out of their way. A trim, fierce-looking man accustomed to being obeyed, Falah told his junior officers, "I'm the law here and JAM are the outlaws."

After Falah cooperated with Miska in arresting a few JAM leaders, an American patrol was attacked near the shrine. A JAM spokesman went on television to decry an American assault against the shrine. When legislators passed a law forbidding coalition forces from approaching within 600 meters of the shrine, Falah decried the JAM deceit and the coalition ignored the law.

JAM turned up the propaganda heat, spreading rumors that all Americans were Jews seeking to steal Iraqi oil. Shiite clerics encouraged their congregations to "damn Falah the enemy." Some spat when Falah's jundis walked by. The jundis began muttering. When Falah was invited to a meeting to work things out, a prominent supporter of Sadr, Imam Hazem al-Araji, pointed at him and raised his cape. Immediately, a dozen men rushed at Falah and his aides, trying to drag them inside, where pliers, a drill, and a bullet in the head were waiting. As the firefight broke out, a police truck swerved out of a side street to block escape. Hearing the shooting, American soldiers raced to the scene, rescuing Falah.

Sending his family away, Falah moved onto the base with Miska and wrote a furious letter to the prime minister. Instead of support,

Falah received a call from the prime minister's office, ordering him to appear before the Kadhimiyah Council.

When his division commander refused to countermand the order, Falah asked Miska to accompany him, prepared to shoot. Miska invited me along. We drove to the council headquarters and strode into an air-conditioned meeting room. To their surprise, the meeting was chaired by Hazem's brother, Baha al-Araji, a prominent member of the Sadr bloc in the National Assembly. Lounging in the outside corridor were a dozen of his 300-man "personal security detachment." Most ministers and Assembly members had PSDs—gunmen-for-hire authorized by the weak government.

Stylishly dressed in a blue blazer and expensive tie, Araji controlled the meeting and put Falah on the defensive, complaining that the Kadhimiyah shrine wasn't properly protected by the army. Hassan whispered to Miska and me, rapidly translating the key points.

"If you're not getting help, call on me," Araji said. "I will punish anyone who breaks the law. Walk with me to the mosque. When the people see us together, that will help you."

"I don't need your protection," Falah said. "I serve Iraq."

"I'm as much a patriot as you," Araji said. "I have a wealthy law practice in London. I don't need to be in the Assembly. The Americans are against me, but no one in Kadhimiyah was involved in the attack on Colonel Miska or you. It had to be outsiders."

"Tell your cousin in the prime minister's office to let me take over this district," Falah said. "I'll do a better job than the police."

The meeting broke up with stiff handshakes. Falah did not smile as he left. In the privacy of their Humvee, Hassan gave Miska his interpretation of what had happened.

"Araji gave us the backhand. His English is perfect, but he spoke only Arabic to signal that we Americans were irrelevant," Hassan said. "He's smooth. The district council will report to the PM's office that Falah has pissed off the people, and that's why he was attacked. No one will file charges against the imam. Araji saved his brother's ass."

"The Shiite politicians don't back the generals," Miska said. "All we're doing with our raids is taking out the bottom feeders, and JAM can restock them."

EAST BAGHDAD: JAM IN THE RUSAFA DISTRICT

In east Baghdad, the influence of JAM was equally pervasive in and around Sadr City. The 1st Battalion of the 18th Regiment, 2nd Infantry

Division, was stationed in the Rusafa district in the middle of east Baghdad, next to Sadr City. At the end of the summer, the commander, Lt. Col. Jimmy Phillips, presided over an uneasy peace. A quiet, middle-class neighborhood with half a million residents, Rusafa had advisory councils and Neighborhood Watches that never reported any suspicious activity. JAM had not thrown the minority of Sunnis out of their houses.

"JAM controls the police," Phillips said. "Each residence pays JAM $7 a month. My base was mortared once and some shells hit a nearby bakery. Two weeks later, JAM rebuilt the bakery. JAM is organized. My outposts prevent sectarian cleansing. But I don't see us pacifying JAM."

Phillips had sent Capt. Bo Dennis and sixty soldiers to establish a joint security station at the police headquarters in the middle of Rusafa. Iraqis and Americans jointly manned the radios in a small operations center with large maps of the district on the walls. There was a coolness between the Americans and the local police. The Americans had spent $14,000 buying lumber and plastic piping to build bunks and showers. On most hot days, a vendor came by to sell ice cream.

"The soldiers spend $25 a day on ice cream," Mikey, the interpreter, said. "The police are jealous. They say the Americans are rich."

Each day, Dennis sent out one dismounted patrol and two mounted patrols, one of which included Iraqis. No one had shot at them in five months.

"Rusafa is light lifting," SSgt. Adam Farmer said. "Some of us were in Ramadi in '05. That was heavy stuff. Engagements don't happen here. Gets repetitive."

The infantry are strange ducks. They understand protecting the population and providing development projects. Veterans like Farmer have no illusions about the gore of battle, the blood, dirt, sweat, screaming, and the loss in combat. That doesn't mean they wouldn't choose the chaos and exhilaration of combat. That's why the grunts cheered Gen. James "Mad Dog" Mattis in 2004 when he said, "I love to brawl. Hell, killing those bastards is fun."

Combat had ceased in Rusafa. In its place, Dennis, Farmer, and the other soldiers were trying to jump-start a moribund economy, while urging the Iraqis to look to their own government, not to the Americans. Still, the soldiers couldn't resist intervening when things went awry.

When a long queue built up outside the district's only gas station, Dennis drove in to find out why. He was astounded to see each car fill up, turn around, and drive back out the same way, blocking the next car in line. Make an exit lane, he said. Drivers will then enter from both sides, the attendants complained. Lay down a board with spikes on a spring, Dennis said.

The next day, the queue was cut in half, but the station closed in midafternoon. No more gas, the manager explained. Worried that Dennis might arrest him, the manager showed us his books. The station was supposed to fill 3,000 cars a day at a subsidized price three times below that of Jordan and half the asking price of the Iraqis lining the streets with bottles of gas. Although a delivery truck left the Bayji refinery with 50,000 liters, the station was receiving about 40,000 liters a day.

An argument had broken out at the pumps, with an attendant yelling at the driver of a Mercedes. When Dennis walked over, the driver gestured at the posted price. Dennis nodded and the driver righteously pulled away as the attendant, beaten out of his cut, scowled. Small-time stuff.

But thousands of truckers, gangsters, tribes, insurgents, militias, army officers, and government officials were running hundreds of similar scams to cash in on the subsidy. Corruption in the energy sector was costing Iraq billions of dollars. Power outages were impersonal calamities affecting entire cities; sitting in a gas line for eight hours and then being turned away with an empty tank, while seeing the attendant shoving dinars into his grubby pocket, affects you personally. More than any other failure, the fuel distribution system provoked nationwide cynicism and distrust of government, because every driver witnessed and suffered from the corruption.

Dennis encountered similar obstacles when he tried to improve the performance of the National Police. The NP had a substation on tony Palestine Street, where shoppers wandered through shops and amidst the sidewalk vendors offering colorful goods behind Jersey barriers. The merchants reported robberies and kidnappings. The NP apprehended no one, while Dennis's soldiers, with only two interpreters, had made ten solid arrests in five months.

The problem was a lack of trust. No cop knew what would happen after he detained someone, whether he would be fired, commended, or shot. Mikey, Dennis's translator, had his cell phone stolen inside the police station. His wife of one month had started receiving taunting calls. Dennis put out the word that if anything happened, he was bringing in the CIA and Special Ops—the unit most feared in Iraq—to polygraph every cop in the station.

Dennis worked with National Police captain Nasir Abdul Raad, thirty-five, a former paratrooper who had been stationed in Rusafa for two years. His family lived with his tribe in Basra. In February, Raad seized five rockets aimed at the Green Zone, receiving congratulations from his colonel and death threats from the JAM.

Raad and fifty police lived on the fourth floor of a seedy walk-up on Palestine Street that looked like a scene from *Blade Runner*. Papers and dust fluttered up and down the windy staircase, occupants slammed shut heavy doors when they heard the tramp of boots on the stairway, the walls were covered with Arabic graffiti, and the voices of women and children echoed down the corridors.

Raad lived in a shabby office with a metal desk, a sagging bed, an air conditioner, a hot plate, a cell phone, a metal wall locker, and an assortment of weapons. When Dennis dropped by, Raad screamed at several lounging police to get away from his door. His colonel had been assassinated a month earlier.

"JAM pays for spies everywhere," he said. "Nothing happens in Rusafa without JAM. It's a germ."

Raad handed Dennis the names of three cops, asking that they be arrested as JAM.

"I can't without evidence," Dennis said.

Raad opened up his locker and lifted out a green metal tube with wires at one end.

"I found this IED near their checkpoint," he said.

"Put it down, slowly!" Dennis said, getting to his feet. "That'll take down this building, with us in it. I'll call the explosive demolitions team."

Saying a hasty goodbye, Dennis left to continue his patrol, walking down Palestine Street. Wherever we stopped, the American soldiers were welcomed by the merchants. The conversations were the same— requests for separating the barriers to allow more shoppers and complaints that the police couldn't be trusted.

ISOLATING THE SOUTHEAST APPROACH TO BAGHDAD

At the southern edge of the city, JAM had extended its control in the area held in 2006 by Lt. Col. Brian Winski. Jisr Diyala, or JD, the market town where Sergeant Weir was killed and two men were murdered for a few chickens, was now a JAM headquarters. A mile outside JD, a combat outpost called COP Castle had been built in the shadow of the enormous berm that enclosed the old Atomic Energy Ministry. The commander, Capt. Brian Gilbert, sent out five mounted patrols a day, taking back roads to avoid IEDs.

"If we stay forty-five minutes inside JD, we're shot at," Gilbert said. "I have sources that call my cell phone, warning where I'm going to be hit. But to get hold of that town, we need an Iraqi battalion. The trouble is the Iraqi generals move their battalions every few months."

Salman Pak, where the man had beaten his daughters for smiling at Winski, had also regressed. The National Police were still living in the best houses, ensuring continued friction with the residents. Because the Sunnis dared not use the roads, Americans had to truck in food and fuel. The American brigade commander's Humvee had been hit by an IED, killing two soldiers.

Restoring stability to Salman Pak and a long swath of farmland along the east side of the Tigris was the responsibility of the 1st Battalion of the 15th Brigade, commanded by Lt. Col. John Marr. With JAM and the National Police controlling the roads, al Qaeda was striking back by blowing up the water pumps along the Tigris that provided irrigation for thousands of farms, owned by both Shiites and Sunnis. Overhead video showed small gangs of al Qaeda driving in cars and sometimes walking, faces wrapped in black balaclavas, from one house to another along the riverbank. Some houses were built with prefabricated tin, imported in the early 1960s from U.S. manufacturers and used by lower-ranking Baathists as weekend getaways.

Marr launched heliborne raids several times a week. Sixty paratroopers would cram into three or four Chinooks and in the middle of the night fly ten or twenty miles to a landing zone. Once on the ground, they trudged through fields and down cow paths to the target houses, their passage announced by the howling and snarling of dozens of dogs. Although the suspects had usually fled, Marr believed the raids disrupted al Qaeda. General Odierno called them "shaping ops," intended to keep al Qaeda off balance until he had sufficient force to occupy and hold the farmlands.

Separating al Qaeda from the people was a long-term matter. "First I have to get the National Police out of the Sunni houses and into their own barracks," Marr said. "If I organized the Sunnis in Salman Pak into a neighborhood watch, I'd light a powder keg. They'd clash with the police, and JAM would exploit the mess."

Two years ago, it had been Winski trying to control the southeast approach to Baghdad; last year, it was Dennis; now it was Gilbert and Marr. Salman Pak–Tuwaitha–Jisr Diyala was like the Hatfield-McCoy feud. It had its own dynamics and insularity. At least AQI couldn't use the east side of the Tigris to rest or dispatch suicide bombers. The human terrain was too unsettled.

BREAKTHROUGH SOUTHWEST OF BAGHDAD

Across from Salman Pak on the west bank of the Tigris, the badlands of Arab Jabour extended north ten miles into Baghdad. For three years, Arab Jabour had served as al Qaeda's nesting ground for suicide bombers. The huge expanse of farmlands laced with irrigation canals channeled vehicle traffic down one main road that was heavily mined. The adjoining farm roads were few, narrow, and also easily mined, forcing security forces to dismount and inspect every bush and hedge, allowing al Qaeda fighters plenty of time to escape.

Maj. Gen. Rick Lynch, commanding the 3rd Infantry Division in the southern belt, believed in the Petraeus plan. "I was here with General Casey in 2006," he told me. "We've changed strategy since then. We no longer commute to work." The only way Lynch's 1,500-square-kilometer battle space could be controlled was by co-opting the Sunni farmers.

Arab Jabour didn't look like much: pockets of concrete houses with a few large villas lining both sides of a sole blacktop road set back a stone's throw from the Tigris. Thick groves of palm trees heavy with dates cast a false hue of tranquil green over the scene.

In April of 2003, the Iraqi police in Arab Jabour had watched as U.S. Marines pummeled and seized Jisr Diyala, across the river. That was enough for them. They fled, leaving local farmers to form a resistance movement. In March of 2004, according to local residents, the first followers of al-Islami showed up. Later known as al Qaeda in Iraq, al-Islami had the names of those they said were traitors—teachers and engineers. Within weeks, all the educated and the wealthy left the area.

Next al-Islami forced the "simple people"—contractors, drivers, cleaning crews—to quit their well-paying jobs working on American bases. Instead, al-Islami paid for lookouts and for help in digging holes for IEDs. When a prominent sheik, Muhi Daldien Hussan of the al Juburi tribe, objected, the insurgents planted an IED near his house and detonated it when a Humvee drove by. Angry American soldiers rushed into Hussan's villa and struck him with a rifle butt. Bleeding from the ears and eye sockets, he fled to Jordan. He returned occasionally to look after his properties, but ceased speaking to the coalition or against the insurgents.

In 2005, the Americans set up an outpost in a villa facing the river named Outpost Thorn. They were isolated, with no local Sunni security forces or links to the population. After being mortared for forty-five days, the Americans pulled out, leaving al Qaeda in undisputed control of Arab Jabour.

In 2006, the locals said, al Qaeda drove all Shiites from Arab Jabour and lobbed mortar shells across the river into Winski's sector. Winski's soldiers occasionally paddled across in small boats to launch a raid. Al Qaeda wasn't troubled, pulling back until the Americans left. To hide from Arab Jabour's snipers, the residents on Winski's side of the river strung black cloth netting across the front of their houses.

Inside Arab Jabour, al Qaeda enforced a Taliban-like set of rules. No smoking outside houses, no American cigarettes, and no cell phones. Women could venture out of their houses only if fully covered by an abaya and were expelled from the middle school. All new cars and trucks were confiscated. "If you're not with us," the local AQI leader, a car thief named Abu Jurrah, proclaimed, "you're against us." Soon, al Qaeda could not accept all the unemployed volunteers. Life was good. The insurgents could take what they wanted, go where they pleased, with enough attacks by Winski's soldiers to add excitement without serious losses.

In June of 2007, Odierno received the last of the five surge brigades, and the 1st Battalion of the 30th Infantry Regiment moved into Arab Jabour. The battalion commander, Lt. Col. Ken Adgie, moved two companies and his headquarters into a mansion on the river formerly used by Saddam's sons for weekend parties.

Winski and Adgie were close friends, having earlier served as company commanders in the same battalion. Winski had several e-mails warning about Arab Jabour. Still, the conditions shocked him.

"When I left in 2005, I thought we had momentum. When I returned, it was like two years had been stripped from history," Adgie said. "We were starting all over again, and we had given the opposition a head start."

Shortly after the battalion arrived, at the outskirts of Arab Jabour two cars stopped a bus carrying workers who had signed up for a coalition contract. Four gunmen forced the bus driver to proceed to the riverbank, where they shot the men and women as they begged for their lives. They dumped the bus and twenty-three bodies into the river, and issued a warning: We told you not to work for the coalition. The Americans in Arab Jabour count for nothing.

Al Qaeda had laced the single hardtop road in Arab Jabour with

IEDs, many weighing over 200 pounds. Most were homemade explosives—concoctions made from mixing and cooking fertilizer and nitric acid. No one, not the villagers and not the insurgents, knew where all the IEDs were. In its first month, the battalion was hit with two IEDs and a sniper attack every day. Not a single Iraqi ventured outside when an American patrol passed near. The second month was worse. Four soldiers died when they were lured into a house packed with explosives.

No police, no Iraqi soldiers, no Iraqi contractors, and no vendors drove into Arab Jabour. The IEDs were indiscriminate. So during the summer, with temperatures above 120 degrees and Arab Jabour without electricity, the American soldiers packed ice into their trucks for the villagers. When Iraqi drivers were afraid to deliver the monthly grain promised to Arab Jabour, the 1-30 battalion provided the vehicles to escort it. Those gestures may not seem like much, but they took an effort when you've lost friends. In nine weeks, Adgie's battalion encountered 115 IEDs and engaged in 66 small arms attacks, lost 11 killed and scores wounded, while reporting 16 insurgents killed.

"If the tribe doesn't want you here," Adgie said, "they're going to drive you out. They're that good with IEDs."

Adgie didn't think the tribe wanted to drive him out. Winski had cordial relations with the al Jibouri tribe in Tuwaitha across the river. Arab Jabour belonged to the same tribe. But the tribe was passive, without leadership, saying not a word about the al Qaeda among them.

"Qaeda's mostly locals, not foreigners," Adgie said. "Punks who've tasted power. The lead man, Abu Jurrah, steals cars. Pulls out fingernails. Sweet fucker."

Energetic, fast-talking, and practical, Adgie deprecated his academic record. He claimed that after his state college was renovated, the dean raised the curtain on the entryway to see new lettering that read, "State Colege." Actually, he was a shrewd grunt who, despite the losses, kept focus on the population and sought advice from the CIA, officially called the Office of Regional Assistance. As in Vietnam, the CIA worked with the battalions at the district level and, for some missions, fell under the operational control of the military. In Vietnam, many CIA operatives used their actual family names. After 9/11, pseudonyms and first names became the rule so that terrorists couldn't track families in the States.

When Adgie, dusty and sweaty in his battle rattle, walked into CIA headquarters in June, Paul, a CIA operative, clean and cool in a polo shirt and pressed khakis, greeted him affably. "Perrier with a twist, Colonel," he asked, "or a latte?"

In the same vein, Adgie quipped, "How about a shot of electricity for my villages?"

Arab Jabour was baking in the heat. Maybe, Adgie suggested, if we do something for them, they'll do something for us. On the spot, Paul called the deputy minister for electricity.

"You'll have up to eight hours a day," Paul said. "It's your call to turn on or off."

Paul then introduced an impressed Adgie to Don, his point of contact. "The keys to the kingdom," Don said, placing on the table a dozen cell phones, "for your own joint security station."

Petraeus had written his Ph.D. about counterinsurgency in Vietnam, where every district had an intelligence center manned by Vietnamese, American, and CIA officers. Petraeus brought the concept to Iraq, installing a joint security station in every district to collect actionable intelligence, such as the location of an insurgent, and launch reaction forces.

A JSS included military radios, local cell phones, high-resolution monitoring cameras, laptop computers, video screens for streaming video from UAVs, and huge, detailed photomaps.

Equipped only with cell phones, Adgie set up the simplest JSS in Iraq. Through the CIA, he met Mustafa Kamel Shabib al-Jabouri, a former brigadier general who lived in a modest house in the middle of Arab Jabour. Mustafa wasn't a sheik or tribal leader, but he was a natural leader in his early fifties with an extended family that included about twenty former soldiers tied to the local resistance group Jesh al-Islami. Abu Jurrah, the local al Qaeda leader, had avoided clashing with the Shabib family. Live and let live.

Mustafa thanked Adgie for providing ice and food and getting the power turned on. Mustafa said he could provide the right men to point out hard-core al Qaeda—provided Adgie sent them away permanently. If they came back, they'd kill everyone they thought was an informer. Although he didn't say it directly, Mustafa assumed he, and not a local sheik, would be treated as the leader in Arab Jabour.

Done. Adgie gave Mustafa the cash to pay $300 a month to 200 men, with a bonus for each IED found. As the only outside employment to reach Arab Jabour in years, the Concerned Local Citizens organization was quickly oversubscribed.

Secretly, Mustafa smuggled eight of his most trusted men onto Adgie's base, where they were handed cell phones and provided a photomap that divided the district into blocks and assigned a number to every house. Called the Bird Dogs, they converted a small brick shed into their living and working area, hidden from the local interpreters and all other Iraqis. They worked the cell phones constantly, receiving about thirty tips a day from Mustafa and other sources. Two intelligence specialists from Adgie's battalion lived with them, sifting and collating the information and calling out the Quick Reaction Force about once every two days, directing them to a house.

In the first ten days, sixteen insurgents were arrested. Dressed in U.S. Army uniforms, Bird Dogs were driven in Humvees through the markets and down back roads, pointing out al Qaeda members. In six weeks, 115 Iraqis were detained. Each detainee was brought to Combat Outpost Murray and held in isolation while the Bird Dogs plied the phones. The American interrogators used the information to impress those arrested with how much they knew. Local residents came forward under various covers to identify individuals, and write sworn statements. The last sentence, written in their hand, would always state that they would testify against the man in an Iraqi court of law. The 115 arrest packages resulted in 60 being sent to Camp Cropper on "the Conair flight," as the troops put it, referring to a movie about hardened criminals.

The residents were providing information but did not yet have the resolve to stand up for themselves. In mid-August, six al Qaeda members beheaded a retarded old man and an eight-year-old boy inside Arab Jabour and no one said a word until they had left. Four sisters were killed four kilometers west of Adgie's base. Al Qaeda's message: We can walk in anytime we want and kill anyone we please.

A few days later, four toughs carrying AK-47s walked down the main street right past the combat outpost. In civilian clothes, they were safe as long as no one informed. Some CLC carried weapons to their checkpoints; others didn't. Stopping an unarmed Concerned Citizen with an orange reflective vest, they pointed at a nearby house with a large dome on the roof. We'll stay there, they said; tell the owner to move out. Tomorrow, we'll deal with all traitors who wear orange vests.

Al Qaeda got it half right. The Concerned Citizens didn't fight them. Instead, someone stepped around a corner, pulled out a cell phone, and called the Bird Dogs inside the patrol base. I was sitting near Adgie in his ops center when the call came in. Four al Qaeda were across the street in the house with the dome—Building 1518 on the photomap. The duty platoon couldn't believe their luck. In conventional war, it's relatively easy to gain intelligence about the enemy; the killing is hard. Counterterrorism is the opposite. Killing terrorists is easy; finding them is hard.

In five minutes, Adgie's soldiers were running out the front gate. Spotting them, the al Qaeda sentry fired a few hasty shots before fleeing down the street. He was shot in the back and killed. Two others leaped out a back window and sped off in a blue sedan. With a dozen Iraqis gawking or leaping out of the way, the soldiers held their fire and called for a helicopter to chase down the car. The fourth insurgent was captured hiding in a back closet.

Ten minutes later, a helicopter pilot reported a blue sedan in a line of cars three miles up the road. The pilot of Light Horse 27 refused to fire, explaining he had "no probable cause." The car pulled off into a copse of palm trees and was abandoned.

The Bird Dogs said the captive was a mortar specialist who also emplaced IEDs, famous locally for trying to kill his father, who had shamed the family by begging for food. Under questioning by the American interrogators, he disclosed the safe house his cell used as a rally point.

Adgie sent out a platoon, which captured four more. When they were brought in, the Bird Dogs exclaimed that one was a son-in-law of Mustafa. Adgie, who often ate dinner at Mustafa's house, reluctantly called him with the news.

"Good," Mustafa said. "I never liked the son of a dog. He was sneaky. When my daughter cries, I will smile."

The next morning, when Adgie dropped by Mustafa's house, the tough old brigadier general was glumly listening to a woman shrieking at him over a cell phone. Mustafa hung up and looked at Adgie, who assumed he would ask for his son-in-law to be released. He didn't.

"Al Qaeda keeps coming back," Adgie said, avoiding the in-law issue.

"We can clear them out of here," Mustafa said, "if the other battalions do like you."

Among the Sunni tribes, the message was spreading to join with the Americans, who pay money and provide services.

"We're leaving in a year, Mustafa," Adgie said. "Remember what the senator asked you."

A few weeks earlier, Republican senator Richard Shelby of Alabama had visited and asked Mustafa what would happen if the Americans left in six months. Mustafa had frozen, unable to conceal his shock. Later, Mustafa pressed Adgie.

"We can't trust the police," Mustafa said. "When you leave, my men must be in the Iraqi Army to protect Arab Jabour."

Adgie didn't respond. The knowledge was widespread of the tension between the Iraqi government and the Americans about recruiting Sunnis.

"The [Iraqi] government won't take responsibility for its own country," Capt. Andrew Kirby, the battalion intelligence officer, said. "Maliki is fighting General Petraeus to stop the Concerned Citizens movement."

The Americans had put behind them the resentment stoked by four bloody years of fighting the Sunnis now aligned with them. The Shiite leaders, including Maliki, couldn't bring themselves to support the recruitment of the Sunnis. The Americans, determined to make it happen, kept chipping away, starting in Anbar, then moving eastward into the Abu Ghraib area, and, with Arab Jabour and Ghazaliyah, moving into Baghdad in the fall of 2007.

TWENTY-THREE

WASHINGTON ASSESSES THE SURGE

FALL 2007

THE HEARING

Petraeus was due to report to Congress in mid-September 2007 on whether he could accomplish his mission. The most important testimony of the Bush administration would be delivered by a military professional who was writing his own script without consulting with the White House.

Petraeus, a graduate of the Woodrow Wilson School at Princeton and member of the Council on Foreign Relations, was comfortable with geopolitics and keenly aware that the Iraq mission would collapse without support back home. Having inherited a strategy that even the president acknowledged was failing, he often mentioned "slowing down the Washington clock" ticking toward a pullout. The public had to be convinced of progress on the military front leading to a satisfactory ending.

In 1967, General Westmoreland, the commander in Vietnam, declared he could "see the light at the end of the tunnel." When the communists launched the large-scale Tet Offensive a few months later, the credibility of the U.S. military crashed. In Iraq, Generals Myers, Abizaid, and Casey had not been that rash. But while avoiding the press when they could, they did allude to gains, only to be proven wrong. As the general in charge of training Iraqi forces under Casey, Petraeus too had cited progress that proved ephemeral.

As the commander in Iraq, he took a different tack, ordering Captain Thomas McCaleb, U.S. Air Force—another in his stable of Rhodes scholars—to systematically array all quantitative measures and double-check them for accuracy. Monthly, they were released to the public.

"I'm not an optimist or a pessimist," Petraeus told me as he prepared for the hearing. "I'm a realist about Iraq, not a cheerleader."

He opened the doors for the press. He invited journalists into his morning briefings and on his visits to units. While fiercely competitive, he had the restrained upper-class manners one would expect of an officer who had married the daughter of the superintendent of West Point. He showed no ego or rough edges, and he didn't preach. He wasn't going to predict progress. The press would judge.

Left to draw their own conclusions, the journalists concluded that violence really was abating rather than oscillating. American fatalities from IEDs had fallen from eighty-eight in May to twenty-seven in September. Suicide bombings were down from fifty-two in August to thirty in September, while overall attacks had dropped by 25 percent. In Anbar, there hadn't been a single American fatality in weeks. The change in tone of the press was conveyed by the analysts Michael E. O'Hanlon and Kenneth M. Pollack when they wrote an op-ed in *The New York Times* entitled, "A War We Just Might Win."

In early September, General Jim Jones, a former commandant of the Marine Corps, delivered to Congress a devastating assessment by a panel of generals and police chiefs on the status of the Iraqi police. Jones accused Maliki of having created in his own office a commander-in-chief position held by a lieutenant general, thus bypassing the Ministry of Defense. Because Petraeus had hosted the commission and provided assessments from sensitive sources, the report boosted his reputation for candor and was interpreted as reflecting his own critique of Maliki's wartime leadership.

On the political front, though, Maliki had shored up his status. Throughout the summer, Petraeus had pressed a special operations campaign against the JAM "special groups" that were killing Americans by using sophisticated roadside bombs supplied by Iran. After American commandos launched raids in a series of southern cities, JAM assassinated several members of the Supreme Iraqi Islamic Council and the Badr militia, accusing them of betrayal. In late August, the

JAM clique in Karbala attacked the guards at the mosques during religious holidays. The guards fought back and in the melee the Sadrists killed over fifty worshippers. The Iraqi Army sided with the local guards, and the Iraqi press blamed JAM for the slaughter. With JAM on the defensive militarily and politically, Maliki flew into the city. Pistol in hand, he arrested a JAM leader and emerged a hero in the Iraqi press.

"The Mahdi Army after Karbala lost popular support," he later said. "No longer can any militia stand against the state."

Secretary Gates shared Maliki's assessment. "There also, it seems to me," Gates said on Fox News, "is growing unhappiness in the Shia area with the excesses of Jaish al Mahdi, the Shia extremist group." Left unexplained was how unhappy residents could disarm JAM.

Sadr relieved the pressure by grandly declaring a cease-fire against the coalition. Unlike in April and August of 2004, the Americans hadn't been fighting the rank and file of JAM. His declaration neither dampened nor increased the amount of fighting in the streets, and didn't halt the American raids against the death squads.

"Sadr called a cease-fire, for whatever it was worth," Odierno said, "because he was losing. Our pressure forced a reaction favorable to us. The cease-fire wasn't a gift from Sadr. It was a means of survival."

While the cease-fire enabled Sadr to sort out his ranks, Petraeus seized on Sadr's words to drive a psychological wedge inside JAM, stressing that he had no animus toward law-abiding JAM members, while branding those he arrested as criminals. Special Operations Forces didn't turn over those arrested to the Iraqi officials, though, because they would be released. In essence, the American strategy toward the militias was limited and reactive, targeting only those JAM leaders suspected of killing Americans or attacking Sunnis.

———

While Maliki enjoyed his moment of personal victory and Sadr scrambled to regain status, President Bush played his own best card in advance of the Petraeus hearings. On September 3, en route to Australia, the president stopped at Al Assad air base in Anbar Province, bypassing Baghdad and forcing Prime Minister Maliki to take a noisy seventy-minute helicopter ride to the remote base. Maliki, nursing an eye infection, wasn't pleased when given only an hour's advance notice to load up and move out.

Bush was rewarding the Sunni tribes for turning against al Qaeda, and forcing Maliki to acknowledge what they had accomplished while reconciliation languished at the Baghdad level. The troops were genuinely excited to see the president, who enjoyed posing for pictures amidst the safest crowd on the planet—armed American soldiers.

The script called for the provincial governor, Mamoon Rashid, to act as host to both Bush and Maliki. For most of the prior two years, Mamoon had been marooned in the sandbagged Government Center in Ramadi, kept alive by Marine sharpshooters who fired through mouse holes on the hallway above his office and defecated in plastic bags because the sewer line had been blown up, leaving a stinking lake outside the front door. Mamoon had survived numerous assassination attempts and gone weeks at a time without a single Iraqi visitor to his "office."

His closest confidants were the marines who kept him alive. When you're with the president, act like you're king of the desert, Brig. Gen. John Allen had advised the governor. Embrace everyone as an honored guest. Smile constantly and say nice things.

The meeting started well, with Mamoon introducing the tribal leaders. Sheik Mishan, whom Allen had enticed back from Jordan and who had lost ten relatives to al Qaeda, told his story. Selected as the tribal guest of honor, Sattar sat two seats away from the president. After the introductions, a genial President Bush asked how things were going, and Allen's script collapsed.

We get nothing, Mamoon exploded, glaring at Maliki. We're on the front lines and Baghdad ignores us.

"I opened my mouth," Mamoon later explained to a furious Allen, "and the words came out by themselves."

Seizing the opening, the Sunni sheiks piled on, berating Maliki for a hundred injustices and years of neglect. Only Sattar rose above the litany of resentments to offer thanks for the sacrifices of the American soldiers. The Anbar tribes, he said, would finish al Qaeda in Iraq, and then go to Afghanistan to help the Americans win there. His speech only partially defused the quarrelsome tone.

———

In Congress, a bitterly partisan mood prevailed as Petraeus and Crocker prepared their testimony. Harry Reid, the Senate's Democratic majority leader, blasted the integrity of Petraeus. "He [Petraeus] has made a number of statements over the years that have not proven to be factual," Reid said, later adding, "Before the report arrives in Congress, it will pass through the White House spin machine, where facts are often ignored or twisted, and intelligence is cherry-picked." The liberal antiwar political action group called MoveOn.org paid *The New York Times* $65,000 to take out a scurrilous full-page ad entitled "General Petraeus or General Betray Us?" It accused Petraeus of "cooking the books for the White House." The anti-military venom of the Vietnam era was seeping back into the American domestic political dialogue.

The fourteen hours of hearings themselves on September 11 and 12 were a letdown because they lacked focus. The Democrats were querulous in confronting a professional soldier and a professional diplomat, Ambassador Ryan Crocker, who did not create policy but were duty-bound to carry it out. Many questions were rants, with the questioners coming across as self-absorbed whiners. Some challenged the veracity of the witnesses.

When a congressman accused him of "cherry-picking" the data, with asperity Petraeus responded, "With respect to the facts that I have laid out today, I very much stand by those. If I did not think that it was an endeavor in which we could succeed, I would not have testified as I did."

In their testimony, Petraeus and Crocker saw a long road (five years or more) ahead. Crocker expected formal reconciliation to move at a glacial pace. Petraeus set out data showing decreasing casualties and attacks, while emphasizing that stabilizing Iraq required a deliberate, slow pace. He projected that five brigades would return to the States by July of 2008, leaving fifteen brigades in Iraq—the same number as before the surge.

President Bush had said in January that the purpose of the surge was to provide the Iraqi government with "the breathing space it needs to make progress . . . pass legislation to share oil revenues . . . hold provincial elections later this year." That didn't happen. The Iraqi leaders failed to reach reconciliation agreements, despite the reduction in violence. No national leader emerged from the sectarian ranks in Baghdad.

Crocker was tepid in his defense of Maliki, whose truculent, secretive management style had antagonized a range of Iraqi leaders. Repeatedly Crocker and Petraeus referred to "frustration" with Iraqis not moving forward on the political front. In the absence of Iraqi top-down leadership, Petraeus introduced a "bottom-up" model for stability, pointing out that the Anbar tribal revolt against al Qaeda had spread to other provinces.

Democrats were unmoved by the testimony. The pollster Andrew Kohut reported that in July, 61 percent of Republicans said that we were making progress in defeating the insurgents; that went up to 67 percent after Petraeus testified. Democrats were not persuaded. Sixteen percent said there was progress in July, and that number didn't change after Petraeus testified.

Five days after attending an Anbar forum, Senator Joe Biden welcomed General Petraeus before the Senate Foreign Relations Committee. After the hearings, the senator went on the *Charlie Rose* show and accused Petraeus of "spinning" and said, "I give the strategy no chance of succeeding. Zero."

When it came to choosing between a politician and a general, the public stood behind the general. In September, a Zogby poll showed Congress with an 11 percent approval rating, while Petraeus's approval rating rose from 52 percent in August to 61 percent after he testified. While strongly united, the Democrats didn't have the votes to force a rapid withdrawal. The Petraeus hearing had strengthened the solidarity of the Republicans in the Senate, and the confidence of the American public in its military leaders.

President Bush was quick to seize the advantage. A few days later, he addressed the nation, citing the military progress in Iraq.

"I ask you to join me in supporting the recommendations General Petraeus has made and the troop levels he has asked for," Bush said. "I have also directed them [Crocker and Petraeus] to deliver another report to Congress in March."

The president set a terrible precedent in ordering a general and a diplomat back into the political arena when the issue was disagreement about policy rather than its execution. Bush had yanked back the nomination of General Pace rather than dispute whether the chairman of the Joint Chiefs had executed his office competently. Now he was shoving forward General Petraeus because the general had exhibited star power. Too weak politically to defend his own policies, the president exploited Petraeus and the military.

After the hearing, the Democrats turned to the race for the presidential nomination. In the intraparty debates on the campaign trail, the 2002 Senate vote authorizing the use of force against Saddam Hussein emerged as the litmus test of Democratic orthodoxy among the three top contenders. Senator John Edwards (D-NC) said he made a mistake in voting to use force and promised to remove all U.S. troops within ten months. Senator Hillary Clinton tried to defend her vote to authorize force as reasonable, given the information and the context five years ago. Pressed by the other contenders, she modified her stance, saying the war was a "tragic mistake" that never should have been authorized. Senator Barack Obama, elected in 2004, declared in stentorian tones that he would have voted against the authorization had he been in the Senate. He promised to swiftly pull all U.S. combat troops out of Iraq.

The Democrats were united in their partisan position. Bush's policy toward Iraq had failed. Therefore America should withdraw. That was the choice to be presented to the voters. The press was satisfied and none of the candidates was pushed about the consequences of withdrawal.

The Democrats used the hearings to show the public that they had made up their minds. Secretary Gates could talk all he wanted about forging a bipartisan approach to Iraq. There would be no compromise when rigid opposition garnered more votes for the presidency. The Democrats wanted out, period, regardless of the defeat the Sunni tribes were inflicting on al Qaeda and regardless of what Petraeus was accomplishing with a new strategy.

IRAN: A MALIGN INFLUENCE UNCHECKED

Upon conclusion of the hearings, Petraeus returned to Iraq with no major alteration to his strategy. The main channel of U.S. military energy remained focused on providing security to the Sunni population and destroying al Qaeda. He wasn't going to be diverted by Iran on one flank or the Jesh al Mahdi militia on the other.

There was no doubt that Iran was training and equipping Iraqi militia factions to kill Americans. For a while the U.S. press, conscious of not having been skeptical enough about Iraq's stockpile of weapons of mass destruction, had been willing to give the top level of Iranian officials the benefit of the doubt. Perhaps the top leaders hadn't been informed by the Iranian Republican Guards, or their Quds Force department conducting the training of Iraqis. But after explosively-formed penetrators—EFPs—with Iranian markings were found throughout southern Iraq month after month, the press aimed its skepticism at the Iranian government.

Since the spring of 2006, resentment toward Iran had smoldered throughout the American ranks from corporals to generals. Lieutenant General Odierno had charged that Iranian EFPs were responsible for 73 percent of American casualties in Baghdad in July, up from 38 percent in January. In early fall, the EFPs took less of a toll, after the discovery of several large caches. During the hearings, Petraeus repeatedly drew attention to Iran's "malign influence." He wanted pressure placed on Iran, lobbying for economic sanctions.

"Iran is not moving forward economically, due to its own actions," he told me during the hearings. "Al Qaeda is the wolf closest to the sled, so that's the one I'm going to kill. In the long term, the Iranian effort to use special groups as Hezbollah in Iraq causes the Iraqi government serious concern."

Asked in the hearings if he would strike training camps in Iran, Petraeus ducked responding, saying that Iran fell under the purview of CentCom, whose outspoken commander, Adm. William Fallon, had made clear his strategic vision. A senior official on a defense advisory board said that soon after his appointment, Fallon had criticized Petraeus, scoffing at his strategy as "nibbling" and declaring that no air strikes against Iran "will take place on my watch." In September, Fallon told the press that "this talk of war against Iran is not helpful," causing one retired official to quip, "The good admiral thinks he's the commander-in-chief."

While Fallon's ego caused a problem, his hands-off view of Iran reflected the administration position. "There's a question of just how much intelligence we have in terms of specific locations," Secretary Gates said on Fox News. Gates then declared Iran off limits to retaliatory strikes, saying, "We can manage this problem through better operations inside Iraq. . . . [We] don't need to go across the border into Iran."

It was odd to declare Iran a sanctuary rather than leave an ambiguous American response. To keep opponents guessing and so perhaps induce restraint, officials usually said they would not take any option off the table. In the case of Iran, the administration promised unilateral restraint, probably in order to avoid a domestic backlash. When directly asked about Iran exporting EFPs, President Bush resorted to an unfathomable circumlocution.

"If the Iranians," Bush said, "are trying to influence the outcome of the political process, or the outcome of the security situation there, we're letting them know of our displeasure."

As Bush sank in the polls with the presidential election looming, American and Iraqi officialdom had perfected a syllogism of diplomatic doublespeak. Iran was not involved in killing Americans; if it were, our intelligence was too poor to locate the EFP factories in Iran; if they were located, they would not be struck because we could "manage" EFP attacks by operations inside Iraq.

Iraqi officials were even more cautious. "Iran is not interfering in our affairs," Maliki said in late September. "If there are any intrusions, they will cease because of improving relations. . . . Interferences used to exist. We have reduced it dramatically. Neighboring countries now understand interference in Iraq is setting a fire that will burn them."

When the U.S. military arrested an Iranian official for smuggling explosives into Iraq, Iran retaliated by closing several border crossings into Kurdistan. Top Iraqi and Kurdish officials then together demanded the United States release the smuggler. Someday the Americans would leave, while Iran would remain Iraq's more powerful neighbor forever.

On the one hand, Bush had justified the Iraqi war on the moral grounds of overthrowing a tyrant. On the other hand, he was winding down the war on realpolitik grounds, accepting that Iranian complicity in American deaths could not be deterred by offensive air strikes.

JAM: BENIGN NEGLECT OR CANCEROUS GROWTH

Petraeus had a systematic strategy for destroying al Qaeda in Iraq by empowering Sunni neighborhoods. There was no corresponding strategy for dismantling the Shiite militias, particularly the JAM in Baghdad. Seventeen of the twenty-four battalion commanders in the National Police had been fired for supporting the militia death squads.

"JAM has its hooks into the ministries," Petraeus told me in mid-September 2007. "It took years to get to this point, and it will take some time to get rid of it. Maliki is working his way through it."

A year earlier, General Casey had voiced similar sentiments to me, saying that Maliki had to take action against JAM. By not arresting Sadr on numerous occasions in 2003–2004, U.S. and Shiite officials had allowed the growth of a social cancer. Although JAM was held in check by the presence of American soldiers, its roots were growing deeper inside Baghdad.

"When we picked up some of their top guys," Odierno told me, "we learned the [JAM] threat was larger than we thought a few years ago."

Neither side—JAM or American—wanted a full-scale clash. JAM would suffer horrendous losses, and the Bush administration would suffer a public relations setback and further erosion of its waning domestic support. When Sadr ordered a cease-fire in August, Petraeus had called it "a positive move."

In the fall of 2007, JAM's leadership was fractious and its objectives jumbled. The special groups killing Americans and Sunnis had to be hunted down, a task the SOF was conducting effectively. Other JAM gangs, involved in extortion and control of the streets, weren't a military threat unless stirred up. Like the warlords in Afghanistan, the militias in Iraq were a problem—as much political as military—that would persist long after American forces had been drawn down and Iraq had faded from the news.

BLACKWATER AND ARMIES FOR HIRE

On September 16, armed U.S. contractors escorting several USAID officials tried to ram their way through traffic in Nisour Square in downtown Baghdad. Becoming ensnarled, the contractors opened fire on the surrounding Iraqi cars, killing seventeen civilians. No contractor was injured and no enemy fire was verified.

The tragic incident was one in a series that extended back to 2003. For two decades, the U.S. military had been contracting out more jobs in order to reduce overall costs. In Iraq, the proportion of contractors to U.S. troops exceeded that of any prior war. Of the 125,000 contract personnel, 60,000 were Iraqis, 45,000 were third-country nationals, and 20,000 were Americans. The vast majority performed logistical duties like trucking and preparing food. Well-trained Peruvians, Ugandans, and other nationalities stood tedious guard duty at the FOBs.

About 2,000 U.S. contractors provided bodyguard and escort services, usually for U.S. civilian officials. This relieved the U.S. military of routine tasks. The size of the force was unusual, but the duties weren't. Since 2003, thirty Blackwater employees had been killed in Iraq, without losing a single U.S. official. Blackwater paid high salaries for skilled former military personnel, some of whom tended to swagger as they rushed about. Combined with their high salaries, this irritated many grunts. In a firefight, though, you could rely on the contractors to pitch in. Armed contractors provided a responsible, cost-effective service.

The tragedy in Nisour Square again illustrated the need for a military command mechanism to oversee the activities, rules of engagement, and judicial issues related to armed contractors in a wartime theater. After several months, the State Department and the Pentagon reached agreement.

It had been the lynching deaths of four Blackwater employees that had provoked the battle of Fallujah after they had driven into the city without coordinating with the Marines. Nisour Square resulted in an oversight arrangement that should have been put in place after Fallujah.

DESTROYING AL QAEDA

Al Qaeda in Iraq was the primary enemy that Petraeus and Odierno intended to destroy by their three-pronged surge strategy. The first was the Baghdad Security Plan, or Fardh al Qanoon, to clear and hold districts like Ghazaliyah and Amariyah in Baghdad, providing security and separating al Qaeda from the population. The second was Phantom Thunder, Odierno's corps offensive to control the farmland belts around Baghdad. The third was Phantom Strike—pursuing and finishing off al Qaeda, a mission that would continue for years. As 2007 drew to a close, Petraeus was doing well on all three fronts.

To the west, Anbar was jolted by the assassination of Sheik Sattar in mid-September, just as Petraeus was returning from the hearings. An officer in his personal bodyguard had conspired to set the fatal bomb, betraying him for a million dollars that was never paid. Al Qaeda had killed Sattar, as they had his father and three of his brothers. Months earlier, al Qaeda suicide bombers had also murdered Lieutenant Colonel Salaam, the key police leader in turning Ramadi around, and Fassal Guood, the wealthy former governor of Anbar who had always been crafty enough to pick the winning side.

Of all the losses to the venomous al Qaeda, Sattar was the most grievous. He was a genuine national leader. In Baghdad, Maliki paused to pay special tribute, as did President Bush in Washington.

His brother, Sheik Ahmed Abu Risha, immediately took over the Awakening movement and its political action arm, the Anbar Salvation Council. Al Qaeda gained no momentum from the assassination. In the last week of September of 2006, there were 350 attacks in Anbar; in that same week a year later, there were thirty-seven. In September of 2006, fewer than a dozen sheiks and forty tribal fighters had attended Sattar's first rally at his compound outside Ramadi. By the late fall of 2007, the Awakening had spread across the Sunni Triangle and Baghdad.

In northern Iraq, the picture was not as bright. The Kurdish areas were stable, but Mosul, the second-largest city in Iraq, was unsettled. Col. Stephen Twitty, commanding a brigade of the 1st Cavalry Division, said attacks in northern Ninewah Province had dropped from eighteen a day in December of 2006 to under ten a day in September. The 15,000 soldiers in the two Iraqi divisions were conducting operations on their own, although the United States provided the fuel, logistics, and maintenance. Twitty considered corruption to be manageable because the division commanders and the Mosul police chief "ran thieves out of the force."

The Sunnis and Shiites in Tal Afar had reached a modus vivendi. Elsewhere in Ninewah Province, there were few Shiites. The Kurds, comprising 40 percent of the population, tolerated no insurgents in their areas. The Sunnis—45 percent of the population—had boycotted the election in December of 2005, allowing the Kurds to take the posts of governor, vice governor, and most seats on the provincial council. Funding went to Kurdish districts, leaving unemployed Sunnis willing to bury IEDs for a few hundred dollars. The local judges released most of the Sunni insurgents brought before them, an indication of continued intimidation.

Maj. Gen. Mark Hertling, commanding the 1st Armored Division, with responsibility for the northern four provinces in Iraq, saw Mosul as a growing problem, due to success elsewhere.

"Al Qaeda has been squeezed out of Anbar," he said, "because the tribes turned under a coherent group of sheiks. Here in the north, I have al Qaeda coming in amidst thirty-seven tribes and fourteen major sheik families who haven't 'awakened.' For them, it's like, what are you doing to support me?"

Hertling was dealing with the Kurds trying to wrest control of Kirkuk from the central government, the skimming of refined product from the Bayji oil refinery, a rash of kidnappings for ransom, and a thriving underground network of chop shops, with thieves from all over Iraq unloading cars to be shipped whole or in parts to Syria.

"I should keep a file called 'You Can't Make This Shit Up,'" Hertling told me. "I see the Tier I enemy as the Qaeda financiers. II are the criminals, and III are the poor kids with no jobs."

———

In the northern belt around Baghdad, al Qaeda was squeezed out of Diyala Province after a year-long fight by Col. David Sutherland and his 3rd Brigade Combat Team of the 1st Cavalry Division. The military historian Kimberly Kagan described the operation in meticulous detail for *The Weekly Standard*.

Diyala, where Sunnis from twenty-five tribes comprised over 65 percent of the province's 1.2 million population, was isolated enemy territory when the 3rd Brigade began operations in late 2006. Sutherland initiated a step-by-step operation to gain control, starting with the Turki village complex just north of Baghdad. By late spring, the brigade had proceeded north twenty-five miles to Baquba. Along the way, they had enlisted the help of dozens of Sunni sheiks and insurgents from the 1920s Brigade who were tired of al Qaeda's version of sharia law.

Capt. Phil Carter, a police adviser in Baquba, believed that to regain control, the police chief, the Iraqi division commander, and the provincial governor, along with the chief aides, had to be removed.

"Diyala was a snake pit," Carter said. "It had to be cleaned out from top to bottom. We're talking five, ten years of sustained presence in the police stations, with advisers working closely, hand in hand with their Iraqi counterparts."

Sutherland put together enough evidence to secure the arrest of the provincial police chief and the relief of the commander of the Iraqi 5th Division. That opened the way to join forces with the 3rd Stryker Brigade of the 2nd Infantry Division to retake Baquba in June; thirty IEDs were found on the main route into the city. He consolidated the gain by installing concrete barriers to impede the reinfiltration of al Qaeda. In a pattern similar to Ramadi and elsewhere, Sunnis volunteered to guard their neighborhoods. Within a few months, over 2,000 Concerned Local Citizens were on the payroll.

In the summer of 2007, Sutherland headed north into the Khalis valley, and then east toward the Iranian border. In some villages, the soldiers fought special groups smuggling in EFP components provided by the Quds Force of the Iranian Revolutionary Guards. In other villages, al Qaeda had to be cleaned out. Following their normal pattern, both Shiite militias and al Qaeda fled as the Americans advanced. Acting on detailed information from Shiites thrown out of their village, the 5th Squadron of the 73rd Cavalry in the 82nd Airborne Division launched a helicopter-borne assault in mid-July, killing twenty-nine insurgents. Following that blow, al Qaeda fled the Khalis area north of Baquba.

To secure the feuding villages, Sutherland convened reconciliation conferences among the hundred-odd tribal leaders in the Diyala River valley. The meetings were contentious, with accusations leveled at specific sheiks in attendance.

"A bomb in one village market," Sutherland said, "would provoke a retaliation against another village. They're all poor, and they'd steal and loot from one another."

Sutherland extracted signed pledges from 118 sheiks to end kidnapping and ransom, and to settle disputes through dialogue. Each village was allotted positions for Concerned Local Citizens. By mid-October, the 3rd Brigade had 4,000 CLC vetted, fingerprinted, and enrolled. Since the beginning of 2007, the brigade had conducted 270 offensive operations in company units or larger.

"Violence is way down in Diyala. There are still some AQI out in remote areas," Sutherland told me. "If they come into the cities, we're tipped off. They're social outcasts. The systematic AQI response is the suicide bomber. My two problems are a total lack of fuel—so the farmers can't move their crops to market—and government foot dragging in allowing the CLC to join the police."

In the area south of Baghdad, Maj. Gen. Rick Lynch and the 3rd Infantry Division were tightening their grip on Salman Pak on the east bank of the Tigris and Arab Jabour on the west, thus blocking the route into Baghdad favored by the suicide bombers.

Inside Baghdad, there was a steady rhythm to American operations, somewhat akin to the old Green Bay Packers sweep. Everyone could see it coming. Every week, the concrete caterpillars advanced across the city, walling people in—or out. You could walk between many openings in the Jersey barriers, but cars were blocked or canalized. While traffic jams increased, car bombings dropped.

Every few weeks, bulldozers and cranes constructed another joint security station or combat outpost. American and Iraqi forces moved in. At first, nothing seemed to change. Then little by little, the residents and the soldiers got to know one another. Cell phone numbers were circulated. Tips started to come in. Worried about betrayal, insurgents and high-profile criminals moved out.

The Sunnis had moved out too, making the American strategy focused on al Qaeda an easier but sadder task. Since the Samarra bombing in February of 2006, by rough estimate, Shiite areas included over 60 percent of the city and Sunni areas about 20 percent, while mixed areas had shrunk from 40 percent to 20 percent. About half of the Sunni population had left the city. The United Nations estimated two million Iraqis had fled the country, while another two million had left their homes and gone elsewhere inside the country. With fewer mixed neighborhoods, it was easier to control homogeneous districts where any stranger stood out. The one-hundred-odd combat outposts and joint security stations in Baghdad blanketed the city, with the major exceptions of Sadr City in the east and Kadhimiyah and Shula in the west. These were the strongholds of the Jesh al Mahdi.

By the end of 2007, about 80,000 Sunnis and 10,000 Shiites had loosely organized into about a thousand neighborhood watch groups. Called Concerned Local Citizens and later Sons of Iraq, the majority were paid about $300 a month by U.S. battalions and coordinated with the local Iraqi forces. Ayman al-Zawahri, the deputy to Osama bin Laden, said that al Qaeda–led insurgents in Iraq were the "primary force" fighting America. The Sons of Iraq posed the mortal threat to al Qaeda in Iraq. Without the support of the Sunni population, al Qaeda could exist only as criminals on the run.

The speed of the Awakening, though, as a social and potentially political movement—potentially a Sunni militia—had alarmed the Shiite-controlled central government. Many Shiite leaders were convinced Sunnis would never accept a minority status. Sooner or later, they would rise up, aided by the Sunni regimes in Jordan, Saudi Arabia, Egypt, and elsewhere. This deep-seated fear transcended rational arguments, leading to a near-paralysis inside the bureaucracies in response to persistent American efforts to recruit Sunnis into the Iraqi security forces stationed near Baghdad.

In a test of wills, the Americans had submitted a list of thoroughly vetted Sunnis to make up 40 percent of a brigade being formed for the Triangle of Death region south of Baghdad. The prime minister's office removed all the Sunnis. Petraeus then replied that he would provide no support to the new brigade. Relenting, Maliki agreed to the original list. But a four-star general does not have the time to be knocking heads with obdurate bureaucrats.

Similar efforts from Petraeus and Odierno down to the seventy-five U.S. battalion commanders in the field to provide services at the district levels were not matched by efforts from Iraqi officials. About half the population was living in absolute poverty. In cities like Fallujah, where unemployment was running as high as 50 percent, the price for fuel in a rich, oil-exporting country was backbreaking. A teacher earning $230 a month had to pay one dollar for a liter of kerosene and $15 for a small tank of propane. Although an $85 million facility provided Fallujah with clean water and sewers, the money came from U.S. taxpayers, while the Iraqi government ran a surplus of $4 billion it refused to spend.

In the States, the military progress hadn't made the war more popular. According to a Pew poll released at the end of November 2007, 48 percent of those polled thought the war effort was going well, up from 30 percent when the surge strategy began in February. Still, 54 percent believed the troops should come home, a figure that hadn't changed in months.

Most of the Republican candidates—Mitt Romney, Mike Huckabee, Rudy Giuliani—scarcely mentioned Iraq, which offered no upside with the president's approval rating for his handling of the war hovering at 31 percent. John McCain marched to a different drummer, addressing the issue head-on in the November/December issue of *Foreign Affairs:*

> The war in Iraq cannot be wished away, and it is a miscalculation of historic magnitude to believe that the consequences of failure will be limited to one administration or one party. This is an American war, and its outcome will touch every one of our citizens for years to come. That is why I support our continuing efforts to win in Iraq. It is also why I oppose a preemptive withdrawal strategy that has no Plan B for the aftermath of its inevitable failure and the greater problems that would ensue.

Barack Obama, writing in the July/August issue of the same magazine, had urged withdrawing rather than continuing:

> We cannot impose a military solution on a civil war between Sunni and Shiite factions. . . . [We should] begin a phased withdrawal of U.S. forces, with the goal of removing all combat brigades by March 31, 2008. . . . We should leave behind only a minimal over-the-horizon military force in the region.

———

By the end of 2007, Sunni and Shiite factions weren't attacking each other. Encouraged by Petraeus, 90,000 Concerned Local Citizens were protecting their neighborhoods. Murders in Baghdad had fallen from thirty a day in January to three a day in December.

The year 2007 was the year of the Sunni Awakening. That changed the dynamics of the war. The Awakening severed the link between al Qaeda and the Sunni population. The war was over in Anbar, where it had begun four and a half years ago. Baghdad was much less violent. Al Qaeda was in retreat, fleeing north.

The year-long campaign had been carried out on the backs of weary soldiers and marines. The Army brigades especially merited praise, extended to fifteen months of daily patrolling in summer heat that turned you into a puddle and winter night winds that chilled with surprising bite. The fighting in 2007 wasn't frequent or fierce. Three thousand enemy were killed, including in attacks by Special Operations Forces and armed helicopters, and 300 battalion operations conducted. On average, a battalion operation resulted in fewer than five enemy killed.

As the violence subsided, the desire grew at the local level for government to provide the basic services and staples that generate productive livelihoods—fuel, power, schools, clean water, and safe roads.

President Bush repeatedly said, "As local politics change, so will national politics."

At the close of 2007, that hadn't happened. Responsible and responsive national-level Iraqi politicians and leaders were the missing link.

TWENTY-FOUR

PROGRESS AND UNCERTAINTY

2008

In January 2008, Petraeus invited Max Boot, a military historian at the Council on Foreign Relations, and me to Iraq. Max had been there several times, and it was my fourteenth trip. We visited with eleven of our brigades operating in areas I had known since 2003. The dominant impression was that of a campaign systematically driving the extremist remnants into smaller pockets.

In the Wild West province of Anbar, Sheik Ahmed Abu Risha had taken over the Awakening movement following the murder of Sheik Sattar. Ahmed had opened up a political wing, called the Sahwa (Awakening) Council of the Sons of Iraq, to prepare for provincial elections scheduled by the end of the year. With the fighting in Anbar having ended, Ahmed was receiving delegations of Concerned Local Citizens from Baghdad, Diyala, and elsewhere, dispensing advice, resolving disputes, calling in favors, and extending his political network.

In Habbaniyah, a police academy was in full swing. With salaries starting at $560 a month, openings in the classes were oversubscribed by overqualified volunteers. The director of the academy, Brigadier General Khalid, said things were quiet on the streets.

"Al Qaeda came to Habbaniyah saying they were the mujahidin," he said. "Then they killed people. You Americans have the power. We know who to inform on."

Due to tribal patronage, the average age of the recruits was over thirty. They weren't shy about expressing their opinions to a visitor. When I asked whether al Qaeda would come back to behead them, as happened in Haditha two years earlier, they shouted a chorus of nos. No more houses for AQ, they explained.

Guerrilla wars have their idiosyncrasies. The Viet Cong habitually dug bunkers and slept in hammocks in the bush. Near the Syrian border and outside Tikrit, earlier in the war some al Qaeda units had pitched tents Arab-style in the desert, underestimating the power of heat-seeking optics in UAVs. The survivors spread the word to sleep inside houses. That meant the neighbors saw when strangers moved in. No more houses for AQ.

ARAB JABOUR

South of Baghdad, the 3rd Infantry Division had methodically organized a Concerned Local Citizens watch in one village after another, with an Iraqi and American battalion in overwatch in each district. On the east side of the Tigris, after the 35th Iraqi Brigade had replaced the untrustworthy National Police, the predominantly Sunni district council moved back to Salman Pak, the JAM moved out of the mosque, and the markets rebounded when the National Police checkpoints on Route Wild were removed.

American casualties had increased through the summer of 2007 because units were going into areas not touched in years and infested with IEDs. Nowhere was that more true than in Arab Jabour, across from Salman Pak, where hundreds of irrigation ditches and palm groves limited vehicles to a few dirt roads. Since I had last visited in the fall, Lt. Col. Ken Adgie had doubled the size of his battle space, which now extended for twelve kilometers along the west side of the Tigris. The 1st Battalion of the 30th Infantry suffered fourteen killed and eighty-two wounded since June of 2007, most due to IEDs.

"We've found 270 IEDs, many buried years ago," Adgie said. "Not even the insurgents know where they are."

To protect against mines, the Pentagon had spent $10 billion to field 20,000 MRAPs, or Mine Resistant Ambush Protected vehicles, which looked like big dump trucks with tank armor. It was the Pentagon's highest priority program. The first destruction of an MRAP, killing one American soldier, occurred in Adgie's zone. Adgie estimated the mine, containing 200 pounds of explosives, had been buried over a year ago.

The loss was a warning that even if all combat stopped tomorrow, mines would continue to take a toll.

Al Qaeda didn't have the time before being betrayed to set in more mines. Instead, they drove around in what the troops called bongo trucks, indistinguishable from any other pickup, intent on killing CLC members. The Bird Dogs had located Adgie's chief adversary, Abu Jurrah, after he had beheaded the son of one of Mustafa's lieutenants. Abu Jurrah died.

"Al Qaeda are local punks," Adgie said. "The outside leaders don't come into Arab Jabour. The guys I'm fighting believe in nothing. They've tasted power. That's it. But they're mean bastards. One punk saying he's AQ puts fear into fifty locals."

With the action slowing down, Adgie was receiving more detainees released from prison than he was sending up.

"We were given nine returnees," Adgie said. "Mustafa said he could live with six of them. Higher told me to take all nine. Mustafa bitched but took eight. I don't know what happened to the ninth."

With no Iraqi police or soldiers yet assigned to Arab Jabour, Adgie had increased his Concerned Citizens to 1,200 employees. Brigadier General Mustafa now had five deputy commanders. The Bird Dog program with a few Iraqis hidden on base running informant networks via a dozen cell phones had expanded.

"We hit targets twelve kilometers away inside twenty minutes," Sgt. Shaun Baker, who ran the program, said. "The British Black Knights from the Special Air Service are unbelievable. They sit by their helicopters, pop in here in minutes to pick up a Bird Dog, and are on the target's house in minutes. Cool."

In Northern Ireland during the 1990s, the British had categorized counterinsurgency as being either covert or framework operations. In Iraq, General Casey had used the same terms. The Special Operations Forces doing the covert work had the advantage of actions that produced immediate, tangible results. Framework ops by conventional forces consisted of an endless routine of daily patrols and guard duty. It was hard on the soldiers when they took losses and didn't have the satisfaction of killing or arresting the enemy on the spot, as SOF did.

To provide some recompense, Adgie involved every soldier in one civil affairs project or another. The Concerned Citizens were the district's largest employer, and 130 tiny stores and roadside stands had sprung up. One, which Adgie called "Wal-Mart," stocked everything from toothbrushes to shovels. A Farmer's Union had attracted 850 members, with the battalion providing $500,000 for 200 grants and projects. The battalion had contracted for fifty streetlights for the marketplace, so that families could shop and socialize after the farm day was done. Adgie took special pride in the repair of four huge pumps that diverted water from the Tigris into 400 square kilometers of irrigation ditches. Whenever Iraqi supplies of fuel ran low, he compensated from American stocks.

"The Maliki government does nothing for us," Kamil Mustafa, the commander of the Concerned Citizens, said. "To get our schools open, we went to Colonel Adgie. We knew he would put pressure on the government."

TRIANGLE OF DEATH

Improved security leading to demands for government services was evident in areas that had in 2006 seemed implacably opposed to an American presence. Five miles southwest of Arab Jabour, Colonel Dominic Caraccilo commanded the 3rd Brigade of the 101st Air Assault Division, which was occupying the Triangle of Death. The prior unit, the 2nd Brigade of the 10th Mountain Division, commanded by Col. Mike Kenshaw, had lost sixty-nine killed, but had done such a thorough job that Caraccilo had lost only one soldier since taking over in November of 2007. On his third tour in Iraq, Caraccilo had dispersed his brigade in twenty-four battle positions across 300 square kilometers holding half a million Sunnis.

Along the road next to the Euphrates where the prior battalion had encountered an IED every day and lost twenty-nine killed, Caraccilo had set in two patrol bases. One base, called Dragon, was in the hamlet of Owesat, where two American soldiers kidnapped in May of 2007 were last seen. An al Qaeda leader, labeled MK-1 in intelligence files, had taken a boat across from Owesat and reconnoitered the road where Humvees were strung out in guard positions several hundred meters apart. The next night, MK-1 returned and pitched grenades into two Humvees, killing six Americans and returning to Owesat with two captives. Equipment belonging to the two soldiers was later found north of Baghdad. The soldiers were never found, and MK-1 was on the run, hunted by special teams.

The tragedy illustrated the need never to lower one's guard. In the entire war, there were only three soldiers listed as missing, while over 4,000 had died. Compared to all prior wars, this indicated extraordinary care.

By 2008, there were no known insurgents inside the village of Owe-sat, where Combat Outpost Dragon was manned by fifty Americans and 500 CLC volunteers.

"I'm trying to get the CLCs paid," Capt. Wendall Stevens, the commander at Dragon, said. "They stand their posts every night. They'd make good village policemen, but I doubt that will happen."

The Ministry of Interior had authorized 600 policemen for the district of Yusufiyah. The Americans had recorded biometric and background data on 3,000 CLCs and submitted them as candidates six months earlier. The MOI had approved none.

"The CLC see us as providing security and money," Lt. Col. Andrew Rohling, commanding the battalion in Yusufiyah, said. "We have to shift those tasks to the Iraqi government before the CLC become disillusioned."

With security improved, the soldiers of the 101st were trying to jump-start the economy. Caraccilo's rifle companies were processing 2,500 microgrants, each with a ceiling of $2,500, for residents to buy seed, fertilizer, and basic goods. Frustrated that a frozen chicken from Argentina cost less than a local chicken, Caraccilo was studying the economics of poultry farming.

ECONOMIC DEVELOPMENT LACKS CLARITY

Caraccilo's brigade was typical of all eleven I visited in 2008. Each was heavily involved in economic projects, advised by EPRTs, or Embedded Provincial Reconstruction Teams, which were made up of five to ten contractors and civilians from the State Department, USAID, and other government agencies.

The role of the U.S. military in economic development was chaotic, uninformed, sincere, and somewhat successful. State and AID provided no doctrine or standard techniques to guide the commanders who were in touch daily at the local level. In the absence of an economic strategy, generals invented their own.

Maj. Gen. Douglas Stone, who was in charge of the U.S. prisons, conducted a survey showing that over 30 percent of prisoners had fought against the coalition for money. Stone described Iraqi Vice President Tariq al-Hashimi as excited about the implications:

There are, you know, by [Vice President Hashimi's] estimation, about 4½ million men that need to . . . get the right skill sets. . . . Put them on a public works program and pay them 300, 350 bucks a month.

Such a program would cost $18 billion a year. Hashimi did not address who would pay that bill. If wishes were horses, beggars would ride.

Stone argued that a jobs program would undercut the insurgency:

> You get them [prisoners]; you BAT [fingerprint] them; you bring them through. But they would then go out and do public works stuff. . . . The number one problem to drain the swamp of the . . . countercoalition guys, the ones that we're rolling up [sending to prison], is jobs.

Paying insurgents not to shoot at you can work, especially in tribal societies motivated by extortion rather than political commitment. It won't buy off nationalists or those who are politically committed. The Iraqi government, on sectarian, political, and sovereignty grounds, consistently turned down American requests for even dollops of aid for Sunni locales. Hashimi's notion of a massive public works program that would include millions of Shiites and Sunnis was politically impossible. Similarly, to release prisoners and give them jobs while the Sunnis who had not rebelled went without jobs guaranteed resentment, violence, and chaos.

Attempting to subdue the insurgency by means of economic stimulants brought to mind Rodney King's piquant quip, "Can we all get along?" Eliminating unemployment was certainly a good idea, and always would be. It was also fanciful and shallow. The U.S. military wasted time and resources, and became distracted from its core competencies, by taking on development projects and making snap judgments about the assumed effects in undercutting the insurgency.

Iraq needed first and foremost to put its own economic house in order. For decades, the Iraqi government had provided free or massively subsidized food grains, electricity, and refined fuels. The United States did little to change this. The export of oil and the delivery of refined products inside Iraq at a cost four times cheaper than across the borders guaranteed massive corruption.

From 2003 on, the military believed correctly that the State Department and the rest of the government weren't applying their fair share of manpower, effort, and sacrifice. Partly this was because the senior leaders at State in Washington kept their distance from the war. That aside, however, no administration leader set the goals and the means for managing America's role in supporting the economy of this oil-rich sovereign nation.

At the practical level, the CERP fund provided commanders with wasta, or immediate influence. The sincerity of sergeants and lieutenants disbursing small sums of money yielded enormous goodwill at the neighborhood level. American soldiers cared. They weren't condescending. They took the time to listen at local meetings and to dole out small loans and grants. Of special significance was the payment of about $350 a month in 2008 to the 90,000 members of the Sons of Iraq, formerly called the Concerned Local Citizens. These payments, which had begun after most of the volunteers had stepped forward, had a multiplier effect in local communities.

As important, the more the Americans learned about the corruption, laziness, and bottlenecks that prevented funds from flowing from the ministries to the provinces and finally to the districts, the more skilled they became in pressuring the sclerotic Iraqi system. By 2008, as a result of State's agreement to provide reconstruction teams embedded in every brigade, the ministries and provinces were confronted by American experts determined to accomplish something before their year was up. The Pentagon agreed to transfer $200 million to State to pay for civilians to support the military. State proposed creating a Civilian Reserve Corps to, in Secretary Rice's words, "volunteer to go to a place like Afghanistan."

The larger question remained unanswered: How did the United States government set goals, limits, and measures when assisting the economic development of a sovereign nation—Afghanistan as well as Iraq—that lacked administrative competency and operated via a system of corruption that lubricated the gears of government?

By 2008, the American military had a system for combating the insurgency. It did not have a system for economic development. While all brigades followed the same basics set forth in the counterinsurgency field manual, there was no equivalent manual for economic development. The U.S. military had complained for years of carrying the burden unassisted, and the EPRTs (Embedded Provincial Reconstruction Teams) were relatively new.

Some EPRTs emphasized microloans, while others favored microgrants. Larger projects depended on local conditions. The brigades praised their EPRTs. Americans, though, could never work their way out of reconstructing Iraq, because an economy is forever expanding. There is always a requirement for additional projects—in Des Moines or in Yusufiyah. It was unclear how American aid weaned the population from supporting insurgents—or how long Americans could substitute for Iraqi officials.

"The problem," Caraccilo said, "is that districts like Yusufiyah have no connection to the provincial government. The Iraqi bureaucrats don't give a damn."

The magnet of profit without work drew power to the center in Iraq and all other oil-exporting countries, creating entrenched interests whose livelihoods depended on maintaining centralized control over the dispersal of revenues. In 2007, the eighteen provinces received $2.3 billion in development funds, or 5 percent of Iraq's $41 billion budget. The ministers and bureaucrats collected the revenues from oil exports without feeling any systemic political pressure to share it. Unlike in the States, Iraqi politicians weren't elected by local or provincial constituencies and didn't have to promise services rendered back in exchange for raising taxes. In 2007, Maliki ordered all ministers shielded from corruption investigations—unless he chose otherwise—and closed forty-eight ongoing cases.

The economic plight of Iraq couldn't be solved by small, temporary doses of aid from good-willed Americans. Oil revenues flowed into Baghdad without any social contract. To political hacks victorious in the Green Zone went the spoils.

———

The pattern of American-local partnering, especially with Sunnis, in the provinces was also evident inside Baghdad in 2008. In the Sunni districts, volunteers had slowly come forward after the Americans had persisted in patrolling daily from their outposts in the neighborhoods. In the Dora district, a cardiologist, Dr. Mouyad al-Jubouri, proposed a few projects and was given funds. Students painted the gloomy concrete barriers with brightly colored art, trash trucks hauled away the garbage, backhoes leveled the dirt for small parks, entrepreneurs opened shops and brought in generators to sell power in the neighborhood. Outsiders were reported to the CLC, who called the Americans. Residents returned, instead of selling their houses. Others wanted to move in. Rental prices tripled.

"An American soldier was blown up outside my house," Dr. Mouyad told me. "The glass came crashing in, the curtains caught fire, my children were screaming upstairs. I said enough! You Americans had your own Awakening. No more rough stuff. It's good here now. The government needs an Awakening."

ABU ABID

When I dropped by Ghazaliyah to catch up with Abu Abid, the former insurgent fighter, the picture wasn't as encouraging. His house had been attacked twice, and he was fatalistic about his chances of surviving.

"Different people are trying to kill me," he said. "We are a victory for the Iraqi government, but they don't support us. If the Americans leave, it will be a disaster."

Abid had summarized the dilemma of transitioning the 90,000 CLCs from American sponsorship to Iraqi ownership. The Sunni tribes weren't fighting the Americans, and neither were tough city gangs like Abid's. Instead, they had joined with the Americans. Across Iraq, advisers and brigade commanders lauded the CLC or Sons of Iraq as key to exposing the insurgents hiding among the population.

"CLC was the top story of 2007," Col. P. J. Dermer, a key adviser in Baghdad, said. "It set us up for success in 2008."

But when the Americans disengaged, this left hundreds of armed neighborhood gangs loosely affiliated through the political arm of the Sons of Iraq. To satisfy worried Shiite officials, senior American staffs had set an arbitrary ceiling for 20 percent of the CLC to join the police, with the rest temporarily employed in public works, like the Civilian Conservation Corps during the Depression in the 1930s. The government of Iraq, though, was offering no money for the CLC to turn in their guns for shovels, while the Ministry of Interior was loath to offer police jobs.

The Iraqi Army was an altogether different case. The minister of defense, Abdul Qadar, was serious about developing a nonsectarian army. Sunnis were recruited and assigned to their home provinces. Leaders were emerging. The commander responsible for Baghdad, Lt. Gen. Aboud Ganbar, has gained widespread popularity by constantly visiting his units, smiling and patting soldiers on their backs as he congratulated them.

SADR CITY AREA

While the CLCs and the Iraqi Army were cooperating with the American units in Baghdad, the Jesh al Mahdi kept their distance. In Kadhimiyah in northwest Baghdad and in Sadr City to the east, JAM operated as a shadow government in the winter of 2008, extorting money and providing local services while sneering at the Maliki clique that accommodated them.

At Combat Outpost Callahan, I visited with the 2nd Battalion of the 325th Airborne Regiment, which had operated in and around Sadr City for a year. These paratroopers from the 82nd Airborne Division were partnered with a National Police battalion that had not arrested a single JAM member in eight months. In the course of eighty-six raids into Sadr City, where two million Shiites lived, the paratroopers had arrested sixty-one senior JAM leaders. Battalion 2-325 had sent almost 1,000 Iraqis, mostly Shiites, to prison—five times higher than the average battalion in Iraq.

Across Baghdad, the Iranian-made explosively formed penetrators used by Shiite "special groups" were the main threat to American soldiers. The paratroopers pounced whenever they got a tip about EFPs.

"We've encountered too many instances," Captain Burroughs, a company commander, said, "of al Qaeda blowing something up in one district, and we hit some EFPs over here when we're reacting. There's collusion between some al Qaeda and the special groups."

Nearing the end of their tour of fifteen months, they had the detached attitude of weary professional soldiers.

"JAM itself isn't bad or good," Burroughs said. "The police have to be JAM to get a job. The average Shiite is exploited by the extreme Shiite. They're criminals. We've arrested the last three commanders of one JAM brigade. I stopped the fourth commander on the street last week and told him to smarten up—play by our rules or go to Bucca."

In addition to raids, they conducted two foot patrols a day in platoon strength.

"In ten minutes, you can have thousands swarming around you out there, screaming," Sgt. Adam Farmer, a platoon sergeant, said. "We're tired of beating our heads against the wall, asking the people to tell us who's shaking them down."

The paratroopers had paid 600 local Shiites to stand guard in their neighborhoods, like the Concerned Citizens. After JAM members paid a few visits, fourteen of the sixteen Neighborhood Watches closed down.

The written mission on the board in the ops center was to "secure the population and improve security by progress in governance, essential services, and economics." That seemed a task more appropriate to the government of Iraq than the United States. The soldiers considered the mission impossibly vague and beyond the capabilities of infantry grunts.

"No one has told us the end state for Sadr City and JAM influence," SSgt. Jerry Byrd, a squad leader on his third tour, said. "We're paratroopers. We're fighters. We've done our job. This is a nonkinetic fight."

The soldiers said the time had been hardest on those affected by "stop-loss," a policy that extended a soldier's enlistment until he completed the fifteen-month tour. They didn't believe their economic projects to generate goodwill had made much of a dent in Sadr City. Like Hezbollah, the Jesh al Mahdi were providing some services and demanding some taxes. They either ignored American aid efforts, or took credit for them.

"I've had two tours as a civil affairs officer," Maj. Olaf Shibusawa said. "Our civilian reconstruction team lives in a bubble. They cause me trouble because they don't know the local structure. My job is to bribe people to get information."

Sadr preached that he was the true patriot who wanted Iraq free of Iranian influence and of all American occupiers. Most JAM members were ambivalent rather than hostile to the Americans. Since September of 2006, a military police company from Fort Bragg had worked in Sadr City with the police, who were, of course, JAM. The MPs confined their daily routine to training. The residents assured the MPs that their vehicles were easily identifiable and would not be attacked.

"JAM has Sadr City in a hammerlock," SSgt. Dale Dukes, who worked there for a year, said. "As individuals, the Iraqis liked us. But as a group, JAM was always saying, you can leave. They didn't shoot at us, and my unit didn't arrest them."

Across the Tigris in west Baghdad, the story was the same. When Lieutenant Colonel Miska packed up to leave the base in Kadhimiyah, to his surprise Brigadier General Falah left as well. "You and Colonel Burton are all I have," Falah said. "My generals don't back me up against the politicians. Jesh al Mahdi controls Kadhimiyah, not the Iraqi Army. When you leave, I'm finished."

Falah had sent his family to Egypt. Miska agreed to sponsor Falah's request for a visa to the States. It would be a long wait.

WEST MOSUL

At the beginning of 2008, Odierno launched Phantom Phoenix in northeast Diyala, the fourth in a series that had driven al Qaeda from Baghdad and the surrounding belts.

"I'm not allowing al Qaeda any rest," Odierno told me. "Wherever they go, I'm going after them."

Al Qaeda cells fled north in their BMWs and other upscale cars, heading up the Tigris valley. Near the top of Iraq, Mosul and the villages stretching west eighty miles to the hospitable Syrian border were shaping up as the final redoubt for al Qaeda.

In the Mosul region, the Kurds held the political power and shared few resources with the disorganized Sunnis. AQI elements converged on battle-torn west Mosul, a thirty-six-square-kilometer cluster of shattered houses and roads pockmarked by IED blasts. The 3rd Squadron of the 3rd Armored Cavalry Regiment was holding west Mosul as an economy of force operation, while Petraeus gave the Iraqi forces time to pull together and prove they could hold the city on their own.

The squadron sent out twenty-four armored patrols a day. In one month, 300 IEDs were found or detonated, in addition to 260 small arms engagements. The odds of a patrol encountering hostile fire were one in three. Max Boot and I accompanied the squadron commander, Lt. Col. Keith Barclay, in his Humvee into west Mosul to meet with Iraqi commanders. Along the way, a radio report came in about a blue van driving erratically down a street parallel to ours. Its occupants had fired at an Iraqi checkpoint. After a helicopter put a Hellfire missile into the van, two survivors hopped out and ran toward a bombed-out house. One was cut down outside and seemed to be wearing a suicide vest. The other had ducked into the house. The soldiers had taken cover and called for a tank.

Barclay and his command group of four Humvees drove over to take a look. The scene was typical of Fallujah in 2005, Ramadi in 2006, and Salman Pak in 2007—blasted-out buildings with no glass in the windows, shuttered storefronts, lifeless streets, the occasional distant cracks of M4s or AKs. The street was empty except for a few men hurrying across the road, away from the firing. When the Humvee in front of us slowed down to creep through a puddle caused by a broken water main, we came up on its bumper just as it sprang into the air like a cat. It crashed down smoking, the hood sailing off as the *BANG!* reverberated off the nearby storefronts and chunks of metal clanged down the street.

The soldiers inside were shaken up but not seriously injured. A chunk from the engine hit an Iraqi civilian hiding in a store and he ran into the street screaming, his left arm ripped apart above the elbow, the blood spurting. A short burst of AK fire came from our left.

"Pull up abreast," Barclay said to his driver.

The Humvee jerked forward to protect its crumbled mate.

"Have PID [positive ID]?" Barclay asked his machine gunner as rounds snapped overhead.

"Negative," the gunner replied, not returning fire blindly.

One in sixteen patrols in contested areas in Vietnam erupted in a firefight, resulting in an average of forty-seven fatalities in a battalion in a year. Once a firefight erupted, despite casualties, your mind was engaged. You had to act. In Iraq, there were fewer firefights. Instead, the IED struck like a bolt of lightning. It played on your nerves, knowing it would happen sooner or later.

After the IED exploded, a tank cut around to the left in front of us and hit a second IED, put in by the civilians who had just crossed the street in front of us. With the tank out of action with a stripped tread, Iraqi soldiers from a nearby outpost rushed forward to protect it. A few minutes later, a second tank rolled up and put a 120mm round into the house where the suicide bomber was hiding.

Each day in Iraq, there were about two such shootouts between American forces and extremists. The Americans used high-tech— airborne sensors, Hellfire missiles—to detect and box in the enemy. A soldier with a rifle then made the arrests or double-tapped the chests of insurgents. Based on intercepts of conversations, what the extremists feared most was not the U.S. technology; it was the grunts who closed with them. The press usually depicted our soldiers as victims, or as nice guys handing out candy. Foremost, though, our infantrymen were hunters. And the al Qaeda types feared them.

On the enemy side, suicide bombers, such as those Barclay's soldiers encountered, distinguished Iraq from prior insurgencies. Without the mass murder of Shiites, al Qaeda could not have provoked the civil war in Baghdad in 2006. And without the mass murder of Sunnis, the tribes would not have turned against al Qaeda. Like Robespierre being consumed by his own Reign of Terror in 1794, the nature of al Qaeda in Iraq eventually locked it into a death struggle with the very Sunni population it claimed to be trying to liberate.

At the start of 2008, al Qaeda had a firm hold in west Mosul. It would take months for dismounted infantry to clear each city block in Ramadi fashion. If the provincial government, dominated by Kurds, provided the Sunni residents with services and won their support, the campaign would go faster. The Iraqi battalion commander working with Barclay doubted that would happen.

"The Sunni people get zero support from this governor," Colonel

Hamid, a burly officer who had been twice wounded, said. "The governor fires anyone who talks for the Sunnis. He says the coalition broke the city and they can fix it, not him."

Maj. Joel Rayburn agreed. He was an intelligence officer on his second tour with an encyclopedic knowledge of Iraqi politics and insurgent groups.

"The problem up here in Ninewah Province," Rayburn told me, "is that the Kurds overreached. They've deprived the Sunni Arabs of any resources. So al Qaeda poses as the Sunni protector. Anbar's all Sunnis. They swung against al Qaeda as a solid bloc. The Sunnis are mixed inside Ninewah with Kurds and inside Diyala with Shiites. When the Kurds and Shiites refuse to share power or money, they create nesting places for al Qaeda."

————

After leaving west Mosul, we visited the dreary city of Bayji, home of an oil refinery generating billions of dollars. Located in Saladin Province 100 miles north of Baghdad, Bayji was a depressed town of 140,000, bereft of home heating fuel, electricity, and jobs. While a few hundred Iraqi police and jundis had barracks on the outskirts, the day-to-day patrolling fell to a 100-man rifle company commanded by Capt. Tim Meadors and 300 Sons of Iraq recruited locally.

With Col. Michael McBride, commander of the 1st Brigade of the 101st Division, we visited the empty market, where a thin, middle-aged man selling cucumbers told us he had served as a colonel. He hadn't applied for a pension, fearing arrest for his former job. Asked how things were, he replied, "Things are terrible! Saddam was better!" Farther down the street, a portly man stood behind a counter piled high with cheap shoes. Asked how was business, he said, "I'd rather be dead." McBride said he hoped we appreciated an honest tour. We were still chuckling when an AK round cracked by. The shot went high, but it cleared the vendors from the street.

"We lost two police here," Captain Meadors said, "so they won't come with us."

His CLC civilians, though, stuck by him as he walked through the market. A few days later, the thirteen-year-old son of a local al Qaeda leader walked into a hall in Bayji filled with CLC supporters and blew himself up, killing seventeen. In the course of January 2008, suicide murderers struck at CLC leaders in Ramadi, Fallujah, Bayji, and Baghdad. These killers weren't foreigners; they were fellow Iraqis known to the locals.

IRAQI RULE OF LAW

Determining who were the murderers, hard-core criminals, and other irreconcilables was vexatious, especially because so many were captured. During the Algerian insurgency, about two guerrillas were killed for each one captured. In Vietnam, about nine Viet Cong guerrillas were killed for each one captured. In Iraq, about one insurgent was killed for every three captured.

Fewer than one in ten captured were al Qaeda fanatics. Most detainees said they fought for money, or were resisting the occupation or the Shiites. This presented a double-barreled problem: a large prison population in which a minority was irreconcilable and a large majority that was not a long-term threat. Under a U.N. resolution, the United States could hold only those Iraqis deemed "imperative risks." In conventional war, prisoners were kept until the war was over. In prior occupations, the United States held military tribunals. In Iraq, the United States could not hold insurgents until the end of hostilities, or punish them for crimes. Only the government of Iraq could impose sentences upon insurgents. But the Iraqi government couldn't be trusted, so the United States kept most insurgents, and then released them.

Since 2003, the coalition had imprisoned 77,000 and released 53,000. With the average prison term being less than a year, commanders complained about fighting the same insurgents twice, while staffs in Baghdad pointed to the astonishingly low rates of rearrest—3 to 9 percent. To the field commanders, this was evidence that the Iraqis—and Americans—were poor at making arrests. Between 2003 and late 2006, the hard-core prisoners were not separated from the general prison population, prompting the troops to refer to Camp Bucca as "Jihad University."

At the beginning of 2008, the United States was holding about 25,000 Iraqis in Bucca and Cropper who had been arrested by our soldiers with sufficient evidence to withstand three levels of review by lawyers before being imprisoned. A task force under Maj. Gen. Douglas Stone had isolated the hard core—about 4,000—and initiated short classes on Islam to reeducate other prisoners.

The prisoners could not be handed over en masse to the government of Iraq, which was apt to abuse many and release others. Iraq's judicial system did not merit trust. The judges had released even the Sadrist deputy health minister, Hakim al-Zamili, and his security henchman, after hundreds of Sunnis were kidnapped and murdered in the Baghdad hospitals under their control.

The Stone task force initiated a program to release 8,000 prisoners in 2008, many accompanied by pledges from families of the prisoners. At his confirmation hearing in 2007, Petraeus had assured the senators that he would end the catch and release program. By 2008, he believed Stone's program of "pledge and release" had caused such "an enormous shift" that it deserved to be taught in counterinsurgency manuals, because less than one percent of those released were rearrested. Recidivism for violent crime in the United States was 65 percent; recidivism of one percent was a world-class breakthrough. Still, in the summer of 2008, the U.S. military was imprisoning thirty insurgents a day, while releasing fifty. Thousands of Sunni insurgents and Shiite militiamen remained unrepentant.

Petraeus had pointed to a disturbing contradiction when he told a Senate hearing that "the prison capacity of Iraq is one-sixth that of the state of Texas, and they [the Texans] are not fighting an insurgency." The murder rate in Iraq was twenty times higher than in the States. Most murderers in Iraq were walking free, yet violence was down. No one knew when murderers stopped killing, or why. Eventually it did happen, as evidenced by the relative stability today in the previous killing fields of Cambodia, Rwanda, and Serbia.

I put the question of recidivism to six battalion commanders directly involved in the turnaround of the Sunni insurgency. The consensus was that the Sunni Awakening meant that many detainees would not attack American forces a second time if released.

"Most Sunni detainees can be let out," Lt. Col. Roger Turner, a two-tour commander, said. "Religious classes in prison don't change them. It's the community attitude at home that changes them."

"The police kill them," Lieutenant Colonel Mullen, who had worked in Fallujah, said. "They come out of prison and they disappear. There's a lot we Americans will never, never know."

Turner gave an example. "In Ramadi," he said, "the top insurgent Bill Jurney and I tried to get for two years was Mullah Katan. The cop who popped Katan had been working with him. He flipped to our side and set Katan up. The cops said Katan was gone, and that was it. No body, nothing. We have our rule of law, and they have theirs."

THE MALIGN INFLUENCE OF IRAN

In mid-March of 2008, Adm. William Fallon resigned as commander of the Central Command. The ostensible reason was an article in which he appeared to be posing as the voice of reason, preventing a rash and intemperate White House from attacking Iran. The actual reason was simpler: Fallon was unable to restrain his ego. National Security Adviser Stephen Hadley had lost confidence in Fallon's prudence. Defense Secretary Robert Gates accepted the admiral's resignation with terse words.

The departure pointed to the unfinished business between the United States and Iran on two fronts: Iran continued on a path toward a nuclear weapon and persisted in training and equipping Iraqis to kill Americans. When Connecticut's Joe Lieberman suggested retaliation with cruise missile strikes, no other senator had endorsed the idea. Although Senators John McCain and Barack Obama agreed that Iran should not have nuclear weapons or support the killing of Americans, neither suggested any military retaliation. At a news conference, Secretary Gates was definitive in ruling out any counterstrikes.

"We are not planning on a war with Iran," he said. "What we are trying to do is, inside Iraq, disrupt the networks that put these weapons in the hands of those who kill our troops. That's it."

Ambassador Ryan Crocker believed Iran was waging a proxy war against the United States, as it had in Lebanon in 1983. The United States withdrew from that country in 1983 after Iranian-sponsored suicide bombers destroyed the American embassy and the Marine barracks, murdering hundreds. In Crocker's judgment, Iran intended to drive out the United States and fragment Iraq's central government by arming and controlling various Shiite militia groups, similar to its control over the Hezbollah in Lebanon.

"I think what the Iranians are doing is pursuing a policy," he told a congressional committee, "of Lebanonization and . . . backing more than one militia."

Col. Jim Rainey, the operations officer of the 4th Infantry Division, told me the Iranian explosively formed penetrator was the major threat to his soldiers in Baghdad. In answer to a question during a Senate hearing, Petraeus testified that it was fair to say Iranian-backed special groups in Iraq were responsible for the murder of hundreds of American soldiers.

There was no support in Congress in 2008 for attacking the training sites in Iran. President Bush repeatedly stressed he had no desire to hit back at Iran. He insisted his role was to "solve these issues diplomatically," with the help of other countries. "You can't solve these problems unilaterally," he said. "You're going to need a multilateral forum."

Bush was acknowledging he could not rally support in America to take action against a country responsible for the deaths of Americans. Senator Obama was quite forceful in saying, "I will do whatever is required to prevent the Iranians from obtaining nuclear weapons." Senator McCain said the same thing: "Iran cannot be allowed to acquire nuclear weapons." Although McCain and Obama said Iran should not have nuclear weapons or support the killing of Americans, neither suggested military retaliation. Iraq had sapped America's will.

VICTORY VIA DEFEAT IN BASRA

Just prior to Petraeus's appearance before Congress in April of 2008, Maliki rushed to the southern port city of Basra to lead an assault upon mafia-style gangs that controlled the city and profited handsomely from oil exports. Several months earlier, Odierno had addressed Basra in candid terms.

"Basra, you know, it's a Shi'a-on-Shi'a power issue," he said. "It's about who is going to control Basra. And frankly, in my mind it's a political issue. The problem is, they tend to use violence right now instead of peaceful means to resolve those political issues."

Since the invasion, Basra had been under the protection of the British, who opted for what military analyst Tony Cordesman charitably termed "not-so-benign neglect." Having failed over five years to protect the population from the criminals and competing militia gangs, the British had withdrawn to Basra's airport, washing their hands of a mess beyond their capabilities. Maliki didn't want to inform the British of his operation, considering them of no consequence.

On March 22, Petraeus met with Maliki, urging him not to rush into a fight and put at risk all the gains of the past year. The respected commander in Basra, Lt. Gen. Mohan Fireji, had already recommended that Maliki adopt a methodical Petraeus-type approach. Maliki had brushed him aside. Now he was ordering two Iraqi brigades to deploy to Basra for an operation Petraeus told him was "not adequately planned or prepared."

It was the second time Maliki had acted peremptorily. In August of 2007, Sadr's followers had provoked a fight in Karbala and killed dozens of pilgrims. Maliki rushed to the scene, arresting a JAM leader at gunpoint and forcing a chastened Sadr to declare a cease-fire in order to regain popular support. The incident had reinforced Maliki's exaggerated sense of power and superiority.

On March 22, President Bush was informed that Maliki was charging ahead, while Petraeus—and any sensible general—knew he had a

90 percent chance of failing. Bush himself had been involved in three urban battles. He had rashly ordered the Marines to seize Fallujah in April of 2004, then agonized before calling them off, then ordered them to attack again in November. He knew firsthand how complex an urban assault was—how you had to marshal sufficient forces, motivate them, warn the population, build political consensus, mold the press, get out your message, control the pace, set military goals that could be met and understood. Maliki had done nothing of the sort.

Yet Bush did not pick up the phone and tell Maliki not to be a damn fool. It wasn't Bush's executive style to move on military matters instinctively, even though Petraeus believed Maliki was making a huge mistake and Bush's experiences confirmed Petraeus's judgment.

On March 24, Maliki flew to Basra and ordered immediate operations against neighborhoods controlled by the Jesh al Mahdi. Provincial elections were scheduled for the fall, with the majority Islamic Supreme Council of Iraq (ISCI) party and Maliki's Dawa Party pitted against the Sadrists and Fadhila, a breakaway Sadr faction. All four parties were taking a cut of the profits from Basra, the oil-exporting port. The list-based political system had deprived Sadr in 2005 of ministerships and Assembly delegates his popularity on the streets had merited. With reason to believe the Basra offensive was aimed principally at his supporters, he called on his followers to fight.

Grandiloquently declaring that Basra was "a decisive and final battle," Maliki vowed to stay in the city until victory. Amidst a flurry of crisis management meetings in the White House, Bush provided Maliki with political cover, calling the assault "bold" and "a defining moment." Although the White House backed Maliki's claim that he was cleaning out the criminals, it was farcical to believe Iraqi battalions were serving warrants as they assaulted Basra. Criminals derived their power from militia factions, not the other way around. JAM was the militia Maliki had targeted.

In Baghdad, the Multi-National Force seethed at Malaki's actions, with Petraeus conveying his anger by saying not one word publicly. Privately, he sent the new coalition corps commander, Lt. Gen. Lloyd Austin, and his deputy, Maj. Gen. George Flynn, to Basra to help out. They scrambled to provide some airlift and several teams of air controllers.

Maliki's carelessness and arrogance quickly caught up with him. The battles of Fallujah, Sadr City, and Najaf showed that the attacking force in a city requires heavy, direct firepower from tanks and infantry determined to clear house by house. Maliki had made scant preparations. Mahdi fighters swarmed into the contested neighborhoods, demonstrating more fighting spirit than the jundis, who weren't sure which generals were commanding them or how to clear a city with a million residents. Over 500 police in Basra refused to fight, with some units making a show of turning their weapons over to the JAM.

JAM gangs initiated fighting in several other cities. For five days, the Green Zone was pummeled by Iranian-supplied rockets launched from inside Sadr City. Secretary Gates had opined that the Shiite residents were tiring of the criminality of the Mahdi Army. One battle in far-off Basra, however, showed who controlled the streets in much of Baghdad. Before the Basra assault, attacks in Baghdad were averaging fourteen a day. One day after the assault began, there were seventy-seven attacks. The American strategy of keeping its outposts outside the JAM redoubts had left the population under the control of the militia and the Green Zone vulnerable to attack whenever JAM leaders wanted to make a point.

The American military used the term "special groups" to distinguish between "good" JAM and supposedly maverick JAM elements who attacked Americans. As JAM fighters rushed around Shula and Sadr City, the distinction proved elastic. Both the "good JAM" and the special groups were shooting at American and Iraqi soldiers.

From Iran, Sadr gave an interview to Al Jazeera. With religious tomes as a prop behind him, he explained he was studying to become a mujtahid, a religious authority held by Shiites in the highest respect. Saying he controlled a Mahdi Army dedicated to liberating Iraq from the occupiers, he dismissed Maliki as a selfish politician disconnected from the people.

Maliki was stuck. He had snubbed the American Army and the Iraqi Army couldn't advance. Some jundis didn't want to shoot at fellow Shiites, and others were concerned that Baghdad had bollixed military death benefits. A macabre joke among the jundis was "Don't get killed before eleven in the morning, or your family won't be paid for the day." The Basra offensive sputtered out.

Yet Maliki had vowed not to leave Basra until the city was under control. Iraqi politicians flew to Iran to negotiate a face-saving exit for Maliki. With advice from the Iranians who were training and equipping "special groups" of JAM to kill Americans, Sadr ordered his troops to stop fighting and disperse. Maliki publicly acknowledged that Sadr was taking a "positive step in the right direction" and ordered a halt to arrests, while a government spokesman said the Iraqi judicial system would "look into the cases" of those Sadrists in jail.

Before quietly leaving Basra, Maliki paid the local sheiks to initiate a Shiite version of the Awakening that had transformed Anbar, hiring 10,000 tribesmen on the spot. Several months earlier, Maliki had objected strongly when Petraeus dispatched his Phoenix team to organize Shiite tribes that were hard pressed by JAM in Diwaniyah. In provincial elections, a Shiite tribal organization would boost local leaders rather than Maliki's Dawa Party. Facing humiliation in Basra, Maliki reversed field in a day.

Nor did President Bush emerge as tough-minded. After Petraeus had laid out the risks in the urban assault, the president had been unwilling to tell Maliki to call off the attack. By year's end, Iraq and the United States had to reach a long-term Status of Forces agreement. Maliki's office was toying with rash terms that would elevate Maliki above American commanders in making military decisions. There was no sense in antagonizing Maliki.

Although Senator Carl Levin had proposed forcing Maliki out of office, the Americans in Baghdad had done their counting. The 137 votes in the Assembly necessary to dismiss Maliki were readily available. One harsh word from Bush and Maliki was out. It took 185 votes to seat a new prime minister. In 2006, the voting for prime minister had paralyzed the government for six months. Maliki's replacement might be an improvement, but the process of getting there was risky.

Casey, Petraeus, Crocker, and Hadley had cautioned Bush about Maliki's unpredictable character. The week before the Basra debacle, *Washington Post* columnist David Ignatius quoted an Iraqi cabinet member as saying, "Maliki laughs at the U.S. government and makes fun of the president as a fool who knows so little about the Middle East." While Bush was relying on Petraeus buying more time by testifying to Congress in mid-April, Maliki was undercutting the case by his rashness. What Bush had called "the defining moment" had defined Maliki as erratic.

Ironically, Maliki's rashness solidified Bush's support. When chastened, Maliki behaved reasonably for a time. Ambassador Crocker made the rounds, urging Iraqi politicians to line up behind their prime minister. You all lose, Crocker argued, if Maliki is beaten by the Jesh al Mahdi aided by Iran. Crocker was successful. Instead of a vote of no confidence, Kurdish, Sunni, and Shiite leaders supported Maliki, who had turned against the major Iranian-backed militia.

When Vice President Cheney visited Baghdad several days before the offensive, Maliki, who resented his dependence on American power, never mentioned his Basra plan. His distrust and secretiveness strained relations with the United States. At the same time, the coalition's support during the Basra fight weakened his inner circle, a font of anti-American sectarianism. Maliki was more quixotic than cynical, fearful of a Baathist revival, deeply suspicious of the motivations of others, believing in a united Iraq and yet unwilling to reach out to Sunnis to get there.

Operationally, the results were positive. Sadr had ordered his followers to cease fighting before they alienated most Iraqis or were crushed by the Americans. Although there were a thousand deserters from the Iraqi forces—Shiites who refused to fight against the JAM— this was less than 5 percent of the attacking force. Sadr, having hidden in Iran for fifteen months, had lost day-to-day control of his Mahdi Army. American commandos continued to kill and arrest that amorphous swarm called "special groups."

The Iraqi Army did not pull out of Basra. Instead, with the aid of American and British fire support teams, it moved slowly forward, gaining gradual control. To avoid being branded as a foreign meddler, Iran felt obliged to distance itself, at least in public, from the militia. Most significantly, Maliki allowed his army to systematically encroach on Sadr City, erecting concrete walls to seal off neighborhoods. Petraeus put the Iraqi battalions in the lead, with American companies a few blocks behind them.

The results of the impetuous Basra assault furthered American goals. Maliki did take forceful action, albeit rashly. Iraqi political blocs solidified against the Sadr movement, while weakening Iranian influence. The repeated strikes of Iranian-made rockets against the Green Zone demonstrated to the U.S. press and Congress what Petraeus called Iran's "malign influence." The Iraqi Army, with American forces in support, brought pressure against Sadr City.

HEARINGS DEBATE THE ENDGAME

In September of 2007, when Petraeus had delivered to Congress his first progress report, he had the attention of the nation. His careful, factual presentation had gained Bush the political support to continue with his policy.

When Petraeus delivered his second report in April of 2008, he had succeeded militarily. The Iraqi Army had expanded to 208,000 soldiers, plus 350,000 police of highly uneven quality and reliability. Sectarian violence had dropped by 90 percent from its height in 2006. The hearings were not a news event. The reporters knew the scorecard in advance. Although Senators Clinton and Reid had insisted eight months earlier that the strategy would not work, they treated as yesterday's news Petraeus's charts showing steady military progress. Instead of again accusing Petraeus of "spinning," Senator Biden said, "The military has done a very good job in this surge. No one ever doubted that."

Petraeus had turned around a losing effort and was widely compared to Gen. Matthew Ridgway, who had prevented a defeat in Korea in 1950. Petraeus was treated with deference during the hearings. A Harris poll showed that 51 percent of the public had a "great deal of confidence" in the country's military leaders, compared with 8 percent for Congress. No senator continued to claim the war was being lost, or that American soldiers were being sucked into the abyss of a Sunni-Shiite civil war.

Petraeus and Crocker testified with caution, qualifying their answers, often long-winded, to the simplest of questions. By their demeanor—sticking to facts and refusing to speculate—they conveyed the impression of professionals untainted by White House politics. The president had taken to calling Petraeus every week, proclaiming that he was guided by "Dave's" advice. Petraeus was particularly careful not to make any remark that anyone could interpret as partisan. His colleagues said he voted for every office except the presidency.

With the full support of the president, Petraeus said the American forces would draw down from the peak surge level of 160,000 to around 140,000 by July. He would then make an assessment about further drawdown. Even with additional force reductions likely in the fall, the next president would take office in 2009 with well over 100,000 troops and 90,000 contractors in Iraq.

In essence, Bush's surge had extended through the last two years of his presidency. Viewed in a favorable light, his insistence on using all available ground forces and stretching the Army beyond sustainable deployment limits enabled the next president to withdraw forces with less risk. Less charitable critics argued that Bush was leaving the hard choices to his successor.

The press was eager to see how the presidential contenders would phrase their remarks. Although he had criticized the Bush administration's wartime leadership since 2003, McCain had firmly supported staying in Iraq, arguing that defeat would be devastating for America's security. He had urged that "Congress must not choose to lose in Iraq" by withdrawing troops prematurely.

Obama suggested that he would keep thousands of troops in Iraq indefinitely and not withdraw precipitously. "But if we had the current status quo, and yet our troops had been drawn down to 30,000, would we consider that a success?" Obama said. ". . . a messy, sloppy status quo but there's not, you know, huge outbreaks of violence, there's still corruption, but the country is struggling along, but it's not a threat to its neighbors and it's not an al Qaeda base, that seems to me an achievable goal within a measurable time frame. . . . Nobody's asking for a precipitous withdrawal."

Obama was later asked if, given the fact that his campaign manager said that the United States would be out of Iraq in sixteen months, he would make a "rock-hard pledge" to withdraw troops. "We are going to have our combat troops out," Obama replied. "We will not have permanent bases there." He offered thin praise of Petraeus, observing that the general had done "a good tactical job."

The hearings set the tone for the presidential election. The Democrats urged withdrawal because the war cost too much, the U.S. Army was stretched too thin, and the Iraqi government did not deserve more help. Hence the American military would pull out under circumstances and rhetoric that bespoke failure. The Republicans argued that a hasty pullout would be catastrophic, resulting in a larger, more costly war. President Bush, with an all-time low public approval rating of 27 percent, kept a low profile.

The rhetoric from each camp was intended to persuade voters who would choose between two candidates and two political philosophies. The Democrats were promising to walk away from Iraq. Yet foreign policy experts discounted the promise, suggesting it was made solely to gain votes. After all, campaign rhetoric rarely predicted presidential decisions.

At a meeting at Harvard, Richard Haass, the president of the Council on Foreign Relations, said he believed the next president of the United States would keep troops in Iraq. The consequences of a total pullout, he argued, would be too damaging for American interests. He drew a sharp distinction between the promises of electioneering and the reality of governing.

Appearing on *The NewsHour,* the columnist David Brooks made the same point. "I think the expectation among serious Democratic foreign policy experts," Brooks said, "is that we're going to have a lot of troops there for a long time, because if the costs of staying are high, the costs of leaving are prohibitive, and there will be a slow, gradual drawdown."

STANDING ON THEIR OWN

In May, the Iraqi high command designated the 3rd Brigade in Habbaniyah as the national Quick Reaction Force, to be moved anywhere to engage in combat. The brigade had fought in Ninewah, Anbar, and Diyala Provinces. In Diyala in early 2008, the brigade was partnered with the 2nd Battalion of the 3rd Armored Cavalry Regiment, led by Lt. Col. Paul Calvert. When fire support was needed, Calvert provided it via the advisers, especially Maj. Chuck McGregor.

The brigade was a seasoned outfit that displayed the potential and the problems of the army. The battalion at Combat Outpost O.K. Corral, advised by Maj. Tom Ziegler and then Lt. Col. Thomas Hobbs, illustrated those problems. The generator for air-conditioning the barracks was set up near the main highway. Within a week, wires were running to nearby houses, and some jundis sold power while the barracks remained stifling. Alex, the advisers' interpreter, noticed that the Humvee guarding the electric power repair truck consistently returned late in the day. Suspicious, he followed the Humvee and snapped pictures of jundis cutting down the electric cable after the repair truck left. The cable was then sold in town, with the jundis and repair crew splitting the proceeds. Furious at being exposed, the jundis donned stolen Marine uniforms and stood at a checkpoint, harassing the women and speaking a little English slang as well as Arabic. Outraged townspeople then demanded that the advisers fire Alex and the other interpreters.

One Iraqi officer consistently found IEDs in unlikely places, receiving commendations and rewards. Another faked reports on patrol routes in order to avoid bad areas, while a third found a weapons cache, turned in some weapons, and left the rest to be "rediscovered" when the next set of advisers rolled in. When advisers believed an Iraqi officer was a "good fighter," they were more apt to overlook his small-time scams. Any Russian-made Dragunov sniper rifle was sold to the JAM. When terrorists were shot, their pockets were emptied in seconds. The battalion commander fined some jundis and sent others home on extended leave, pocketing the difference from their full month's pay.

Hobbs patiently collected evidence and raided the barracks at midnight, arresting three officers. There was an uproar the next morning, but Hobbs held his ground and passed out copies of photos and payroll records. One officer did jail time, one ran away, and the third, a lieutenant colonel, was transferred but kept his rank. The jundis and honest officers held Hobbs in high regard because he tried to clean out the stables, and he succeeded to some degree.

Alex had served with four Iraqi battalions. He estimated that in a good battalion perhaps three of the dozen officers with the rank of captain or above were dirty, taking pay from the jundis, stealing, shaking down the locals, or selling weapons, fuel, or power. Even a powerful commanding officer was loath to investigate those who were corrupt. Collecting proof was hard, and no one worked alone. Because you didn't know who was in on what scam, being dismissed from the army without apparent cause was one concern. And since everyone went on leave in civilian clothes for weeks at a time, the threat of assassination was another concern. In such conditions, it was the advisers who acted as the unit's conscience to prevent egregious corruption.

This description of petty thefts and scams, of course, fit the armies in a hundred countries. The issue was how to know when corruption undercut battlefield performance. The U.S. military had no clear standards stipulating when advisers were to act as the guardians of ethical behavior. Once a unit seemed capable of fighting, the advisers were withdrawn.

After fighting in Diyala in late winter of 2008, the 3rd Brigade was sent to Baghdad—without its advisers. An adviser told me in an e-mail, "The Iraqis are thrilled to get rid of us pesky Americans, and reluctant to fight without us." In early June, the brigade moved into Sadr City. Sadr's movement was far from crushed, but it now confronted improved Iraqi battalions, backed by American firepower. When Sadr City quieted down, the 3rd Brigade was sent to Mosul.

The story of the 3rd Brigade illustrated a prudent way of withdrawing U.S. forces. The advisers were pulled out once the brigade seemed competent. Two battalions were sent into a violent area. The third took up a position outside a quiet town to provide a Quick Reaction Force for the police. This created, of course, a natural tension between the Iraqi Army commander and the police chief over wasta, or influence. Pride, prestige, and resources were at stake. Both the police chief and the army commander had to take care of their followers.

For years, American colonels like McFarland and Nicholson had been the shock absorbers that buffered such clashing interests and extracted resources like fuel and pay from sclerotic Baghdad ministries. As the American advisers and combat units moved back to remote bases, the Iraqis would have to work out their differences on their own.

The high-level Iraqi leadership certainly wanted fewer pesky Americans. By the summer of 2008, Maliki, safe in the Green Zone, had re-

gained his exaggerated sense of power and his sectarian advisers were
once again lobbying for a Status of Forces agreement that would give
the erratic government of Iraq too much control over U.S. forces. Grat-
itude and humility weren't characteristics of the government. Such
diplomatic wrangling, though, was normal among nations.

The singular accomplishment in 2008 was victory on the battlefield.
In a remarkable turnaround since 2006, violence and casualties had
plummeted by the summer of 2008. Al Qaeda in Iraq was being hunted
down. The Iraqi Army was in the lead, with American forces pulling
back into a support role. The steadfastness of soldiers like Adgie and
marines like Zembiec had brought stability to Iraq.

Doug Zembiec had a manic grin, as if he wanted to spring up and grab
you in a bear hug, maybe breaking a rib by accident, just for the sheer
hell of it. "I'm never so alive," he told me, "as in a firefight. Time slows
down for me. I can see it all, sense what they're going to do next."
Doug Zembiec, full of life and energy.

Lt. Col. Ken Adgie shared Doug's infectious love of the rough life.
When Ken, big as a tank in his armor and Kevlar, dragged me into the
local "Wal-Mart" in Arab Jabour, he couldn't have been prouder. He
clapped the proprietor on the shoulder and gestured expansively at the
shovels, toothpaste, toilet paper, cooking oil, and coloring books. Donald Trump showed off gold-plated faucets in Trump Tower; Ken Adgie
beamed about plastic showerheads in Arab Jabour.

In 2004, Doug showed me his snipers; in 2008, Ken showed me a
grocery store. I have an image of the two of them striding down Arab
Jabour's hardtop road beside the Tigris, arguing about where to put in
the streetlights and how to hook up speakers to pipe Springsteen into
the market. Their corporals break in, pleading for sensible sounds like
Guns N' Roses. Back at the combat outpost, the Bird Dogs grab their
cell phones to make a pitch for their favorite music. Brigadier General
Mustafa breaks in from the Ops Center to report that a nearby hamlet
is taking harassing fire. Zembiec hustles off with the Quick Reaction
Force, while Adgie allows that he'll wait for the gun truck. Why run
with a rifle when you can drive with a .50-cal?

Adgie and Zembiec, the warrior kings.

TWENTY-FIVE

THE STRONGEST TRIBE

2009

During the fierce battle for Fallujah in 2004, an Iraqi colonel pointed at a Marine patrol and said, "Americans are the strongest tribe."

In this book, I have tried to explain why American soldiers so impressed the colonel. "I tell our soldiers," Odierno said to me, "that it's the hundred things they do at the tactical level that make strategic success." This book has described those tactical, human things within a framework for understanding the war. American society seems frivolous and soft, yet it produces the world's toughest warriors. American society is fickle, yet its warriors keep coming, year after year. Without encouragement from society, especially its elite, our warrior class—the Adgies and Zembiecs—selects itself.

By the fall of 2008, America's fighting role in Iraq had largely run its course. Petraeus was taking over at Central Command, while Odierno was returning to run a war he knew well. Although corruption pervaded the ministries and the police were widely incompetent, the Iraqi Army was progressing satisfactorily. Sadr's Shiite militia was on the defensive, harried by Iraqi rather than American forces. Al Qaeda had fled northward. The Marines had pulled back in Anbar, returning the former heartland of the Sunni resistance to local control.

From this narrative of five years of fighting, what can be learned about the American way of war? And what are the choices going forward?

Role of Commander in Chief. The president, advised by his National Security Council, determines war policy and approves strategy. In this war, President Bush presided more than decided, acting like the chairman of the board rather than the chief executive. He waited for his staff to produce consensus options. Once he selected an option, he considered his job done.

In President Bush's view of history, presidents and prime ministers determined the fates of their nations. The leaders decided and the people followed. The insurgency in Iraq was the opposite model. The will of the people—tribes, militias, and terrorists—shaped the course of the war. Officials at the top scrambled to respond to events at the bottom. High-level teleconferences between Baghdad and Washington had as much influence over the war as did television correspondents. An insurgency is a bottom-up war, impervious to the egos and theories stroked in the court of Washington.

While Bush exaggerated his own influence, he failed to understand that the Pentagon disagreed with his vision. U.S. forces entered the war with a doctrine of destroying an enemy force by decisive battle. They quickly shattered Saddam's regime. Defense Secretary Rumsfeld then insisted that the Pentagon be put in charge of Iraqi reconstruction, although he and his key generals opposed a long-term presence. "The American military," he said, "does not do nation building." Yet nation building was precisely what Bush and his energetic viceroy, Bremer, had undertaken.

The result was an incoherent strategy. In 2003, the Pentagon wanted to hand Iraq back to Iraqis, while the State Department wanted to leave Iraq in Bremer's hands. When weapons of mass destruction weren't found, Bush changed the war's rationale to liberation and democracy in Iraq. He wanted Iraq rebuilt and the insurgency quelled, requiring a long-term U.S. military involvement; Rumsfeld and the generals, on the other hand, sought a quick exit, letting Iraqis deal with insurgents.

From one year to the next, the administration lacked unity and consistency. Condoleezza Rice, as the national security adviser, glossed over the basic contradiction between the White House and the Pentagon in 2003 and 2004. Then, as secretary of state in 2005, she endorsed a military strategy of clear and hold, opposing the Pentagon strategy of standing up Iraqi forces and leaving. In late 2006, she again reversed course in favor of declaring victory and leaving—just as the Pentagon finally embraced the concept of clear and hold.

Bush, who criticized President Lyndon Johnson for meddling in military matters, believed a president should remain above the details of strategy. But when a war becomes of prime importance for the nation, a president must understand the details. During World War II, Roosevelt discussed strategy daily with the generals. Any number of sergeants, colonels, and generals could have told President Bush that the military strategy on the ground contradicted his policy goal.

Only by intense study and the cultivation of conflicting ideas can a president ride, if not channel, the inchoate currents called "the will of the people." Although the bully pulpit provides a president with a powerful tool to persuade the public, Bush took pride in being inarticulate. The president's first duty as commander-in-chief was to persuade the American people to support the war. Bush failed to do so.

NSC Process. Policy is supposed to direct the selection of a war-making strategy. That didn't happen during the Iraq War until President Bush decided on a surge in 2007. Washington existed inside its own bubble, showing no humility in the face of a fiendishly complex war. Until late 2006, the interagency process in Washington concocted policy theories that were disconnected from the military strategy actively being pursued. High-level policy discussions didn't influence insurgent actions. To his credit, Stephen Hadley infused discipline and focus into the NSC system and presented clear options.

The Secretary of Defense as Risk Manager. In wartime, a secretary of defense must decide what his chief role is. Robert McNamara was the worst secretary of defense because he didn't believe in the mission he was sending American soldiers to carry out in Vietnam. Melvin Laird as secretary of defense in the early 1970s skillfully extracted U.S. forces from Vietnam. James Schlesinger in the mid-1970s took on the role of moral leader, solicitous of the morale inside the services as Vietnam fell apart.

Before the Iraq War began, Rumsfeld sought to transform the services into an agile high-tech force, a role quite different from the plodding tasks of nation building. Once the war began, he relied on logic and hectoring, rather than direct orders to reach a unified point of view about quick withdrawal with the top generals.

"I was on about fifteen video teleconferences with Mr. Rumsfeld," said Maj. Gen. Timothy Donovan, Casey's chief of staff in Iraq. "He questioned everything. He really stressed numbers. He wanted to win the war with one bullet left in the magazine."

In substituting debating skills for in-depth study, Rumsfeld over-looked his role as risk manager. In the 1970s, Secretary Laird set up an analytical office to assess the military reports from Vietnam. Rumsfeld set up no such office. In addition, the chairman of the Joint Chiefs or the commander of the Central Command should have provided risk assessments independent of the coalition commander in Baghdad. Instead, the Pentagon had no risk manager from 2003 through 2006. Based on the campaign assessments coming directly from the coalition headquarters in Baghdad, Rumsfeld had no independent means of assessing risk and warning when things were going awry.

The president must have someone—either the chairman of the Joint Chiefs or the secretary of defense—who has the clear responsibility for assessing risk separate from the commander in the field. Robert Gates, the new secretary of defense, competently took on that role in 2007, demanding evaluations from the chairman of the Joint Chiefs, the Central Command, and the command in Baghdad. But Gates did not establish his own office of risk assessment. During war, a secretary of defense should have a small staff assigned permanently to provide continuity of follow-up, solicit outside judgments, and assess risk.

How the War Turned Around. In dealing with an insurgency, controlling the population is distinct from protecting the population. In 1921, the British did not protect the Irish population from the Irish Republican Army. In 1941, the Germans did not protect the population of France from the resistance movement. In 1951, the British forced the Chinese in Malaya to live inside hamlets surrounded by barbed wire. By the end of 2004, U.S. operations in Iraq had been rough enough to antagonize the Sunni population without imposing the draconian methods armies habitually employ to control a population.

In the spring of 2006, the coalition was losing on the two major fronts that accounted for most of the fighting. In Anbar to the west, al Qaeda controlled the population; in Baghdad to the east, Shiite death squads were driving out the Sunnis, while al Qaeda's suicide bombings continued.

Yet the conditions had already been set for a turnaround without precedent in combating an insurgency. In less than three years, two giant institutions steeped in 200 years of traditions—the Army and Marines—adopted new doctrines and turned around a losing war. This was equivalent to GE and Ford starting afresh in new business lines and turning a profit in three years.

The western front in Iraq turned first from the bottom up, due to partnerships between local leaders and U.S. battalions. Half a year later, the eastern front turned, due to strategic change at the top that enabled partnerships at the bottom.

Back in 2004, the Sunni tribes in the west had welcomed al Qaeda with its call to jihad. Though a small minority, AQI quickly dominated by ruthlessness. Anbar, according to conventional wisdom, would be the last province to be pacified, if ever.

The conventional wisdom didn't factor in that the Marines were sending the same battalions back to the same cities on seven-month tours. Over the years, the Americans and Iraqis grew to know one another, while Marine tactics improved. They persisted in small patrols as the population went through a cycle of opposing them (2004), resenting them (2005), and seeking their protection (2006) after experiencing al Qaeda's reign of terror.

The key to the turnaround on the western front was bottom-up partnership between local leaders and U.S. battalion commanders. The locals knew who were AQI; the Americans brought the hammer. The public face of the turnaround was Sheik Sattar, leader of the Sunni Awakening. His partner was Col. Sean McFarland. In Tal Afar, the partnership was between McMaster and Sheik Najim; in Haditha, between Tracy and police chief Farouk; in Qaim, between Alford and Sheik Kurdi; in Ramadi, between Jurney and police chief Salaam; and in Fallujah, between Mullen and police chief Faisal. By the fall of 2006, such local partnerships were springing up across the west.

The turnaround on the eastern front followed in 2007. The same bottom-up partnerships eventually emerged, shaped by three decisions at the top. First, President Bush sent 30,000 more troops, mainly to control Baghdad. Second, Odierno chose to deploy most of them in belts around the capital in order to crush al Qaeda countrywide. Third, inside Baghdad, Petraeus moved his soldiers off the large bases and into neighborhoods, especially along the fault lines where the Sunnis were being driven out or where al Qaeda was in control.

Petraeus was impressed that thousands of Sunnis were joining tribal units in Anbar, with many accepted into the police or the army. He authorized battalion commanders across Iraq to recruit similar irregular forces. By 2008, U.S. battalions were paying 90,000 Iraqis, mostly Sunnis, who had volunteered for neighborhood watch groups. Al Qaeda fled and Shiite death squad attacks greatly diminished. These bottom-up partnerships placed Americans in daily contact with local leaders who complained about poor services. In turn, the Americans pressured the government to respond to local needs.

In Shiite areas under militia control like Sadr City, the population didn't dare to accept American protection. Petraeus largely left those areas to Maliki to deal with. By mid-2008, Maliki was seriously trying to break the power of Sadr's militia.

In sum, on both the western and eastern fronts, bottom-up partnerships caused the war to turn around. The antecedent was a change in attitude of the Sunni population, which had experienced al Qaeda's whip hand.

Myth About the Lack of U.S. Troops. A lack of soldiers is frequently cited as the basic flaw after the invasion. This is mistaken. There were 140,000 soldiers, plus 100,000 contractors in support roles, in Iraq in 2003. Adding troops would not have accomplished much because the two-headed command of Bremer and the inept Lieutenant General Sanchez lacked a plan, a counterinsurgency doctrine, and proper training. With the Pentagon's agreement, Bremer had disbanded the Iraqi Army, and the Iraqi police were ineffective. More American troops operating alone under a doctrine of attack and destroy would have exacerbated the rebellion.

Sovereignty Took Away Critical Leverage. The Marine Corps *Small Wars Manual,* based on decades of combating insurgencies, stressed the selection of competent combat leaders in the host nation. That central lesson was not heeded in Iraq. When sovereignty was handed back in 2004, the coalition did not insist upon a role in promoting or firing Iraqi commanders. As a result, sectarian and incompetent Iraqi leaders prolonged the war. President Bush conflated sovereignty with sanctity, refusing to interfere in supposedly Iraqi affairs. But a nation incapable of defending against internal threats is not truly sovereign. As long as the coalition remained responsible for Iraq's security, it had a legitimate right to sanction incompetent or malign Iraqi security leaders. That did not happen on a large enough scale.

Was a Faster Turnaround Possible? In 2003, an Afghanistan-type loya jirga, including Sunni tribal leaders, was recommended by Rumsfeld and by the field. Bremer and the State Department spiked the idea. We'll never know whether power sharing among Iraq's tribes and factions under a strong leader, backed by 170,000 coalition solders, would have nullified the insurgency and prevented the growth of al Qaeda.

After that, it was doubtful that the United States could have won over the Sunnis. "The Sunnis needed to go through pain," Maj. Ed Sullivan, an Arabic-speaking intelligence officer, concluded after two tours in Anbar. "The best way to extinguish a jihadist revolution is to experience it."

It took two years of al Qaeda dominance, from mid-2004 to mid-2006, for the Sunnis to gain trust in the Americans and hatred toward the extremists. "We Sunnis," Sheik Sattar said, "had to convince ourselves."

Inapt Imposition of Western "Rule of Law." Morality does not change, but governments frequently change the rules of war. In Iraq, the *Counterinsurgency Field Manual* stated that a key goal was establishing the rule of law, to include "a government that derives its powers from the governed, sustainable security institutions and fundamental human rights." That mission was beyond the skill set of soldiers and did not match the conditions on the ground. On the one hand, Iraq, as a sovereign nation racked by corruption, did what it pleased. On the other hand, American soldiers had to act as arresting officers subject to strict rules of evidence, while Iraqi judges, U.S. review boards, and the Iraqi National Assembly flouted the rule of law and let prisoners go whenever it suited them.

Eight out of ten insurgents sent to prison were released within ten months. The high command claimed that only between 1 and 9 percent of those sent to jail were ever rearrested. That statistic alone was proof of terrible police work, given that the rate of violent crime—murder, kidnapping, robbery—in Iraq was staggering. An insistence upon the liberal American rule of law resulted in a catch-and-release cycle that prolonged the war and angered the troops. Imprisoning insurgents for less than a year in the course of a multi-year insurgency did not make sense.

Advisers: An Uncertain Past and Future. From the start, the role of advisers in Iraq was ill defined. In Vietnam, advisers were valued because they were the link to fire support. In Iraq, fights requiring fire support were rare. Some adviser teams improved Iraqi staff planning functions, while others set the combat leadership example by daily circulation on the battlefield.

The aggressiveness of adviser teams varied broadly because there was no shared standard about their proper role. In late 2006, the Iraq Study

Group recommended replacing U.S. brigades with a corps of advisers embedded in Iraqi units and supported by U.S. firepower. Since that was the road not taken, the Iraq War provides few clues as to whether advisers with indigenous troops can substitute for U.S. conventional units, assuming the advisers have a role in deciding promotions.

The U.S. command does not envision advisers remaining with Iraqi units. As U.S. combat units pull back, so will the advisers. The absence of advisers runs the risk that deterioration may creep in from the bottom up—fewer arrests, fewer patrols, taxing drivers at checkpoints, and so on. But with the war winding down, Iraqi officials do not want the daily presence of pesky Americans. As a result of the removal of advisers from the level where the insurgency is fought, the risk of American casualties will decrease, as will the supervision that limits corruption, inspires aggressive operations, and provides a warning when conditions are falling apart.

Iraqis marvel at men like Hobbs who stride into IED-infested areas without blinking and raise holy hell when they catch anyone stealing or abusing civilians or jundis. The physical and moral fortitude of a protean adviser impresses hundreds of Iraqis and sets a standard they seek to emulate. It would be a grave mistake to pull out the advisers too early.

Interpreters Neglected. The Bush administration, to its shame, erected a maze of wickets that prevented interpreters who risked their lives for America from obtaining visas. U.S. officers resorted to running underground railroads to aid their interpreters. This was a disgrace that went uncorrected.

New Tactics. Most of the time, American soldiers weren't out on the streets. Protecting the force resulted in larger—and many fewer—patrols per battalion than was the case in Vietnam. With each soldier wearing eighty pounds of armor and gear, patrols were of short duration. For several years, the battalions lacked an agreed-upon template of operational procedures for counterinsurgency. This led to a marked variation in tactics and operating tempo, even in the same sector.

By late 2006, though, a standard technique was applied in urban areas. Cities were divided into bite-sized chunks. Neighborhoods were walled off to exclude strangers and prevent car bombs. "The way to leave is to stabilize the situation in each area," Petraeus said, "and each will require a slightly different solution—in some cases, literally using cement T-walls to secure the neighborhoods." Although they restricted commerce, the "gated communities" worked, with loudspeakers the best means of communicating immediately to the local people. Tips from the locals provided the chief means of finding insurgents.

The rural areas could not be walled off. They were pacified only when the tribes, emboldened by the strength of the pack, turned against the insurgents. No technique emerged to prevent the insurgents from routinely using Iraq's excellent network of highways.

The U.S. Military as Police. Although the American military adapted counterinsurgency methods, it erratically applied the techniques appropriate to a police-style war. Western armies lack the doctrine, training, and inclination to do police work. The problem in Iraq (and in Afghanistan) was that the nature of the combat demanded police skills on a scale that the police program run by the State Department could not handle.

"Counterinsurgency is a police war," Maj. Rory Quinn wrote in 2007, summarizing two tours as a company commander. "We don't like thinking of ourselves as police, but the system has to change if we are going to succeed in the long term. A company commander has to become an expert on police techniques. That's the only way to combat the flawed strategic policies we operate under, like catch-and-release. Start your own database immediately, with maps hyperlinked." The fact that company commanders like Quinn write to advise other company commanders indicates a gap in military training.

Insurgent cells were like Mafia gangs. Thrust into communities without local police willing to identify the gang members, American and Iraqi battalions seldom engaged in firefights and made few arrests compared to police in the States. "Winning Iraq is what cops do," Lt. Col. Norm Cooling, who brought police chief Farouk back to Haditha, told me. "The Iraqi Army wasn't any better than us at sorting out the locals."

Due to congressional restrictions and bureaucratic resistance, it wasn't until 2006 that the U.S. military turned serious attention to the Iraqi police. In 2008, U.S. and Iraqi forces together were holding in prison about 40,000 insurgents and criminals. Given the level of violence in Iraq, there should have been twice that number. Too many killers in Iraq were walking free because Iraq had no credible system of justice and because from the beginning U.S. strategy did not define Iraq as a police war and align resources accordingly.

The Greatest Technical Failure. The greatest technical failure in the police war was the inability to identify the male population. Even the arch-terrorist Zarqawi was stopped and let go because he was not identified. The Pentagon adapted electronic intelligence and armor to greatly lessen the IED threat. The Pentagon, however, did not grasp what the company commanders understood: Counterinsurgency was the process of separating the insurgents from the population. This required determining the identification and address of each male—commonly called a census. Every serious study of insurgencies has stressed the need to identify the male population and to conduct a census. Hundreds of company commanders designed their own databases and conducted local censuses. But the top level never grasped the importance and tied together the local efforts.

The Pentagon failed to apply its knowledge base to overcome the insurgents' central advantage of anonymity. The National Defense University wrote a devastating report about the failure, and the MITRE Corporation, a Pentagon think tank, suggested changes. But year after year, corporate and military special interest groups persuaded the generals that a census, to include fingerprints, of military-age males was impossible, even though most Iraqi males were stopped twice a year for identification checks. In Vietnam, it took two years to conduct a census that greatly restricted Viet Cong agents' movement among the hamlets. In Iraq, a census was rejected because, as a four-star general told me in 2005, "a census could take two years."

A hybrid biometric device to take fingerprints was used in 2008 at the company level. The Pentagon, however, did not develop handheld devices that enabled the squads to send in prints and receive back a report, as police do in cities in the States. The concept of Web sites like Megan's Law on Google, which showed the locations of convicted child molesters, was never applied to the battlefield. The military fought a police war without the basic police tool of fingerprints, let alone databases linking pictures of individuals to their addresses.

Insurgents and death-squad militia members walked right by our troops every day. The U.S. military needed a technical means of identifying enemies at the level where the fighting occurred. Every squad must be equipped with a handheld fingerprint device linked to a master database.

Excellent Logistics Support. Support was superb from both U.S. soldiers and contractors, most of whom were not American. Congress was generous in its appropriations, despite partisan bitterness. Fixed-wing and helicopter support in night operations was continuous, despite the dust and high winds. Unmanned aerial vehicles provided terrific video coverage. Attack helicopters accounted for a surprisingly high percentage of enemy kills and made emplacing IEDs on the highways a hazardous occupation.

Special Operations Forces. SOF tracked down al Qaeda and Shiite special group leaders, combining tips from informants like the Bird Dogs in Arab Jabour with electronic intelligence and helicopter lift. Though they constituted less than 10 percent of the coalition force, SOF accounted for about 70 percent of the killings and arrests of senior terrorists and special group members.

Economic Development Without a Plan. The military developed a doctrine for counterinsurgency. No comparable doctrine guided the $21 billion in U.S. reconstruction expenditures. Iraq in 2007 received $60 billion from oil revenues, hoarding $20 billion while U.S. tax dollars were spent. The United States lacked a sensible economic strategy for Iraq.

American Society Divided. While the American military was adapting, American society was disconnecting from its martial values. Lessons from each war affect expectations about the next. The literary historian Paul Fussell observed that the "cautious use of infantry only after elaborate air and artillery bombardments" in World War II was a reaction to the deadly frontal assaults during World War I. The word "cautious" would surprise many World War II veterans. In the last year of the war in Europe alone, the U.S. Army sustained 760,000 casualties. But in World War I, the losses were much higher. In the Third Battle of Ypres, the British took 250,000 casualties. By war's end, England had lost 700,000 men, while France had lost 1.7 million and Germany 2 million.

Today we cannot imagine such losses, or even those of Vietnam, where we lost almost 60,000. Fatalities in Iraq were fourteen times lower than in Vietnam. The impact, though, of seeing the fresh young faces of the fallen on nightly television evoked anger and frustration. "Back in Washington, I think it is once a week," Senator Dianne Feinstein (D-CA) wrote in *The Atlantic*, "they run the photographs of the American men and women killed in action. . . . And at some point you say, 'Enough is enough.' "

The nation was more caring of the wounded than in any prior war. By some estimates, one in five soldiers returning from Iraq needed treatment for post-traumatic stress disorder. After World War II, treatment and payments for tens of millions with psychological as well as physical wounds would not have been possible. The American public holds an unrealistic expectation that the next war will be fought with few fatalities and with extraordinary health care. And if the focus of the press is as intense in showing each casualty, maintaining support for the war will be difficult.

The martial values of our society have deteriorated. During World War II, the press scarcely mentioned and never photographed the dozens of public hangings of American soldiers, and never mentioned the shootings of German civilians or captured prisoners. The press considered such stories to be out of bounds. In Iraq, the killings of civilians in Haditha, trumpeted as a massacre, received vastly more press attention than any valorous action in the war. The hue and cry was not motivated by a thirst for justice; when investigations exonerated most of the marines involved at Haditha, the press wrote little and said less.

In World War II, our nation highlighted courage and quietly accepted mistakes. Today, we highlight mistakes and quietly accept valor. On Iwo Jima in 1945, almost 6,000 Americans died, many more than in five years in Iraq. Iwo Jima was a strategic blunder. Today, the press and Congress would be apoplectic about such a blunder. Courage, Aristotle said, is the virtue that makes all other virtues possible. Geopolitical wisdom is admirable, but martial valor is essential to sustain a democracy. American society takes courage for granted, and the press ignores it. When we fight the next war, this attitude will poorly serve the nation. Will soldiers risk their lives if society ignores courage?

Instead of praising our own troops, we focused concern on how we treated our enemies. The 400 prisoners at Guantánamo received remarkable pro bono legal attention and lavish press coverage. "Elite political culture," CIA director Michael Hayden said, "seems to be squeezing, at least psychically, that operational space; . . . [the CIA's] legitimacy is being questioned by certain segments of the population." If the press and Congress extended to the prisoners in Iraq the same legal protections and front-page stories as are the case with Guantánamo, the military legal system would grind to a halt.

There were 400,000 prisoners of war in the States during World War II. Had they not been wearing uniforms, their cases would still be pending in state and civilian courts. An enemy who wears a uniform while fighting Americans is foolish. By wearing civilian clothes, he can hide among the population and, if detained, demand an array of civil rights beyond the capacity of the United States judicial system to administer.

In five years of war, the president asked for no sacrifice by the American people. "I think a lot of people are in this fight," Bush said. "I mean, they sacrifice peace of mind when they see the terrible images of violence on TV every night." Terrible images weren't sacrifice; instead, they turned viewers against the war, making it easy for politicians to repudiate their earlier votes authorizing the invasion. Without sharing in any sacrifice, the voters had scant stake in the war.

Conversely, there was no evidence that American society was willing to sacrifice, whether the issue be Iraq, Afghanistan, or anywhere else. As measured by casualties or costs in terms of the gross domestic product, Iraq was not a major war like Vietnam, let alone World War II. Society is disconnected from the military. Less than one in a hundred high school graduates serves in the infantry mentioned throughout this book. Three quarters of high school graduates do not meet the military physical or mental entry standards, while Ivy League graduates no longer feel an obligation to serve a tour in the military before getting on with their careers.

Although sacrifice on a national scale is not required for every conflict, a healthy society does not treat war as an extension of domestic political competition. Secretary of Defense Gates took the post at the Pentagon intent on bringing Democrats and Republicans together on Iraq, where he said steady progress was being made. Far from promoting reconciliation in the States, progress in Iraq increased the bitterness at home.

"I say to our soldiers," Odierno told me, " 'You're finishing it so it wasn't in vain for those who came before.' " Despite Odierno's sentiment, some politicians did insist the sacrifices were in vain. Senator Harry Reid's comment in 2006 that the "war is lost" disgraced America. Another senator cited polls questioning the military's support for the war. Had a poll reported low morale on the beaches of Normandy in June of 1944, would the Senate have voted to end the war?

National security cannot be sustained when domestic party affiliation and ideology determine the support for a war. Iraq was a symptom, not the cause, of the ideological polarization of American society.

The Endgame in Iraq. Believing Iraq possessed weapons of mass destruction, a majority in Congress authorized the president to use force. While that intelligence proved incorrect, America owes no apology for removing a murderous tyrant. At the grand strategy level, however, invading Iraq weakened America's resolve and strengthened Iran's confidence and regional influence. In this book, I have laid out failures and shortcomings. But you can't undo the past. As we look forward, the question is whether America quits in Iraq. In making that decision, four factors should be considered.

First, we're in Iraq for the sake of ourselves. A stable Iraq advances America's interests. American steadfastness evokes more respect from adversaries than does fecklessness. Reliable oil exports are preferable to a stunning price spike. Aligning with the Sunni tribes to crush al Qaeda in Iraq diminishes al Qaeda's global reputation and its recruiting appeal throughout the Islamic world.

In 2008, Iraq, though beset with problems, is on the road to stability. The American military, roundly criticized for its performance in the early years, deserved credit for a remarkable turnaround. The counterinsurgency strategy of Petraeus and Odierno worked. The Iraqi government was functioning better, and casualties had decreased.

Second, reducing the U.S. force in Iraq can be done prudently, as long as we don't promise a total withdrawal that signals America has given up. That makes no sense given the progress that has been made. The strain on the U.S. Army caused by repeated deployments eased when the surge strategy ended in the summer of 2008. "The risk of overextending the Army is real," Secretary Gates said. "But I believe the risk is far greater—to that institution, as well as to our country—if we were to fail in Iraq. That is the war we are in. That is the war we must win."

Maintaining, say, five brigades in Iraq at an annual cost of $12 billion would be sustainable. In Anbar, for instance, marines will remain in a few remote bases even when the province is handed over to Iraqi control. Similarly, the United States has thousands of troops in Kuwait, as well as in Germany, the Balkans, and South Korea.

The dollar costs of the war have been largely paid. The war has been expensive, but not exorbitant. The Congressional Budget Office estimated the five-year cost as $608 billion, less than one percent of GDP per year. The entire defense budget is 4 percent of GDP, far lower than in past decades. Defense consumed 12 percent of GDP during the Korean War, and 9 percent during Vietnam. It is the growth in entitlement programs, not defense spending, that imperils the next generation.

Third, an abrupt pullout may shatter Iraq. It is illogical to withdraw because the Iraqis are not united while assuring the public that withdrawing will cause the Iraqis to unite. Centrifugal forces can speedily gain momentum. Pledges made in the fever of a presidential campaign can turn Iraq into a self-fulfilling prophecy of failure. In April of 2004, Iraq almost lurched out of control. In 2008, the fighting in Basra provoked by Maliki's hasty decision quickly spread to Baghdad. In 1975, President Thieu ordered one division to pull back; in short order, South Vietnam fell apart.

Fearing abandonment, Maliki could issue an impetuous order with the same result. As chaos spread, American forces would pull out without dignity, while Iraqi oil exports would plummet and energy prices would skyrocket. Al Qaeda would seize West Mosul. With the world watching America's humiliation, it's doubtful that the next president would respond by bombing an Iraqi city.

Fourth, if Iraq held together in the face of a total pullout, it would resent America for having given up. It is not reasonable to assume increased cooperation from Muslim states following a swift and total pullout. Instead, Iraq and the other countries in the region will expect Iran to replace America and respond accordingly.

America controls how Iraq ends. The endgame can occur with a total pullout. Vietnam ended in 1975 when the last helicopter flew out of Saigon, leaving behind a panic-stricken mob. If Iraqis believe America is abandoning them, they will fall apart. Or the endgame can occur when the press places Iraq next to Afghanistan on the back pages. If Iraqis believe America is standing by them, they will hold together and violence will abate.

Some American forces will be needed for years, in steadily decreasing numbers. But Americans cannot be sheltered from combat. Iraq is a small-unit war where the brief firefights reflect tribal and gang rituals for establishing dominance rather than war to the death. After six years observing the dynamics on the streets, I am convinced that a few stalwart Americans like Hobbs make a huge difference as they circulate around the battlefield.

Wars turn on confidence. Iraqis—soldiers, police, and citizens—want to believe Americans will aid them in extremis. Gradually that feeling will diminish. To use Petraeus's phrase, the definition of victory is "sustainable security that the Iraqis can take over by themselves."

Both Democrats and Republicans agree on withdrawal, but follow different paths. One party advocates a pullout based on conditions as judged by the military commanders. The other promises a pullout of all combat units in sixteen months, regardless of military judgment. Every American brigade commander knows the score in his area. To order all brigades to withdraw without asking their evaluation of risk would be reckless and unworthy of the president of the United States. Avoidance of catastrophe in Iraq is a national security objective.

Beyond Iraq. Decades from now, historians will point out how Petraeus saved Baghdad. More important, they should describe the sturdiness of marines like Zembiec and soldiers like Adgie, trudging along under suffocating heat, ready to shoot any attacker or to aid any civilian. The poet W. H. Auden wrote, "Teach the free man how to praise." In that vein, what deserves our fulsome praise is the steadfastness and decency of the American soldiers.

It is clear why the Iraqi colonel called our warriors the strongest tribe. They were unified in battle and took care of one another. This book has recounted many frustrating situations that mocked the strategic mission. At such times, the members of a squad have to dig down, hold on to one another, and fight on, while cursing the stupidity or futility. Wars are strewn with blunders. Mistakes are not a reason to abandon the mission.

While the American military adapted to overcome mistakes, American society became more divisive. As Rome and Athens demonstrated two thousand years ago, every military, no matter how strong its internal code, eventually mirrors its society. Society was not unified in supporting the battle in Iraq. It was easy to decry the Bush administration with all its faults. It is less easy to question whether our society retains sufficient unity to be the world's strongest tribe. We can dodge the question by protesting that the notion of tribe is archaic, or that diplomacy, economics, goodwill, and the like constitute national strength. In the end, though, America will again be tested by force of arms under circumstances as ambiguous as those in Iraq.

The burden and pain of Iraq were borne by only a few, like Jim and Maria Simpson, who lost their son Abe, and Abe's best friend and cousin, Jonathan. Both died fighting in the Habbaniyah-Fallujah corridor.

"Just a few families stepped forward," Jim Simpson told me. "I think we're losing the sense of being a nation."

Losing the sense of being a nation should concern us all. We fought the war in Iraq as a nation divided. If we are as divided in the next war, we will be defeated. No nation can sustain its values by claiming to support the soldier while opposing his mission. The truth is that the nation determines the mission.

ACKNOWLEDGMENTS

In Iraq, correspondents are routinely invited into the operations centers and into briefings. The ground rule is simple: Don't write anything that endangers the soldiers or the operations. While I received my share of phone calls and e-mails when I wrote something that angered generals, our disagreements were professional rather than personal. In the field, the U.S. military is confident in the mission and in the decency of its actions.

As in many bureaucracies, there was less openness farther from the front lines. To put it bluntly, official records were guarded by the bureaucratic instinct to hoard. Asking Central Command and historical divisions in the States for simple things like information on the disposition of forces and major operations in the war was an exercise in frustration. A major reason was that the computer net was secret, automatically marking most documents secret. To the historian's dismay, it will take an army of clerks years to wade through and declassify millions of documents now reposing somewhere in ether space.

Special thanks go to Betsy West, my wife and editor-at-large; Will Murphy, my editor at Random House; and Dan Mandel, my agent at Sanford Greenberger. Also at Random House, Steve Messina and Courtney Turco turned the thousand edits from Betsy and Will into book form.

We are all shaped by the example of others. I would like to acknowledge Dr. Francis West, Lt. Thomas Boland, Friar William Boland, Lt. Walter West, James Schlesinger, Lt. Gen. John Chaisson, Sgt. Hugh D. "Yusha" Auchincloss, Maj. Gen. Ray Smith, CIA field officers Rudolph Enders and R. Campbell James, Capt. Henry H. Anderson, Jr., Lt. Tyler "Toby" Field II, Lt. Jonathan Pardee, RADM Dennis McCoy, Seaman 1st Class John Hall, Col. Ted Gatchel, VADM Thomas Weschler, and Admiral James Hogg—warriors of firm mien.

Because an insurgency by its nature grows from the bottom up, to describe it you must work at the bottom. No one can spend time with American soldiers on the lines without appreciating their cocky spirit, camaraderie, and adaptability. For six years, I have benefited from the hospitality, openness, and guardianship of hundreds of marines, soldiers, and police, American and Iraqi. What struck me as I returned to the same places was how our soldiers learned, and how the Iraqis learned about us.

IN APPRECIATION

Lt. Col. Mohamed Abas
Brig. Gen. Abbas
Col. Abbas
Lt. Col. Salaam Abbas
Brig. Gen. Abdul
Ali Muhamed Abdul
Kais Abdullah
Capt. Muhamed Abdullah
Lt. Gen. Abedi
Lt. Col. Josslyn Aberle
Abdul Abid
Adel Abouhan
Abdel Abouhana
Brig. Gen. Robert B. Abrams
Sheik Abdul Sattar Abu Risha
Sheik Ahmed Abu Risha
Col. Tony Acuri
Anwar Addas
Mr. Addel
Lt. Col. Kenneth Adgie
Maj. Gen. Abdul Afar
Col. John Ahern

Alex al Bayaa
Fouad al Bazi
Salam al Hadi
Maj. Kais al Haidori
Mario al Sadria
Brig. Gen. Robert Alardice
Allah Alarki
Dr. Adnan al-Asadi
Lt. Col. Rafea Alawani
Col. Alexander Alderson
Mazin Al-Eshaiker
"Alex"
Lt. Col. Brian Alexander
Lt. Col. Ali
Capt. Allahs
Brig. Gen. John Allen
Craig Alley
Sheik Hamid al-Mhana
Bassim Altaee
Lt. Yarub Altawee
Sgt. Maj. Joseph Altman
Sheik Dhari al-Zobaie

Col. Dan Amaya

Capt. Tim Anderson

CSM Jesse Andrews

Chris Andros

Andy from Beirut

Capt. Jeremy Anzevino

Rayson Arashidi

Capt. Siddahartha Arias

Capt. Mike Armsted

Capt. William Arnold

Capt. Jason Arthand

Bruce Ashe

Brig. Gen. Assam

Gunnery Sgt. Kevin Austin

Mayor Sa'ad Awad

Brig. Gen. Ayad

Sheik Hamid Aymen

Vincent Azzarelli

Col. Donald Bacon

Maj. Bahub

Sgt. Sean Baker

Lt. Col. Robert Balcavage

SSgt. Brian Bandini

Lt. Col. Keith Barclay

Capt. Max Barela

Capt. Ty Barger

SSgt. Anthony Barnes

Sgt. Kody Barnes

Sgt. Maj. Michael Barrett

Cpl. Robert Barrickman

LCpl. Alex Bartoli

Mr. Bassam

Col. Al Batschelet

Maj. Randy Baucom

Maj. Eric Baus

Lt. Col. Kenneth Beebe

Col. Michael Beech

Chris Beeson

Capt. Tyson Belanger

Col. Michael Bell

PFC Juan Beltran

Hassan Benkato

John Bennett

Maj. George Benson

Cpl. Abdil Bent

LCpl. Omare Beury

Stephen Biddle

Capt. Matt Biel

Lt. Col. James Bierman

Maj. Todd Birney

Sgt. Maj. Roger Blackwood

SSgt. Hubert Blevins

Lt. Devon Blowes

Brig. Gen. Dan Bolger

Cpl. William Boone

Max Boot

Spec. Jonathan Borgwing

LCpl. Kenneth Boss

Lt. Daniel Bourke

Capt. Richard Bowen

Capt. David Bowers

Col. Steven Boylan

Brad from Special Ops

Ahmed Brahim

SSgt. David Brandgaro

PFC Nicholas Brudevold

Lt. David Brunais

SSgt. Anthony Bryant

SSgt. Kevin Buckley

Sgt. Lyle R. Buehler

Capt. Jeffrey Burroughs

Col. J. B. Burton

Maj. Ben Busch

SFC James Butler

SFC Jerry Byrd

Capt. Pat Byrne

Tom Calabro

Lt. Gen. William Caldwell IV

Maj. Luke Calhoun

Col. Michael Callaghan

PFC Brian Callahan

Maj. Brann Calvetti

Dr. Joseph Campbell
Saasdon Cardon
Brig. Gen. Edward Cardon
Capt. Sam Cartee
Capt. Philip Carter
1st Sgt. Tracy Cartwright
Gen. George Casey
Sgt. Warren Cash
Maj. Chris Cassibry
Col. Tom Cathy
LCpl. Corey Catizera
Cpl. Anthony Celano
Col. John Charlton
Lt. Col. M. P. Cheme
Lt. Gen. Peter Chiarelli
Chico in Salman Pak
Sgt. Maj. Neil Ciotola
Col. H. S. Clardy
SSgt. Vincent Clinard
Col. Bob Coates
Maj. Adam Cobb
Prof. Eliot Cohen
CWO Scott Colburn
Alex Connors
PFC Frank Contreras
Capt. Warren Cook
Lt. Col. Norm Cooling
Cpl. Michael Cortez
SFC Edward Cote
Col. Scott Cotrell
Cpl. Dennis Couture
Sgt. Maj. Eric Crabtree
Cpl. David Cracker
Conrad Crane
LCpl. Richard Crane
Rich Crawford
Lt. Col. James Crider
J. D. Crouch
Col. Blake Crowe
Christopher Crowley
Sgt. Vincent Cruz

Maj. John Cushing
Dahm from Salman Pak
Maj. Gary Dangerfield
Sgt. Joseph Daniels
Dar from Special Ops
Col. William Darley
Dave from Baghdad
Maj. Bo Davenport
David "Slim"
SSgt. Nicholas Day
Lt. Col. Todd DesGrossiers
Maj. Luis Del Valle
Capt. Andrew DelGaudio
Lt. Gen. Martin Dempsey
Lt. Col. Ron Dennard
Capt. Bo Dennis
Maj. Jeff Dennis
Lt. Raymond Derek
Col. P. J. Dermer
Kathleen Devine
Sheik Dhari
Maj. Kevin Digman
Lt. Col. Jeffrey J. Dill
Lt. Col. Donald Dinger
Col. Alessandro Dochnal
Lt. Col. James Donnellan
Maj. Chris Dowling
Gen. Wayne Downing
Lt. Phil Downs
Col. Dennis Doyle
Lt. Gen. James Dubik
1st Sgt. John Dudas
Maj. Doug Dudgeon
SSgt. Dale Dukes
Lt. Andrew Duncan
Lt. Gen. Joseph Dunford
Sgt. Michael Dunn
Lt. Col. Brian Durant
Lt. Cassidy Eaves
Capt. "Eba"
Lt. Barry Edwards

Maj. Brian Ellis
LCpl. Christopher Erbe
Maj. Steven Espinoza
"ET"
Master Sgt. Gary Evan
Sgt. Jason Fabrizi
Col. Abbas Fadhil
Darawam Faris
SSgt. Adam Farmer
Maj. Abdul Farouk
Maj. Gen. Fastabend
Chief Feisal
Maj. Tom Feltey
Lt. Col. Howard Feng
Col. Terry Ferrell
Sgt. Derek Fetterolf
"Fouad"
Mr. Fouad
Capt. Christian Franco
Frank from Dora
SSgt. Marquis Franklin
Col. Paul Funk
Lt. Luke Gaffney
Brig. Gen. Abdul Gainey
Capt. Brendan Gallagher
Col. Jerry Galloway
Col. (ret.) John Garrett
Cpl. Joseph Garrity
Maj. Gen. Walt Gaskin
SSgt. David Gauthier
LCpl. Brandon Gayle
Lt. Clint Gebke
Capt. Lester Gerber
Col. Nasir Ahmed Ghanam
Brig. Gen. Ali Ghazi
Col. Ricky Gibbs
LCpl. Brian Gibson
Capt. Brian Gilbert
Capt. Scott Gilman
Lt. Col. Ben Gipe
SFC Michael Glancy

Lt. Col. Kerrye Glass
Maj. Eric Glassie
Brig. Gen. Stephen Gledhill, U.K.
Lt. Jonathan Glover
Capt. Tom Goettke
SSgt. John Gonzales
Lt. Col. Barry Graham
Maj. Chris Graves
HM3 Jesse Gray
Dan Green
Col. Tom Greenwood
Capt. Leo Gregory
Theresa Grencik
LCpl. Amarinder Grewal
Capt. Nick Griffiths
Col. Wayne W. Grigsby
Maj. John Grimm
Brig. Gen. Will Grimsley
Lt. Col. Ben Gripe
Col. Gronski
LCpl. Justin Gross
Maj. Henry S. Groulx
PFC John Gunderson
Maj. Gen. Mark Gurganus
Lt. Nicholas Guyton
Mayor Abdul Hakim
Maj. Chris Hall
Col. Hamid
Sheik Hamid
Michael Hankey
Lt. Col. Jeff Hannon
Maj. Ala Harat
Col. Farouk Hardan
SSgt. Jeff Harilson
Cpl. Randall Harper
Sheik Talib Hasnawi
Col. Raad Ali Hassan
Brig. Gen. Baha Hassan
Capt. George Hassetine
LCpl. William Hawkins
SSgt. Robert Hays

Lt. Bobby Haywood
Capt. Clint Haywood
Col. Jim Henderson
1st Sgt. Kenneth J. Hendrix
Cpl. Sean Henry
Sgt. Jason Hermenau
Master Gunnery Sgt. Luis
   Hernandez
Maj. Gen. Mark P. Hertling
Pamela Hess
Maj. Woody Hessler
Hhado from Ghazaliyah
Col. Hickey
Col. William Hickman
Capt. Neil Hilderbrand
Sgt. Maj. Henry Hines
Sgt. Jeffrey Hitt
Lt. Col. Thomas Hobbs
CWO Wesley Hofferek
Maj. Christopher Hofstetter
Lt. Roger Hollenbeck
Col. Thomas Hollis
Cpl. Matthew Horn
Capt. John Horning
Maj. Stanley Horton
Sgt. Maj. David Howell
Capt. Michael Hudson
Brig. Gen. James Huggins
Col. Frank Hull
Zuhair Humadi
Maj. Robert Hunter
Col. Feisal Hussain
Farouk Hussein
Sheik Jai Ibrahim
Sheik Abdul Ikthar
Brig. Gen. Ishmael
Maj. Muhamed Jabar
LCpl. Patrick Jackson
Col. Mary Ellen Jaddick
Maj. Gen. Jamal
Col. Ali Jasam

Capt. Mohamed Jasim
Brig. Gen. Moutaa Habeeb Jassim
Lt. Ilah Jawal
HME Zach Jennings
Joe from Special Ops
SSgt. Johnson
Sgt. Brian Johnson
Gunnery Sgt. Eric Johnson
Tech Sgt. Julian Johnson
Cpl. Kenneth Johnson
Lt. Col. Mike Johnson
Maj. Rick Johnson
Sgt. Robert Johnson
Sgt. Robin Johnson
Capt. Court Jones
Lt. Col. Matt Jones
Maj. Gen. Michael Jones
Lt. Regan Jones
Joseph from Jordan
Capt. Kevin Joyce
Lt. Col. Bill Jurney
Capt. Khodar Juwad
Namk Nuri Kaleb
Azi Kalif
Brig. Gen. Mustafa Kamel
Brig. Gen. Falah Hassan Kanbar
Deputy Police Chief Kareem
Col. Abdul Kareem
Lt. Col. Karousal
Howard Keegan
Maj. John Kelley
Lt. Donovan Kelly
Capt. Eric Kelly
Sgt. Maj. Kent
LCpl. Luke Kern
Lt. Benjamin Kesling
Cpl. Michael Kessler
Brig. Gen. Khalid
Sammy Basam Khazivya
Salam Kiasvbien
David Kilcullen

Capt. Andrew Kirby
Chris Kirchoff
Cpl. William Kittell
1st Sgt. Kenneth Klinger
Capt. Wesley Knick
Gunnery Sgt. James M. Knuckles
SSgt. Ryan Kohrig
Sgt. Joseph Kolniak
MM2 Louis Kost
Capt. Nick Kron
Lt. Col. Dale Kuehl
Lt. Col. Christopher Landro
Maj. Jason Lange
Cdr. Jon Lazar
Lt. Col. Paul Lebidine
Capt. Andrew Lee
1st Sgt. William Lefever
Sgt. Alexander Lemons
Maj. S. D. Leonard
Lt. Col. Joseph L'Etoile
Brig. Gen. Levin
Capt. William Lewis
Lt. Col. R. J. Lillibridge
1st Sgt. Robert Lillie
Lt. Jimmy Lindemann
Maj. Lippo
Capt. Mark Liston
Lt. Michael Lobach
Capt. Andrew Lockett
Col. Jon M. Lockey
Lt. Michael S. Loveless
Lt. Gen. Douglas Lute
William Luti
Col. Joe Lydon
Capt. Andrew Lynch
Maj. Gen. Rick Lynch
"Mac"
Lt. Col. James MacVarish
Maj. Toby Magsig
Capt. Todd Mahar
Col. Mahid

Governor Mahmoon
Col. Stephen Mains
Lt. Gen. Ali Qidaan Majeed
Col. Abdul Majid
Majid of Tuwaitha
Col. Malik
Prime Minister Nouri al-Maliki
Lt. Col. Robert Manion
Maj. Mike Manning
Jeff Manshaur
Col. Peter Mansoor
Lt. Keith Marifore
Tech Sgt. Franklin Marquis
Lt. Col. John Marr
Lt. Col. Gary Martel
Col. J. D. Martin
Capt. David Martino
Col. Mark Martins
Lt. Cdr. Buzz Mason
Lt. Col. Doug Mason
Spc. Gene Matson
Matthew from Karbala
Maj. Kevin Matthews
Gen. James Mattis
Col. Michael McBride
Col. Sean McBride
Capt. Tom McCaleb
Lt. Col. Robert McCarthy
Col. (ret.) Jeff McCausland
Capt. Reginald McClam
Maj. Megan McClung
Capt. Jeff McCormack
Col. Sean McFarland
Lt. Col. Brandon McGowan
Col. Paul McHale
SSgt. Scott McLaughlin
Tech Sgt. Matthew McLead
Col. H. R. McMaster
Phil McNulty
Lt. Col. Jim McVarish
Gunnery Sgt. Andre Meade

Capt. Tim Meadors

Lt. John T. Meixner

Lt. Col. Robert Menti

Lt. Cdr. Chris Merwin

Sgt. Matthew Merz

Col. Clark Metz

Maj. Pat Michaelis

Sgt. Serge Michaud

Mikey from Baghdad

Col. George F. Milburn

Lt. Jason Miller

Maj. John Miller

Lt. Col. Monica Miller

Capt. Sean Miller

Sheik Mishen

Lt. Col. Steven Miska

Capt. Dustin Mitchell

Maj. William G. Mitchell

Lt. Michael Mixon

Capt. Casey Moes

Maj. John Moloko

LCpl. Eric Montanez

LCpl. Robert A. Montgomery

Sgt. James Moore

Sgt. Maj. Mark Moore

SSgt. Matthew Moore

Cpl. Michael Moore

Maj. Tom Moore

SSgt. Robert S. Morris

Ralph Morten

PFC Michael Moses

Capt. Seth Moulton

Lt. Jon Mueller

Lt. Col. William Mullen

Maj. Michael Muller

John Mulligan

Jeff Mumshaur

Col. Munam

Col. Sam Mundy

Lt. Nicholas Murchinson

Maj. Tim Murphy

LCpl. Joshua Murray

Col. Murray

Maj. Gen. Murthi

Amar Dahan Nael

Lt. Col. Muhamed Nashmi

Nathan from Baghdad

Lt. Col. Lloyd Navarro

Lt. Col. Steven Neary

Lt. Col. Mike Negard

Brig. Gen. Robert Neller

Chaplin Rob Nelson

Cpl. Michael Nemis

Maj. Edward Nevgloski

Col. Bob Newman

Lt. Newton

Col. Larry Nicholson

Brig. Gen. Niman

Cpl. Ian Norris

Col. John Norris

Brig. Gen. Robert Nutter

Col. Robert Oates

Sheik Ahmed Obeidi

Lt. John O'Brien

Col. Brian O'Connor

Lt. Gen. Raymond Odierno

LCpl. Joshua Oldman

Col. Mark A. Olsen

Maj. Gen. (ret.) Rick Olson

Cpl. Randy Ortiz

LCpl. Joseph Osborn

Meghan O'Sullivan

Maj. Clay Padgett

Sgt. Steven Palmer

Sgt. Dean Paris

Col. Issmi Parrulli

Capt. Travis Partiquin

Col. Dave Paschal

Lt. William Patrick

Capt. Scott Patton

Sgt. Maj. James M. Pearson

LCpl. David Pelaez

Lt. Col. Bob Peller
SSgt. Nicholas Pelter
Lt. Ian Peoples
Capt. Giovanni Perez
Maj. Brad Permella
Dr. Rasheed Perry
Maj. Lee Peters
Capt. Eric Peterson
Maj. Gen. Joseph Peterson
Gen. David Petraeus
Brig. Gen. Dave Phillips
Lt. Col. Jimmy Phillips
Capt. David Pine
Maj. John Piroq
Brig. Gen. Dan Pittard
Col. John Pollock
Maj. Gen. Alessandro Pompegnani
Maj. Jeff Pool
Cpl. Benjamin Potts
LCpl. Benny P. Poybal
Brig. Gen. Douglas A. Pritt
Maj. Pat Proctor
Gen. Abdul Qadar
Sheik Jamal Ra'ad
Capt. Nsir Abdul Raad
Col. Jim Rainey
Sgt. Teodoro Ramos
Col. Bill Rapp
Fadil Rasheed
Gov. Mamoon Sami Rashid
Maj. Joel Rayburn
Lt. Col. John Reeves
Lt. Col. Sparky Renforth
John Reynolds
Lt. Col. Nick Reynolds
SSgt. Jason Richardson
LCpl. Adam Riddle
Capt. Jonathan Riggs
ILPO Jim Riley
Capt. Paul Robbins
Lt. Col. Andrew Roberto

Col. Pat Roberts
MG Mastin Robeson
Sgt. Rogelio Rodriguez
Maj. John Rogan
Lt. Col. Andy Rohling
Maj. Dan Rouse
Maj. William Rummel
Maj. Rich Russo
Maj. Wilson Rutherford
Col. Sean Ryan
Maj. Saeh
Maj. Gen. Abdul Salam
Dennis Salcedo
Cpl. Ismael Saldano
Brig. Gen. Saleh
Deputy Prime Minister Barham Salh
Lamil Salman
Sheik Ahmed Salmon
Maj. Rob Salome
Mr. Sam
Sam in Fallujah
Ambassador David Satterfield
Cpl. Aaron Sawyer
Chris Schaubelt
MSG Brian Schlatter
Hon. James R. Schlesinger
Lt. Eric Schneider
John Schnittker
PFC Richard Scott
SFC Robert L. Sepulveda
Maj. Todd Sermarini
Sgt. Sam Severtsgaard
Brig. Gen. Sha'aban
Marwan Shaalan
Capt. Ryan Shaffer
Oubai Shahbanvar
Capt. Ahmed Sharki
Maj. Shavan
Maj. Gen. Jonathan Shaw, U.K.
CWO Rex Shelton
Maj. Olaf Shibusawa

Maj. Gen. Hamad Showka
Lt. Rob Shuford
Lt. Col. Scott Shuster
Sgt. Ray Sifford
LCpl. Neil Silvestro
Col. Richard Simcock
Lt. Col. Michael Simmering
Spec. Joshua Simpson
Sgt. Kenneth Sineath
Khamis Sirhan
Lt. Andrew Skinner
Gunnery Sgt. Brandan Slattery
Gunnery Sgt. John Slattery
Capt. Kyle Sloan
Capt. Tom Sloan
Col. Smart
Chris Smith
Lt. Col. Eric Smith
Sgt. Matthew Smith
Lt. Nathan Smith
Maj. Niel Smith
Lt. Col. Jeff Smitherman
Lt. Col. Rob Smullen
James Soriano
Maj. Joseph Sowers
Lt. William Speicher
Capt. Matthew Stanley
Col. Martin Stanton
Capt. Michael Starz
Karen State
Maj. Charles St. Clair
Lt. Eric Steiner
Lt. Michael Stempead
Col. Phil Sternhagen
Maj. Eric Stetson
Lt. Col. Wendall Stevens
Pvt. Cody Stewart
Capt. Jay Stewart
LCpl. Nathan Stinnett
Maj. Gen. Doug Stone
Sgt. Michael Storey

Maj. Jarrod Stoutenborough
Capt. Cecil Strickland
LCpl. Matthew Sullivan
LCpl. William Sullivan
SSgt. Charles Summers
Maj. Jeff Sutherland
Tech. Sgt. Barron Swayer
Capt. Matt Swindle
Maj. Steve Sylvester
CWO2 Robert Tagliabue
Brig. Gen. Taha
Col. Talebe
Sheik Talib
Maj. Gen. Tariq
Capt. Bobby Taylor
LCpl. Paul Tdelle
Cpl. Ryan Thibodeau
Lt. Col. Dan Thoele
SSgt. Keith Thomas
Brig. Gen. Tony Thomas
SFC Christine Thompson
Capt. Harry Thompson
Capt. Richard Thompson
Sgt. Robert Thompson
Mark Tokola
SSgt. Stuart Toney
Capt. Gordon Toppey
Cpl. Paul Torocco
LCpl. Jose Torres
Lt. Jared Towles
Capt. Matt Tracy
SSgt. Lake Traut
Capt. Sean Troyer
Cpl. Frank Turco
Capt. Joseph Turgeon
Lt. Col. Roger Turner
Col. Stephen M. Twitty
Lt. John Urquhart
Lt. Col. Chuck Van Heusen
SSgt. Gordon Van Schoick
Lt. Col. John Velliquette

Maj. Bruce Vitor

Maj. Jason Vos

Maj. Tom Voytko

Capt. Nathaniel Waggoner

Brig. Gen. Hussein Wahed

Walid at Casino

CWO Terry Walker

SSgt. William Walker

Capt. Wallace

Maj. Richard Wallwork, U.K.

Lt. Jeremy Walter

Maj. Vaughn Ward

Maj. Steve Wargo

1st Sgt. Albert Washington

Col. Watson

Lt. Wazam

SSgt. John Wear

Maj. Eric Weis

Cpl. Tyler Weiser

Sgt. Devon Welcher

Maj. Owen West

Lyle Westin

Capt. Jody White

Sgt. Devon Wilcher

Lt. Col. Pete Wilhelm

Brig. Gen. Terry Wilks

Sgt. Aaron Willardson

Lt. Col. Willoughby

LCpl. Brian Wilson

Lt. Frank Wilson

Col. Marty Wilson

SSgt. Martyn Wilson

Capt. Sean Wilson

SSgt. Christopher Winship

Lt. Col. Brian Winski

Col. Jeff Witsken

Sgt. Ryan Wood

1st Sgt. Bobby Woolridge

Capt. Dave Wray

Rear Adm. Gar Wright

Maj. Steven Wright

Brig. Gen. James Yarbough

Cpl. Steven Yarra

Fareed Yasseen

Gunnery Sgt. Tim Ybay

Maj. Gen. Zahner

Maj. David Zappa

Capt. Doug Zembiec

Sgt. Gregory J. Zieba

Maj. Tom Ziegler

Maj. Gen. Richard Zilmer

Capt. Kevin Zimmerman

Sheik Dhari Zobaie

Capt. Fahed Zoher

INSURGENCY AND UNITY OF COMMAND IN VIETNAM

BY BING WEST, DECEMBER 2003

PREMISE

This appendix addresses Vietnam, where the author spent years involved in the pacification effort. Two U.S. wars were fought in Vietnam. From 1965 to 1969, U.S. regular Army and Marine units engaged against North Vietnamese and, to a lesser extent, Viet Cong battalions. During that same period, U.S. advisers and some squads (113 at peak) were involved in counterinsurgency operations.

Vietnam fell to a conventional onslaught of eighteen North Vietnamese divisions equipped with Chinese artillery and Russian tanks.

In 1970, Americans in single vehicles could safely drive through most of the countryside of Vietnam. The internal insurgency did not topple that country and lessons can be learned from the counterinsurgency effort.

DISCUSSION

Given its experiences on the massive battlefields of World War II and its recent experience in Korea, the U.S. Army in the early 1960s held guerrillas or insurgents in low regard. "Any good soldier can handle guerrillas," Army Chief of Staff General George Decker told President John F. Kennedy. Guerrillas had been handled with ease in the previous two wars, compared to the epic battles fought against German, Japanese, and Chinese soldiers. In 1962, the U.S. advisory effort in South Vietnam assigned only five advisers to the regional forces; in 1964, it had assigned 100, compared to 1,700 advising the regular army, or ARVN.

The theory underlying counterinsurgency was to "pacify" the rural countryside by winning the hearts and minds of the peasants while providing them with security. With the introduction of both U.S. and North Vietnamese regular units in 1965, pacification was assigned a low priority in a war characterized by search and destroy missions and the clash of main force units. Nonetheless, with a population of eighteen million, South Vietnam by 1966 fielded 300,000 local forces, called Regional and Popular Forces. These RF/PFs, throughout the next nine years of war, sustained higher casualty rates than the ARVN. There were also 60,000 police, half in the 250 towns and cities and half assigned to the villages.

From 1962 until 1967, there were three separate American hierarchies providing advisers in the forty-four provinces: MACV (Military Assistance Command, Vietnam) handled the RF/PF; the CIA advised the 35,000-man Revolutionary Development Cadre (and later the Provincial Reconnaissance Units, or PRUs); and AID, Agency for International Development, advised the police. There was no single coordinator at the province level.

At a meeting with Vietnamese leaders in Hawaii in mid-1966, President Lyndon Johnson laid out his vision of pacification in Great Society terms: "How are you building democracy in your rural areas?" he asked the Vietnamese. "Have you improved credit, handicraft, light industry, rural electrification . . . have you coonskins on the wall?"

To ensure impetus to the pacification effort, President Johnson appointed a special assistant in the White House charged with coordinating the agencies in Washington, with another special assistant of ambassadorial rank in Saigon in the office of the American ambassador to South Vietnam. This unwieldy organizational arrangement yielded few concrete results and in 1966 the Pentagon lobbied the president to place pacification under control of the military. The State Department, AID, the CIA, and the U.S. embassy in Saigon argued for a separate but consolidated civilian agency, called the Office of Civil Operations, reporting to the ambassador in Saigon and not to Gen. William Westmoreland. The agencies pointed out that civilians comprised a majority of the 1,000-man U.S. pacification staff and controlled most of the budget.

After the Office of Civil Operations failed over several months to achieve progress in the countryside, Johnson decided to appoint General Westmoreland as both the U.S. ambassador and the U.S. military commander. When State, Defense, the Joint Chiefs of Staff, and Westmoreland all objected, Johnson shifted responsibility for pacification under Westmoreland, assigning a civilian deputy with ambassadorial rank and the single responsibility of pacification, called Civil Operations and Revolutionary Development Support—CORDS. At the same time, the president sent Gen. Creighton Abrams to Vietnam as the military deputy to Westmoreland, anointed to be his eventual successor. Johnson told Abrams his top priority was to revamp and motivate the ARVN.

The deputy chosen for CORDS was Robert Komer, and his charge was to function as the component commander for pacification, with control over all its resources, inside the U.S. military chain of command. As a deputy to a four-star general, he reported not to the U.S. ambassador, but to General Westmoreland, who could relieve him if he so desired. The reasons for the change were organizational pragmatics. Pacification conducted by civilian agencies under the aegis of the U.S. ambassador had proved sluggish due to bureaucratic turf wars, egos, and adherence to slow procedures. In contrast, the military had a "mission-first" ethos, uniform procedures, and a clear chain of command and rank structure. After the reorganization, there were still two chains of command in Vietnam. The U.S. ambassador, charged with nurturing political stability and acceptance of democratic principles by the political leaders of South Vietnam, and the U.S. military commander, charged with prosecuting the war and making pacification work. Komer concentrated on rural security and local forces, Abrams focused on the ARVN, and Westmoreland directed the overall strategy and deployments of U.S. forces. While U.S. advisers to ARVN remained in the military chain of command, reporting to Abrams, responsibility for training and advising the RF/PF local forces rested with Komer, as did allocating resources and advisers to the provinces.

There was now unity of command inside the military structure stretching down through the forty-four provinces to the 240 districts. Each had a composite advisory team of civilians and military, each with a single manager. The province senior advisers were split roughly 50-50, with a U.S. colonel heading the advisory teams in the less secure provinces and a State Department or AID official in charge in the more secure areas. Foreign service officers received fitness reports written by military officers and vice versa. CORDS, Civil Operations and Revolutionary Development Support, pulled together, under one undisputed authority, all the complex, competing, and often redundant U.S. civil and military pacification programs.

CORDS had its own army of several thousand PF platoons and several hundred RF companies, as well as the police and the CIA-trained Revolutionary Cadre, several thousand strong.

District advisers were expected to be walking encyclopedias of local knowledge, to include the district's political, social, and educational structure; the local economy; the typical patterns of graft and corruption; which officials could and could not be trusted; the professionalism, or lack thereof, of each PF platoon (five to fifteen) and RF company (two or three); the patterns and orders of battle of local VC; which villages were friendly and which were not; and so forth. Each month the adviser had to fill out a long checklist, called the Hamlet Evaluation System, or HES. While widely mocked as the press became disenchanted with the war after the Tet Offensive in 1968, HES actually was a fair tool for evaluating overall trends. District advisers also supervised the allocation of U.S. resources to a multitude of development projects. These resources, together with immediate radio links to U.S. ground forces and fire support, were the principal points of leverage to persuade Vietnamese officials to do what they otherwise would not do.

The CIA established and managed corps-level and Provincial Interrogation Centers (PICs). These functioned well as long as the supervisor of the Vietnamese interrogation teams was an American who persisted in eliciting and filing an enormous database on each prisoner, complete with wire diagrams of organizations, associations, family ties, times of movement, and other pertinent information. Eventually the CIA published a handbook for interrogators that showed diagrams of typical Viet Cong organization at the district and village level. The regional troops cooperated by calling the PICs when they captured Viet Cong, rather than brutalizing them with crude methods that elicited scant information. The interrogation technique that worked best was sympathy and kindness, the path least expected by the Vietnamese, who were accustomed to inflicting and absorbing pain. A favorite ploy was to tell a prisoner that the information was for the Americans, not for the South Vietnamese.

The backbone of area security was the Popular Forces, assigned to a village, and the Regional Forces, assigned to district headquarters.

Establishing a strong RF/PF base had been opposed by Prime Minister Tran Van Huong, who was concerned about creating local warlords who would challenge the authority of the central government after the war ended. General Abrams proceeded despite Huong's misgivings and by 1968 there were three types of training being given to the RF/PFs. The first was combined action with Marine squads in I Corps. These squads lived in the villages and associated with the Vietnamese as soldiers and fighters twenty-four hours a day for six to eighteen months. An American in a Combined Action Platoon had a 17 percent chance of being killed and a 75 percent chance of being wounded, yet the odds were 60 percent that he would extend in Vietnam for at least six months after his one-year assignment was finished—the highest extension rate in Vietnam. The second type of training was the Mobile Training Team of two officers and three enlisted Army soldiers who stayed with an RF company or PF platoon for six weeks, then moved on. The MTTs saw their role as trainers and providers of equipment, not as fighters. The third type of training was done by the District Advisory Teams, who often went on an operation with the RF companies and provided radio communications and fire support. Frequently the district adviser would become the de facto co-leader of the operation.

Whether training with advisers leads to success is a complex matter. Raising a Haitian gendarmerie of 2,700 soldiers in Haiti after World War I took three years to certify as ready and one-third of eighty-eight U.S. marines serving as advisers were shipped out as unsatisfactory trainers, due to cultural differences and attitudes toward the Haitians. Training the Guardia in Nicaragua proved technically easier. In the Vietnam case, both the VC and the RF/PF came from the same cultural stock, as did the North Vietnamese, perhaps the finest light jungle infantry of the past century. The willingness to fight was there. Indeed, eventually all Combined Action Platoons moved out of their village forts in order to meet the Viet Cong as equals in the night. This concept of perpetually mobile units was recommended for all RF/PF forces, but was not implemented.

In addition to the RF/PF, in each province the CIA raised a force of fifty to 100 Vietnamese, usually ex-soldiers and ex-VC. Called the Provincial Reconnaissance Units, or PRUs, these soldiers reported to the CIA and were advised by U.S. Special Forces, SEALs, or marines. While accused in the popular press of being assassins, most PRU units were praised by their CIA managers and rewarded with perquisites such as treatment at U.S. military hospitals and permission to keep any money found on fallen VC. In the mid-1980s, a variation on the PRU model, called Tactical Task Forces, was set up in Honduras and El Salvador. The TTFs, which employed helicopter gunships followed by a heliborne landing by commandos, met with considerable success.

The presence of American advisers in Vietnam also reduced corruption. Payoffs for protection to local forces becomes endemic if the leaders are involved because the payoffs trickle down and permeate all ranks. That diffusion, however, leads to rumors, quarrels, and complaints, which in turn come to the attention of the advisers. The advisers usually knew when a district or village chief was involved in some sort of shakedown or falsification. Ordinarily, it was small-time graft, like reporting thirty soldiers on the payroll when there were only twenty. When Saigon fell, the Vietnamese officials who managed to flee eventually secured work as cab drivers and hotel clerks. The image in the popular press of a corrupt hierarchy accumulating wealth was incorrect.

The normal course an adviser pursued upon finding evidence of fraud or graft was to indicate to the official that his scheme was known. Usually it persisted and the adviser would ask the province adviser to arrange the relief of the district chief. In most cases, the chief would be transferred to a like or better position and become someone else's headache. As foreigners, Americans in Vietnam could never understand the skein of tribal and familial relationships that extended from the capital to the most wretched district.

MEMO TO GEN. GEORGE W. CASEY, USA

FROM: BING WEST
SUBJECT: SECURITY IN IRAQ, AUGUST 2004

1. The Sunnis are the heart of the insurgency. To them, we are the conquerors who changed the natural order of dominance. In Sunni heartlands, the insurgency is genuine and deep-rooted. In cities like Ramadi, the people, whether intimidated or in sympathy, actively support or passively do not inform upon the insurgents.

2. The insurgency has gained combat experience and confidence over the past year. Their morale is intact and they can quickly defeat and embarrass any Iraqi Security Force (ISF). Hence in the net, the last year has been a security loss to us.

3. The Allawi approach to counterinsurgency via an "Iraqi solution"—based on political deals supposedly backed by a few hard guys sneaking around in the night to shoot someone—is naive. The idea of seizing back places like Fallujah without a fight by inserting former Baathist generals and stirring up internecine fights has, to paraphrase de Gaulle, "a brilliant future—and always will." Sooner or later, the Iraqis must fight to regain control of Fallujah.

4. Sadr is a menace to the Shiite dream of democratic political control. Sistani's medical treatment in England conveniently gives

Allawi the freedom to finish the fight and not to allow another Fallujah to grow in Najaf.

5. War requires killing people. The glaring defect of the ISF is their refusal to kill a fellow Iraqi, no matter how murderous he may be. Too many in the ISF are complicit in, or passively countenance, attacks upon U.S. troops. The ISF lacks leaders at all levels. Particularly, the ISF needs tough battalion and company commanders and city district police chiefs. The numbers needed are small—maybe 400. But the task is daunting—going into battle.

6. The ISF has not one hero, not one single battalion commander who has taken the fight offensively and persistently to the enemy. So far, there is no example of success, no emerging U.S. Grant. This is scary. On the U.S. side, the battalion and brigade commanders ride to the sound of the guns. On the ISF side, no one responds.

7. Surrounding Allawi are officials who believe Iraq had a fine army and needs less U.S. advice and fewer advisers. That is fine talk, but it hasn't budged one insurgent. No ISF general has gone into battle. Conversely, if the insurgency coalesces around a charismatic leader, there will be real trouble.

8. Every effort should be made to find and to shove into battle ISF tactical commanders in places like Samarra, Ramadi, and Fallujah. Baghdad is a sump hole and a refuge for those who talk and avoid action.

9. Firm U.S. firepower support will be required if the ISF ever goes into battle. This means insisting upon clear written orders down the proper military chain of command from the SecDef. Alleged verbal orders have been a disaster.

10. Currently, ISF soldiers and police die passively as victims of bombings. Instead of being victims, they must be infused with the spirit of taking the fight to the insurgents. The Iraqi Army will follow a few leaders. Unlike the U.S., the NCOs in the ISF count for little; it is a few officers who can make the difference. So far, we haven't found and empowered them.

11. The strength of the coalition lies in the fighting spirit of our troops. Because they react so ferociously, they keep a firm lid on the level to which the insurgency can rise. Every time the insurgents rise to engagements at the platoon level and above, they are hammered. Hence the coalition defines the limits of growth of the military insurgency. So I don't see how we lose this war. I do hope we apply the pressure and incentives to turn it over quickly to the ISF, be-

cause as long as we are protecting the MSRs [Main Supply Routes] to sustain ourselves, we will be the targets.

12. While avoiding a Lam Son 719, we must leverage the ISF to undertake offensive actions, backing them up in battle in return for having a strong voice in the replacement of leaders who do not lead. My concern is that the ISF has no incentive to do battle, because we have promised to stay without conditions and do the fighting for them. How we get them to go into battle, while sustaining their morale when they absorb casualties, is a great challenge. This is not foremost a matter of equipment or length of training; it is a matter of battlefield leaders.

BING WEST'S COUNTERINSURGENCY LESSONS

1. **Partner Always.** Don't fight someone else's battles for him. The goal of U.S. units and adviser teams is to nurture armed units—army and police. If a U.S. unit is not combined with a local unit, it cannot succeed.
2. **Fire Incompetents.** Americans go in because the host nation failed. Insist on a mechanism to relieve those who fail. Sovereignty should not shield failure.
3. **Act as Police.** The key is identifying the insurgents, not redressing their political grievances. Installing "good government" is not a U.S. military mission. The U.S. military has neglected basic police metrics and methods. It is foolish to fight an insurgency without conducting a census and employing biometric tools.
4. **Be Aggressive.** A unit or advisory team must set the example and spend most of its time outside the wire. Force protection is not a mission. The goal is a clearance rate (kill or capture) of over 50 percent for violent crimes—shootings, bombings, kidnappings, etc. The insurgent must know he will die or be captured.
5. **Don't Catch and Release.** Insist on a system of incarceration based on common sense rather than democratic ideals. It is crazy to catch insurgents and let them go a few months later.

6. **Bribe.** The U.S. military has no competence to restructure an economy. Every platoon and advisory team should have a monthly allowance of several thousand dollars to disperse for goodwill and information.

7. **Treat Everyone with Respect.** First, do no harm. The task—that will take years—is to separate the people from the insurgents, not to act like a thug and recruit for the insurgents. If you wouldn't push someone around at home, don't do so anywhere else. No Better Friend comes before No Worse Enemy. If foot patrols by local police require more than four men, the area has not been cleared. If you don't have a confident, competent police chief, the area is not being held.

8. **Barriers Work.** "Gated communities"—walls, concrete barriers, etc.—greatly impede commerce, but they impede the entrance and exit of assassins.

9. **Fight the Top.** In Iraq and Afghanistan, as in Vietnam, the high-level officials were the most resistant to change. The top levels of the U.S. government have failed to establish tough practices to force change, particularly in ripping out corruption at ministerial levels. If sovereignty guarantees massive corruption, sedition, and recalcitrance that undercut the war effort, then American soldiers should not be committed.

10. **A Divisive Society Will Not Remain the Strongest Tribe.** As a society, America's martial values of patience, sacrifice, and unity have declined. Iraq was as much a symptom as a problem. We fought in Iraq as a nation divided, with many of our elected leaders willing to lose. No nation can sustain its values by claiming to support the soldier while opposing his mission. The nation determines the mission. If we are as divided in the next war, we will not succeed.

NOTES

PREFACE

xviii **"Battle is decided":** Leo Tolstoy, *War and Peace* (New York: Norton, 1996), p. 1051.

CHAPTER 1: HOW TO CREATE A MESS, SUMMER 2003

6 **Franks applauded:** Tommy Franks, *American Soldier* (New York: Regan Books, 2004), p. 531.

7 **"driven to the brink":** George Tenet, *At the Center of the Storm* (New York: HarperCollins, 2007), p. 428.

10 **"a classical guerrilla-type campaign":** Vernon Leob, "Guerrilla War Acknowledged," *Washington Post,* July 17, 2003, p. A1.

12 **Yet the JTF estimate:** Data from Iraq Index, Brookings Institution, January 9, 2004, p. 9.

17 **"The thing that did not happen":** Conway interview in *Leatherneck Magazine,* July 2007, p. 21.

CHAPTER 2: DESCENT INTO CHAOS, SEPTEMBER–DECEMBER 2003

18 **Abizaid opposed:** Douglas J. Feith, *War and Decision* (New York: HarperCollins, 2008), description of Pentagon meetings, October 26–28, 2003, p. 465.

21 **By October, twenty-four police trainers:** William McMichael, "Iraqi Police Trainer Calls Program a 'Complete Failure,' " *Military Times,* April 25, 2006.

22 **"It will require"**: Senator John McCain, press release, November 5, 2003.

22 **"In the late fall of 2003"**: Yasin al-Dulaimi, "Violence Slashes Ramadi Property Prices," ICR No. 179, May 31, 2006.

23 **If they couldn't control**: Patrick J. McDonnell, "Town Preoccupies the Occupation," *Los Angeles Times,* November 17, 2003, p. 1.

23 **"The Arab tribe"**: John Bagot Glubb, *The Story of the Arab Legion,* p. 176.

23 **Maj. Gen. Charles H. Swannack, commanding**: Associated Press, "In Iraq, Treading Carefully While Fighting Insurgency," *Baltimore Sun,* November 16, 2003, p. 1.

24 **"The Coalition Provisional Authority deliberately"**: David Kilcullen, *Small Wars Journal* blog site, December 3, 2007.

24 **"CIA's old pals"**: Tenet, *At the Center of the Storm,* p. 441.

25 **"War Criminal!"**: Tom Ricks, "Holding Their Ground," *Washington Post,* December 23, 2003, p. C1.

CHAPTER 3: A NEAR COLLAPSE, JANUARY–JUNE 2004

26 **Yet at the same time**: Thom Shanker, "G.I.'s to Pull Back in Baghdad," *New York Times,* February 2, 2004, p. A1.

28 **up to 90 percent**: Brookings Institution, Iraq Index, January 9, 2004, p. 9, first footnote.

28 **"We are taking"**: DEBKAfile, "Falllujah Raids," February 14, 2004.

29 **"We've made significant progress"**: Hamza Hendawi, "US Marines Handed Authority of Fallujah," Associated Press, March 24, 2004.

31 **"a symptom of the success"**: Sewell Chan, "General Calls Insurgency a Sign of US Success," *Washington Post,* April 15, 2004.

31 **Maj. Gen. Charles Swannack**: Swannack, press conference, March 19, 2004.

31 **according to Sanchez**: Lt. Gen. Ricardo S. Sanchez, *Wiser in Battle* (New York: HarperCollins, 2008), p. 365.

32 **"It's not an accident"**: McCain on CNN News, April 16, 2004.

32 **"No, this was not an uprising"**: Myers, Sanchez press briefing, CNN, April 15, 2004.

34 **According to then–undersecretary of defense**: Feith, *War and Decision,* pp. 482, 483.

34 **The descriptions of the televideo conferences**: L. Paul Bremer III, *My Year in Iraq* (New York: Threshold, 2006), pp. 338–42.

35 **"We shouldn't be focused"**: Feith, *War and Decision,* p. 483.

36 **"This is the right way"**: Thomas Ricks, " 'We're on the Brink of Success,' General Says of Iraq Situation," *Washington Post,* May 22, 2004.

37 **"no courts-martial"**: Stephen E. Ambrose, *Citizen Soldiers* (New York: Simon & Schuster, 1998), p. 352.

38 **"disgraceful conduct"**: Bush, speech at the Army War College, May 24, 2004.

39 **Addressing the Army War College**: Ibid.

41 **"His [Bremer's] biggest error"**: Peter W. Galbraith, "The Mess," *New York Review of Books,* March 9, 2006.

CHAPTER 4: WAR, JULY–DECEMBER 2004

45 **"there were 75 ways":** Alistair Horne, *A Savage War of Peace* (New York: New York Review of Books, 2006), p. 331.

46 **"we've got a really bad":** Bob Woodward, *State of Denial* (New York: Simon & Schuster, 2006), p. 319.

47 **"Victory in the next war":** Ambrose, *Citizen Soldiers,* p. 90.

48 **The Arab League was antagonistic:** Reuters, "Arab League Head Does Not Rule Out Arab Troops in Iraq," May 31, 2004.

53 **The provincial governor:** Ann Scott Tyson, "Sadr's Militias Regrouping," *Christian Science Monitor,* July 15, 2004.

60 **From the beginning of the struggle:** Bing West, *No True Glory* (New York: Bantam, 2005), p. 316.

60 **"we have broken the back":** Rowan Scarborough, "US Declares Insurgency Broken," *Washington Times,* November 19, 2004, p. 1.

61 **"there has never ever been":** Sanchez press briefing, CNN, April 15, 2004.

61 **Bremer had recommended:** Bremer, *My Year in Iraq,* p. 106.

63 **"a long-term project":** Ibid., p. 112.

CHAPTER 5: INADEQUATE MEANS, 2005

64 **accepted it reluctantly:** Tenet, *At the Center of the Storm,* p. 489.

65 **"flawed and senseless":** Ayad Allawi, "How Iraq's Elections Set Back Democracy," *New York Times,* November 2, 2007, p. A23.

65 **According to columnist David Ignatius:** David Ignatius, "Bush's Lost Iraqi Election," *Washington Post,* August 30, 2007, p. A21.

66 **"The elections had":** Petraeus testimony, House Armed Services Committee, January 23, 2007, p. 18.

66 **Prodded by U.N. advisers:** David L. Phillips, *Losing Iraq* (San Francisco: Westview Press, 2005), p. 218.

67 **"Before, I sold water":** Solomon Moore and Christian Miller, "Before Rearming Iraq, He Sold Shoes," *Los Angeles Times,* November 2, 2005, p. 1.

67 **"the largest theft":** Patrick Cockburn, "What Happened to Iraq's Missing $1B?," *The Independent* (U.K.), September 19, 2005.

67 **One annual index:** Damien Cave, "Nonstop Theft and Bribery Stagger Iraq," *New York Times,* December 2, 2007, p. A1.

68 **The Nobel Prize–winning economist:** Roger B. Myerson, "Foundations of the State in Theory and Practice," University of Chicago Web site, p. 15.

69 **"Corruption exists":** Col. Juan Ayala, "Reflections," *Marine Corps Gazette,* March 2008, p. 53.

69 **"Corruption in this part":** Abizaid remarks, Senate Armed Services Committee, August 3, 2006, p. 49.

70 **"Shiism is the looming danger":** CPA translation of Zarqawi letter given to Ikenberry Study Group, February 2004.

71 **"rapid progress":** Eric Schmitt, "New US Commander Sees Shift in Military Role," *New York Times,* January 12, 2005, p. 10.

75 **"We can hold it":** Dan Murphy, "In Fallujah's Wake, Marines Go West," *Christian Science Monitor,* February 24, 2005.

75 **"We've gone from":** Associated Press, "President Prays for Peace, US Soldiers," *Washington Post,* March 28, 2005, p. A2.

77 **"Voting in Iraq":** Ann Scott Tyson, "Iraqi Insurgency Is Weakening, Abizaid Says," *Washington Post,* March 2, 2005, p. A05.

77 **"huge amount of work":** Eric Schmitt, "U.S. Commanders See Possible Cut in Troops in Iraq," *New York Times,* April 11, 2005, p. A10.

77 **"becoming a reality":** Donna Miles, "Two Years in Iraq: 2005 to Be Pivotal," American Forces Press Service, March 23, 2005.

78 **"I've never been":** "II MEF Takes Over Fallujah," MilitaryCity.com, March 28, 2005.

78 **Chiarelli wrote:** Maj. Gen. Peter W. Chiarelli and Maj. Patrick R. Michaelis, "The Requirement for Full-Spectrum Operations," *Military Review,* July 2005, p. 14.

79 **"a direct correlation":** Ibid., p. 10.

82 **"The MSCs were":** Clay, *Iroquois Warriors in Iraq,* p. 153.

82 **"What was unclear":** Dominic J. Caraccilo and Andrea L. Thompson, *Achieving Victory in Iraq* (Mechanicsburg, PA: Stackpole Books, 2008), p. 150.

83 **In November, he told the Senate:** Kirk Semple and Edward Fong, "Major Offensive Hits Insurgents," *New York Times,* November 6, 2005.

CHAPTER 6: WIDESCALE FIGHTING, 2005

84 **The troublesome insurgents:** Lt. Col. Christopher M. Hickey, 2-3 ACR, "Commander Estimate of Situation AO Sabre (Talafar)," January 10, 2006.

85 **In September, after enclosing Tal Afar:** Col. H. R. McMaster, Pentagon televideo press conference, September 13, 2005.

86 **After a month of patrolling:** Maj. Niel Smith, "Retaking Sa'ad," *Armor Magazine,* July 2007, pp. 28–33.

98 **Having decided the 12,000 Sunnis:** "Command Chronology," II Marine Expeditionary Force, March 2005, p. 21.

98 **"The goal is not":** Jacob Silberberg, Associated Press, "Forces Pound Foreign Fighters," *Washington Times,* June 19, 2005.

98 **Iraqi civilians told the marines:** Dan Murphy, "After Temporary Gains, Marines Leave Iraqi Cities," *Christian Science Monitor,* March 3, 2005.

100 **"You're going to have":** Tom Lassiter, "US, Insurgents Locked in a Stalemate," Knight-Ridder, August 25, 2005.

100 **"We leave these marines":** Biden, *CBS Early Show,* August 4, 2005.

100 **"It's the truth":** Kimberly Johnson, "Towns Left Vulnerable After Being Secured," *USA Today,* August 12, 2005.

100 **"This is not":** Kirk Semple, "US Forces Try New Approach," *New York Times,* December 5, 2005.

101 **In October and November:** Brookings Institution. In October–November 2005, there were thirty-six U.S. KIA in the Upper Euphrates and thirty-five in the Lower

Euphrates. Multiple fatality bombings increased from eighteen in February 2005 to thirty-nine in February 2006.

102 **At the end of 2005:** "Command Chronology," II Marine Expeditionary Force, January 2006.

102 **The number was sufficient:** Ibid., #5757.

CHAPTER 7: CONTRADICTORY GOALS, 2005

106 **"I think in the west":** Tony Perry, "Marine General Gives an Upbeat Report," *Los Angeles Times,* March 29, 2005.

107 **"there were not signs":** Anthony Cordesman, *Iraqi Force Development* (Washington, D.C.: Center for Strategic and International Studies, March 10, 2006).

107 **By year's end:** Jason Campbell, Michael O'Hanlon, and Amy Unikewicz, "Iraqi Scorecard," *New York Times,* March 18, 2007. Based on Brookings data.

107 **"no plans for enduring bases":** Excerpt from "Commanding General's Decision Brief," November 26, 2005.

108 **Most of the $21 billion:** "MNF-I 2005 Campaign Review," December 20, 2005.

110 **"our political-military strategy":** Rice testimony, Senate Foreign Relations Committee, October 19, 2005.

110 **From the start of his tenure:** See, for instance, Rumsfeld's press statement of September 28, 2004.

110 **"As they [the Iraqi forces] stand up":** Bush, speech at Annapolis, November 30, 2005.

110 **"We will never accept anything":** Bush speech, November 30, 2005.

111 **"last throes":** *Larry King Live,* June 5, 2005.

111 **"Too often we've been told":** McCain, *Meet the Press,* June 19, 2005.

112 **"not intellectually curious":** Woodward, *State of Denial,* p. 419.

CHAPTER 8: THE SECOND WAR BEGINS, 2006

113 **"I am confident":** Bush, January 31, 2006.

114 **"The biggest difference":** Thomas E. Ricks, "In the Battle for Baghdad, US Turns Over War on Insurgents," *Washington Post,* February 26, 2006, p. A01.

117 **Since the bombing at Samarra:** "The Struggle for Iraq," *New York Times,* January 2, 2007, p. A8.

117 **Inside the city:** *New York Times,* August 5, 2006.

118 **"the largest since":** Walter Pincus, "Corruption Cited in Iraq's Oil Industry," *Washington Post,* July 17, 2006, p. A12.

119 **"The president must remember":** Condoleezza Rice, "Campaign 2000: Promoting the National Interest," *Foreign Affairs,* January/February 2000.

120 **"the natural tendency":** *Counterinsurgency Field Manual 3-24/mcwp 3-33.5,* Headquarters, Department of the Army, December 15, 2006, p. A7.

121 **"single narrative":** Ibid.

122 **"I think that sometimes":** Nelson Hernandez, "Attacks Rock Foundation That Marines Built," *Washington Post,* February 7, 2006.

123 *The New York Times* ran an op-ed: Paul D. Eaton, "A Top-Down Review," *New York Times,* March 19, 2006.

123 "President Bush would have": Fred Kaplan, "The Revolt Against Rumsfeld," *Slate,* April 21, 2006.

124 "The president has the right": *East Valley Tribune,* 415/2006 http://www .eastvalleytribune.com/story/63311.

CHAPTER 10: HADITHA: EXPLOSION ON THE HOME FRONT, 2006

153 "But I will not excuse murder": Steve Soto, *The Left Coaster,* May 2006.

153 Murtha abused his office: Robert Pear, "Lawmakers Put Out New Call for Earmarks," *New York Times,* February 14, 2008, p. A18.

153 "Raging in Iraq": Reid, speech on the Senate floor, June 5, 2006.

154 "During the Clinton years": Reid addressing the annual Yearly Kos meeting, 2006.

155 "The most important": Max Boot, *War Made New* (New York: Gotham, 2006).

157 "Who Will Be Punished": Brian Bennett, "Who Will Be Punished for Haditha?," *Time,* October 11, 2007.

CHAPTER 11: A FLAWED ASSESSMENT, MID-2006

160 But the decrease didn't hold up: For the difference in civilian casualty figures for April and May, see Multinational Forces Iraq chart on page 35 of the DoD Report to the Congress on Iraq, August 29, 2006, compared to the data entitled "The Struggle for Iraq: A Year of Strategy and Sectarian Strife," *New York Times,* January 12, 2007, p. A8.

162 "I have come": Bush remarks, June 13, 2006.

162 While the president was in Baghdad: icasualties.org Web site, Iraqi civilian casualties for May and June 2006.

162 By comparison, battalions in Vietnam: M. E. Arnsten and F. J. West, "A Tabular Method for Comparing Friendly and Enemy Casualties: A Case Study of Marine Mortalities Resulting from Patrols and Six Offensive Operations in Quang Nam Province," RAND Corporation, RM 6378-ARPA, December 1970, p. 33.

163 "new government of national unity": CNN transcript of Pentagon press conference, June 22, 2006.

163 The Baghdad coroner's office: DoD report to Congress, August 29, 2006, p. 34.

163 "I'm not comfortable": Pace, SecDef Roundtable press conference, February 2, 2007.

164 A CNN poll: CNN poll, August 2, 2006.

165 "being subjected": Zalma Khalilzad, "The Battle of Baghdad," *Wall Street Journal,* August 23, 2006, p. A10.

165 "If there is seen": I Marine Expeditionary Force Press Release #0814-06-0857, "Iraqis Must Step Forward in Anbar Province, General Says," August 13, 2006.

166 "He has made it": Snow, White House press briefing, September 12, 2006.

166 "The current force": Robert Burns, "Pace: Bigger US Force May Stabilize Iraq," Associated Press, August 14, 2006.

CHAPTER 12: AL QAEDA: MURDER AND INTIMIDATION, FALL 2006

171 **Of every 1,000 patrols:** Arnsten and West, "A Tabular Method," p. 33.

CHAPTER 13: THE TURNAROUND BEGINS, FALL 2006

174 **Media-savvy:** Khalid al Ansary and Ali Adeeb, "Most Tribes in Anbar Agree to Unite," *New York Times,* September 18, 2006.

180 **According to Michael Frank:** Michael J. Frank, "US Military Courts and the War in Iraq," *Vanderbilt Journal of Transnational Law,* Volume 30, May 2006, p. 746.

181 **Of 58,000 Iraqis:** Data from several meetings in 2006–2008 with Task Force 134 in Baghdad.

181 **Between June 2004 and June 2006:** Multi-National Force briefing paper, Baghdad, April 2007.

181 **During the same period:** Multi-National Force briefing, October 20, 2006, citing twenty-five murders/kidnappings a day, plus 110 insurgents killed between September 1 and October 18, plus 1,330 detained. The number sent to prison was unknown.

185 **"AQI is the dominant organization":** Thomas Ricks, "Situation Called Dire in West Iraq," *Washington Post,* September 11, 2006.

CHAPTER 14: THE CIVIL WAR, FALL 2006

187 **"The center of the problem":** Lisa Burgess, "Abizaid: Iraq Troop Levels to Hold Steady Until 2007," *Stars and Stripes,* September 15, 2006.

188 **When former secretary of defense William J. Perry:** Perry, testimony, House Armed Services Committee, July 18, 2007, p. 5.

188 **"In Iraq, we cannot afford":** Notes from Robb, received May 2, 2007.

195 **In September, there had been:** "A Year of Strategy and Sectarian Strife," *New York Times,* January 2, 2007, p. A8.

195 **"ineffective to non-existent control":** Multi-National Force, Baghdad Security Plan draft outline, December 25, 2006.

195 **"sliding toward chaos":** Michael Gordon, "Military Charts Movement of Conflict in Iraq Toward Chaos," *New York Times,* November 1, 2006, p. A1.

CHAPTER 15: BUSH WEIGHS HIS OPTIONS, FALL 2006

199 **"I said: General":** Bush, October 11, 2006.

201 **"The U.S. Army is past the point":** Richard Oppel, "Sectarian Rift," *New York Times,* November 12, 2006.

202 **"the inability of the government":** Bob Woodward, "CIA Said Instability Seemed Irreversible," *Washington Post,* July 12, 2007, p. A01.

204 **"I believe that more":** Abizaid remarks to McCain, *The NewsHour,* November 16, 2006.

207 **The report contained:** Peter Baker and Robin Wright, "Bush Appears Cool to Key Points of Report on Iraq," *Washington Post,* December 8, 2006, p. A01.

207 **"not going to outsource"**: Sheryl Gay Stolberg, "Bush Reassures Iraqi," Associated Press, October 17, 2006.

207 **"We've got to get"**: Undated White House working paper, "Iraq Strategic Review."

207 **"George, do you have"**: Ibid.

CHAPTER 16: THE WAR TURNS, NOVEMBER 2006

212 **"the coalition forces"**: Sterling Jensen, "Terp Lessons from an Anbar Sheik," *Washington Post*, September 29, 2007, p. A19.

212 **"Of his courage"**: Jack Weatherford, *Genghis Khan* (New York: Crown, 2004), p. 240.

212 **"We've got to get"**: From the dialogue in a western called *At Gunpoint*.

CHAPTER 17: WASHINGTON TURNS, DECEMBER 2006

217 **"the situation in Iraq"**: Gates, Pentagon press briefing, September 17, 2007.

217 **"We have done everything"**: DoD press briefing with Lt. Gen. Peter Chiarelli, December 8, 2006.

218 **"One of the most important"**: Fred Barnes, "How Bush Decided on the Surge," *Weekly Standard*, January 28, 2008.

218 **"nation building"**: Andrew Gray, "Army Nation Building," Reuters, June 24, 2007.

218 **"Bush bears heavy responsibility"**: Jim Hoagland, "The Spies Strike Back," *Washington Post*, December 9, 2007.

218 **"I believe a gift"**: David Brooks, "Heroes and History," *New York Times*, July 17, 2007, p. A21.

219 **After the December 13 meeting**: Pace, remarks, SecDef roundtable with the press, February 2, 2007.

222 **"It is clear"**: Bush address, January 10, 2007.

CHAPTER 18: THE SUNNIS CHANGE SIDES, WINTER 2007

224 **"Victory is no longer an option"**: "Legislating Leadership on Iraq," *New York Times*, editorial, March 29, 2007.

224 **"Friends of mine"**: David Brooks, "Breaking the Clinch," *New York Times*, January 25, 2007, p. A23.

225 **"seventy percent of the troops"**: Webb, Senate Armed Services Committee hearing, January 23, 2007, p. 46.

225 **"I hope it succeeds"**: Hillary Clinton, *New York Times* transcript, March 14, 2007.

225 **"This is a tactic"**: Excerpt from *Meet the Press*, January 14, 2007.

225 **"This speech given last night"**: Ibid.

225 **"situation in Iraq"**: Petraeus, Senate Armed Services Committee hearing, January 23, 2007, pp. 4–5.

227 "The existing strategy": *Meet the Press,* January 14, 2007.

228 "We cannot allow": Petraeus, letter to the troops, February 10, 2007.

228 Overall, the number of civilians: Brookings Institution, Iraq Index, August 30, 2007, pp. 11–12. In January 2007, 285 Shiites were killed by suicide murderers, and 459 in February. In January, there were 1,415 murders, euphemistically called Extra-Judicial Killings, reported in Baghdad; in February, there were 800.

242 "start your own database immediately": *Company Commander Lessons,* Marine Corps Combat Development Command, November 2007.

CHAPTER 19: MOMENTUM, SPRING 2007

247 "This war is lost": Jeff Zeleny, "Leading Democrat in Senate Tells Reporters, 'This War Is Lost,' " *New York Times,* April 20, 2007.

248 The only good news: Alissa Rubin, "70 Killed in Wave of Revenge," *New York Times,* March 28, 2007.

249 "I think he's": Crocker, comments at Sharm el-Sheikh, Egypt, Associated Press, May 3, 2007.

250 On the political front: Edward Wong, "6 in Iraq Cabinet Resign," *New York Times,* April 16, 2007, p. A1.

254 One million Algerians: Horne, *A Savage War of Peace,* p. 359.

259 Relations between: Ned Parker, "How Ghost Soldiers Are Bleeding the Iraqi Army," *Financial Times,* January 19, 2007.

266 In 2006, of the 5,300 Iraqi translators: Karen DeYoung, "Stalwart Service for U.S. in Iraq Is Not Enough to Gain Green Card," *Washington Post,* March 23, 2008, p. A01.

269 Ten percent of the troops: Pauline Jelinek, "Stress Linked to Battlefield Misconduct," Associated Press, May 5, 2007.

269 "We treat noncombatants": Petraeus, letter to the troops, May 10, 2007.

269 On the Iraqi side: Pentagon report to Congress, "Measuring Stability in Iraq," March 7, 2008, p. 5.

271 "I think, in that area": Robert Burns, "Commandant: Anbar Has Turned the Corner," Associated Press, April 9, 2007.

272 "Anbar is a place": Jim Garamone, "Marines in Anbar Express Optimism," American Forces Press Service, April 19, 2007.

272 In May, there were thirteen American fatalities: ICAS Web site, "American Fatalities from Hostile Fire," May 2007.

CHAPTER 20: OVERVIEW, SUMMER 2007

273 "I've committed more than": Bush, speech, January 10, 2007.

273 A corps is generally comprised: "Private Sector's Tramping in Iraq," *New York Times* editorial, March 24, 2008.

274 "It is an open-ended operation": Jim Garamone, American Forces Press Service, June 22, 2007.

274   **In the first week of Phantom Thunder:** Multi-National Corps data for June 15–22, 2007. The number of detainees was 721. Most of these, however, did not yield in arrest packages sufficient to send the detainees to the prisons at Bucca or Cropper.

274   **The average American battalion:** According to data from MNF-I, in 2007, 7,400 insurgents were killed and 45,000 were detained, of whom 19,000 were sent to prison, while 7,300 were released from prison. Special Operations Forces accounted for 3,000–4,000 imprisoned and 1,000 killed. Attack helicopters killed several thousand. There were about seventy-five battalions involved in combat.

275   **In the second week in July:** Stephen Farrell, "Around 150, Death Toll Among War's Worst," *New York Times,* July 9, 2007.

276   **"But an increase":** Michael O'Hanlon and Jason Campbell, "Measuring Progress in Iraq," *Wall Street Journal,* July 13, 2007, p. A13.

276   **"There's extreme unhappiness":** Thomas Ricks interview, ABC On Line, August 31, 2006.

277   **"out of touch":** *The NewsHour,* June 15, 2007.

278   **The report:** Initial Benchmark Assessment Report to Congress by DoD, July 12, 2007.

278   **"The big negative":** Petraeus e-mail, July 12, 2007.

278   **"I can't deal with you":** Damien McElroy, "Iraqi Leader Tells Bush: Get Gen. Petraeus Out," *The Guardian,* July 29, 2007. See also *Newsweek,* July 30, 2007; Steven R. Hurst of Associated Press, July 30; and John Burns, *New York Times,* August 14, 2007.

278   **"non-functional":** Leo Shane, "Sen. Levin: Iraqi PM Needs to Be Replaced," *Stars and Stripes,* August 22, 2007, p. 6.

278   **"If the government doesn't respond":** Michael A. Fletcher, "Bush Turns Up the Heat on Maliki," *Washington Post,* August 22, 2007, p. A01.

278   **"extremely disappointing" and "I heard more people":** Shane, "Sen. Levin: Iraq PM Needs to Be Replaced," p. 6.

CHAPTER 21: VICTORY IN ANBAR, FALL 2007

286   **"And it is the case":** Keith Mines, "Memo to the Administrator," November 4, 2003, p. 3.

286   **In June of 2007, Mullen launched:** Cpl. Joel Abshier, "2/6 Kicks Off Op Alljah," *Marine Corps News,* June 12, 2007.

290   **This was a paltry sum:** The White House, Iraq Fact Sheet on Capital Spending, March 27, 2008.

290   **What exasperated Senators Levin and Warner:** James Glanz, "Senate Committee Seeks Audit of Iraq Oil Money," *New York Times,* March 9, 2008.

291   **In 2007, Iraq received:** Monisha Bansal, "War Reconstruction: Senators Call for Iraq Oil Revenue Audit," CNSNews.com, March 11, 2008.

291   **The Council on Foreign Relations reported:** Curt Tarnoff and Nina Serafino, "US Occupation Assistance Iraq, Germany and Japan," Council on Foreign Relations, March 23, 2006.

292 "The American people can't want peace": Armed Forces Press, "US Senator Tells Iraqis to Sort Out Future or See US Leave," September 7, 2007.

CHAPTER 23: WASHINGTON ASSESSES THE SURGE, FALL 2007

318 American fatalities: *Washington Post,* October 3, 2007.

318 Suicide bombings: "The Measure of Progress," editorial, *Wall Street Journal,* September 2, 2007, p. A14.

318 The change in tone: Michael E. O'Hanlon and Kenneth M. Pollack, "A War We Just Might Win," *New York Times,* July 30, 2007.

318 Jones accused Maliki: "Report of the Independent Commission on the Security Forces of Iraq," September 6, 2007.

320 "He [Petraeus] has made": Matthew Jaffe report, ABC News, September 8, 2007.

321 The liberal antiwar political action group: *New York Times* advertisement, September 10, 2007.

321 "the breathing space": Bush, address to the nation, January 10, 2007, p. 3.

322 In September, a Zogby poll: Newsmax.com, September 19, 2007.

322 "I ask you to join me": Bush, address to the nation, September 13, 2007.

322 "tragic mistake": "Clinton Vote," MSNBC.com, February 12, 2007.

323 Lieutenant General Odierno had charged: Odierno, Associated Press interview, August 5, 2007.

324 several large caches: Odierno, National Press Club interview, October 2, 2007.

324 "Iran is not moving forward": Maliki meeting at the Council on Foreign Relations, September 2007.

328 The military historian Kimberly Kagan: Kimberly Kagan, "Securing Diyala," Iraq Report #7 for the Institute for the Study of War and Weeklystandard.com, December 4, 2007.

330 Since the Samarra bombing: See the *New York Times* map of June 25, 2006, versus sectarian maps provided by MNF-I in January of 2008.

330 The United Nations estimated: Associated Press, "UN Report on Iraqi Displaced Persons," June 5, 2007.

330 The one-hundred-odd: Edward Wong and Damien Cave, "U.S. Troops to Open 100 Garrisons Across Baghdad," *New York Times,* March 15, 2007.

331 Ayman al-Zawahri: Associated Press report of audiotape posted on the Internet, April 21, 2008.

331 A teacher earning: Ali Fadhily, "21st Century Guernica: Fallujah Under a Different Kind of Seige," IPS News, November 27, 2007.

331 According to a Pew poll: Perry Bacon, "Very Little War in Republicans' Words," *Washington Post,* November 30, 2007, p. A06.

332 president's approval rating: CNN poll, December 2007.

332 The war in Iraq cannot: John McCain, "An Enduring Peace Built on Freedom," *Foreign Affairs,* November/December 2007.

332 We cannot impose: Barack Obama, "Renewing American Leadership," *Foreign Affairs,* July/August 2007.

333 **Three thousand enemy were killed:** MNC-I operational results from June 15, 2007, to March 28, 2008.

CHAPTER 24: PROGRESS AND UNCERTAINTY, 2008

336 **In Northern Ireland:** Daniel Marston and Carter Malkasian, eds., *Counterinsurgency in Modern Warfare* (New York: Osprey, 2008), p. 177.

338 **"There are, you know":** "Battle of the Minds: An Interview with Major General Douglas Stone," MountainRunner blog, September 19, 2007, http://mountainrunner.us/2007/09/battle_of_the_minds_an_intervi.html.

339 **"You get them":** Ibid.

340 **"volunteer to go":** Rice, testimony before the House Armed Services Committee, April 15, 2008.

341 **In 2007, the eighteen provinces:** Michael Knights and Eamon McCarthy, "Provincial Politics in Iraq," Washington Institute for Near East Policy, April 2008, p. 18.

341 **In 2007, Maliki ordered:** Walter Pincus, "Shh—There Is Corruption in Iraq," *Washington Post,* June 25, 2007, p. A17.

346 **One in sixteen patrols:** Arnsten and West, "A Tabular Method," pp. 13, 33–34.

348 **During the Algerian insurgency:** Horne, *A Savage War of Peace,* p. 337.

348 **The judges had released:** Alissa Rubin, "Charges Are Dropped Against 2 Shiite Ex-Officials," *New York Times,* March 4, 2008, p. A14.

349 **The Stone task force:** Alissa Rubin and Stephen Farrell, "Bomb Kills U.S. Soldier in Baghdad," *New York Times,* April 19, 2008.

349 **At his confirmation hearing:** Petraeus, Senate Armed Services Committee hearing, April 8, 2008.

349 **"the prison capacity of Iraq":** Petraeus, Senate Armed Services Committee hearing, January 23, 2007, p. 23.

349 **The murder rate in Iraq:** Memo from Capt. Thomas McCaleb, USAF, MNF-I, January 14, 2008.

349 **than in the States:** "Prison Population Around the Globe," *New York Times,* April 23, 2008. The murder rate in the United States was 6 per 100,000 population.

350 **"We are not planning":** Jim Garamone, "Gates, Pace Talk About Iranian Involvement in Iraq," American Forces Press Service, February 15, 2007.

350 **"I think what the Iranians":** Crocker, House Armed Services Committee hearing, April 9, 2008.

350 **In answer to a question:** Petraeus, reply to Lieberman, Senate Armed Services Committee hearing, April 8, 2008.

350 **"You can't solve":** Karen DeYoung, "Iran Top Threat to Iraq, US Says," *Washington Post,* April 12, 2008.

351 **"Basra, you know":** Odierno, remarks at National Press Club, October 2, 2007.

351 **"not-so-benign neglect":** Anthony H. Cordesman, "A Civil War Iraq Can't Win," *New York Times,* March 30, 2008.

351 **On March 22, Petraeus met:** Michael Gordon, Eric Schmitt, and Stephen Farrell, "US Cites Gaps in Planning of Iraqi Assault on Basra," *New York Times,* April 3, 2008.

351 "not adequately planned or prepared": Petraeus, Senate Armed Services Committee hearing, April 8, 2008.

352 "a decisive and final battle": Robert Reid, "Sadr Defies Iraqi Government," Associated Press, March 29, 2008.

353 One day after the assault began: Sudarsan Raghavan, "Attacks on US Forces Soared at End of March," *Washington Post,* April 2, 2008, p. A12.

353 With religious tomes as a prop: Hamza Hendawi, "Al Sadr: I Am in Control," Associated Press, March 29, 2008.

353 "positive step in the right direction": Sholnn Freeman, "Relative Calm Returns," *Washington Post,* April 1, 2008.

353 ordered a halt to arrests: Ammar Karim, "Iraqi PM Expects More Assaults," *Armed Forces Press,* April 3, 2004.

353 "look into the cases": Dr. Ali Dabbagh, press conference, Baghdad, March 31, 2008.

354 Before quietly leaving Basra: Stephen Farrell and James Glanz, "More Than 1,000 in Iraq's Forces Quit Basra Fight," *New York Times,* April 4, 2008.

354 "Maliki laughs at the U.S. government": David Ignatius, "Waiting Games in the Middle East," *Washington Post,* March 16, 2008, p. B07.

356 "The military has done": Biden, *The NewsHour,* November 27, 2007.

356 A Harris poll showed: Harris poll, February 28, 2008.

356 "Congress must not choose to lose in Iraq": Yochi Dreazen, "Democrats Decry Cost of Staying in Iraq," *Wall Street Journal,* April 8, 2008.

357 Obama suggested: Obama, Senate Foreign Relations Committee hearing, April 9, 2008.

357 "We are going": ABC News debate coverage, April 16, 2008.

357 "a good tactical job: Fox News Channel, April 27, 2008.

357 At a meeting at Harvard: Richard Haass, meeting of the Council on Foreign Relations, Harvard University, April 17, 2008.

357 "I think the expectation": *The NewsHour,* April 11, 2008.

CHAPTER 25: THE STRONGEST TRIBE, 2009

364 In 1951, the British: John A. Nagl, *Learning to Eat Soup with a Knife* (San Francisco: Westview Press, 2005), p. 98.

367 "a government that derives": FM 3-24, *Counterinsurgency,* Department of the Army, December 2006, p. D8.

369 "Counterinsurgency is a police war": Maj. Rory Quinn, "Company Commanders' Observations," Marine Corps Combat Development Command, October 12, 2007.

371 "cautious use of infantry": Paul Fussell, *The Great War and Modern Memory* (New York: Oxford, 1975), p. 317.

371 In the last year of the war: Stephen Ambrose, *Citizen Soldiers* (New York: Touchstone, 1997), p. 281.

371 But in World War I: William Moore, *Gas Attack* (New York: Hippocrene, 1987), p. 140.

371 **By war's end:** John Keegan, *A History of Warfare* (New York: Vintage, 1994), p. 385.

371 **"Back in Washington":** Dianne Feinstein, "On Iraq," *Atlantic,* October 2007, p. 56.

371 **By some estimates:** Lizette Alvarez, "Nearly a Fifth of War Veterans Report Mental Disorders," *New York Times,* April 18, 2008, p. A16.

372 **"Elite political culture":** Michael Hayden, at Council on Foreign Relations, New York, September 21, 2007.

372 **"I think a lot of people":** Samantha Power, "Our War on Terror," *New York Times Book Review,* July 29, 2007.

374 **"The risk of overextending":** Thom Shanker, "Gates Says New Arms Must Play Role Now," *New York Times,* May 14, 2008, p. A18.

374 **The Congressional Budget Office:** Rep. John Spratt, House Armed Services Committee hearing, April 9, 2008.

BIBLIOGRAPHY

Addington, Larry H. *The Patterns of War Since the Eighteenth Century.* Bloomington: Indiana University Press, 1994.

Affourtit, Thomas D. *Communion in Conflict: The Marine Advisor in the Middle East.* USMC Advisor Publications, 2006.

———. *Communion in Conflict: The Marine Advisor Vietnam, 1954–1973.* Volume 3. USMC Advisor Publications, 2006.

Ajami, Fouad. *The Foreigner's Gift: The Americans, the Arabs and the Iraqis in Iraq.* New York: Free Press, 2006.

Allawi, Ali A. *The Occupation of Iraq: Winning the War, Losing the Peace.* New Haven: Yale University Press, 2007.

Ambrose, Stephen E. *Citizen Soldiers: The U.S. Army from the Normandy Beaches to the Bulge to the Surrender of Germany, June 7, 1944, to May 7, 1945.* New York: Simon & Schuster, 1997.

Army, Department of the. *Counterinsurgency.* Marine Corps Warfighting Publication. Washington, D.C., 2006.

Axelrod, Alan. *Miracle at Belleau Wood: The Birth of the Modern U.S. Marine Corps.* Guilford, CT: Lyons Press, 2007.

Boot, Max. *War Made New: Technology, Warfare, and the Course of History, 1500 to Today.* New York: Gotham Books, 2006.

Bremer III, L. Paul, with Malcolm McConnell. *My Year in Iraq: The Struggle to Build a Future of Hope.* New York: Threshold, 2006.

Brown, Timothy C. *The Real Contra War: Highlander Peasant Resistance in Nicaragua.* Norman: University of Oklahoma Press, 2001.

Caraccilo, Dominic J., and Andrea L. Thompson. *How to Win in Iraq.* Mechanicsburg, PA: Stackpole Books, 2008.

Clay, Steven E. *Iroquois Warriors in Iraq.* Fort Leavenworth, KS: Combat Studies Institute Press, 2006.

Coogan, Tim Pat. *Michael Collins: The Man Who Made Ireland.* New York: Palgrave, 1990.

Counterinsurgency Handbook: Multi-National Force, Iraq. Baghdad, 2006.

Davidson, Phillip B. *Vietnam at War: The History, 1946–1975.* New York: Oxford University Press, 1988.

Defense, Department of. *Iraq Country Handbook.* 1998.

Frank, Tommy. *American Soldier.* New York: Regan Books, 2004.

Galula, David. *Counterinsurgency Warfare: Theory and Practice.* New York: Frederick A. Praeger, 1964.

Gordon, Michael R., and Gen. Bernard E. Trainor. *The Generals' War: The Inside Story of the Conflict in the Gulf.* New York: Little, Brown, 1995.

Halberstam, David. *The Coldest Winter: America and the Korean War.* New York: Hyperion, 2007.

Horne, Alistair. *A Savage War of Peace: Algeria, 1954–1962.* New York: New York Review of Books, 2006.

Independent Commission on the Security Forces of Iraq, Report of the. *The Independent Commission on the Security Forces of Iraq.* Washington, D.C., 2007.

Kaplan, Robert D. *Hog Pilots, Blue Water Grunts: The American Military in the Air, at Sea, and on the Ground.* New York: Random House, 2007.

Kimmage, Daniel, and Kathleen Ridolfo. *Iraqi Insurgent Media: The War of Images and Ideas.* Washington, D.C.: Radio Free Europe, Radio Liberty, 2007.

Levitt, Steven D., and Stephen J. Dubner. *Freakonomics: A Rogue Economist Explores the Hidden Side of Everything.* New York: HarperCollins, 2005.

Lind, Michael. *Vietnam, the Necessary War: A Reinterpretation of America's Most Disastrous Military Conflict.* New York: Simon & Schuster, 1999.

Marston, Daniel, and Carter Malkasian, eds. *Counterinsurgency in Modern Warfare.* New York: Osprey, 2008.

Metz, Steven. *Learning from Iraq: Counterinsurgency in American Strategy.* Washington, D.C.: Strategic Studies Institute, 2007.

Millen, Lt. Col. Raymond A. *Command Legacy: A Tactical Primer for Junior Leaders of Infantry Units.* Washington, D.C.: Brassey's, 2002.

Moyar, Mark. *Phoenix and the Birds of Prey: The CIA's Secret Campaign to Destroy the Viet Cong.* Annapolis, MD: Naval Institute Press, 1997.

Nagl, John A. *Learning to Eat Soup with a Knife: Counterinsurgency Lessons from Malaya and Vietnam.* Chicago: University of Chicago Press, 2005.

Parker, F. Charles, IV. *Vietnam: Strategy for a Stalemate.* New York: Paragon House, 1989.

Phillips, David L. *Losing Iraq: Inside the Postwar Reconstruction Fiasco.* San Francisco: Westview Press, 2005.

Report to Congress. *Measuring Stability and Security in Iraq.* June 2007.

Ricks, Thomas E. *Fiasco: The American Military Adventure in Iraq.* New York: Penguin, 2006.

Ridgway, Matthew B. *The Korean War.* New York: Da Capo, 1967.

Roberts, Andrew. *A History of the English-Speaking Peoples Since 1990*. New York: HarperCollins, 2007.

Schaffer, Howard B. *Ellsworth Bunker: Global Troubleshooter, Vietnam Hawk*. Chapel Hill: University of North Carolina Press, 2003.

Sorley, Lewis. *A Better War: The Unexamined Victories and Final Tragedy of America's Last Years in Vietnam*. New York: Harcourt Brace, 1999.

Tenet, George, with Bill Harlow. *At the Center of the Storm: My Years in the CIA*. New York: HarperCollins, 2007.

Tolstoy, Leo. *War and Peace*. New York: W. W. Norton, 1996.

U.S. Marine Corps Combat Development Command. *Tentative Manual for Countering Irregular Threats*. Draft. Quantico, VA: 2006.

Vincent, Steven. *In the Red Zone: A Journey into the Soul of Iraq*. Dallas: Spence, 2004.

West, Bing. *No True Glory*. New York: Bantam, 2005.

———. *The Village*. New York: Simon & Schuster, 1972.

Woodward, Bob. *Plan of Attack*. New York: Simon & Schuster, 2004.

———. *State of Denial*. New York: Simon & Schuster, 2006.

ABOUT THE AUTHOR

BING WEST, a marine combat veteran, served as assistant secretary of defense in the Reagan administration. Based on fourteen extended field trips over six years, *The Strongest Tribe* is the third book in West's trilogy chronicling the war in Iraq. A correspondent for *The Atlantic,* he is the author of the Vietnam counterinsurgency classic *The Village.* His books on Iraq have won the Marine Corps Heritage Foundation's General Wallace M. Greene Jr. Award for nonfiction, the Colby Award for military nonfiction, and the Veterans of Foreign Wars Media Award. He appears on *The NewsHour* on PBS and is a member of the Council on Foreign Relations and St. Crispin's Order of the Infantry. He lives in Newport, Rhode Island.

www.westwrite.com

ABOUT THE TYPE

This book was set in Sabon, a typeface designed by the well-known German typographer Jan Tschichold (1902–1974). Sabon's design is based upon the original letter forms of Claude Garmond and was created specifically to be used for three sources: foundry type for hand composition, Linotype, and Monotype. Tschichold named his typeface for the famous Frankfurt typefounder Jacques Sabon, who died in 1580.